THE COLOR OF STRENGTH:
EMBRACING THE PASSION OF OUR CULTURE
AN ANTHOLOGY

Frederick Williams
Editor

THE COLOR OF STRENGTH: EMBRACING THE PASSION OF OUR CULTURE AN ANTHOLOGY

Frederick Williams
Editor

Divine Literary Publishing
San Antonio, Texas

DIVINE LITERARY PUBLISHING
8023 River Valley
San Antonio, Texas 78249

ISBN: 978-0-9709957-3-5

2nd Printing July, 2011

Cover art: Dr. Melissa Duvall
Inside text design: Mark Mayfield
Printed in the United States of America

Dedication:

This anthology is dedicated to the memory of the beautiful four little girls who gave their lives in the Sixteenth Street Baptist Church bombing in Birmingham, Ala. in 1963. It is also dedicated to the two boys who were murdered on that same day in Birmingham.Their sacrifices have helped to make us all free. This is for you, Denise McNair, Addie Mae Collins, Cynthia Wesley, Carole Robertson, Virgil Ware, and Johnny Robinson so that your sacrifice will never be forgotten as long as the stories in this anthology are read. Its title, *The Color of Strength*, is in remembrance of the strength you represent over the generations of Black people who have struggled and suffered, and ultimately won the battle for dignity, love, and forgiveness.

Acknowledgements

As founder of the The Divine Literary Tour (DLT), Toschia Moffett thanks and acknowledges her fellow board member, Professor Frederick Williams, for his insight in taking the DLT to the next level and for undertaking the awesome task as Managing Editor of this anthology as well as The Divine Literary Tour Publishing. You are truly one of the, "Winds beneath my wings and I love you dearly." Toschia also would like to thank and acknowledge her friend and fellow board member Rhonda Lawson. No matter where she is deployed for military service she is always loyal and steadfastly working for the DLT. She would like to acknowledge our student intern, Dauun Bradley from San Antonio College, for her hard work in marketing. She also thanks Mrs. Latisha Floyd for her website design and Dr. Melissa Duvall for designing the book cover and Priscilla Cooper at The Civil Rights Institute in Birmingham, Ala., for hosting our kickoff event. To Dr. Victoria Santiago, thanks for your editing services. Thanks to Mark Mayfield of Litho Press for going the extra mile to make sure the text design was done right. To the wonderful authors that participated in this anthology, to her wonderful friends, family and her supportive Sorors, thanks for all your support in everything I do. Toschia says, "I was truly blessed with two of the smartest parents that ever walked the earth. Thank you."

Michael Booker would like to send acknowledgements to Fostoria Pierson, his mother, for her unwavering support.

Margaret Patton Brown would like to acknowledge her daughter Rhonda Young, her son Emerson Bradley Brown, and her brother and sister-in-law Mr. and Mrs. Joseph D. Patton III.

Taj Matthews acknowledges God as his guiding force. He also sends a special thank you to his wife, Cheryl; his children, De'Asia and Taj Omari; his sister, Chatney; and his nephew, Montero. He also acknowledges with a special love his grandparents, Rev. Claude Black, Zenora Black, and Mary Ann Matthews. He sends a special thank you to his local church, Mt. Zion First Baptist in San Antonio, Texas, as well as Faith Christian Center in Jacksonville, Florida; his pastors, Bishop George Davis and Rev. Otis Mitchell; and to all his brothers and sisters in Christ.

Alexis Williams would like to acknowledge 1st Sgt. Donald Halford, "the only father figure I have ever had in my life." She wishes to acknowledge her sister Rachel Williams for always supporting her; Jennifer Pearson, her former probation officer who, unlike the system, never gave up on her; Jackie Tovar; Missy Singletary; and Rashawn Smith, her best friend.

Fattah Muhammad would like to acknowledge the Nation of Islam (MM#48), Black Men United for Reading and Writing, and M.U.S.I.C., the video and audio production and education company.

Anthony Prior would like to acknowledge and thank his parents for supporting him in all his endeavors.

D. L. Grant would like to acknowledge Tilford Grant Sr., who told him that he could do anything he wanted to do, and to Lisa, his sister, for believing in him.

Chris Cannon would like to acknowledge Professor Frederick Williams for being the spark that fueled the fire of a movement for positive change.

Dr. Loren Alves acknowledges his late Vietnam veteran hero and brother, Donald Alves, who persuaded him to get into college and out of the uncertainty of a factory career in Dayton, Ohio. Unequivocally, he also pays a special tribute to his wife of forty years, Phyllis Arnold-Alves. They were high school sweethearts and she is still the love of his life. Phyllis was instrumental in his success as a college student, a parent, and a successful dentist.

The family of the late Dr. James William Sanders Sr. wishes to acknowledge the legacy of his life. They also wish to acknowledge his best friend, Rev. Malachi Duncan. They further acknowledge the congregations of Bethel Baptist Church in Gaffney, S.C. and Island Creek Baptist Church in Cowpens, S.C.

Margaret Richardson extends a special acknowledgement to her mother, Mrs. Patricia F. Adams Taylor for serving as the strength that keeps her going and pushes her to soar higher. She also sends a special thank you to her nieces, Kimberli, Tiarra, Tara, her nephew Isiah, and godsons Devin, Donovan, Darren, and Damien for uplifting her soul.

Lenton Collins extends a special acknowledgement and a thank you to his mother, Mrs. Mattie C. Fields, for her love, support, and encouragement. He also thanks his wife Charmaine and children for always being the lights of his life and his reason for living. Lastly, Lenton extends a special thank you to his "sis" Margaret for including him and working with him on this project.

Calvin Thomas gives thanks and acknowledges his mother, Elizabeth "Bessie" Thomas. She shared her gifts of understanding with him, allowing him to reach heights he never thought possible, which has allowed him to pass down the wisdom received from his mother to the younger generation in his family. He hopes their accomplishments may become a celebration that honors her and inspires our race.

Our Griot, Leslie Perry, extends acknowledgement to his high school drama teacher, Mrs. Berdevick, who gave him the opportunity to develop his talents at a time when such opportunities were denied young Blacks. He also acknowledges his late brother, Claude Ware, who stressed to him that a prejudiced world can only hold someone back when they incorporate that bigotry into their life.

Rhonda Lawson sends a very special thank you to the people in her life who thought she wasn't listening to their words of advice. Her contribution to this historic work is proof that she really was listening. Her works are a gift to the next generation so they will not only know our history, but also embrace it.

David Floyd sends a heart-felt acknowledgement to his mother, Wanda, his brothers, the late Ronnie, James, and Levi, and to his sister Nicole. Through all the turbulent times they have faced, they remained intact as a loving family. Finally, to his sons, David and Daniel, he offers special praise knowing that their struggle will be less than his because they can learn from what he had to endure to make it in this country.

Michael Smith wishes to acknowledge his late father, Earl Smith Sr. who taught him how to be the father and man he is today. His mother Mildred Smith, who taught him how to show compassion and love, his older brother, Earl Smith Jr., his oldest sister, Lori Luster, his twin sister, Marilyn Smith, his wife, Monisha and children, Motranique, Deandre, Devonte, and the baby, Shayla. He sends a special thank you to Lee Dawn, Charles Parker, and Frederick Williams, three men who have served as mentors to him.

Frederick Williams with great pride acknowledges the twenty-six writers who put the passion for writing, the love for their culture, and their concern for our children's future above any other consideration and helped make this anthology a reality. He is especially thankful to Toschia Moffett who is his closest associate and friend in these endeavors. He also sends out a very special thank you to Sharon Shelton-CoAngelo who lent her extreme knowledge as a grammarian to this project. She transposed this from a rough manuscript to a real work of art. Finally a very special thank you to his wife, Venetta Williams. She recognized the importance of this project and was willing to sacrifice her time with him.

Finally and most important of all, every author who has contributed to this anthology acknowledges God as their inspiration for participating in this work. In our efforts to uplift our young people, we are very much aware that we are doing God's work, and any success in this on-going struggle to save our children and our culture is due to His intervention on our behalf.

TABLE OF CONTENTS

CONTRIBUTING AUTHORS

Caleb Alexander is a successful *New York Times* Bestseller List ghost writer and author. He is responsible for some of the biggest titles in the Urban Fiction genre. Recognizing that he wanted to change the genre of his writing, he abruptly decided to write stories of hope and uplift and since has published three works, *Eastside*, *Two Thin Dimes*, and *Belly of the Beast* that contribute valuable lessons for our youth. Caleb's short story, "The Gift," represents one of the best-written works in the anthology. It is a well-crafted story about the importance of family and heritage for the success of our youth.

Dr. Loren Alves is a pediatric dentist who is presently writing his autobiography about his rise from poverty and living in the projects of Dayton, Ohio, to a successful dental practice. He served twenty-one years in the US Army Dental Corp, retiring as a Colonel. He retired with the Distinguish Legion of Merit Medal. Dr. Alves has lectured internationally and within the United States on "How to Meet Special Needs and Challenges in Life." and on the "TEAM Approach to Success." He devotes much of his time as a mentor and a volunteer for the Omega Psi Phi fraternity and as a charter member of the One Hundred Black Men of San Antonio. A chapter from his autobiography, "Coming of Age to Manhood," is included in the anthology.

Michael Booker played collegiate football at the University of Nebraska and for the Atlanta Falcons and Tennessee Titans of the National Football League. He was an outstanding defensive back for University of Nebraska when they won back-to-back National Collegiate Championships in 1994 and 1995, and when they defeated the University of Miami in the 1994 Orange Bowl and the University of Florida in the 1995 Fiesta Bowl. Both years the team was undefeated. They also defeated Virginia Tech in the

1996 Orange Bowl. He was selected to play in the 1997 Senior Bowl Game as well as the 1997 Hula Bowl. Michael was drafted number eleven in the 1997 NFL draft by the Atlanta Falcons. He played three years for them and an additional two years for the Tennessee Titans.

Jayme L. Bradford is an assistant professor and mass communication coordinator at Voorhees College in Denmark, S.C. She began her teaching career as a communications professor at Florida Community College in Jacksonville, Fla. In addition, she taught English and Journalism at William M. Raines Senior High School. She is the former communications chairperson and assistant professor at Edward Waters College, the oldest historical black college in Florida. Before embarking on a teaching career she worked as a features/entertainment writer for the *Florida Times-Union* and an education writer at the *Muskegon Chronicle*. She was voted "Journalist of the Year" by the Florida Rehabilitation Association and served on the board of directors for the National Association of Black Journalists. Ms. Bradford received a Bachelor's Degree in Mass Media Arts from Clark Atlanta University, a Master's Degree in Communication Arts from University of West Florida and a second Master's Degree in English Education from Jacksonville University. She has written a short essay, "KKK: The Real Boogeyman," recalling the brutal murder of a young Black man in Mobile, Ala.

Rosalind Patton Brown is a native of Spartanburg, S. C. and a graduate of South Carolina State University. She taught school in the Spartanburg Public School System, at Spartanburg Methodist College, and was also a school administrator. She is the president of The Links, Inc., Spartanburg Chapter, and continues to work with at-risk students. She also works very closely with the Sickle Cell Foundation and has served as the Director of Alumni Affairs at Barbara Scotia College in North Carolina.

Chris Cannon acclaimed author of *Winning Back Our Boys* has become nationally recognized for his award-winning interactive youth presentations. Once labeled an at-risk youth, Chris spends countless hours training, transforming, and speaking to teens across the nation regarding the pressures of sex, relationships, drug/alcohol, and self-identity. He skillfully shows young people how to go from tragedy to triumph, from pitiful to powerful, and from regrets to rewards. His essay, "Testing Positive: What I did to Have Sex with Her," is a cleverly constructed essay for the young that delivers a very different message than what the title might suggest.

Cary Clack is a well-respected columnist for the *San Antonio Express News*. He writes on local and national events. Before his writing career with the newspaper, Cary was a Scholar-intern at the Martin Luther King Jr. Center for Nonviolent Social Change in Atlanta, Ga. He wrote CNN commentaries for Mrs. Coretta Scott King from 1988 to 1995. He also served as a trainer in non-violence at King Center workshops for high school and college students. He has won the Dallas Press Club's Katie Award for Best General Column and the 2008 Friends of the San Antonio Public Library's Arts and Letters Award for writing. Cary has done a short essay for the anthology on the history and importance of the Tuskegee airmen as a part of Black culture and pride.

Lenton Collins served a four-year tour in the United States Navy and is presently working in San Antonio, Tx.. with the underground music scene. Lenton is also a free-lance writer, specializing in the rap music field. He has teamed with Margaret Richardson to write the moving and beautiful short story about the love shared between an elderly Black couple. The story is told from the viewpoint of the couple's grandson.

David Floyd is a full-time faculty member at Austin Community College. He teaches courses in Accounting for freshmen and sophomores. He received his Bachelor of Science Degree from Huston-Tillotson College in Austin, Tx., his Masters of Science in Accountancy from Bentley University in Boston, Mass. and is presently working on his doctorate degree. He is the author of *Through My Mother's Tears*, a heartfelt story about growing up in poverty and achieving his goals in life against insurmountable odds. His contribution to the anthology is an excerpt from his autobiography.

D.L. Grant is assistant branch manager of the George Washington Carver Branch Library in San Antonio, Tx. Mr. Grant is presently working on his doctorate degree in Library and Information Sciences. He is a member of the American Library Association, and is the chair-elect of the Black Caucus of the Texas Library Association. Mr. Grant was recently elected to the Executive Board of the Black Caucus of the American Library Association and is also a member of the Beta Phi Mu Library and Information Studies Honor Society. He was recently awarded the

President's Call to Service Award, presented by President Barak Obama's Council on Service and Civic Participation. Mr. Grant's short story tells of a young fourteen-year-old boy's determination to get a library card from the local library in the segregated south.

Rhonda Lawson is the award-winning author of *Cheatin' in the Next Room*, *A Dead Rose*, and *Putting it Back Together*, three exciting and well-written novels. She has another novel due out in 2011, *Some Wounds Never Heal*. Ms. Lawson is a United States Army journalist, garnering several journalism awards, including the 1997 Training and Doctrine Command Journalist of the Year Award. Currently she is serving with her unit in Iraq, supporting Operation Iraqi Freedom. Rhonda is an active member of Zeta Phi Beta Sorority and a board member of the Divine Literary Tour. Rhonda contributed one of the six outstanding short stories in the anthology, "A Lesson in Life and History." In this well-written story a young Black girl who has just graduated from high school is taken south to learn about the foundation of her culture. It is a learning experience for her.

Taj Matthews is author of *Grandpa was a Preacher: A Letter to My Grandson*. This is the story of Taj's grandfather, Rev.Claude Black Jr., who was one of the greatest and most respected civil rights leaders in the entire state of Texas. Taj currently serves as Executive Director of the Claude and ZerNona Black Developmental Leadership Foundation, which works to revitalize inner-city communities and provides special services to at-risk teens, seniors, and needy families. Taj has contributed an important essay about the courage his grandfather showed when he challenged the San Antonio city council's banning the great poet Langston Hughes from reading his poetry in the city in 1960, and when he challenged Rev. Billy Graham's support of a segregationist to appear on the podium with him during Graham's visit to San Antonio in 1952.

Toschia Moffett is the principal founder of the Divine Literary Tour. An attorney and author, Toschia is undoubtedly one of the brightest young African American females in America. She graduated from Duke University in three years and passed the bar exam by the age of 24. She is also an entrepreneur and marketing guru.Toschia has many hats and wears them all well. She also has written one novel, *You Wrong for That*, and is presently completing her second novel for publication in 2011. Toschia has contributed to several anthologies and written several magazine articles.

She has two outstanding offerings in the anthology. The first is a short story, "Whose Shoulders Are You Standing On?" She also contributed an excellent essay linking the past to the present, "You Can Learn a Lot from Dead People."

Fattah Muhammad is a brilliant young brother who has mastered the use of mathematics as a method to understand human behavior and historical events. Brother Fattah co-founded a very progressive student organization seeking to unite all the Black students around university issues affecting them. During his three years as a student at the University of Texas at San Antonio, Brother Fattah addressed issues of race, religion, and Black history and garnered support for implementation of Black Studies courses at the university. He presently lives in Dallas, Tx., where he is authoring several articles and books analyzing the meaning of numbers, human relationships, and human history. Brother Fattah's essay is entitled, "The Mathematic Make-Up of SELF: The Self Within."

Leslie Perry has been a modern day Griot for over 30 years and has performed throughout his home state of California and many other states. He is a shaker and mover in the storytelling community in the greater Los Angeles area and is a founding member of the Los Angeles Storytelling Festival. Long before his life as a storyteller, Leslie was a theatre man, and among his creative works was a performance of Frederick Douglass' famous Fourth of July speech. His one-act play *History Man* was performed at the University of Texas at San Antonio during Black History Month in 2009. Leslie recently published a series of short stories and plays entitled, *The Story Man.* In this anthology, Leslie has three folk tales, usually performed in a story-telling format, but changed to written format and a short story. His folk tales include: "Door of No Return," "Sunshine and the Gummy Man," and "Stone Gumbo Soup," and his short story is "A Time Remembered."

Anthony Prior played seven years in the National Football League and four years in the Canadian Football League. Anthony still holds the speed record, having run the 40-yard sprint in 4.2 seconds for the New York Jets. He is now an author of three series of essays criticizing the manner in which Black athletes are treated in professional sports. For this anthology Anthony has provided our young readers with a short autobiographical account of his pursuit of his dream to play in the National Football League. "Forty Yards in 4.2 Seconds" is about one young man's successful fight against the obstacles of life. There is a deeper message about responsibility: One must always be aware there is something more important than sports in our life and that is a need to be a good person.

Margaret Richardson is a local scholar who has recently received her Masters Degree from the University of Texas at San Antonio in Political Science. She was awarded a Ruth Jones McClendon internship to work in the Texas State Legislature 2005 and worked on the staff of State Representative Jose Menendez. Margaret has written a beautiful short story that brings tears to your eyes, "Passing the Torch." It is about the love shared by a couple that lasted for over fifty years, and it is told from the voice of their grandson. In her story she points out the importance of family, heritage, and culture.

Dr. James William Sanders Sr., was an educator and Senior Pastor for 61 years at Bethel Baptist Church in Gaffney, S. C. He served as Moderator of the Thickety Mountain Baptist Association. Dr. Sanders was listed in *Who's Who in America,* and *Who's Who Among Top Executives*. He was a member of Omega Psi Phi Fraternity, a Mason, and a recipient of the NAACP Hall of Fame Award. The Governor of South Carolina presented him with the Order of the Palmetto, the highest award that the state gives to a civilian. He was a member of many esteemed boards and was a role model to many. He passed away on July 6, 2010, shortly after completing his short essay which is an excerpt from his forthcoming autobiography entitled, *Moving from Obscurity to Prominence.*

Nevil Shed was a member of the historic Texas Western basketball team that won the National Collegiate Athletic Association Men's Division One Basketball Tournament in 1966. Their team made history for being the first to start five African American players. Nevil was one of the players featured in the Disney movie, *Glory Road*, which was about that victory. The team was honored at a White House ceremony in 2007. After playing for Texas Western, Nevil went on to play briefly for the Boston Celtics until he suffered a career-ending injury. Nevil now tours the country as a motivational speaker and conducts a summer league basketball camp for the San Antonio Spurs. Nevil's contribution to the anthology is the first in a series of essays under the heading "Legacies of Courage."

Contributing Authors

Sephira Bailey Shuttlesworth is a former teacher and elementary school principal of 23 years. In 1966, Sephira and two of her siblings integrated their county's school system. She began college at Union University in Jackson, Tenn. while still a high school student. She earned a Bachelor of Science Degree in Elementary Education in less than three years. In 1986, she met the civil rights icon Rev. Fred Shuttlesworth, and they remained friends for over 20 years, finally marrying in a candle-lit ceremony at the church he founded in Cincinnati, Ohio. Following her husband's stroke in the fall of 2007, the couple returned to his home, Birmingham, Ala. in early 2008 where she now devotes her time to taking care of him and securing his legacy as one of the big three of the Civil Rights Movement with Dr. Martin Luther King, Jr. and Rev. Ralph Abernathy. Her essay tells the reader of the courage that her husband had in order to confront the racist Birmingham police in the 1960's.

Michael Smith has lived an exciting but dangerous life in the past. He worked as an undercover agent for a major police force in an East Coast city. After years of doing this work, Michael was bothered by the number of innocent people who happened to be at the wrong place at the wrong time and were taken down just like the criminals. He watched as the guilty cut deals with the district attorney's office and walked away with no time served if they agreed to turn snitch, while others with no significant involvement in the drug trade had their lives destroyed. Michael has used his experience as an undercover agent to write a novel, *Pieces of a Broken Man*, to be published in 2011. Excerpts from the novel are included in the anthology under the title, "Losing the Game."

Brenner Stiles is the Program Manager for the Moving to Work Project at the San Antonio Housing Authority. Moving to Work is a special Housing and Urban Development Program with the purpose of facilitating and promoting education and job training for the residents of public housing. Brenner recognizes the importance of our youth knowing the rich history of their heritage and culture. For that reason she has written a short biographical sketch of Fannie Lou Hamer for the section "Legacy of Courage."

Calvin Thomas grew up in Helena, Ark. during the era of segregation in the South. As a young man he often heard older men and women say, "Out of every five Blacks maybe two would succeed in life because life's odds were so stacked against them." He grew more and more aware that there was a huge discrepancy between the way Black people viewed themselves and their actual importance to society—a discrepancy he termed "mental illness." In his first publication, *The Long Road from Slavery to Mental Illness*, he analyzed the specific reasons for the collective mental illness that is pervasive in the Black world. In his essay, "The Authentic American Culture," he writes about the strong and beautiful culture that belongs to Black America and in essence is an intricate part of the American culture. He urges young Blacks to be proud of that culture and to protect it from many of the negative forces trying to destroy it.

Alexis Williams is our youngest contributor to the anthology. At seventeen years old, she had the courage to write about a tragic period in her life. Her essay, "I Have Overcome," is a strong message to other young girls that despite the tragedies they may experience, there is always hope for success in their future if they do not lose faith in who they are and their worth to the Black race and culture. Alexis is a beautiful young Black girl with a gift as a writer and an excellent career in her future

Carrie Williams is our second youthful writer (no relation to Alexis). Carrie, at nineteen, is a student at Virginia Union University, one of the original historical Black colleges. It is the university attended by one of our major cultural icons, James Weldon Johnson. Carrie is majoring in Clinical Psychology, but also has a love for writing poetry. She has a book of poems she wrote as far back as the seventh grade. Carrie, in a collaborative effort with her father, Frederick, wrote the essay on the four little girls brutally murdered in the Sixteenth Street Baptist Church bombing in September, 1963.

Frederick Williams received a Masters Degree and worked on his Doctorate in Political Science at Indiana University prior to receiving a political appointment to serve as a Legislative Aide on the staff of Senator Birch Bayh, a Democrat from Indiana. While a member of Senator Bayh's staff he helped manage the first Senate bill to make Dr. Martin Luther King Jr's birthday a national holiday. He also served on the staff of Congressman Parren Mitchell. Frederick helped establish the African American Studies minor at the University of Texas at San Antonio. He designed and taught a number of courses including African American Political Thought, African American Politics, African American Literature from Phyllis Wheatley to the Present, Politics of the Civil Rights

Movement, and a course on the Harlem Renaissance. Frederick is the principal founder of Black Men United for Reading and Writing whose mission is to enhance young Black men and women's understanding of their culture and heritage through reading and writing about it. He is the author of three novels, has ghost written an autobiography, and has edited numerous works. In 2011, he was named one of the five "Men of the Year" by *San Antonio Magazine* for the excellent job he did in managing the editing of this anthology. Besides being the creator and managing editor, he has contributed two short stories, "Scottie's Journey" and "In Perpetuity (Always)," a short autobiography about his involvement in the passage of the King Holiday legislation, and with his daughter, Carrie, an essay in the "Legacies of Courage" section.

Prologue

Frederick Williams

The *Color of Strength: Embracing the Passion of Our Culture* is the work of twenty-six African American writers who share one common goal and that is to present our youth with a range of stories, essays, and short autobiographies about the grace, beauty, and strength of their culture. As we move into the second decade of the 21st Century, it is becoming increasingly important that young Black Americans know their history. We can no longer afford to ignore our past. Knowledge of the sacrifices our ancestors made so that we can enjoy more liberties and freedoms than they had, will help us recognize our obligation to do the same for future generations.

As I travel around the country, more often than not I observe the same hedonistic, selfish behavior among many young Blacks from Boston to Los Angeles. Some feel responsible to no one but themselves. An eighteen-year-old drug pusher will sell drugs to a ten-year-old with no remorse. They will shoot each other down with the ease of a hunter shooting prey. Getting pregnant or getting someone pregnant, to some, makes you a woman or a man. And doing time, either in jail or prison, is a rite of passage. These attitudes are shared all over this country and if they are not put in check, someday there will be no Black America. If our ancestors had taken the same kind of attitude, we would not be here today. The writers of this anthology all speak in a collective voice, and that is a voice from the past demanding that we do something to counter this pathological road to destruction. Our works are a beginning that can possibly serve as the first dose of medicine desperately needed for a cure.

This particular anthology is very unique in that it consists of contemporary works written by a group of artists ranging in age from 17 to 89. We decided early on in this process, that it was important to find writers who shared a common vision and goal. We were careful to ensure that our collective thinking centered on the need to produce a literary product that delivered a message: Black culture grew out of a deep and abiding love our ancestors had for themselves and each other, despite the constant barrage of negative portrayals of them in the dominant media outlets. They understood the tremendous obstacles facing them on a daily basis during the years of slavery and Jim Crow. It is our contention as writers that under the most horrendous conditions any race of people have confronted over such a long period of time, 400 years, they remained a very gifted, innovative, and strong people. That belief is expressed throughout the anthology.

In one of his more insightful poems, the great literary icon of the Harlem Renaissance, Langston Hughes, captured the essence of the Black struggle, "Well son, I'll tell you, life for me ain't been no crystal stair...But all the time I'se been climbin' on... And reachin' landings. And turning stairs." In this classic poem, "Mother to Son," Hughes captures the tragedy and the potential triumph in Black America. When our forebears walked into the 20th Century, they had been free of slavery for only 35 years. They entered a new century and confronted a hostile people who ruled over them as tyrants, determined to block their road to prosperity, equality, and cultural sustainability. The irony of their condition and those people so hostile toward them was that only because of their blood, sweat, and labor did the United States become a major world industrial power.

When we look back at our ancestors' dilemma, we can only be in awe that they survived. Every major institution in this country, from all geographical sections, lined up against them. The national, state, and local governments, the courts, the police force, even the military, were of one accord, and that was to keep the Black race subservient. Their actions were justified, according to them, through the portrayal of Black people in movies, novels, magazines, and newspapers. Still our ancestors survived. They made it up the "rough side of the mountain" and kept fighting back and praying to a just God that conditions would get better for them and their children. They were a spiritually endowed people who never turned to hate, even though they would have been justified to do so. Instead they turned to love, prayer, and an uncanny determination to never give up, never quit, and never succumb to the evil all around them. Langston ends his poem, providing us with the collective will-power of our ancestors to fight the battle, "So boy, don't you turn back cause you finds it's kinder hard… For I'se still goin' honey, I'se still climbin'…And life for me ain't been no crystal stair."

Our forebears' spirit, strength, and love are the foundation for this anthology. These works are about them and how we must follow in their footsteps to sustain this beautiful culture and also improve upon it.

The *Color of Strength* is divided into three sections. The first section includes eight short stories and three folk tales. The overarching message in each of these stories is consistent with the theme of the anthology. Fiction is an entertaining art form through which to deliver a message. One of the key components of that message must provide hope for the future. An additional component of the message is that past is prologue for the future. If we are to present new ideas to protect our culture from this onslaught of negativity, we must look to our past to find answers. The great historian, John Hope Franklin, taught us just how important our past was to the future. Each of our writers delivered that message in their entertaining and informative short stories.

Section Two consists of essays and short autobiographies. These works complement the short stories in the first section by supporting the messages delivered in fiction with real life experiences through a non-fiction genre. Their messages are also very clear and succinct. Black Americans regularly overcome obstacles and accomplish goals they have set for themselves all over this country. The old folks used to tell the young that they had to be twice as good to make it in this country. Theirs was a very basic message that you could never quit and no matter how difficult the road, through sheer will power and determination, you could make it. Our authors have passed that message on to our young readers through their words of encouragement, based on their own personal will to overcome and achieve.

The saying "we saved the best for last," might be appropriate when describing the third and final section of the anthology. There is a special quality found in the pages of "Legacies of Courage." When you survey the names and titles included in this section you are instantly impressed. This section consists of short essays on Rev. Fred Shuttlesworth, the Tuskegee Airmen, Nevil Shed and his teammates who won the 1966 National Collegiate Athletic Association Basketball Championship, Ida B. Wells, Rev. Claude Black, Rev. James W. Sanders Sr., Ella Baker, and the sharecropper's daughter the great Fannie Lou Hamer. Each of these giants of the Black race were heroes in their own right of whom we can be proud. Their deeds convince us that we all must embrace the passion of our culture and that the future of our people will be determined by how well we incorporate what they did as part of our being Black and American, which is an exceptional combination.

PART ONE

SHORT STORIES AND FOLK TALES

Scottie's Journey

Frederick Williams

Monday morning couldn't come fast enough for fifteen-year old Scottie Brown. When the alarm clock rang at 6 a.m., he sprang from his bed and rushed to the bathroom. Scottie lived in a two-bedroom apartment in a public housing unit off Fair Oaks Avenue in Pasadena, California. He shared a small bedroom with his younger brother Alex. His mother Wanda occupied the bedroom on the other side of the apartment. They lived off Wanda's welfare check because there was no child support from Scottie's father, who abandoned the children right after Alex's birth. Despite their financial struggles, the family maintained a positive attitude about life, something Wanda insisted on. At some point she knew that she would get off welfare and move her family into a home in a better part of the city. Scottie was determined to help her and that's why this day was so important to him.

He had to beat his younger brother to the bathroom so that he could wash up and be out of the apartment by seven. He noticed his mother's bedroom door still closed. She was sleeping later than her usual five o'clock wake up, something she would often do if she had gotten in late from her part-time job. Scottie closed the bathroom door, stripped out of his underwear, and poured hot water in the bathroom sink. He splashed water over his upper body and face, then grabbed a towel and patted the water off his body.

Scottie turned and stared at his physique in the full-length mirror on the back of the bathroom door. His 5-foot-6-inch frame was slim, but muscular. He'd shaved all the hair from his head, just like the professional basketball players did. All he wanted to do in life was play basketball, and he modeled his appearance after his favorite players who all had clean-shaven heads. The only missing symbol was the earring. His mother insisted that he not wear one and that he not get his ears pierced. But once he made his high school basketball team and she saw all the other players with pierced ears and earrings, she'd come around. That's why he had to hurry and get to school so he could learn the outcome of last week's tryouts for the school's basketball team.

He slipped on his underwear and hurried back to the bedroom where Alex sat on the side of his bed.

"What position you think they going to let you play?" Alex asked.

"Don't jinx me," Scottie shouted. "I ain't made the team yet and you talking like that might bring me bad luck." Scottie scolded his brother for jumping the gun even though he knew darn well there was no way he wouldn't make the cut. He had two great practices and no one looked better than he did in front of the coaches.

"Oh man, you ain't got to worry. Can't none of them dudes throw up the ball like you can. You a shoo in. I can't wait to come to your games.

"We'll see." A big smile spread across Scottie's face. "You'd better get ready before Mamma comes in here," he said. He watched his brother head toward the bathroom as he put on his FUBU sweats and jersey. He again glanced at his physique in the mirror, and then slipped into his Nike tennis shoes. Scottie was now ready to take on the day.

When he entered the kitchen, Wanda stood over the stove preparing bacon and eggs for him, but he shot right by her and toward the front door.

"Where you going, boy?' she asked without looking his way.

"Mamma, I ain't hungry this morning."

"What you mean, you ain't hungry. You'd better get back over here and eat this food that I got out of the bed to fix you," Wanda scowled.

Scottie stopped and sauntered back to the kitchen table. Wanda placed his plate on the table in front of him.

"What are you in such a hurry for anyway?" she asked taking a seat across from him at the table.

"I'm just in a hurry, Mamma," Scottie said. He got up and hurried over to the refrigerator to get a glass of milk. He then returned to the table and started gulping down his food.

"Slow down boy. What's wrong with you? I ain't ever seen you in this much of a hurry to get to school. You found some young girl that's got you all twisted?"

"No way Mamma. Today they tell us who made the basketball team for this year."

"Boy don't get your hopes all built up around a game," Wanda admonished. "I wish you could get just as excited about your grades as you are about a game."

"Mamma, I'm going to go pro and get us out of here. You just wait and see."

"Whatever happens, just remember your Mamma loves you and I want you to be a good student as well as a good ball player. You understand?"

"Yes Mamma." Scottie pushed his plate away. "I'm finished so can I go now?"

"After you put that plate in the sink and rinse it off. You boys act like you got a maid around here."

Scottie got up and strolled over to Wanda. He kissed her on the cheek and then placed his dishes in the sink. "Okay, I'm gone now and you going to be real proud of me when I get home."

"I'm proud of you anyway."

After closing the apartment door, Scottie jumped down the steps taking three at a time until he got to the first floor of the apartment building. He then pushed open the door to the building and stepped out in the California morning sunshine. As he headed for the street he ran into John Ambrose, the manager of the complex as well as one of the coaches at the local boy's club where Scottie learned to play basketball. He had the upmost respect for his coach and mentor John who had been a great athlete at John Muir High School in Pasadena. Scottie thought of him as a surrogate father, a replacement for the one he'd never known.

"Hey Uncle John," Scottie shouted. "This is the big day."

"Oh yeah, you find out your fate don't you?" John asked as he placed his arm around Scottie's shoulder and walked next to him.

"It's going to be on now, Uncle John. Me and my boys going to kick somebody's butt in the conference."

"Don't get ahead of yourself," John admonished. "Check the

list first and then celebrate when you see your name there."

"My name will be there," Scottie said. "I tore them suckers up during tryouts."

John removed his arm from around Scottie's shoulder and stood there. "Just remember someone else makes that decision and basketball isn't everything in life. It's just a game."

"It was for you, Uncle John."

"Yeah, but I never went pro and I made sure I got a half-way decent education. Just think if I had concentrated on school instead of ball and finished my college education, I'd be Director of the Boys Club by now instead of just the assistant. Keep that in mind, young brother." John gave Scottie a tight hug. "Remember ball isn't everything. You have so many more things to accomplish in life. Don't limit yourself." He finished and headed back inside the building.

Scottie stood motionless as he watched Uncle John enter the manager's office to the building. What if his name wasn't on the list? That couldn't be possible. He'd kicked too much butt in the tryouts not to make the team. Sure, he'd missed a few shots and one of the boys had scored at will over him. He still looked good and, anyway, his life would be over if his name was not on the list. Determined that he'd be reporting to practice that afternoon, he turned and started up Fair Oaks Avenue to catch the bus to school.

When the bus pulled up in front of John Muir High School, Scottie jumped from his seat. He pushed his way by a number of other students, bolted off the bus and headed for the gym.

"Hey, Scottie man," a young brother walking out of the gym shouted to him.

"Not now," Scottie shouted back. "I got to check out what's happening." He ran right by the brother and up the steps into the gym.

"But what I wanted to tell you was--"

Scottie slammed the door closed and didn't hear what the brother tried to tell him. He ran down the hall to the gym and swung the locker room door open. He spotted a half-dozen boys standing around a window that had a paper taped to it. Scottie watched as a couple of the boys, who'd been pretty good in practice, slapped hands, did a high five and patted each other on the back. Apparently they had made the team. Suddenly they stopped celebrating as he approached them. Something was wrong. He slowed down, as he got closer to the window. The other boys said nothing to him. It felt like a ton of gravel pulled at his heart and Scottie's legs went weak as he looked at the twelve names of the players who'd made the junior varsity basketball team. He looked again and then a third time and a fourth time. Tears welling up in his eyes. His name was not on the list.

The young boy who had scored all over him in the tryouts said, "Sorry, dawg, but you can always try out next year." He and the other two boys turned and walked away.

"Too bad, Scottie, but there's always next year," one of the other young brothers added. He turned and strolled up the stairway, leaving Scottie alone and crying inside.

The day dragged on forever. It seemed like the entire freshman class offered their condolences to him. With each student that approached him, he slid further down in his chair and deeper into his state of depression. He was a failure, and now his life meant very little to him. How could he possibly tell his mother, Uncle John, and his younger brother that he didn't make the team?

When the bell rang and his last class for the day was over, he hurried back down the stairs and stood outside the gym. He stared through the window and watched as the twelve players chosen for the team lined up and began shooting lay-ups. Again, his eyes filled with tears as he finally turned and walked away. He was in no hurry to go home, but at some point knew he would have to deliver his disappointing news to his family. He still had time to catch the last bus, so he rushed to the front of the school and climbed aboard. This would be the longest ride of his life.

Scottie ran past Uncle John's apartment, rushed up the stairs and into the apartment. He could hear Tupac's "AllEyez on M*e*," and that meant Alex was in the bedroom. He couldn't face his little brother who thought the world of him. Alex considered his older brother an all-star who some day would be as good as Michael Jordan. Now he had to tell him that he didn't even make the junior varsity team. But he just didn't have to do it right then.

He swung the bedroom door open and Alex looked up at him from his bed where he was stretched out listening to the rap song. Scottie tried to ignore him. He went to his side of the room and fell out on his bed. He could detect Alex's eyes on him, and he knew what was coming.

"Well, don't keep me in suspense," Alex said. "Did you make the team?"

Scottie turned his back to him.

"Come on Scottie tell me, you going to be playing point guard or shooting guard? Or maybe they put you right on the varsity team?"

"Naw, they didn't put me on varsity."

"That's okay, cause you can really shine playing junior varsity. You better than all those chumps put together."

"I ain't better than nobody," Scottie snapped. "So just leave me alone. I'll tell you what happened later."

Alex jumped from his bed and turned the music off. "You ain't got to bite my head off," he said and walked out the door. "Way you actin' don't sound like you even made the team." He slammed the door behind him.

Scottie lie there staring at the ceiling. How could God be so cruel to him? He had given him a rotten father who never came around to see him and as far as he knew, never sent any money to help his mother. That's why she had to work all the time doing menial jobs so they could make ends meet. Now God had denied him the one dream he really wanted to come true. That was to be a great basketball star, make plenty of money, and then move his mother into a better house and neighborhood. Someplace where they wouldn't hear neighbors fighting all the time and hear shooting right outside their windows. Now that would never happen because he had no other ability or talent. Like his buddies, it was basketball or nothing. So for him, it would be nothing.

****

Scottie didn't know if he had fallen asleep and captured the images that appeared in a dream or if they were real. Suddenly Uncle John stood before him, but he was dressed differently. He looked like some kind of psychic or holy man. It scared Scottie and he drew back when Uncle John sat on the side of his bed. He placed his large hands on Scottie's shoulder.

"So, little brother, you didn't make the team," he said.

Scottie froze up because he knew Uncle John would be angry

with him. But the tone in his voice was soothing and reassuring. He tried to speak, but the words wouldn't come.

"Don't try to say anything," Uncle John admonished. "My last words to you this morning was to let you know things may not be as you want them to be. Don't be discouraged. I want to take you on a journey. And when we return, you'll reconsider your entire life and the feeling that you are a failure because you didn't make the basketball team. Now close your eyes, take my hand and journey out into the world from which you came centuries ago."

Scottie trusted Uncle John so without hesitation, he reached out and grabbed his mentor's large and strong hand. Instantly, he felt his body moving, but knew he was still lying in bed. He experienced a smooth, fast, and relaxing movement. The pace continued to increase and he felt the distance between his reality and the world to which they traveled.

"Wait, wait," Scottie screamed. "Where are we, Uncle John? Where are we and what's happening?"

"Trust me and relax," Uncle John whispered. "Just feel the bright light and let it take over."

The faster and further they went the brighter the light. Scottie closed his eyes and enjoyed the exhilarating feeling of existence outside of his physical body. They were caught up in the center of a light that was warm and non-threatening. Suddenly, they descended toward the ground. He had no idea where they landed. From what he'd seen in books at school, it appeared to be some kind of farm or plantation. He stared off to his left and there was a large white house with pillars out front, a beautiful green lawn and a carriage off to the left side. To the right there were a number of men sitting atop horses with rifles in their hands. They took off riding toward the woods.

"Uncle John where are--"

"Ssh," Uncle John interrupted him. "We can't make any noise or those men over there will take us in and we'll never get back to Pasadena." Uncle John pointed in the direction of the men who had just taken off riding toward the wooded area.

Scottie took Uncle John's warning seriously. "Where are we?" he whispered.

"We're back in time. The year is 1831 and we're on a plantation in Virginia." Uncle John led him around the side of the big white house.

When they reached the back, Scottie saw rows and rows of old beat up wooden cabins without windows. There was no green grass, only dirt all around them. A number of chickens, along with some pigs and a couple of straggly looking dogs wandered from cabin to cabin as if looking for scraps of food.

They approached the second cabin in the first row and Uncle John swung the door open. They both stepped inside and Scottie saw three Black men sitting on the dirt floor inside. One of the men jumped to his feet and pulled out a knife. He was a big muscular, dark skinned man, with thick coarse hair and fire burning in his eyes. Scottie thought what a powerfully good-looking strong Black man. The kind of man they never saw in their history books. He must have put the fear of God in white people. No wonder they needed the extra advantage of guns and numbers in order to subdue men like the strong Black man standing in front of him.

"We mean no harm," Uncle John said. "This boy comes to you because he has a few questions for the revolutionary prophet Mr. Nat Turner."

"What is it you want with me?" Nat asked in a deep and commanding voice.

"Prophet Nat, this boy is concerned about his future. You see in his time era many of our young brothers are more concerned about honing their basketball skills, a sport where people throw a ball into a net, instead of their learning skills. A test of a young man's worth in some of our communities is how well he plays a game. So Scottie thinks--"

"What is this basketball?" Nat interrupted. "Is it something needed to fight our oppressor for our freedom? Will it help to defeat him?"

"No sir," Uncle John said with humility. "What you're about to do will eventually lead to a war that will end slavery. So this boy lives in a free world and his only concern is that he be able to play this game better than the other boys. He feels that his world will crumble if he doesn't win at this game?"

"A game," Nat shouted. He turned and stared at the other two men. He then walked over to Scottie and placed his hand on the boy's shoulder. "Young brother, these men and I are getting ready to go to our death tonight fighting for Black folks' freedom.

Does your game help free Black people in your world? Does it benefit the race or just the individual? That game will someday be forgotten, just like it is not known to us now, but what we do here tonight will be remembered forever. Forget that game and go back to your place in time and do something to help your people. Don't let our deaths be in vain." Nat ended his words of wisdom and waved his arms back and forth.

Scottie felt his body caught up in the power of Nat Turner and it lifted Uncle John and him right out of the cabin and back into the bright light of time. Again, he felt his body floating through space to a different part of the country but still one filled with danger. Scottie could see a heavily wooded area with no houses or roads. As they started down into the dark of night he saw a campfire with ten Blacks, all dressed in raggedy clothes, huddled around the fire for warmth. He knew the leader of the group was the Black woman with a red bandana around her head and a pistol in her hand. She appeared to be fussing with one of the others in the group. Scottie and Uncle John landed right next to the woman. She jumped back and aimed her pistol at both of them.

"Wait Mrs. Tubman," Uncle John pleaded. "Please don't shoot. We come from another time era seeking your advice."

"What is it that you want with me and my people?" Harriet scowled. "I just got these folks this morning off the Peabody plantation outside Natchez, Mississippi. We got a long ways to go to freedom. And our enemy already done put the slave hunters and them dogs on our trail. So what is it you want? Hurry, man. We don't have much time." Harriett glared at Scottie. "Well, what is it, boy? What do you need to know?"

Uncle John spoke up. "Mrs. Tubman, we come from the time space of 2011. Your tireless work and bravery in bringing Blacks to freedom has since helped to do away with slavery. This boy comes from a free world, so he thinks. His biggest concern is that he didn't make the basketball team, a sport at his school."

"School for Black children," Harriet shrieked. "You hear that, my fellow brothers and sisters? This boy goes to a school." She now turned and glared at Scottie. "Why are you so concerned about this team? Is making this team more important than learning to read and write, something these beautiful people have been deprived of all their lives? They'd sacrifice their life if they knew their kids could learn to read and write someday in the future. On the plantation we aren't allowed to do those things. Our enemies are scared that if we know how to read, then we can study about the great Nat Turner's sacrifice he made years ago for us." Harriett suddenly stopped talking as they heard a twig snap in the woods. "Everyone quiet," she whispered.

Scottie felt a shiver run through his body. What if he got caught with the others? Would he ever be able to return to his time frame? He was beginning to get a better understanding of what his ancestors went through at the hands of an evil and brutal system of oppression. He watched as Harriett crept over to the area where they heard the sounds. She checked it out with pistol drawn, no doubt ready to be used if necessary. As he followed her every move, he recalled one of his teachers telling the class that often times the slaves were very happy and content with their station in life and the slave owners were kind. Now, as he experienced the fear of oppression, he knew that was all one big lie.

After checking out the area where they heard the sound, Harriett returned to the spot next to Uncle John and Scottie.

"These people here will never give up their rights to be educated. That's why they risk their lives to escape from slavery, even with the white oppressors on their trail." She moved in closer to Scottie and stared directly into his eyes. "And you're worried about some game. Please don't tell me after all this struggle that our future generations going to worry about if they can play a game?"

Scottie was frozen in place. He felt ashamed, and knew he could do nothing but stand and listen.

"Boy, go back to your time and master the ability to read and write so that you can continue the work we've started for our race's survival. Go help some Black folks, then you'll also help yourself. Now get out of here before you get caught and can't go back and do your job. Please tell our people that these monsters were never our masters. That is a lie they tell. We call them that for fear of severe beatings. But know that behind their backs, we call them exactly what they are, monsters and oppressors." Harriett clapped her hands together and instantly Scottie felt the air under Uncle John and him lifting and moving them forward in time and location.

The force carried them at such a rapid speed Scottie had no idea where they would end up. He traveled through the dark and light with Uncle John by his side. He tried to talk, but words failed him. He finally closed his eyes and just waited for them to land at their next destination.

It didn't take long. They landed with a thud on the floor of what appeared to be a library or study in someone's home. Scottie lie flat on his back and when he raised up on his side he saw a light skinned man with long gray hair and a matching beard sitting at a desk surrounded by more books than he'd ever seen in his life. He had no idea that Black men read that much. In his neighborhood, everyone watched television and listened to music. He also saw a bunch of newspapers, with the heading *North Star* scattered on the floor. The man looked from his reading and writing at Scottie and Uncle John sitting on the floor.

It surprised Scottie when Uncle John called out the man's name.

"Mr. Frederick Douglass, please forgive us for this intrusion."

Frederick Douglass glowered at the two of them. Despite his fierce stare, Scottie felt attracted to the man. Douglass resonated a feeling of comfort and security. Scottie didn't want Uncle John to spoil that feeling by talking about basketball. He didn't want this man to think as the other two had, that his only concern was for himself. Scottie began to feel embarrassed because of his childish behavior when he found out he didn't make the team. That all seemed irrelevant now as he listened to Black men and women who did great things for Black people. To his chagrin, Uncle John did not spare him.

"Mr. Douglass, my young friend has been feeling low and depressed because he--"

"Don't tell me," Douglass interrupted. "He didn't make some kind of team and now he thinks his life is over."

"How did you know?" Scottie conjured up enough courage to ask.

"You've already visited with my friend Nat, who that same night you met with him struck a mighty blow for freedom. He'll live in the minds and hearts of Black folks forever. He'll be there even after your game is no longer around." Douglass stood up, sauntered over to the window and stared out. The silence lasted for over a minute. He then returned to his chair, sat down and crossed his legs. He stared directly at Scottie. "It's good to feel a passion for something. Just like Nat and Harriett, I feel a passion for freedom for my people." Suddenly Douglass raised his arm and brought his balled fist crashing down on the table. The noise startled Scottie, but he didn't fear this man.

"We have to be free in this century and we have to prosper in generations to come in the next centuries. Make no doubt about it, this is our country just like it is for any other group. Nat, Harriett, and I can help with the freedom, but you, young man, and your generation must help us prosper. I guess this game is going to help some, but what about the other millions of our people? What's going to happen to them while these few players prosper? Take that passion you have for this game and direct it toward your people. And you can help them only if you learn to work the white man's system. This game won't teach you how to do that. School and education will. I was forced to sneak in order to learn how to read. You can do it freely and with no restrictions except the one you impose on yourself. Understand what you have to do young man and go back to your time and direct that passion to benefit all the people and not just you."

"Thank you, Mr. Douglass," Uncle John said as they got up and prepared to leave.

"What are you writing?" Scottie asked as he also got to his feet.

"I am writing a Fourth of July speech that I will read on that historic day. I will, in my speech, point out the hypocrisy of this country that has the nerve to celebrate a day of freedom while keeping others in bondage. Hopefully, it will help serve the abolitionist cause against slavery. And, hopefully, someday you and your generation will read it and realize that we did not like slavery and were not happy in bondage. But first, you and your generation must learn to read before you can understand what we endured just for you."

With those final words, Scottie and Uncle John swooshed back out the door and into the time dimension. Now accustomed to the trip they were on, Scottie felt comfortable asking Uncle John about what was happening to them.

"How is this all happening, Uncle John?"

"We are traveling through the time funnel of the Black experience in this country. The totality of these experiences is what constitutes our culture. Each one of the individuals you have met did something of great importance to help build that culture that we all should be proud of, but just don't know a lot about."

"So we are all connected through these experiences that go back way over a hundred years."

"Exactly and they go back much further than that. They go all the way back to the continent of Africa when our ancestors were brought over here in the bottom of slave ships. They held on to many of the great achievements of their ancestors, and then added the ones we have accomplished here in this country. That is what constitutes our culture. It is on loan to each new generation and it is their duty to preserve it, add something new and exciting and positive to it, and then pass it on to a generation after them."

"Amazing," Scottie mumbled as they slowed down for the next visit.

This time they landed in a classroom with approximately thirty students sitting at desks, totally concentrating on every word spoken by the scholarly looking professor. Like Douglass the man was light skinned in color with a moustache and Van Dyke beard. The man appeared to be soft and warm.

Scottie and Uncle John scrambled to their feet and stood against the wall. All eyes were riveted on them. The professor spoke first.

"Young man, I see that you have been to see Nat, Harriet, and Frederick. How fortunate you are. These students study about them and you actually had the chance to meet them. What an honor."

"Who are you?" Scottie asked.

"What do you mean, who is he?" a number of the students shouted at Scottie. "Where have you been and what are you learning at your school? This is our leader and the greatest scholar in the country, Dr. W.E.B. DuBois. He's the first Black man to receive a Doctorate Degree from Harvard University. He's teaching us here at Atlanta University how to understand the world so that some day the entire race can prosper and graduate from schools like Atlanta University and Howard University."

One of the young students wearing overalls and no shirt jumped to his feet and stuck out his chest. "He has designated us as the Talented Tenth with the enormous, but critical responsibility to go out and educate the rest of our race once we finish our studies. How well he does and how well we do depends on you all in the future. Have you all taken the same serious attitude about the Black race here in America as we have?"

Scottie began to feel intimidated by these young men. They were about his age, but only one hundred years earlier. Their commitment to the future of the Black race far surpassed any commitment coming from his friends at John Muir High School. Scottie wondered when and where had all this fervor been lost.

"Quiet," Dr. DuBois admonished the class. He turned and stared at Scottie. "I know why you are here?"

"How do you know that?" Scottie asked in a somber tone.

"You're searching for your own way. You've been disappointed because you didn't make the basketball team at your high school."

"You know about basketball?" Scottie asked

"Yes, young man, I certainly do. In fact, I've thrown up a couple of hoops in my later life."

"Dr. DuBois, what advice would you give Scottie about his future?" Uncle John finally asked.

"You see these young men in this room?" DuBois asked, pointing to the students. "They'll do anything to get an education because they know it will help them and it'll help the race. I tell you to stretch your mind and your imagination. Test the limits of your ability and when you feel you reached that point, keep on going. Don't ever quit and be twice as good as the other race. Read, study, and understand that you are a part of a mighty people who know how to struggle and win. You can't do that just shooting hoops all day."

"I'm not sure I understand," Scottie said.

"Don't worry. It'll come to you in time. Here's a copy of my writings, *Soul of Black Folks*. Take it and study it." DuBois handed Scottie a copy of the book. He then placed his hand on Scottie's shoulder. "Play your game for fun and exercise, young man. But read and study for your survival. Now you all must be on your way." DuBois turned and sauntered back to his desk in front of the class. "I have squandered twenty minutes of these student's time and that's twenty minutes they must make up." DuBois took his pointer and struck it against the blackboard. Scottie felt himself lifted up and taken out of the room.

As they floated through space, Scottie and Uncle John could

actually see days, weeks, and years pass by. The force carried them to a large hall with a podium up front and rows of seats lined up for the audience. A tall, thin man with flaming red hair, a short beard and wearing black rim glasses stood in front of the podium and stared out at the crowd. Scottie and Uncle John took seats in the front row. The man spoke with fire in his voice.

"You just left Dr. DuBois, a real scholar and a tribute to the Black race," the man said.

"Aren't you Malcolm X?" Scottie asked with excitement in his voice.

"Yes I am, my young brother, and I am pleased that you came to see me about your concerns," Malcolm X answered. "I assume by now that after visiting my fellow heroes of the race, you do realize you have a problem, but it can be resolved."

"How did you know?" Scottie asked, but this time he was pretty sure how the great man knew.

"We have quite a network set up for our communications between generations," Malcolm X answered. "We are worried about you and your many young brothers and sisters of the future."

"Excuse me, sir," Uncle John interjected. "This boy thinks that his life is over because he didn't make the basketball team at his high school."

"I know," Malcolm X said. "You count yourself fortunate, young brother, that your uncle has taken the time to save you from your own destruction. Basketball is right for some, but that number is so small that it is doing our race a disservice."

"What do you mean?" Scottie probed.

"You kids are buying the hype that the National Basketball Association is waiting to make you all super stars and super rich. You see a few great players like Michael Jordan and Kobe Bryant, and the new young super phenom, Lebron James, and you think that's the life for you. Here is a statistic for you and it is right out of your time period." Malcolm paused and pulled a paper out from his inside jacket pocket. He continued, "For every 5,000 boys who play junior high basketball, only 500 play high school. And out of that 500 only 50 play college ball. Now I'd say the chances of hitting it big are not good, but you have every young buck out there putting all their chips on making it to the pros. When they don't even make it to college, they got nothing, but maybe a chance to play ball on the concrete inside the prison." Malcolm X paused to let this message settle in with Scottie. "While you are concentrating on basketball, they are busy building new prisons cause the man knows the real deal. He checks out attendance at inner city schools so he'll have a good idea how many prison beds he'll need in the future. Once you don't learn how to read cause you're so busy playing ball, then you turn to crime. I know cause I did." Malcolm spoke with emphasis. He looked up at the crowd sitting patiently waiting for him to finish with Scottie so he could get on to addressing them. "It's okay to feel bad about not making your team, but you have to get over it and continue to pursue your studies. Read history and learn about your people. Study government so someday you can run the country. Learn mathematics so you'll be able to function in a technological world. If you can accomplish these disciplines, your pride and feeling of self-worth will far exceed any reward you get from playing a game. Now I have a very important speech to deliver this evening, and you all must excuse me." Malcolm slapped his hands together, and Scottie with Uncle John took off on their way to the final destination of the journey.

They landed right at the front of the Lincoln Memorial in Washington, D.C. It was mid-day and Scottie looked out at thousands of people standing around evidently waiting for someone to speak. He then looked up at the steps of the Memorial. A number of men and women mingled around the microphone that was set up at the front of the stage. Suddenly, a man he knew from the history books and the picture in his grandmother's house hurried toward him.

"I only have a few minutes to talk with you," the man said.

"You're Dr. Martin Luther King Jr., aren't you?" Scottie asked in astonishment.

"Yes I am," Dr. King answered. "In a few minutes I have to address the multitude of people who want to know about our future. I have a dream I want to share with them. But before I do, let me share a private dream with you."

Scottie and Uncle John moved in closer to Dr. King so that they could better hear every word spoken.

"My dream is that someday there will be no prisons to house our youth in such large numbers," he began. "My dream is that we will have more of our children born in two-parent families than those just in one-parent households. My dream is that someday young Blacks like you will go to the library like you run to the basketball court. My dream is that there won't be any more crack houses and crack heads, heroin addicts, and for that matter any other drugs in our communities. My dream is that our hatred will be replaced with a love and respect for one another." Dr. King paused and took Scottie's hand. "Scottie, help me to make my dream come true. Return to your time and make a difference. Still play your basketball, but also play in the real game of life and that is for our survival." With those words King disappeared, as did all the surroundings.

Scottie shot straight up in the bed. Uncle John sat next to him and his mother stood at the bedroom door.

"How you doing, young fellow?" Uncle John asked.

"I don't know," Scottie answered. "I had the weirdest dream." He glared at his mother and then at Uncle John. "You were in the dream with me, Uncle John, and we were on a trip and I met all these famous people."

"I know," Uncle John said. "And you now know what you have to do."

A big smile crossed Scottie's face. "I sure do."

"You think you can handle it?" Uncle John asked.

"Just watch me, because I know I got history on my side. I got so much to be proud of and to talk about that I can't wait to get to school in the morning.

"How about basketball?"

"It's just a game. Just basketball."

The Gift

Caleb Alexander

Dr. Shelby Cole stormed through the antiseptic smelling halls of the Johns Hopkins Medical Center searching anxiously for a water fountain. She found one and drank incessantly, trying to quench her parched mouth and dampen her frustration.

"How could he?" she whispered.

Shelby clenched her teeth first, then her fist and pounded it against the off-white colored wall in front of her. How could she have accepted, she wondered?

"Shell, what's the matter?" A voice called out to her.

Shelby turned to see her friend, Dr. Holly Griffon, standing behind her.

"Nothing really," Shelby answered with a rush of air flowing out of her words.

"It didn't look like nothing just a few seconds ago," Holly said.

Shelby lifted her hand and raked it through her hair sending it back over her shoulders. She couldn't hide the truth from Holly. They had been best friends and roommates all the way through undergraduate school at Spelman and then again at Howard Medical School where they both studied to realize their dreams of becoming pediatricians. Holly knew her better than she knew herself.

"Dwight just invited me to spend Christmas with his family in Maine."

Holly crossed her thick arms, and rested them lightly over her hefty midsection. She then leaned forward and engaged her friend with a raised eyebrow.

"And?" she asked

"And I accepted."

"And?"

Shelby raised her arms, lifting her palms toward the sky. She shrugged her petite shoulders.

"And...well...I don't think I'm ready for that yet."

Holly smacked her full, burgundy colored lips and shook her head forcefully, causing her thick gold hoop earrings to shake.

"Girl, ready for what?" she asked.

"For that kind of commitment."

"He didn't ask you for your hand in marriage," Holly scowled. "He just asked you to spend Christmas with his family."

Shelby again raked her hand through her hair and blew out a breath of frustration.

"You know how these things are. I mean he's taking me to meet his family."

"Okay, let me get this straight." Holly lifted her hand and ran her well-manicured finger through her small, perfectly round Afro. "Dwight Cheikh, eligible young bachelor, educated doctor, fine as all outdoors, nicer than the church house deacon, sweet as a stalk of Jamaican sugar cane, has asked you to go meet his family? Now this is the same Dwight who sends you candy, cards, and flowers like they are going out of style? The same Dwight who calls you every night just to tell you how much you mean to him and how much he cares for you? Dwight, who every eligible female doctor, nurse, and technician in this hospital would die to have a man like?"

"Yes, like!" Shelby agreed. "But not Dwight. He's more like a good friend, close buddy type guy. The kind of guy that you call when it's snowing outside and you have a flat tire in the middle of the night."

"Oh yeah, good old reliable, dependable, trustworthy, faithful Dwight. Who would want a man like that?" Holly pursed her lips and tossed her head towards the ceiling. "Girl what on earth was I thinking?"

"You don't understand. Dwight's nice, he's sweet, but--"

"But what?" Holly interrupted her.

"But… he's Dwight. No depth, no coordination, no fashion sense, no excitement, and no fire."

"Then let him go," Holly said flatly.

Shelby folded her arms and turned away from her friend. She took several steps down the hall before stopping and turning to face Holly.

"You don't understand."

"Shell, what is it to understand?"

"I like Dwight. He's a good friend, a wonderful companion, a really sweet boyfriend, but--"

Holly raised her eyebrows encouraging Shelby to continue.

"Lets just say Dwight's a BMW, but I want to marry a Ferrari. I want to be surprised. I want a little salsa, a little spice, and a little spontaneity. I don't think Dwight's capable of those things."

"Wrong! First of all sweetie, salsa and spice will give you heartburn. Unless you want your heart to get burnt, you'd best stay away from those things. Second, you're running around looking for a Ferrari, when you already have a Rolls Royce. Dwight's not fast, maybe not even exotic, but he is rare, and he is the epitome of class. He's a good man. Girl, don't lose a bag of platinum, trying to go for a fist full of gold."

Shelby smiled. Somehow, Holly always knew the right things to say. It was her wisdom that got them through medical school and kept them out of trouble at Spelman.

Holly smiled back with a knowing smile, and ready arms because she knew what was coming next.

Shelby stretched out her arms and wrapped them around her friend. "Why do you always get to be right?" she asked. "Why can't I be right sometimes?"

"Oh, Shell, just do the right thing." Holly squeezed Shelby's petite frame. She stared into her friend's deep chocolate brown eyes. "Remember the promise we made when we graduated from med school?"

"To listen to our patients?" Shelby asked.

Holly nodded. "Uh-huh, that's one of them. Another was to always listen to our hearts. Listen to your heart, Shell. Don't go through life detached, neutral and always analytical. Don't plan out every single thing that's ever supposed to happen to you."

"I don't do that," Shelby protested.

"Oh yeah you do, Girl. I'll bet you know exactly what you want this mythical salsa and spice Ferrari man to be wearing when he comes to drive you off into the sunset."

They both laughed.

"So, don't rule out Mr. Dwight?" Shelby asked after they stopped laughing.

"What does your heart say?"

"I care about him a whole lot."

"Then go. Give him a chance."

"I guess you're right," Shelby admitted. "I mean it's not like I have any other big plans for Christmas."

Holly nodded and smiled. "Good."

Shelby slapped her hand against her forehead. "God, I hope he doesn't get up there and embarrass me."

"Embarrass you how, Shell?"

"I don't know…any number of ways. By dancing for one. Girl, you remember the last time we went to the club with him. He got up and started shaking his narrow butt, doing that old rhythm-less herky-jerky dance that he does."

"Paging Dr. Griffon," the loud speaker interrupted their conversation. "Paging Dr. Griffon. Please report to pediatrics."

While they walked down the hall Holly started shaking and twisting convulsively. "Do the herky-jerky! Do the herky-jerky!" She started singing as they turned the corner. "Do the herky-jerky!"

****

Shelby laid her head back on the headrest as Dwight pulled into a long driveway and proceeded to the front of a magnificent white Victorian-style mansion. Maine was beautiful in the winter. Snow covered the grounds and was piled on the individual branches of the bare trees. The small stream that flowed along the side of the mansion was frozen solid, the white picket fence matched well with the snow, and the low pink clouds in the sky looked like puffs of cotton candy. Smoke was coming from the chimney indicating that the fireplace was ablaze inside the mansion. It was simply Christmas card beautiful as they pulled up and Dwight parked the car off to the left in the driveway.

The Gift

As he got out of the car to come around and open the door for Shelby, Dwight spotted a small group of young adults helping a larger group of children build a round and robust snowman. He then gazed at the other cars parked in the cobblestone driveway. There was a Porsche, Range Rover, Navigator, and a Mercedes, all belonging to members of his family. The crew was all there and ready to celebrate the holiest of days.

The first person out to greet Dwight and Shelby was a young girl, bundled from head to toe in a soft pink Oshkosh snowsuit. Dwight opened his arms wide to receive her.

"Meghan." Dwight took her by the arms and lifted her high into the air.

"Uncle Dwight," the young girl giggled.

Dwight managed to spin Meghan through the air once, and then found himself surrounded by the rest of the troupe.

Shelby laughed and smiled uncontrollably as she watched Dwight descend to one knee and pass out hugs and kisses like candy. He obviously was one of the family favorites. She saw four other young women run out of the house and right up to Dwight. She figured they were family.

"Dwight," the first young lady shouted.

Dwight hugged each of the four, and then turned to Shelby. He grabbed her hand and pulled her close to him. "Shell, I'd like you to meet my sister Stephanie, my sister Erykah, my cousin Sydney, and my cousin Terri. Hey y'all this is Dr. Shelby Cole."

Shelby extended her hand to them, but was pulled into a series of embraces. Tight ones.

"It's good to finally meet you," Stephanie said.

"Dwight has told me so much about you. I feel like we're family already," Erykah said.

"Already, already!" The words bounced through Shelby's mind like a tennis ball at the Williams' sister's home. She could still feel the force of them when Terri stepped forward and hugged her.

"Dwight talks about you all the time," Terri said.

Shelby felt she already knew Terri. She was not only Dwight's cousin but also one of his best friends. She held her hug a little longer than she did the others.

Sydney took her turn and leaned forward to hug Shelby. Her embrace was interrupted by a call from the front door of the farmhouse.

"You kids get in here before you catch a cold," an elegantly dressed older woman with a head of beautiful gray hair said. She wore a long pleated forest green skirt that stopped just above her ankles to reveal a matching pair of suede boots. She also had on an oversized multi-colored sweater with a Christmas motif that complimented her skirt and boots. Her ears were adorned with a set of pearls surrounded by tri-clustered diamonds. Her deep burgundy lips contrasted well with her pearlescent smile and her rich sandstone colored skin. But her most striking feature was the way she stood and moved with grace. An aura of dignity emanated from her very presence.

"Aunt Marjorie," Dwight said as he approached the porch. "How is my ninth favorite aunt?"

"There are only eight of us," Marjorie said as they embraced. "How is my twenty-first favorite nephew?"

"There are only twenty of us," Dwight answered with a smile.

"Oh well." Marjorie shrugged her shoulders. "And who is this?" She asked looking at Shelby.

"Aunt Marjorie, this is my very close friend, Shelby." He placed his arm around Shelby. "This is my Aunt Marjorie, Terri's mom."

Shelby extended her hand, but instead Marjorie took her into another hug. Shelby wondered had this family ever heard of a handshake?

They broke their embrace. Marjorie stepped aside and waved her arm inviting them inside. Shelby entered first, with Dwight right behind her.

As he passed by, Marjorie whispered in his ear, "Not bad, pumpkin. A little thin if you ask me, but not bad."

Shelby overheard Marjorie's comment. She wanted badly to turn around and say, "You're not so bad yourself, toots," but she resisted the urge.

Most of Dwight's family had gathered inside the exceptionally large living room. Shelby calculated its size and concluded that it was larger than her entire apartment back in Baltimore. A tall brightly decorated tree stood majestically in the center of the room with plenty of beautiful decorations, and the massive, mahogany trimmed, brick fireplace with logs ablaze crackled off to the left. It was surrounded by dozens of bright red stockings. Shelby took in the pine mixed with burning log from the fireplace. It smelled just like Christmas throughout the room. Two men and three women stood around the tree drinking hot apple cider out of beautifully engraved glass cups.

The sounds emanating from the piano grabbed Shelby's attention. Several young adults had gathered around a Steinway Baby Grand, while one young lady played Stevie Wonder's "Ribbon in the Sky."

"Here," Dwight said, startling her. He handed Shelby what appeared to be a cup of eggnog.

"Thank you." She took the cup and sipped from it. "This is a lovely home," she said in between sips.

"It's our family homestead," Dwight said. "Been in the family for generations. Come on, I'll show you around and introduce you to everyone."

They strolled into the kitchen where a number of the women stood at the kitchen table preparing the Christmas meal even though it was still a couple days off. The aroma from the various foods teased Shelby and made her hungry. She wanted to eat right then and there. It always seemed to be the older women who were in charge when the food was being prepared. It was no different here. It reminded Shelby of the many Christmas celebrations she had spent at home with her family.

Dwight took her hand and led her over to an elderly lady sitting on a chair in the corner of the room. It seemed to Shelby that the woman's deep, rich brown eyes penetrated right through her as she stood in front of the old lady.

"Shelby, this is my Grand Dora. She is my great grandmother and she is one-hundred-and-one years old."

"Boy, don't be telling my age cause I still look like I'm young and only eighty." Dora's voice resonated across the room in sharp, unbroken tones of authority. She reached out to hug Shelby. "Where did this boy find someone as pretty as you, young lady?"

"Thank you, ma'am," Shelby said. What an absolutely beautiful woman. I can't believe she is over one hundred years old, she thought. "I work with your grandson at the hospital."

"You his nurse?" Dora asked.

"No ma'am, I'm a doctor. I'm a pediatrician."

"Praise to Jesus, look what progress this race is making. We don't only have men doctors, which was the case in my day. We now got our women as doctors. I need another hug, honey."

Shelby hugged Dora one more time and they moved over to two ladies who looked quite alike with one appearing to be just a little older than the other. She especially noticed how the older lady was dressed with her long pleated skirt, and suede boots. She wore a burgundy double-breasted top with double rows of pearl and diamond clustered buttons and a large burgundy and black paisley scarf hanging loosely over her left shoulder. The younger lady wore an elegant navy blue dress with double rows of gold buttons that accentuated her large gold earrings and then gold bracelets that hung loosely around her wrist. She sported double rows across her hair in a twist and joined at the back forming a V. Shelby thought that these ladies really did know how to dress. The two ladies stood over the kitchen sink cleaning a bunch of greens.

"Shelby, I want you to meet the other two ladies who are the most important in my life right now." Dwight placed his arm around the one who looked to be younger. "This is my mother Dr. Bernadette Cheikh and this other gorgeous lady is my grandmother, Granny Grand."

The three ladies hugged and Dwight continued. "Shelby is my dearest of friends and is a pediatrician at the hospital."

"I heard you tell Grand Dora that," Bernadette said. "That's just wonderful. We ladies got it going on, don't we Shelby?"

"Yes ma'am, we sure do," Shelby concurred and they all laughed.

The piano playing came to an end and was replaced with sounds from the radio. The Mighty O'Jays blared through the speakers singing, "Family Reunion." Dwight's sister Erykah, his cousins Tracey, Terri, and Brittany, and his sister-in-law Lauren jumped up and started dancing. To Shelby's horror, Dwight joined them.

Shelby's hands flew to her face and covered her mouth in embarrassment as Dwight danced off beat with the others. Dwight's cousins, aunts, and everyone else in the room began laughing.

"Dwight, sit your no-rhythm-having butt down somewhere, boy," Aunt Connie shouted.

"Nope, and this is all your faults. Y'all sent me to boarding school in Canada, and so now you have to reap what you've sown." Dwight spun around and flailed his arms through the air like a spasmodic harem dancer. "So now you have to watch, and eat your hearts out."

Dwight's dancing had everyone laughing, including himself.

Shelby felt good watching Dwight having a lot of fun. He couldn't dance, but that didn't stop him from enjoying himself. Shelby laughed so hard she developed a slight headache.

When they finally sat down, Dwight's dancing was the topic of conversation.

"Dwight, I'll never forget the time when we were in Medical school at MeHarry, and we all went out to the club," Terri said. She turned toward the rest of the family and Shelby. "Dwight got up to dance, and my goodness, he cleared the entire dance floor. Everyone just stood around watching him, like they were in shock."

"I remember that time," Brittany chimed in. "I was down there visiting with you all. And when Dwight started dancing I didn't know whether to applaud or run for help."

"Hey y'all," Bernadette shouted in her strong West Indian accent. "Stop teasing my baby boy. Him can't help it cause him don't have any rid-dem. You blame it on his far-der, not me." She was a thin lady, but had an overwhelmingly strong voice.

Shelby knew from conversations with Dwight that his mother had also attended MeHarry along with his father. They met during medical school. There were so many successful people in this family. How do they do it? When she thought she had been sufficiently awe-struck by this family's credential what she learned next shocked her even more.

"Shelby, Dwight told us you're specializing in pediatrics?" Dwight's Aunt Colleen asked.

"Yes ma'am."

"Great," Aunt Colleen replied. "You know my husband and I are both pediatricians, and so are our daughters, Sydney and Robyn. If there's anything we can do to help you, don't hesitate to give us a call."

"Thank you," Shelby said somewhat tongue-tied. "Are all the members of your family doctors?" She turned to Dwight and asked.

"Just about," he said and smiled, as did the rest of the family. "All my aunts and uncles are doctors, I got a couple cousins who have Doctorates in Aeronautical Engineering, in Physics and Economics. My cousin who isn't here yet is a lawyer. We just don't know how she went astray. Majoring in something outside the sciences."

"I'm very impressed," Shelby said. She then got up and stretched. "Dwight, could you show me where I'm going to be sleeping?" She asked. "That long drive up from Baltimore has just worn me out."

"Shame on you, Dwight," Bernadette interjected. "You should have already shown her to the special guest room overlooking the lake. I'm sorry, darling, but my son is not acting like a Cheikh. You'll get the opportunity to meet his father tomorrow who is a real gentleman, you know from the old school. He would have been up here but had a late emergency at the hospital."

"I'm looking forward to it," Shelby said. "You all have quite a family."

"Come on, I'll show you where you can tuck away for the night," Dwight said as he led Shelby out of the room.

"Good night, all. I'll see you in the morning." Shelby followed Dwight out of the living room.

"Good night, Shelby," the family said in unison.

Shelby lay in the bed with several troubling thoughts on her mind. Who were these people? Where did they come from and how did they all become so successful? What was their secret? She drifted off to sleep with that question burning in her mind.

That morning Shelby woke up to a fantastic picture window view of the trees covered with snow and the lake frozen solid and also snowed over. It was a perfect view of nature at her best. She showered, dressed, and hurried down the spiral staircase into the dining room area. As soon as she hit the bottom steps she could smell the fried potatoes, bacon and eggs, along with the coffee. Dwight wasn't up yet, so she sat with Terri at the kitchen table and devoured her breakfast.

The Gift

After breakfast she walked outside into the brisk morning air. Shelby tilted her head towards the new morning sky and smiled at the sunbeams as they broke through the clouds and tickled her face with their warmth. It was a wonderful morning. She never imagined that this holiday would turn out to be so pleasant and so full of surprises. To actually see a Black family as successful as Dwight's was as refreshing as the morning air. They seemed to stay under the radar and no one even knew they existed. This family was the equivalent of the 1980's Huxtable's in 2010, but the difference was they were the real deal.

She was glad that she'd gotten up early even though she'd been quite tired from the long drive yesterday. Why in the world would I want to sleep when there is so much to enjoy in the environment, she thought. Sleep is a waste of time. I want to take in as much of this as possible. Shelby strolled back up to the porch and into the house.

The family had gathered in the living room, and they were threading strings of popcorn and candy to add to the already decorated Christmas tree. Dwight's Uncle Major was stringing additional lights around the tree, while his Aunt Beverly passed out cups of hot chocolate. The kids were buzzing like wasps around a fiery nest, and the rest of the adults were gathered inside of the living room trying to remember old dances.

"Come on Shelby," Sydney said as she entered the room. "We're about to do the Electric Slide."

Shelby shook her head. "I forgot how to do that one," she lied.

Dwight's cousin Lauren beckoned for Shelby to join them. "Girl, you remember the Electric Slide?"

"Honey, stop being shy and get up there and join the fun," Aunt Connie said. "You're practically family."

Again, Shelby shook her head. "I think I'll go back outside and get some more of this Maine fresh air."

"It is really beautiful out there." Connie nodded.

"Here, take my jacket." Aunt Marjorie handed Shelby a large blue, down filled parka. "It's still a bit cold out there."

"Thank you," Shelby said and then headed back out doors.

Shelby spotted Dwight outside with his brothers, Brian and Kirby, and the rest of the children, building a snowman.

"When is Uncle Sig coming?" Meghan asked Dwight.

"I think he'll be here today," Dwight answered.

"Is he going to be wearing his red suit?" Cheyene asked

"Of course," Princess said. She, at six, was the oldest of the children outside. "It's a tradition."

"Is he going to bring the big red bag?" Emily asked

"Yep," Dwight answered.

"Is he going to bring the gifts?" Pria chimed in with the question.

"Yep," Dwight again answered and smiled.

"What about the story?" Amber walked up next to Dwight and took his hand in hers. "Is he going to tell the story?"

"Definitely," Dwight answered. "Uncle Sig tells the story every year."

"Why does he always tell it?" Amy asked.

Dwight stopped working on the snowman. "I don't know. Uncle Sig has always told the story. Ever since I was a little boy."

Paige, Dwight's niece, jumped into his arms and wrapped her arms around his neck. "I want you to tell the story," she said.

"I can't," Dwight said.

Paige's sparkling doe-like eyes glistened as she titled her head. Their hazel color shifted towards a soft green as the sun struck them. "But I want you to tell them," she said.

"Yeah," Pria agreed.

"Yeah," Amber joined in.

"Yeah," Cheyenne added her two cent.

"We'll see," Dwight said. He sat Paige down and turned towards Shelby. "How about a walk?"

Shelby nodded and accepted Dwight's hand as he led her across the lawn and into a wooded area right next to the lake. Shelby wanted to ask Dwight about this Uncle Sig, the stories, and the red suit. If Uncle Sig was going to wear the suit and carry a bag of gifts, why was he going to do it on the 23rd instead of on Christmas morning? And why did the kids know it was him?

Dwight led Shelby to a small covered beach swing, which sat next to a large frozen duck pond. Together, they sat and began swinging.

"How do you like it out here?" Dwight asked.

"It's beautiful Dwight and your family is so nice. Thank you for asking me to be your guest."

"No, thank you for coming." Dwight rose from the swing, reached inside his large, green down parka and pulled out a small black, felt box. He dropped down slowly on one knee, and took Shelby's hand into his. "Shell, we've been going together for almost a year now. We're close friends, we know each other really well, and we've shared so much together. I don't have to look any further. I don't want to look any further." He hesitated to clear his throat and get his words just perfect. "I've found everything that I'm looking for, everything that I need in you."

Dwight opened the small black box and held it out for Shelby to look into.

She coughed. It was a rock big enough to choke a horse.

"Shell, grow old with me," Dwight said. "Do me the honor of becoming my wife."

Shelby was breathless, speechless, in shock. First things first, she thought, breathe. That's it girl, breathe!"

"Dwight, I don't know what to say," she whispered.

"Say yes."

"I care about you tremendously, Dwight, but--"

"But you don't love me," Dwight said as he rose up from his knees.

"That's not what I was going to say. I do love you, Dwight."

"But not in a marrying sort of way?"

"Dwight, please let me finish."

He nodded.

"I do love you, but I can't give you an answer right at this moment. This is a big surprise, Dwight, and I'm going to need some time to think."

"I can accept that answer, but I'm putting you on notice, Ms. Shelby Cole. I love you and so you get prepared to be romanced, wined, dined, pampered, loved, cuddled, protected, and flowered from this day forwaard.."

She laughed. She knew that Dwight was serious and was one of the nicest, sweetest men in the world. She often told herself that Dwight would be a real catch, and definitely make some woman really happy, she just didn't know if she was that woman.

Dwight and Shelby made it back to the house and into the living room just as his cousin Sydney had organized the five other members into a contest of "name that tune."

"Come on, you guys have to join in this," she said to the two of them. "You got out of doing the Electric Slide, but you're not going to get away this time." Sydney directed her comments at Shelby.

Shelby and Dwight took seats on the large leather couch and listened as Sydney took them on a trip down memory lane. Shelby was swept away by Billy Paul, Rolls Royce, Teena Marie, Betty Wright and Luther Vandross. She listened as Marvin Gaye, the Isley Brothers, The Manhattans, and Teddy Pendergrass serenaded her and everyone else in the room. She listened to the strong voices of Natalie Cole, Aretha Franklin, Gladys Knight, and Diana Ross, Earth, Wind, and Fire, the Mighty O'Jays, LTD, The Commodores, and the Isley Brothers swept her away. Smokey Robinson and the Miracles, Tina Turner, The Four Tops and The Stylistics, and James Brown all took her to another time and place. She was lost in the good times, the times of Motown. It lasted all the way until the sun gave way to the moon, and no one noticed the time.

"He's here!" Brittany shouted. "Uncle Sig's car just pulled up."

The kids ran to the door and stared out bursting with anticipation. Shelby clasped her hands together to hide her nervous curiosity. She just knew Uncle Sig was going to come through the door with a bright red Santa suit, screaming, "Ho! Ho! Ho!"

Uncle Sig strolled to the door, stood just at the entrance and posed, allowing the doorsill to frame him. Shelby's mouth fell open in shock.

Uncle Sigmund Chiekh wore a tailor-made double-breasted, crimson red, designer suit with a white ascot button-down shirt, and a crimson red, silk tie. At the end of his cuffed red trousers, Shelby saw a pair of crimson red alligator skin shoes by Mauri. On his head, he sported a crimson red fedora, tilted just to the right. His smile looked as though it could light up Manhattan.

Dwight leaned over and whispered into Shelby's ear, "Uncle Sig's suits are legendary. They are like a quirky family tradition. Don't worry, we're not crazy."

Suddenly, everyone inside the house burst into applause. They whistled, clapped, and laughed as Uncle Sig posed and bowed over and over again.

Shelby laughed and clapped enthusiastically. Every family had their own quirky little tradition, she told herself. This one was fun. She was really enjoying herself.

The children surrounded Uncle Sig and led him into the living room to his special seat near the fireplace. He smiled and placed his bright red bag next to him then motioned for Dwight to come over.

"What's up, Uncle Sig?" Dwight asked.

Uncle Sig made a slashing motion across his throat. "I'm hoarse and I've lost my voice," he whispered in a croaking, rasping voice. "You're going to have to tell the story."

Dwight's eyes flew open wide in disbelief. "Me? Uncle Sig I can't tell--"

Uncle Sig's raised eyebrows cut off Dwight's protests as he handed the bag over to Dwight.

Shelby moved in closer to Dwight wondering what the big deal was, and why Uncle Sig couldn't pass out these gifts even with a sore throat.

Dwight opened the red canvas bag and began to remove large bundled albums and bundled papers. Shelby remained at a loss, despite the fact that everyone's enthusiasm remained high, even the children.

When Dwight unrolled one of the large scroll-like pieces of paper, she understood. It was the Chiekh family tree.

"Okay," Dwight said in a slightly high-pitched and broken voice. "We're going to play the game first, and then I'll tell the story."

The adults moved slowly to the rear of the huddled group and allowed the children to gather up front. They formed a semi-circle around Dwight.

"Who was Grand Dora's mom?" Dwight asked.

"Mamma Jewel," Emily answered.

"Right, two points for Emily," Dwight said. "And who was Mamma Jewel's mamma and daddy?" he asked.

"Mamma Sweet and Grandpa Timmy," Meghan shouted.

"Good!" Dwight said. "Four points for Meghan. Now who was Grandpa Timmy's mamma and daddy?"

"Mommy Eddie Mae and Grandpa Louis," Princess answered.

Shelby was suddenly short of breath. She had to get out of the room and out of the house; she needed air. She raced onto the front porch and sat down on the swinging porch bench. Shelby understood now. It all came together; it all made sense. She had expected toys, clothes, and other types of gifts. But what Uncle Sig had brought was more precious than all of the toys and the clothes in the world. He had brought with him a real gift, the gift of family, of history, of roots.

Shelby fumbled with her hands before interlacing her fingers and rocking back and forth in the swing. She had wondered how this family was able to turn out generation after generation of successful, educated, well-rounded individuals, and now she knew. They gave each new generation a foundation to stand on, a legacy to uphold, roots to nourish, and a supporting, nurturing, loving environment in which to flourish.

She could hear Dwight through the living room window. He told the story of his family's history, recounting each generation and their struggles and their accomplishments, all to the claps and cheers of the children. This man, the man she thought had no depth, no history, no rhythm, no soul, was now recounting the history of a family whose service, dedication, and sacrifice to their people dated back hundreds of years.

Shelby buried her head into her hands and began to weep. She had been so wrong, so silly, and so shallow. Her tears flowed steadily for several moments before she felt a tap on her shoulder. Startled, she raised her head quickly to find Uncle Sig standing before her with his gigantic smile.

"What's the matter, young lady?" he asked.

Shelby quickly wiped away the tears streaming down her cheeks. "Oh, it's nothing," she said. She glanced back over her shoulder and peered through the blinds of the living room window.

"Your family, it's just so…so beautiful."

Uncle Sig smiled and waved his hand toward the bench. "May I?" he asked.

Shelby nodded yes.

Uncle Sig sat down next to her and produced a soft, white silk handkerchief. He handed her the handkerchief and then wrapped his arm around her.

"Everything is alright, young lady. You just cheer yourself up. It's Christmas."

"I know, I know," Shelby said. "I was just sitting here thinking, and, well, my emotions got the best of me. Hey, wait a minute… your voice!"

Uncle Sig smiled and lowered his head. Shelby looked at his puffy cheeks and noticed the twinkle in his deep brown eyes. She knew he was embarrassed.

"I'm not getting any younger," Uncle Sig said. "It was time to pass on the story-telling to the next generation."

"So you pretended that your throat was sore!"

"That's the way it was passed on to me," Uncle Sig said with a smile. "If it wouldn't have been for my Uncle Lamar's sore throat I would have never taken over when I did."

"And a whole generation would have missed out on those fabulous red suits!" Shelby said.

They laughed together.

"Wait a minute, is Dwight going to have to wear those things?" she asked.

Uncle Sig laughed again. "No. Every generation adds their own flair, and has their own style of presentation. My Uncle Lamar's suits were green." Uncle Sig leaned over and nudged Shelby's shoulder with his own. "Can you imagine me wearing a green suit?"

Again they laughed.

The big white door creaked open and Dwight stepped out. "What's up guys?" he asked.

Uncle Sig grabbed his throat and whispered in a raspy voice, "Just getting some advice on this old throat of mine." Having finished, Uncle Sig got up and headed back into the house.

Dwight sat down on the bench next to Shelby and smiled at

her. "What's up Shell?" he asked.

Shelby turned her body on the bench facing him. She took his hand into hers. "Dwight you have a wonderful family. And, well… they remind me a little bit of my own. They are always there for you, always willing to help out, and give advice. I remember one piece of advice my mother gave me when I was younger. She told me to never be afraid to admit when you're wrong. You'll lose friends and sleep if you do."

She released Dwight's hand and crossed her arms as the chill of the evening air struck her. "My mother used to give me a lot of advice," she continued. "We used to talk about relationships, and about finding true love. I always pictured my Knight in Shining Armor, my Romeo, and my Prince Charming, coming and sweeping me off my feet, and carrying me off into the sunset. I never thought my Romeo would sneak up on me, or that he would be so comfortable, so easy to talk to. I didn't know that he would start off being my dear, sweet, kind friend."

Shelby threw her head back in laughter, and raked her hand through her hair, sending it over her shoulders. "I was told that love blindsides you, not creeps up on you and wraps itself around you like a warm, comfortable old blanket on a cold winter's afternoon. And that's why I didn't know, that's why I didn't recognize it. I didn't see it. I was looking in all the wrong places, for all of the wrong signs."

She took Dwight's hand into hers again. "I, Shelby Denise Cole, love you, Dwight Antoine Chiekh. And I would consider myself the luckiest woman on earth if you would have me as your wife."

Dwight pulled the small, felt box from his pocket, opened it, and removed the ring. He placed it on her finger.

Shelby giggled the whole time he was placing the ring on her finger. She felt dizzy, like she was floating.

"Did my uncle have anything to do with this?" Dwight asked suspiciously.

Shelby laughed. "No, silly. Your uncle and I were discussing something else."

"Him pretending to have a sore throat so that he could pass the story-telling on to me?" Dwight raised an eyebrow.

"Dwight!" Shelby said, surprised. "Now what makes you think

that?" They hugged, got up and went back into the house to share their good news with the family.

That night Shelby lay in the bed and thought about the day's events. How odd, two days before Christmas and gifts were passed out like there was no tomorrow. She had a fiancée who was going to make a wonderful husband. Dwight was given the honor of being the guardian of his family's treasured history, the librarian of all that is sacred to them and makes them who they are. The children received the best gift of all. They were given a foundation of dignity, a legacy of accomplishment, and an abundance of family love to stand on. Shelby knew that it was a precious gift that they would be given every year until they went off to Fisk, Howard, Spelman, and Morehouse to become doctors, lawyers, and scientists. Judging from their enthusiasm, they understood what a precious gift they were being given, as well.

After Dwight had proposed to her earlier that afternoon, they went back inside and she was officially welcomed into the family. The warm hugs, the kisses, and the advice from the older women who had married into the family would be invaluable. She also smiled as she thought about the celebration they had after the announcement. Dwight's family loved to have a good time. They cranked up the CD player and danced down memory lane for the rest of the evening. They did the Electric Slide again, and the Wop, the Calypso, the Jerk, the Penguin, the Camel Walk, the Flirt, and every other dance they could think of. Dwight even joined in and did his little rhythm-less herky-jerky. Eventually, even Granny-Gran danced a little.

Shelby rolled on her side and laughed heartily as she visualized Granny-Gran's dancing. She performed the most elegant rendition of the Butterfly and the Tootsie Roll Shelby had ever seen.

A Lesson in Life and History

Rhonda M. Lawson

A gust of exasperated air escaped from seventeen-year-old Michelle's lips as Delta Airlines Flight 1081 began its descent into Savannah, Ga. airport. She stared out the window, her eyes transfixed on the city as the little map-like shapes turned into recognizable buildings, houses, and trees. A few minutes later, a woman's voice, sounding too cheerful, came over the intercom.

"Welcome to Savannah, Ga., we're glad Georgia's on your mind."

Michelle rolled her eyes upward and sucked her teeth. "Let the country-ness begin."

"Watch your mouth, little girl," Louise, her mother mumbled. "I know you're not happy about coming to the South, but don't let your mouth get you into trouble."

"I don't understand why I had to come," Michelle replied, pursing her lips.

"Michelle, look at me."

She whipped her head toward her mother and cupped her forehead with her hand. The speed of her descent mixed with attitude shot a pain from the back of her ear to just over her right eye. "Mamma, can this wait until we land? My head is killing me."

"You keep actin' like that, and your head won't be the only thing killing you," Louise scowled while leaning back against the headrest. She closed her eyes, and Michelle knew that the conversation was temporarily over.

The plane hit the ground with three thuds and then coasted to the gate.

"It is now okay to use cell phones and other instruments," the stewardess said.

Louise sat straight up in her seat, pulled out her cell phone and powered it on. Michelle watched her mother as she scrolled through the address book on her cell phone and tapped the desired number. It took only a few seconds before Louise morphed into her alter ego.

"Hey girl," Louise sang, a little too loud for Michelle's liking. She could only hope the beep signaling the passengers to unfasten their seatbelts and prepare to exit the plane would drown out her mother's outburst.

Michelle looked around at the people shuffling past them with their duffle bags and suitcases, hoping her mother's loud voice didn't attract too much attention.

"I betcha she'll be late," Michelle mumbled. "They're always late."

Louise cut her eyes at her daughter as she asked, "All right, Cheryl, how long you gonna have us waitin'? Black folks know they ain't never on time."

Michelle's small victory over-rode the wave of embarrassment she felt when her mother berated an entire race of people in front of an airplane full of strangers. Mostly white strangers. Although her mother was right, the entire world didn't have to know. Besides, she only meant *Southern* Black people were always late. Her mother had taken it to another level by applying her family's ineptitude to everyone. Back home in New York, no one was ever late. In fact, being on time was late.

"Well, hurry and get here," Louise said. "Lord knows I don't wanna be standin' on that curb all night." She pushed the END button and dropped the phone back into her purse. "Your Auntie Cheryl is on the way, but she's gonna be awhile."

"That's not surprising." Michelle rose up from her seat, reached into the overhead bin and grabbed her shoulder bag. "We'd better get off this plane before they kick us off."

The two gathered their belongings and strolled off the airplane, bidding a heartfelt "bye-bye" to the captain and flight attendant. As they walked through the airport, Michelle took note of the people who seemed to move in slow motion through the corridors. No wonder people are always late here in the South, she thought.

They don't move fast for anything.

They made it out of the main corridor and into the baggage claim area and down to the carousel where the luggage had already started to go around in a semi-circle.

"This airport is tiny," Michelle said.

"It's a small city," Louise quipped. "Not every airport in the South is like this. The Atlanta airport is huge and so is the one in Dallas."

A smirk showed on Michelle's face. "I don't think every city in the South is backwards. I'm sure there are a few progressive cities around here."

Louise glared at her daughter and shook her head. "I can't believe I've let 16 years go by without bringing you to the South. Your family didn't always live in New York."

"Yeah, but enough of my family did that I didn't have to experience this stuff." She looked around with disgust. All of the men looked like wannabe thugs with their white T-shirts, gold teeth and scruffy faces. And the women were no better. Did the words Twenty-four Hour Fitness mean anything to anyone down here? "Why am I here anyway?" she asked.

Before Louise could answer she spotted one of their suitcases rounding the carousel. She stepped forward, grabbed the black Louis Vuitton garment bag before it could pass her by. A matching suitcase came out of the end of the carousel. Instead of waiting for it to move in front of her, Michelle shuffled a little closer in and grabbed it, nearly losing her balance once she snatched the suitcase in her hands.

"You all right, honey?" an elderly Black man asked. The scruffiness of his face, although a bit greyer, was characteristic of what she'd seen in the less than thirty minutes she'd been in Savannah, but he was well dressed in a casual tan suit, white shirt with a brown tie.

"Yes, thank you," Michelle answered, managing a friendly and apologetic smile. "I guess my suitcase was a little heavier than I thought. I hope I didn't hurt you?"

"No, I'm fine," the man said with a smile. "I was just makin' sure you were fine, too."

"Michelle, you all set?" Louise asked, approaching them while

43

pushing a luggage cart.

Michelle picked up the heavy suitcase and placed it on the cart, thankful for the assistance. "Yes," she said. "I was just talking with this gentleman. He kept me from breaking my neck when I tried to pick up the suitcase with my clumsy self."

"I don't know why you packed so much anyway," Louise said with a chuckle. "We're only going to be here for the weekend."

The man smiled as he looked directly at Louise. "I've had the same kind of conversation with my own daughter. She would always tell me, 'Daddy, a woman has to have options.'"

Michelle and Louise both laughed at the manner in which the man mimicked his daughter. Michelle was sure the girl would be horrified at the way her father portrayed her to strangers.

Louise stuck out her hand. "My name is Louise Anderson, and this is my daughter, Michelle."

The man took her hand and shook it. "I'm Charles Perry. Welcome to my city."

Louise smiled.

Michelle groaned.

"My sister lives here," Louise said. "I haven't been here since I was a teenager, but I still love Savannah." She pulled her hand back and asked, "Is this your home?"

"Yes it is," Charles answered. "I've lived in Savannah all my life. My daughter moved to New York from here a couple of years ago after she got married. I just returned from visiting them."

"I'll bet New York was a big difference from Savannah?" Michelle said.

"Yeah it was," Charles replied. "But I have to tell you, it's good to be home. There was way too much hustle and bustle in New York. It seems like everyone's always in a hurry. It's a beautiful city, though, but there's nothing like being home."

"I love New York," Michelle said bursting with pride. "There's no place like it."

"Is this your first time in Savannah?" Charles asked.

"Umm…" she stuttered and looked at her mother. Back home a New Yorker knew better than to tell a stranger it was their first time anywhere. Most of them could tell an out-of-towner from a mile away, and also knew they could easily be victimized if they trusted the wrong person.

"Excuse my child, Mr. Perry," Louise said, touching her daughter's shoulder. "This is not only her first time in Savannah, but it's her first time in the South. She has a touch of Big City-itis."

"You have to take a tour of the city while you're here," Charles said. "Savannah is known as the most beautiful city in the country, and there's a lot of history here."

"That's true," Louise agreed. "I haven't been here in years, but I do remember the moss hanging from the trees in the squares. River Street, the cobblestone streets--"

"Yes, all of that, but don't forget the history," Charles interrupted. "Savannah was a major port in the Trans-Atlantic slave trade. Savannah was also a stop on the underground railroad."

"Big surprise," Michelle mumbled, looking away. "A southern city famous for slavery."

Suddenly she felt a sharp sting on her arm. "Ouch!" she exclaimed and tried to rub away the pain. What was intended to be an inner thought must have been voiced a little too loudly and Louise made her pay for it. Her eyes quickly focused on Charles, more embarrassed by the reprimand than the words that caused it. He didn't seem to be upset at all, but he sure wasn't smiling.

"That's enough, young lady," Louise snarled through clenched teeth. "Now don't let your mouth get you in trouble." Louise looked directly at Charles. "I'm sorry, Mr. Perry. Like I said, this is her first time in the South. But that's no excuse. I know I taught her better than that."

Charles raised his eyebrows and nodded his head. His comforting smile returned. "I'm sure you did. No offense taken. Just make sure you show her around so she can see what we southern folks have to offer."

"Sorry, Mr. Perry," Michelle said, almost in a whisper. "No offense."

He smiled and nodded again, then picked up his suitcase. "It was a pleasure meeting you ladies. Michelle, I hope you'll enjoy your stay in Savannah."

"It was nice meeting you as well, Mr. Perry," Louise said before Michelle could say anything else.

Charles disappeared out the revolving door, Louise turned to her daughter and glared.

Michelle looked away. "What, Mamma?" she asked, her shoulders hunched in resignation. "I said I was sorry."

"You shouldn't have even had to say you were sorry. One of these days you're going to learn to watch your mouth."

Louise picked up her garment bag and charged toward the door, leaving her daughter to trudge behind pulling the heavy suitcase. It felt as if the entire airport had witnessed the exchange. Some onlookers were blatant. They stared as Michelle walked past, some with looks of compassion, others with contempt. A couple of men even had the nerve to snicker. She rolled her eyes at them, mumbling, "Ignorant, bamas."

Michelle finally caught up with her mother standing at the curb with her arms folded looking towards the oncoming traffic. Michelle didn't know what her Aunt Cheryl's car looked like, but judging from her mother's tense stare and locked jaw line she knew the vehicle wasn't on the horizon. She placed the suitcase down on the ground and sat on top of it, refusing to look up because she knew Louise's tirade was far from over. A few minutes went by and still no Aunt Cheryl and the longer it took her aunt to show up, the more her mother's speech would become intense. Louise didn't disappoint her.

"Sometimes I wonder if you sit in your room and invent new ways to embarrass me," Louise said, her gaze still transfixed on the passing vehicles. "You still haven't figured out that what you do and say reflects on me." She chuckled and shook her head. "I sound like my grandmother now. She used to tell me, 'Remember you're Helen's grandchild.'" She didn't let any of us represent her wrong. And we didn't."

Louise turned and glared at her daughter, the look of scorn still intact. "I guess I should have used more of her rules in raising you. You're a good girl, but that attitude that you're better than other people has got to stop. What makes you think you're so much better than southerners? You're only a couple generations removed from the South yourself."

Michelle jumped up and pleaded, "Come on, Mamma. What is really so special about living in the South? All you ever talk about is slavery, segregation, and the Civil Rights Movement. It doesn't sound to me like the South was all that great a place to live."

Louise's glare intensified as if regarding her daughter for the first time. "I really should have brought you back here sooner. All those years of letting you hang out with your friends, going to summer camp when I should have been sending you back home in the summer. Now here you are, about to graduate from high school, and I'm seeing that you have absolutely no respect for anyone without a New York zip code."

"Mamma, that's not true. I just don't like the South. What's wrong with having preferences?"

"Nothing, but you don't have preferences, you have prejudices. You don't know a darn thing about life in the South, but you have such a strong judgment that you're not even giving the place a chance." Louise switched her garment bag from one hand to the other and flung it back over her shoulder, "which makes me wonder, if you have this type of disregard for the place where I grew up, do you have the same disregard for me? And if you disregard me like that, what must you possibly think of all the women who came before you?"

Did the few misplaced words about the South deserve this lecture, Michelle wondered as she chose to remain quiet. There was no need to raise the ire of her mother an additional notch. She so wanted to tune her out that she didn't notice the white Cadillac CTS pull in front of them.

"Hey, hey, HEY!" Cheryl called out to her sister and niece, punctuating each word with a honk of the horn. "What's going on?"

"Aunt Cheryl," Michelle whispered with a sigh of relief. "Thank goodness."

"Don't think Cheryl is going to save you," Louise spat out, losing none of the fervor from her tirade. She headed for the back of the car. "Pop the trunk, Cheryl."

"All right."

The trunk popped open and Michelle followed her mother to the back of the car. As Louise placed the bags in the car, Cheryl stuck her head out the window and shouted, "You ain't going to bite my head off too?"

"You shut up." Louise finished placing the bags in the trunk and closed it. "Because if your tail would've been on time, your niece wouldn't have embarrassed the mess out of me.

"Here we go," Michelle grumbled and climbed in the backseat.

"You're right, 'here we go," Louise said looking over her shoulder. "Now just keep on talking." She turned to her sister and recounted the incident that set her off. "Can you believe that girl?"

Cheryl eyed her niece through the rear view mirror. "Not too crazy about the South, huh?"

"It's all right." Michelle shrugged her shoulders.

"Just not New York, right?" Cheryl retorted and turned her attention back to Louise. "You know this is your fault, right?"

"How you figure?" Louise challenged.

"You kept her away too long," Cheryl said. "I know Mamma and Daddy moved to New York years ago, but here is where our history lies. The South is where nearly every Black person's roots are. You stayed away too long, and now your daughter has grown up believing every stereotype the media has to offer about us down here."

"Cheryl, don't act like you've been here all your life. You only moved back to Savannah five years ago."

"And I'm glad I did. A lot of people leave the South thinking they can get a better education somewhere else, just like Condoleezza Rice. I don't take anything away from her, but I'ma tell you like this, I didn't really grow until I came back home."

"What do you mean?" Michelle asked, scooting closer to the armrest separating her aunt and mother.

"Chelle, New York is full of history," Cheryl explained. "There's so much culture in New York that almost anyone feels at home there. I grew up in New York, so I used to think it was the capital of the world."

"It is," Michelle exclaimed. "We had the Harlem Renaissance, we had Malcolm X, we have Broadway, and we have the Schomburg. Just about all our Black leaders either came from Chicago or New York. If you really want to get technical, New York is where the slaves came to be free. Shoot, people are still coming to New York to try to make it. So I don't see how you feel like you grew up by coming back to the South. If anything, you stepped back."

"You see what I mean?" Louise threw her hands up in

frustration. "This girl really does need to take that tour that man told us about."

"What, the Black history tour?" Cheryl asked. "That tour is awesome. I take my students on it every February."

"What's so awesome about seeing a bunch of spots that remind you how your people were oppressed?"

Cheryl and Louise exchanged a look that Michelle couldn't tell if it was from anger, hurt, or frustration

Cheryl quickly made a right turn. "You will take the tour," she said with a firmness that Michelle did not want to challenge.

She slumped in her seat, realizing her mouth had gotten her into trouble again. Why couldn't she just leave well enough alone? Why did there seem to be some type of pipe in her head that let every thought she had slip between her lips? Why couldn't she and her family just agree to disagree? There was nothing she could say to make them think the South wasn't wonderful, and nothing they could say to convince her that it was. Although she had to admit Savannah grew more and more beautiful as they drove along. The urban area began giving way to the rural splendor. Stores and restaurants slowly turned into proud live oaks draped in Spanish moss.

"This kind of looks like a scene from the movie *Forrest Gump*," Michelle said.

Cheryl and Louise laughed.

"Funny you should say that," Cheryl spoke up first. "We're about to pass Chippewa Square where the bench scenes took place."

"Really?" Excitement exuded from Michelle's voice. "Can we stop and see it?"

"Maybe another time," Cheryl replied. "Right now, you need to learn about your own history."

They drove a few more blocks and then parked at a parking meter on a side street.

"Where are we?" Michelle asked, looking all around as if finding herself in another world. In New York, they would never have found a parking spot so easily. If they did, it would cost them thirty to forty dollars to take it. As she exited the car, she gazed at the buildings. They looked modern, but they also looked historic.

It was strange and exciting all at the same time.

"This is downtown Savannah," Louise said smiling. "I haven't been down here in years, but I could never forget it."

"We'll have time to walk down memory lane later," Cheryl said. "Right now I have to give your daughter a history lesson. The child is lost and doesn't even realize it."

She ushered them across Bay Street, the main road in downtown Savannah, and pointed to a set of rickety-looking brick steps that seemed to lead underground. Michelle looked beyond the steps at the river paralleled by a cobblestone road. A ship coasted by, which astounded her, but it wasn't enough to keep her mind off the rickety steps.

"Is this safe?" she asked nervously, her eyes transfixed on the steps with no railing. She could just see herself toppling forward and gasping for air. She would die in the South, tripping down some old weak steps. A heck of a death.

"Girl, hush up and get down those steps," Cheryl fussed with no sympathy reflected in her voice. "You really think I would purposely put my only niece in danger?"

"Come on, Michelle," Louise encouraged. "I'll hold your hand."

Michelle sighed and grabbed her mother's hand. Slowly they descended the steps, one at a time. She clung to the wall next to her with the other hand. The further down they went, the tighter she held her mother's hand. She must have squeezed a bit too hard because once they reached the bottom, Louise snatched her hand away and rubbed it, prompting Cheryl to chuckle and shake her head.

"Here we are. Welcome to your history," Cheryl said, walking ahead of them. She led them to a statue depicting an African American family of four, clinging protectively to each other. Broken shackles lay at their feet, but that wasn't what struck Michelle most. It was the brave, defiant look on the boy's face. While the rest of the family looked at each other, he stared off into the distance, holding his sister's arm as she held his shoulder. To Michelle it seemed that he knew his destiny lay ahead and wasn't afraid to face it, head on.

"Wow," she mumbled, captivated by the scene. Music from a saxophone played a few feet away, but it didn't have enough power to steal Michelle's attention. She just couldn't take her eyes off the little boy.

"When did they erect this?" Louise asked. "I don't remember?"

"That's because you haven't been on River Street in a while," Cheryl replied. 'They built this back in 2002. Isn't it gorgeous? Take a look at the inscription?"

Michelle, now very curious, knelt down to get a better look at the words carved into the concrete pillar underneath the statue and read aloud, "We were stolen, sold and brought together from the African continent. We got on the slave ships together. We lay back to belly in the holds of the slave ships in each other's excrement and urine together, and our lifeless bodies were thrown overboard together. Today, we are standing up together, with faith and even some joy."

The words impacted her, as did the inscription's author. "Maya Angelou wrote this?"

"Yep," Cheryl replied smiling. "So not all northerners look down on us little people." She then leaned against the statue to get a better look at her niece. "But that's not even my point in bringing you here. Look at that inscription. What's the one word that continues to be repeated?"

Michelle looked at the words and mouthed the one most frequently used. "Together."

"Which means we can do nothing by ourselves," Cheryl added. "No one can say they reached their success on their own. Even as wonderful as New York is—and I do miss the Big Apple sometimes—it took strong people from the South to make it the diverse place that it is."

"This is so true," Louise agreed. "Look at the great Zora Neale Hurston. She might be best known for her work during the Harlem Renaissance, but she is the product of the South, born in Alabama and grew up in Eatonville, Florida."

"And just so you'll know, Eatonville was the first all-Black town in the United States," Cheryl added.

"Yes I did," Michelle protested. "But she went to school up North."

"That's true, but she did most of her activism in the South," Cheryl countered. "Like I said, we can do nothing by ourselves.

New York couldn't do it alone, but neither could the South." Cheryl paused to place her arm around Michelle. "Think about Mary McCleod Bethune. She not only helped found Bethune-Cookman College in Florida, but she also founded the National Council of Negro Women. And she was born in South Carolina. There is Dorothy Height, born in 1912 in Richmond, Virginia, who served under Ms. Bethune and eventually replaced her as President of the National Council of Negro Women and was active until the day she died this past summer. Now that is history. Can you start to feel the link from our past to our present?"

Cheryl paused and squeezed her niece's shoulder. "Then we have Mae C. Jemison who grew up in Chicago, but it took the influence of two southern parents from Alabama to make her into who she is today. Wilma Rudolph is another one. She was born in Tennessee with polio, and still wound up winning three gold medals in the 1960 Olympics. There was also Bessie Coleman. She was born in Texas to two sharecroppers and still went on to become the first Black licensed airplane pilot and the first person of any race to get an international pilot's license. And then there is Fannie Lou Hamer a sharecropper from Mississippi, who challenged the powerful President Lyndon Johnson at the 1964 Democratic National Convention, and we must mention Barbara Jordan from Texas, who made the stirring speech during the hearings on the possible impeachment of President Richard Nixon."

"Cheryl," Louise cut in. "You're on a roll. Take a breath!"

"Girl, you just don't know," Cheryl replied. "I'm passionate about this. These little girls out here who walk around thinking they own the world but can't string two sentences together about their history just kill me."

"Aunt Cheryl, I know my history," Michelle protested. "I've heard of all the people you talked about."

"Yeah, but you don't appreciate it. You know their glory, but do you know their story?"

Michelle opened her mouth to speak, then stopped. There was no response to that question. She really didn't know. She was a shoe-in for Valedictorian of her graduating class, but in a matter of less than an hour, she felt clueless. Ashamed. She looked away and stared at a couple boats passing by each other just as her history and culture had passed her by.

"I know it's not perfect down here," Cheryl continued. "We don't have the excitement of a New York City and Lord knows it took me a long time to get used to that. And the way some of these kids dress is just shameful. But you know what? I love it here. The lifestyle is just right. We take it easy, but we get the same results. We value our families. There are a few butt holes, but for the most part, people are respectful and courteous to each other. The young respect their elders, as it should be. They say yes and no ma'am, yes and no sir. People wave at each other as they walk past. Another thing, it took me coming here to realize that we come from a long line of women who did what they had to do for their families, their friends, and themselves. And they did it without compromise."

"A prime example is not too far from home," Louise added. "Dorchester Academy is about an hour from here. It used to be a school for African American kids. They would walk miles to get to that school just to get an education. These days, kids complain about walking a few blocks. Try seven or eight miles a day, despite the weather, while on the lookout for kidnappers and lynchers!"

Michelle shook her head. She just couldn't imagine having to endure such conditions.

"There's a church here in Savannah that's known as the first Black church in North America," Louise continued. "It was built by former slaves. Those slaves would work all day, and then in the evening they would work on the church. Later that church was actually used as a stop on the Underground Railroad, which is what Mr. Perry, tried to tell you about earlier. I'll never forget how I felt when I walked into the basement and saw the air holes in the floor where the slaves would hide. It was dark, probably scary, and very hot, but they saw the big picture. One sound could stand between them and freedom."

Michelle nodded. Suddenly, her struggles didn't seem so bad like studying until the wee hours of the morning or catching the bus because she didn't have the car her mother refused to buy her. Now visiting her southern relatives instead of attending that music festival with her friends didn't seem so bad. She realized she was able to do all she could and have all she had because of those who struggled before her.

The statue again caught her attention. This time, she focused on the woman. She was the supportive wife, the caring mother and would do what she had to for her family. Without compromise. No matter in what region or area of this country they resided, she would take care of them. And she would take care of herself while pulling up those around her. In this powerfully beautiful woman, Michelle didn't just see the past. She saw her present-day heroes, Alexis Hermann, Katherine Dunham, and Mariam Wright Edelman. She also saw what the little boy seemed to see—her destiny.

"Mamma, can I take that tour Mr. Perry was talking about?" she asked.

"What?" Louise smiled. "Is the great Michelle Anderson actually requesting a tour of the city of Savannah? A *southern* city?"

"I think we got through to her," Cheryl said and hugged her niece.

"Yeah, yeah," Michelle said, laughing a bit. "I guess the South isn't so bad."

"Girl, watchu talkin' bout?" Cheryl asked. She slapped her hands on her hips. "We the bomb!"

"Oh, God," Michelle groaned. She covered her eyes, hoping to shield her identity from a curious passer-by. "You two are just intent on embarrassing me, but I love you anyway."

In Perpetuity

Frederick Williams

Young Marshall Taylor stared up at the clock on the wall. It was a little after 6 p.m. and he had to be home before seven. He had been in the Carver Library for over two hours and in that time had completed all his homework with the exception of his geometry assignment due the next day in his third period class. Later on that evening, he'd go over to Tanika's apartment and get the assignment from her. She was a whiz in math and always helped him. He knew she really liked him and so he played on that fact to get what he needed from her. And that was always the homework assignment for geometry. He hadn't hit that yet, but would probably have to sometime in the near future just to keep her doing those things he needed from her. The problem was that she had nothing to attract him physically. She was black with nappy hair and extremely big lips, nose, and just not attractive. But then again, ugly girls needed loving too.

Marshall closed his history book and packed it and the other books he'd spread out on the table into his book bag. He had an hour to kill before he'd have to get home. Going to the Carver Library after school was not his favorite thing to do. He'd rather hang out with his niggahs and his dawgs. But Mamma insisted that he spend time in the library instead of on the street. The only good part about being in the library was that he could get on one of the computers. With no computer at home he liked to spend at least a half hour on one at the library. His mother had promised that sometime soon she'd buy him and his younger sister Angela a computer. Marshall knew that probably wouldn't happen anytime soon. They survived on the very little money his father James gave them whenever they could catch up with him and the money

Phyllis earned working the counter at the local McDonald's on Walter Street. They struggled to make it from week to week with the basic necessities and there was no way Phyllis could find money to buy a computer.

Marshall got up and sauntered over to the computer room filled with others like him who needed to get on the Internet and also retrieve e-mails. He found one empty spot, sat down, and turned it on. He searched "My Space" until he found the one person he communicated with at that same time everyday.

"Hey Dawg, wuzzup?" The message read.

"Usual, being hassled by my Mama for doing what comes natural," Marshall replied and waited for another message.

"Yeah I know, these old people can't get right with us cause they don't want to let us be us."

"I know that's right. I'm still tripping about last Sunday at church and then when I got home."

"Oh yeah, what's that all about?"

"It was a real B day for me. Let me run it down to ya. Here goes."

That particular Sunday the church had been packed. Marshall, Phyllis, and Angela found seats in the back pew. They usually sat up front, but this day they were late arriving and were fortunate to find enough room to sit together. Marshall entered the row first and made his way until he was right next to a young, pretty Black girl, who sat there with a child. Marshall sat down and left a little room between him and the girl. He noticed the disdainful glare Phyllis shot at the young lady. She grabbed Marshall by the shoulder and forced him to slide toward her. She then moved past him and took the seat next to the young lady.

After church Marshall worked up enough nerve and asked his mother, "Mamma, why did you make me move in church?"

"Because I don't want you sittin' next to no sinner," Phyllis scowled. "That girl, the one that had that baby and ain't married. I ain't goin' have you getting' caught up in no mess like that." Phyllis turned and glared at her son.

"Yes, ma'am," Marshall replied in a whisper. He didn't really understand his mother. She had never married his father so she was also looking down on them as a family. It made no sense because just about everyone who lived in their apartment complex was single. There were no fathers and it was just like the families where he lived existed of only a mother and the children. Why be so hard on that young girl when she was doing just like all the other young girls? Whenever he did decide to get with Tanika, he'd have to be careful; he sure didn't want to get her pregnant.

Marshall hustled up the steps to their apartment, leaving his sister and mother behind. He unlocked the door, hurried to his room and changed clothes. He hit the ON button on the radio and instantly the room filled with the words from the rapper, Too Short. Immediately, a barrage of "niggahs," "bitches," and "dawgs," poured out of the radio.

He heard his mother walking outside the room and knew what was coming.

"Marshall, turn that junk off," she shrieked. "How dare you just come from church and started playing all that profanity?"

"But, Mama, it's our music, just like you all had your music in the past," Marshall said as he complied with his mother and turned the radio off. He got up and walked out of the room. "Why you so hard on us cause we got our choice in music? I bet Grandma was just as hard on you with your music."

"Don't matter, our music wasn't filled with all that filth," Phyllis said as she walked into the kitchen and started to put dishes up in the cabinet. "You're not going to insult Black women by listening to that junk in my house. And that's just my rules. When you grow up you can do what you want in your own place."

"Mama, they're just words," Marshall said making his last appeal and knowing it would do no good. "You old people need to get up with the times. It's just words." Marshall finished and went back into his bedroom."

"Say, young brothah, how long you going to use this computer?" A man standing directly behind Marshall asked.

Marshall jerked and looked at the man. "Just a little longer," he answered. "I got a friend on Face Book who I talk with every day right about this time."

"I was wondering cause there are a few things I'd like to show you."

Marshall studied the man in some detail. He'd never seen him in the library before. And he dressed differently than what most folks did in his neighborhood. He appeared to be from another time in history. Most of the brothers in Marshall's neighborhood would crack up laughing if this man walked down his street. He was tempted to ask the man where he came from, but had learned long ago not to delve into other people's business. His mother always told him what he didn't know he shouldn't know.

"Say, little brothah why you looking at me so hard, something you want to ask me?"

"No sir," Marshall said as he turned back and signed off the computer. Suddenly he swung back around. "Yeah," he said to the man. "Why you dressed like that and where you from?"

"It's the way we dressed during my time and I'm from the same Black community that you live in."

Marshall leaned away from the man and looked for Mary the librarian. This man was acting weird and he wanted to make sure other people were still in the library even though he knew they were.

"What you talking about man? I ain't ever seen you in my neighborhood."

"I visit your classroom on occasion and know your instructor teaches you better than to say ain't." The man moved in closer to Marshall who jumped up and moved further away.

Marshall, are you all right?" Mary asked as she walked toward him. "And who are you talking to?"

Marshall jerked his head to the right and glared at the man, and then looked at Mary. "What do you mean, who am I--"

"Stop," the man interrupted. "I'm afraid you may appear to be silly to the lady."

Marshall turned away from Mary and again concentrated on this strange man who obviously he could see, but no one else could.

"Marshall Taylor, who are you talking to and what is wrong with you?" Mary again asked him.

"If you tell her that a man is standing over here next to you, she's going to think you're on drugs and are hallucinating," the man warned Marshall before he could respond to Mary.

The young boy sat back down and looked straight ahead. Now he was more curious than he was afraid. There wasn't much this strange person could do in the library and why would he want to do harm to him.

"Who are you?" Marshall whispered and quickly glanced over at Mary to make sure she didn't hear him.

"I am In Perpetuity," the man answered as he put his large, strong hand on Marshall's shoulder.

"You're what?" Marshall shrieked and quickly put his hand over his mouth as he looked in Mary's direction. She didn't look up.

"In Perpetuity means always. It might be a stretch but I use it for emphasis with young Black men like you."

Marshall no longer feared this strange man, but instead wanted to know more about him. He glared at the clock. He needed to be home by six to start dinner and see about his sister. Phyllis would be home by seven; he had to get there before she did, but he couldn't let this man get away. He felt a strong attraction to him.

"You trying to tell me that you been on earth forever?" Marshall quipped and again shot a glance over at Mary.

"I'm not telling you that at all. You know the physical body cannot last forever. That was not the purpose the Lord had for the body. What I am telling you is that I carry with me the essence of our culture." The man stopped for a moment and took in a deep breath. "It is ideas of who and what we are passed on through the generations. It defines the meaning of a group of people who have coalesced in a survival mode. It is also agreed upon behavior patterns, speech, music, dance, and most importantly how they treat each other. It is respect for all the individuals in the group."

"How do you define yourself?" Marshall didn't know where that question came from. It's not something he would ask in a normal conversation. This man had affected him to reach deep in the depths of his own thinking he never knew he possessed.

"Good question." The man smiled. "I am already having an influence on you. No doubt you'll be an excellent student after our discussion. I define myself on the behavior of all our people. I am a composite of all our people from the inception of our existence here in this country until this day, right now, right here with you. I am the collective body of all the years and vast experiences both pleasant and unpleasant of Black people. Unfortunately, most of our experiences in this country have been unpleasant and that is part of the reason why we treat each other the way that we do."

"Why do you say that most of our experience here has been unpleasant?" Marshall asked. "I've had a pretty good life, even though we are poor."

"You are a part of a collective body," the man said. "The Black experience in America did not begin with you, you are only an extension or continuation. You are only 15 and your collective experience goes back to the first time back in 1619 when the first African landed on the shores of this country and had his past wiped out. He had no past, but only a present and future."

"That sounds real confusing to me," Marshall whispered as a young girl walked past him.

"Let me explain it to you in this fashion. We arrived in this country in 1619 and from the middle of that century until 1865 we were forced to be slaves against our will. From 1865 until right to this day in 2011 we have been out of slavery but forced to exist under a horrendous system of apartheid until about 1964 when Dr. Martin Luther King Jr. helped end segregation. So let's calculate, from 1650 to 1865 is two-hundred-and-fifteen years, and from 1865 until 1964 is another ninety-nine years. Let's see, that adds up to three hundred and four years, as opposed to forty-six years of real freedom. With those kind of numbers no wonder we struggle with our own identity. We have a lot of years of oppression to overcome and we're just getting started. I have a great deal of work in front of me."

Marshall again perked up and wanted to shout out his next question but he was very much aware of Mary sitting at the desk. He toned it down and asked, "Is that why we talk so harshly and ugly about each other?"

"Exactly! It reflects all the negative experiences we encountered in a country that oppressed us and has never liked us as a people."

"You should've been in church with us a few Sundays ago when my mother--"

"I was there," the man interrupted.

"How do you feel about the way my mother referred to that young girl sitting in our pew?"

"She is simply a reflection of what has happened to us for those first three-hundred-and-four years."

"I need a better answer than that." Marshall felt he could get aggressive in his discussion with this man who claimed to be the collective experience of Black people in America. "Culture is supposed to be something good. You can't tell me the way she acted and the words she used was a positive thing."

"You're getting pretty deep into this young man. I'm impressed."

"Mister, I don't mean to be rude, but I don't have much time. I got to get home, look after my sister, and on top of that get supper started before my mother gets there. If you can answer my question it would sure help me out a lot. I want to understand how my Mamma can look at another woman in that light?"

The man took in a deep breath and slowly released it. "You have centuries of a race insecure within themselves but powerful people with all kinds of weapons of destruction, tearing down your ancestors in order to build themselves up. Blacks have been forced to succumb to a distorted view as projected by these insecure people. After a while we began to believe their lies."

"Why do white people hate us so much?" Marshall asked. "If you really look at what happened, we should be the ones full of hate, but instead we want to be like them, you know, dress like them, talk like them, and most of all look like them."

"You're way ahead of your time," the man said. "That kind of thinking and understanding should only come to you much later in life. But since you are already at that point, let me show you the truth."

The man gestured for Marshall to get up. He then sat down and punched some codes into the computer. When the site popped up on the screen, he got up and let Marshall sit back down. "Watch, listen, and learn."

The site illuminated a scene from sometime in the past. Five men wearing long white wigs and dressed in colonial garb, sat at a large table reading some kind of document. Marshall turned up the volume just loud enough for him to hear what they were saying, but not disturb the other people using the computers next to him. He listened intently.

"What is this, Thomas?" one of the men asked.

"It is the results of my experiment I carried out on my slaves," Thomas Jefferson answered. "I needed to find out if Africans who are our slaves are really human beings just like us or are they closer to the animal kingdom." Jefferson paused and allowed the magnitude of his comment to sink in with the others. "If they are human beings created by God in the same manner that He created us then based on what I wrote in the Declaration of Independence and what we claim in the new Constitution, we cannot keep them as slaves. We cannot have men and women equal to us as our slaves. It is against the laws of human nature and God."

The other men stirred around in their chairs and looked with much more intensity at the document.

"What are you saying and doing, Thomas?" one of the men spoke up. "We can't afford to prove that the African is our equal. It'll be the ruin of us all. We need our slaves to maintain our standard of living and our life style."

John's right, Thomas," another man spoke up. "And furthermore, who'll do our work in the fields?"

"Yeah, and who'll do all the work in the kitchen for my wife?" the fourth man added. "She'll divorce me if she has to lift a pot and sweep a floor."

All the others laughed.

"Don't worry men," Jefferson said reassuring them. "My findings vindicate us and actually prove that we are doing these poor beasts a favor." He stopped, picked up the document, and turned to a certain page. "Look at my findings on page 15. I have proof that these poor creatures are by nature lazy, slow thinking, over-sexed, and easily frightened."

The men grunted in unison. They smiled their approval.

"As you may have noticed, if you get too close to one of them," Jefferson continued. "They have the most vile body odor."

"You're being nice, Thomas," the fourth man said. "They just plain old stink."

"And there is a reason," again Jefferson spoke up. "Unlike normal human beings like us, they have trouble passing material out of their bodies."

"They just can't take a good crap," one of the men said.

Marshall suddenly jerked back, turned and stared at the man.

"I know, it's hard to stomach," he said. "Every time I reveal this to a new neophyte like you, I get angry. But anger won't change our condition; knowledge will. And knowledge is nothing more than knowing and learning. So turn back and learn."

Marshall followed the stranger's instructions. He knew he should be home by now, but he had to know more, even at the risk of a whipping when he got there. He turned his attention back to the men, anxious to know how much more damage one of the country's greatest leaders, one he was taught to admire and respect, had really done to the image of his people.

"Since they have trouble passing material out of their bodies," Jefferson continued. "It backs up in their system and comes out in their pores. That means they are not fully developed as human beings. If placed on God's scale of human development, they would fall lower than man, but just above animals. In fact, it is the truth that an African woman would be just as content and happy being married to an ape."

Again, all the men in the room got a good laugh.

"So my friends, when I said all men are created equal I was referring to all human beings. God made human beings equal, and since my study has proven that Africans are not fully developed human beings, but a cross between humans and animals, we do not have to look upon them as equals."

Smiles spread across the collective faces of the other men. One of them spoke for the rest.

"Then that means we are not going against the word of God or against our beloved Declaration of Independence and Constitution if we don't treat these people as equals."

"Correction my friend," Jefferson interjected. "Not people, but subhuman's."

The men again burst out laughing and the image before Marshall faded away.

He sat there and stared at the screen. "Did they really believe that?" he asked the strange man.

"It doesn't matter whether they believed it or not," the man said as he leaned over Marshall's shoulder and pulled up another site. "What matters is that they acted on their misguided beliefs and as a result millions of our people suffered." He pointed at the screen as another picture appeared. "Look, listen, and learn," the man instructed.

Marshall stared with anger and trepidation as the scene developed before him.

Twenty-five to thirty haggardly looking white men stood in front of a large platform lifted a few inches off the ground. To their right were at least ten Blacks; five men, three women, and two children about five years of age. Four guards with shotguns held high stood at each end of the Blacks, intently staring at them.

A neatly dressed white man entered the yard and hurried to the front of the group of white men. He smiled at one of the men in the front of the line.

"Hey Sam, I see you right up front. Guess you want a close up view of these niggers, especially the winches." He laughed. "Guess you probably going to buy the wench with the biggest back side."

The other man broke out in a loud laugh. "Gotta get mine," he said. "But I've got to buy two good size bucks and one of them bitches for a client down in Natchez. I should make a pretty good profit. He was desperate to git some niggers to work his fields. Seems that they had some kind of epidemic down there. Killed off a bunch of their niggers and they got to replace them right away. Can't get behind on working the fields. Too much money involved.

"I'll see if I can help you out, make sure you git the best of the bunch. Then maybe you'll give me a little something extra," the auctioneer said as he signaled for the guard to bring the first slave to be sold that day.

The first slave, a young naked woman who appeared to be about sixteen was forced up on the platform by one of the guards.

Marshall turned away when he saw the naked girl, but the strange man grabbed him by the shoulders and forced him to look back at the screen.

"Look and learn," he said.

Marshall glared at the man, but knew what he was doing for him would be beneficial in his understanding of what really happened to his people and the brutality of it all. He turned his attention back to the screen.

He couldn't help but to notice the sorrow written all over the young girl's face as she lowered her head down looking at the ground instead of what was happening all around her. It struck him as interesting that many of the young girls in his school and neighborhood often walked with their heads down and backs slumped just like this young girl. The girls in his neighborhood needed to see this young girl who was also Black but lived over 150 years ago. Too bad she couldn't come back to this world today and let some of her sisters in the future see how much better they had it than she did in such a vicious and oppressive system. Bingo! It dawned on Marshall that is exactly what the strange man had done. No wonder he forced him to look back at the screen. What Marshall didn't understand is why he had been picked to have so much of his people's past revealed to him?

"Git your head up, bitch before I lay this whip to your back," the auctioneer shouted. "Act like you happy that these fine men would consider even buying your lazy behind."

The young girl held her head up but still looked away into the distance, just as if she was dreaming of a place across the ocean.

"Come on boys, let's start the bidding on this fine, young and healthy wench. She a good worker and she got a whole lot of child rearing years ahead of her." None of the men immediately responded. The auctioneer continued. "Come on men, get in closer to this bitch. Feel on her strong and healthy breasts, her firm back side and she got all her teeth."

The auctioneer now looked up at the girl. "Open your mouth so these men can see how healthy your teeth is." The young girl complied with the man's instructions.

Five of the men, including the man the auctioneer was talking with before the bidding opened, moved in much closer and surrounded the girl.

"Bend over," one of the men instructed her.

She did.

Another of the men felt on her legs and another squeezed her breasts. Finally another man popped her on the backside. They all laughed.

"You see how that meat just bounce like jelly?"

Again all the men laughed then moved back to their original positions so the bidding could begin. The man the auctioneer had talked with started the bidding.

"Three hundred dollars," he shouted.

"I'll go six hundred," a man from the back, who hadn't come up front to examine the girl, shouted.

"How you going to bid from way back there," the first man said. "I'll go seven hundred and no higher. Anyone want to go higher than that, then you can have the bitch."

"Seven hundred and fifty," the man who had slapped the young girl on her backside said. "It's worth that to have her around just to be able to slap that rear end."

"Okay, seven hundred and fifty, going, going, gone," the auctioneer cut the bidding off. No further discussion was necessary. It was no one's business how he planned to use the young girl. All that mattered was that he got a good price for her, which meant a nice profit for the owner, which would result in a nice bonus for the auctioneer.

The scene slowly faded out and Marshall, now angry, turned to face the strange man.

"Why are you showing me this?" he asked. "It's really making me mad. Makes me want to go out their and kick some white butt."

"Remember young man, not anger but knowledge," the man instructed. "When you get angry, they win. When you get knowledge, you win."

"I think I'm beginning to understand why we treat each other the way we do," Marshall said. "Is there anymore I need to see in order to understand much better?"

"Take this final trip with me," the stranger said and hit the proper keys on the keyboard to bring up another scene.

Marshall was already late, his mother would fuss and probably whip him, but it would all be worth it for the knowledge. He turned and faced the screen and anticipated the next scene.

Three figures, a woman and two children, ran along the banks of the river. Snow covered the ground and a strong wind blew in their face. It slowed them down, but they appeared determined and would not be stopped. She saw the house on top of the hill and the lantern in the window. She had to get there before the men chasing from behind caught up with her and returned her back across the river into Kentucky.

Marshall turned and stared at the man as if to question why the woman and two children were running. But the man held his hand up as a signal to just look and learn. He turned his attention back to the scene before him.

Snow blurred the woman's image but she seemed to know the house on the hill would protect them. The woman looked behind her but could not see much. She did know, however, that the pursuers weren't far behind them.

"Mamma, I'm cold and I can't run anymore," the younger of the two children, a girl about seven, said.

"No, baby, you can't stop," the mother pleaded. "We have to keep moving. We can't go back. We just can't go back." She grabbed the girl's hand and jerked her forward. She held her other hand out, and the boy, who was a little older, took it.

Marshall again turned his attention away from the scene developing before him. He compared what he was watching with his family, a mother with two children, the oldest a boy, and the youngest, a girl. They were frightened and were desperately trying to find their way to safety. He had to find out how this would turn out.

"I'm okay, Mamma," the boy said. "All we have to do is make it to that house and we'll be safe?" he asked.

"Yes, baby, that's all we have to do," she answered then looked behind her. She knew it would happen. Images of men on horseback were visible. She looked straight ahead and the house on the hill was still some distance from them. The woman looked in all directions for a place to possibly hide, but nothing was there.

The young girl's legs went out from under her and the mother had to drag her along. She finally lifted her into her arms and that slowed them down considerably. The snow was getting heavier and the wind had picked up. No doubt the wind chill had to be close to zero. The young girl began to cry. Finally, they fell down in the snow knowing that soon the slave hunters would be on them and their desperate attempt to escape their personal hell would be over. No doubt they would be returned to Kentucky and the children would be sold or traded to one of the Deep South plantations. The woman hugged her two children tightly and prayed that God would take them out of this misery.

She could now hear the barking dogs that would lead the men right to them. She held her children tightly and cried.

Marshall took his open hand and hit the computer, practically knocking it off the stand. He stared at the strange man who had a solemn expression.

"Did that kind of thing really happen or is this some kind of mean game you're playing on me?" he asked.

"It happened all the time under the laws of what was called the Fugitive Slave Law of 1850. Any white man could capture a Black person, didn't matter if they were a slave or not, and take them back into the South and slavery."

"Why did our government let that kind of thing happen?"

"Because they looked at our ancestors as niggers and bitches. Called them those names no different than that music you think is so cool and, as you told your mother, just words, nothing more. They made jokes of our physical features and the color of our skin and used it as a reason to do what you just saw. They used our beautiful Black women in the same manner that you have used Tanika."

"How do you know about Tanika?"

"Because I am culture perpetuity and a hundred years from now I will let some young Black men know how you treated a beautiful Black sister, Tanika, in the same manner that those animals treated our women back then."

"No, you can't--"

"Yes, I can, and, yes, I will. In fact, I'll be obligated to do just that. I will tell the future generations that you used Tanika because you saw her as being ugly and your concept of beauty is copied after the very people who have oppressed us for hundreds of years. Do you know that we are the only race of people who want to look like the people who committed some of the most atrocious crimes in history against our people, against Black women who looked like Tanika, and because they didn't meet a certain standard of beauty, it was all right, just like it's all right for you to disrespect that young lady." The stranger reached over Marshall and hit the play button creating another scene on the computer screen.

"Watch this last scene, brace yourself for what you are about to see, and wake up young man."

"I don't think I want to," Marshall said and tried to turn away from the computer. "I should have been home a half hour ago."

The stranger placed his large hand on Marshall's shoulder

68

preventing him from getting up.

"You're all right," he said. "Your mother is okay with you being late because she knows you are caught up in a knowledge blast. After we finish, she also knows that you will be converted from the ignorance of your history and culture to the light.

Marshall sighed then reluctantly turned and stared at the computer.

A very dark skinned young woman stood handcuffed and surrounded by a group of white men. They appeared to be drunk. The leader of the men moved closer to a tree with a long extended branch about ten feet off the ground.

"This one will do," he said to a man holding a rope. "Throw it over the top of this branch and tighten it up."

The man moved under the tree branch and tossed the rope over the top. He tightened it with the end of the rope in a noose.

"That's it sheriff. It's ready to do the job," the man said.

"Okay, boys, throw that old bitch up top of the horse and let's get that rope around her Black nigger neck. Sass me, will you?" he said as he glared at the woman who just stared at the ground.

Two men grabbed the young girl and threw her on top of the horse. They then placed the noose around her neck. One of the men laughed and said.

"Hey sheriff, we ain't killin' jest one nigger. This bitch is pregnant. We goin' git rid of two of them. Two for one, and the world is a better place."

The men laughed.

Marshall turned his head away from the scene. He didn't want to see what was about to happen.

"Okay mister, I've seen enough. I get your point, now I'm going home."

The stranger again placed his hand on Marshall's shoulder and that locked him in place. Sternly he said, "Look and learn. Learning is knowledge. You young boys don't know, and it is our fault. If you knew you wouldn't dare use the same terms and misuse our Black women the way you do. That terminology led to tremendous suffering for your ancestors."

Marshall couldn't do anything but sit and stare at the monitor. He grimaced as one of the men slapped the horse. It sprinted forward and the woman dangled from the branch. Her body began to convulse.

One of the men smiled and took a drink from a bottle. He then snatched a long Bowie knife out of his belt and strutted up to the woman.

"Y'all watch what I'm goin' do." He took his knife back and then swung it forward. It came down and across the front of the woman's stomach. Blood shot everywhere and the fully developed baby fell to the ground.

"What have you done?" one the men shouted.

"Kill the little nigger. Stomp on it," another man shouted.

The man smiled, lifted his big boot and brought it crashing down on the baby's head.

"NO!!!" Marshall shouted.

"Young man what in the world is wrong with you?" Mary asked from behind her desk.

Marshall buried his head between his hands and sobbed.

The librarian got up and rushed over to him. "Why are you crying? What's wrong?"

He pointed to the screen without saying a word.

Mary stared at the blank monitor. "Are you all right? There's nothing on this monitor."

Marshall looked up at a blank monitor. He turned to his left and the stranger was gone. He then glared at Mary.

"I'm okay," he said.

"Why were you shouting?" she asked. "You know that kind of behavior is not allowed in here. Please don't do it again." She turned and walked back to her desk.

Marshall stared at the blank monitor. He wanted that old and funny-dressed Black man to come back. He was due an explanation for what he had to endure from all four of those visuals. Marshall smiled as he thought it all had been some kind of a joke. Because if what he'd just witnessed really did happen and the words nigger and bitch helped facilitate that kind of cruelty, he would swear off, not only those two words, but all music that used them. He needed some kind of sign, something left behind as proof. Without some kind of verification he would assume that this had been nothing more than his imagination at work overtime.

Now he had to rush home and take his punishment. But the stranger said that his mother knew why he was late and would not be upset. If when he arrived home, she did not fuss at him that would be proof of the stranger's existence in the library and proof that what he saw was the truth.

Marshall ran up the two flights of stairs, unlocked the door, and rushed inside the apartment. He braced for the explosion as he walked into the kitchen area where Phyllis was preparing dinner.

"Mamma, don't go off. I met some crazy guy who showed me all these ugly things that happened to Black people in the past."

"I know," Phyllis said without looking up.

"You ain't mad at me, Mamma? You ain't going to whip me?"

"Not at all," Phyllis answered. "Now go get ready for dinner."

A shocked Marshall hurried to his bedroom. This was all getting too crazy. What he experienced at the library couldn't have really happened. It was too cruel and ugly. And it would make him feel bad for all the times he'd enjoyed music that used words that brought extreme pain and suffering to his ancestors. His music meant too much to him. He needed more evidence in order to believe what happened. He needed physical proof. Marshall would become a convert if the stranger came back and gave him something more to hang on to.

He hesitated before he went into the bedroom. Marshall let out a big sigh and opened the door. After turning on the light he froze in place. There on the bed was a small trinket with the inscription "IN PERPETUITY."

Losing the Game

Michael Smith

Malik Williams sped his Mustang into the parking lot outside
the downtown Metropolitan Police Department. He shot a glance
at the clock on the dashboard in his car. It read 3:58, and roll call
for the afternoon shift would start at 4:00 p.m. He knew Platoon
Sergeant Dennis Washburn would commence to call roll right on
the hour. The man was like clockwork. He never deviated from his
procedure. And he never deviated from the hard cold stare he gave
any officer who was late. Sergeant considered any arrival after
the second hand had passed the number twelve, indicating it was
four o'clock as late. That's why Malik was pushing hard to find a
parking space and get inside. He finally found one, pulled into the
space, jumped out of his car, and ran into the building. It was now
3:59, and he had one minute to spare.

Today was especially important because Sergeant Washburn
would make the monthly announcement of new assignments.
Malik had put in a request to be transferred to the Community
Service Unit. As he ran through the long corridor and finally burst
into the roll call room, he knew his chance of getting that transfer
was slim to none. He had been a beat cop for only three years
and hadn't paid his dues for such a plush transfer. But he had to
try, simply because of his promise he had made to himself when
he first joined the force. At some point in his career he wanted
to help save young Black kids instead of throwing them in jail
to waste away and become yet another statistic of a lost young
man or woman, who under different circumstances might have
become a doctor, lawyer, or scientist. Instead of arresting them he
wanted to save them. And that's why the afternoon's roll call was
so important to him.

"Welcome, Malik" Sergeant Washburn called out. "I'm glad you could make it just seconds before roll call."

Malik found a seat in the very back of the room. "You got it, Sarge," he said. "As long as it's a few seconds before the hour and not after, I'm okay."

"I can't argue with that," Sergeant Washburn replied. "But that's got to be awfully hard on your nerves knowing you were so close to getting the stare."

Malik relaxed back in his chair and smiled. "You right about that. Nobody in this room wants to get that stare."

"All right, men and ladies, today we announce the new promotions and transfers," Sergeant Washburn said, abruptly changing the subject and getting to the business for the afternoon.

Malik sat quietly praying and held his breath as if those acts would deliver the new assignment he wanted to him. Dead silence engulfed the room and you could hear a pin drop. There were over a hundred officers in that room and way over half were hoping to hear their name called.

"Okay, listen up," Sergeant Washburn's voice increased a couple decibels. "The officers who have been transferred to..."

He stopped and stared, with a frown on his face, at the paper in front of him.

Sergeant Washburn knew exactly what he was doing, Malik thought. He's just messing with us. He deliberately stopped in order to make us suffer just a little bit longer. But Malik didn't care what silly games he played just as long as his name was called.

"Officers Parker and Hernandez," Sergeant continued, "and Officer Roberts have all been transferred to the Community Services Unit."

"All right, way to go," Officer Parker said. He got up and reached to slap hands with the other two. Dejected, Malik watched as the three men congratulated each other then sat back down.

"Congratulations, gentlemen," Sergeant Washburn now shouted above the chatter coming from all over the room. "The effective date of your new unit assignment will start after completion of your shift today."

Malik's head dropped and his shoulders slumped. The transfer would have meant so much to him, and now he would have to wait another six months before he could even apply again. The razzing from the other officers hadn't started but it was coming. They all knew how badly he wanted that transfer, and the fact that he didn't get it would leave him vulnerable to some serious teasing. The older men on the force had labeled him "bleeding heart" and stayed on his case. They knew he dedicated his spare time visiting the high schools, detention facilities, and going to community events advising children about the dangers of gangs and drugs.

"Hey, Malik, now you can take your mind off saving these bad little juvenile delinquents and concentrate on throwing them behind bars where they belong," one of the officers shouted out loud enough for all to hear. The officers busted out laughing.

"Yeah, if they gave awards for saving souls instead of locking up gangsters, he'd be a sure winner," another officer shouted.

"And then we'd all be looking for jobs," a third man called out. "People like him go around trying to save these hoodlums, and then we won't have nobody to arrest, and that'll put us in the unemployment lines."

Again, the officers laughed. They seemed to be enjoying themselves at Malik's expense.

The laughter and the sounds faded as Malik drifted off into his own world. Growing up right in the inner city, he could relate to the kids they were talking about. Some of the crimes they committed he had actually done himself as a young man and at the time honestly didn't know they were illegal. It made him feel like a hypocrite. How could he possibly take them downtown for things he had done on the same streets of Cleveland, Ohio. Some of the infractions went on so much and often in his neighborhood growing up they had become socially acceptable to the community. But to the other officers who worked those same streets with him but had grown up in a different environment, things that seemed petty, were crimes to them, and the offenders received no understanding or sympathy regardless of age.

Malik took in a deep breath and sighed as he listened to the Sergeant take back control of the room.

"You know, I'm still conducting roll call," he shouted. Sergeant's face turned beet red as he stared down at the second list of names for transfer. "The following men have been promoted to the status of detective and assigned to the Criminal Investigation Unit." He paused and waited for the officers to give him their attention. They stopped bantering Malik and stared up at him. "Officer Lee, Officer Robinson, Officer Bond and Walker, and last but not least, Malik will get the last laugh on you all because he, with the others, has been promoted to detective and will be working undercover in narcotics."

Malik's drooped body came to full attention. He stared at the Sergeant as if in disbelief. Surely it was a joke and any minute Washburn would admit as much. He could feel all eyes in the room on him. He never made a request for undercover work and knew the other officers were probably wondering how he, of all people, could work undercover. He was too soft for that kind of high-level intrigue and danger. Malik waited for Washburn to bust out laughing, but he didn't.

Instead he said, "Congratulations, gentlemen, the lieutenant from CI will be contacting you as to when they want you to report for your new assignment. Again, congratulations and be safe out there today. Roll call is over."

Malik sat dumfounded. He tried to ignore the taunts from the older officers who filed by him on their way out.

"You ain't got no business in the detective unit," the first officer who commented on his not getting promoted earlier said. "You're still learning patrol."

"You rookie," another officer taunted. "Good luck, but I doubt you'll last a day in undercover."

"Yeah, he'll be so nervous that he'll give himself away," a third man added.

" Now you'll get a chance to throw some real bad guys under the jail where they belong," still another officer said and then laughed. The men giving him a hard time patted each other on the back as they left the room.

Malik sat there as the afternoon shift of police officers left the room, leaving him alone to think further about what had just happened to him. Undercover work meant busting drug dealers, something he didn't mind doing. After all they were a real menace to the Black community with no conscience and no concern for the damage they were doing to his people. But he preferred to be at the other end of the process, that is saving the youth from becoming drug dealers and especially drug users. Malik knew he would be good at mentoring young brothers who had no role models in their lives and often no hope for the future according to how they viewed life. Why hadn't they given him an assignment for which he was best suited and where he could help prevent crime instead of fighting crime? Because he loved police work he would accept this assignment, but would still look for the day when he could serve his community in a more positive role. In the meantime he would go undercover and fight the bad guys just like in the movies.

Malik slowly pulled himself out of the chair and strolled out of the roll call room. He picked up his pace as he headed down the long corridor toward the cafeteria. Before leaving for the day's assignment he always bought an Evian water. His thoughts were still on what had just happened when Lieutenant Wendell Hampton, head of Criminal Investigation Unit approached him.

"Welcome aboard," Hampton said as he slapped Malik on the back. "We're glad to have you join us in C.I. I've heard good things about you."

What good things could he have possibly heard about me, Malik wondered. He hadn't done anymore than any other beat officer. It was probably just part of the con game. Make him feel good and say things that would force him to perform at a higher standard. By telling him that good things were being said about him would force Malik to live up to the hype.

"Thanks, Lieutenant," Malik replied. "Glad to be aboard."

"I'm taking you off patrol immediately," Hampton said. "How about you take the next two weeks off. Just relax and get ready for the change, you know, like grow your hair out, change up your appearance, and start to look a little gruffy." Hampton placed his hand on Malik's shoulder. "You'll get a five-hundred-dollar clothing allowance. You're going to be back in the middle of the hood on the other side of the law so buy clothes that fit the environment." Hampton tapped Malik on the shoulder and then moved back a few steps. Go on and take off. When we see you back here be ready for a another couple week's training and then your first assignment. How does that sound to you?"

"Sounds just great," Malik answered with little enthusiasm.

"Good, son. I'll let your Sergeant know you're being

transferred immediately and won't be working your shift today. Stop by tomorrow and see Sergeant Hall so you can get your undercover vehicle." Hampton finished, turned and called out to Sergeant Washburn. "Hold up, Sarge, I need to talk to you. We're pulling Malik off his beat today. He's now officially transferred to CI."

Malik watched as Hampton caught up with Sergeant Washburn and the two men disappeared around the corner. Hampton's words to Washburn reverberated over and over again with Malik. He really had been transferred to undercover, but he didn't quite understand why. What was it in his behavior or his performance for the past three years that convinced these men that he would serve the department better putting criminals in jail? And many of these criminals would be just like many of his friends he grew up with in Cleveland. Many of these young men that he would send to long prison terms had never gotten a decent break in life and turned to a life of crime as their only option. What they really needed was a mentor to help them understand who they were and their worth as young men. But instead they would get a long prison sentence and the system wouldn't have to worry about them at all. That's not what he wanted to do, but at this point, Malik had no choice. How long he could do this kind of dirty work he just didn't know.

The next morning Malik pulled into a parking space at the police warehouse right at eight o'clock. As he got out of his car he watched the large metal door swing open. He spotted Sergeant Hall, chief of the warehouse, on the other side.

"Congratulations, I hear you made detective." Hall greeted Malik.

"Sure did," Malik replied. He walked into the large warehouse and shook the Sergeant's hand.

"Man, you going to be working undercover in narcotics," Sergeant Hall continued. He patted Malik on the back and walked toward the area where the undercover vehicles were stored. "You go for the exciting and dangerous kind of action, don't you?"

If only he knew, Malik thought. "It beats writing traffic tickets on little old ladies, who most of the time shouldn't be driving anyway." Malik stared at the twenty various models of cars parked in three rows. He felt like a kid in the candy store. He could pick any one of the twenty. What a decision.

He spotted a black Nissan Maxima with twenty-inch chrome rims and blacked out tinted windows.

" Can I have this one?"

"I don't see why not. We can do up the paper work real quick and get it assigned to you."

"Yeah, Sarge this is the one I want."

"Well, let's get it done."

The two men walked back to Sergeant Hall's office. He grabbed some papers off the shelf behind his desk, sat down at his desk and started filling them out. Malik sat across from him with a sense of anxiety. This was really happening and for the first time he felt a tinge of excitement. This was not what he wanted to do, but since he had to do it, why not find some enjoyment in it?

Sergeant Hall slid the papers across the desk and handed Malik a pen. "Sign where I put the check marks," he said.

Malik took the pen and signed his name in four different boxes and slid the paperwork back across the desk.

"Okay you're all set," Sergeant Hall said as he took his pen back from Malik, separated the papers, folded one set and handed them to Malik. "If the vehicle gets burnt, bring it back to the warehouse and we'll trade it out for another model." He stood up. "If the vehicle doesn't get burnt, you can still change it out in three months. You know, nothing like a little variety, free of charge."

The two men walked over to the car and Hall handed Malik the keys. "Good luck and be safe out there."

"Thanks, Sarge." Malik opened the door and climbed in the driver's seat. He smiled as he ran his hand over the smooth tan leather upholstery. The car was loaded with a Bose sound system and upgraded woofers, television in the headrest and dash. Malik started out of the garage and headed to the mall. He had one more chore and that was to buy some new clothes to match his new position. With the five hundred the department gave him, he was about to make that transition.

The department gave Malik two weeks of uncharged leave in order to allow him to grow a beard, let his hair grow long and allow for mental preparation. During the two weeks he spent a lot of time meditating on this life-changing experience he was about to undergo. He also spent time with his girlfriend, Jonetta. She was adamantly opposed to the change and had no problem expressing her dissatisfaction. One night over dinner their relationship almost came to a breaking point.

"This isn't fair," she scowled while sipping on a Margarita. "I guess I'll just have to accept the fact that your job is more important to you than our future."

"Don't say that, because it just isn't true." Malik reached across the table and tried to take her hand.

She jerked her hand away and slid it under the table. "You didn't think enough about me to discuss making this change. You just did it."

"It's not what I wanted, Jonetta. You know that."

"But it's what you accepted."

"I didn't have a choice. You turn down a promotion and it'll be a long time before you get another offer."

"I don't want you working for the stupid police anyway. All you going to be doing is sending our Black kids to jail. Doesn't that bother you at all?"

Malik reared way back in his chair. Maybe his decision to accept this job didn't make any sense because he did agree with Jonetta. Their love of kids and their shared concern for young Blacks was what attracted them to each other. He knew she never would have agreed to a relationship with a policeman if he hadn't convinced her that he viewed the job as a way to help save boys who were victims of the pathological environment they lived in. She had believed him when he told her that as soon as he was eligible for a transfer to community service work, he would do it. And now he had to convince her that was still his intentions when his actions pointed in the opposite direction. He didn't want to lose Jonetta and in fact, he planned to marry her once he achieved the financial stability so that she wouldn't have to work if she didn't want to.

"Are you listening to me or am I just talking to myself?" Jonetta's harsh words ended Malik's musing.

"Yes, sweetheart, I hear you," he said. "But wouldn't you agree that some of our boys need to be locked up?" He scooted in closer. "Don't get me wrong. I know our boys get a bum wrap in life, but we can't let the ones who blame everything on the system or the white man and use that as an excuse to rob, steal, and sometimes kill other kids spoil it for the rest. It's important that we save the potentially good ones, but there is also a bunch beyond saving. As long as I have to do this kind of work, those will be the ones I'll go after.

He noticed his explanation seemed to relax Jonetta.

"Just as long as you don't forget that," she said in a much softer tone.

Malik got up and walked around the table, leaned down and kissed Jonetta on the forehead.

"I won't," he said. "I promise you that I won't." He walked back to his chair and sat down. "Let's order."

****

A surge of excitement shot through Malik's emotionally charged body as he pulled the Maxima into one of the many parking spaces reserved for 'Detectives Only." It made him feel special. He was now a part of a select cadre of law enforcement officers. Reserved parking was one of the privileges that went along with that selective category. Malik had to check himself or he could really begin to enjoy the special attention that he was about to get.

He entered the headquarters building at 8:00, but was stopped before he got through the door by a security guard.

"Hey, you, this is for police officers only," the guard said gruffly. "What do you want?"

Malik smiled and flashed his badge at the guard.

"Malik, is that you?" the guard asked.

"Yeah, it's me, Smitty."

"Man, you sure look different. What happened?"

"Special assignment. I've been moved to undercover so I had to alter my appearance, and no more uniforms."

"You did one heck of a job," the guard said with a broad smile. "You sure fooled me."

"Isn't that the nature of what I'm going to be doing?" Malik asked rhetorically. "Fooling people?"

"You know you right." The guard raised his hand and Malik slapped it and then went inside.

As he strolled down the long corridor, other officers stared at him. Evidently, they also didn't recognize him. The more it seemed that he could fool people who actually knew him with his altered appearance, the more secure he felt about going out into the community. If he could get over this easily on trained policemen, he sure would be able to do the same out in the world.

Malik made it to his new home, the Criminal Investigation Unit of Detectives. When he entered the office, his new sergeant seemed to be waiting for him.

"Good morning detective," Sergeant greeted him. "It's amazing what two weeks can do. You sure don't look like Patrolman Williams anymore." The Sergeant got up, reached across the desk and shook Malik's hand.

"You think I'll fit in okay out there with the criminal element?" he asked.

"You'll do just fine. Just remember though, you're one of the good guys."

"No problem," Malik said in a terse tone. He kind of resented the implication. He watched as the Sergeant reached in his desk and pulled out a detective's gold badge.

"Let me have that patrolman's badge," he said.

Malik handed him the patrolman's badge and took his new one.

"That should make you feel real special," the Sergeant said.

"It does."

"Are you ready?"

"As I'll ever be."

The sergeant placed his arm around Malik's shoulder and they both headed out of the room.

"Good cause the next two weeks I'm going to train you to be the best undercover detective in this unit."

Sergeant wasn't kidding about the training. It was two weeks of the most intense work Malik had ever encountered. But when he finished and finally reported to work that evening for the real thing, he was ready. Working in community service was now behind him. He was anxious to get out in the field and test his newly acquired skills. The Friday of his last day of training, he was told exactly what he'd be doing. When he arrived at headquarters, he met up with Detective Wendell Booker, the man he was replacing.

"I hear you came through the training with flying colors," Booker greeted him.

"I guess I did all right," Malik replied.

"Let's get going into the real world," Booker said as the two men headed toward the Maxima. "Fun and games are now over. You're getting ready to play in the big leagues and face some real major league criminals. And remember no errors." Booker paused for a moment as he climbed into the passenger seat and fastened his seat belt. "In this game, errors will get you killed."

Malik climbed behind the wheel and they started off into a place where there was a possibility there would be no return. They drove the five blocks south out of the downtown area and turned left onto Martin Luther King Boulevard. What a contrast just a few blocks could make. They'd left the busy downtown area with its tall buildings, people dressed in business suits hurrying into their offices, with brand new cars filling the streets and entered an area with rundown boarded-up store fronts. Trash was strewn across the streets, and there was dirt where there should have been grass. Within a three-block area they passed three pawn shops, two liquor stores, and two older storefront buildings. One of the buildings had a worn out marquee with the words, "JERUSALEM BAPTIST CHURCH: COME HERE AND FIND JESUS, REVEREND WILLIE JACKSON, PASTOR." A couple blocks further down Martin Luther King Boulevard, Malik saw another run down building serving as a church. The glass in the marquee was broken. It also had a message to the passersby: "COME FIND JESUS. HE IS YOUR HOPE AND SALVATION, BETHEL BAPTIST CHURCH, DR. PASTOR ROSCOE ANDERSON, MINISTER."

Malik looked back at the road just in time to slam on his brakes, stopping in front of a disheveled man who had staggered out into the street. He glared over at Booker, and they both shook their heads.

"It never ends," Booker said.

"And I wonder will it ever?" Malik asked.

"I don't know," Booker said and then jerked his head to the right. "Hey, there's our man standing over there in that Church's Fried Chicken parking lot. Pull in over there."

"You sure this guy is all right?" Malik asked as he stared at a dark-skinned man who looked to be six feet tall, very thin, and about thirty years old. He had a clean-shaven head, imitation diamond earrings in each ear. He wore black slacks and shirt with rundown black shoes.

"Been a snitch for me for over three years. He knows his way around. Claims he's not hustling anymore. But I believe he's turned informant as a way to get rid of his competition."

"Real nice guy, huh?"

"He's not trying to be nice. Just trying to hustle," Booker said. "Pull over there to that parking space." He pointed to an empty space facing the boulevard inside the church's parking lot.

Malik followed Booker's instructions and pulled the Maxima into an open space.

"I'm going to turn him over to you. I got no need for him since I'm finished with undercover. His name is Mello and he's going to test you." Booker hit the button and the window rolled down. "So put him in his place right off and it's okay to joke a little with these guys, but never, not ever trust them, and always let them know who is in charge." He finished and called out. "Mello, over here."

Mello stared over at Booker and then Malik. His brows furrowed as he hesitated before making a move.

"He's trying to figure out what's going on," Booker said. "He's really checking you out. Wouldn't you hate to live this life? Never knowing who to trust and always suspicious. Sometimes you wonder how these guys ever sleep."

"Maybe they don't," Malik said as he stared at Mello. There was nothing really different about him. He looked like any other Black man hanging out in a fast food parking lot with no job and nothing to do all day but find ways to hustle. For Black men like him, hustling was a full time job. Malik knew this same scene was playing out all over this country in every inner city. Given a different set of circumstances and a different break in life, Mello might have been a banker or president of some large corporation. Instead, he was a hustler.

"Get over here," Booker shouted. "I ain't got all day to deal with you. It's all good."

Mello sauntered over to the driver's side and glared inside.

"Get in the back," Booker instructed him.

"Who is this guy?" Mello asked as he looked at Malik.

"Your new contact. Now get in."

Mello hesitated for another minute and then got in the backseat right behind Booker.

"Let's get out of here," Booker said.

"Where to?" Malik asked.

"Don't matter, just drive anywhere." Booker turned back toward Mello, handed him a package and continued. "This is your new inside contact. His name is Malik."

Momentarily, Malik took his eyes off the road and extended his hand back to Mello.

"How you be?" he asked.

Mello slapped his hand. "I'm here," he said, then snatched his arm back and turned directly to Booker. "So we got a new green hornet? I don't know if I can work with no young buck."

"What's up with this fool?" Malik blurted out. "What makes this loser think I want to work him?" He abruptly pulled over to the curb, slammed on the brakes. "In fact, get this fool out my car."

Just as abruptly as he stopped, he hit the gas and the car jerked at high speed back onto the street. "No, as a matter of fact, let's drop this fool off right in the middle of the hood, so when we put him out everybody going to know he's a snitch."

Booker broke out in a hearty laugh. "That'll work for me." He turned and looked back at his snitch. "I'm finished with him, so it's up to you, partner. If you don't think you can work with him, we might as well give him back to the dealers he's been snitching on."

" Y'all stop foolin' around," Mello scowled. "That ain't one bit funny."

Malik now had Mello's attention. He pulled over to the curb, turned and looked back at the snitch.

"Now you ready to put the work in?" he asked.

"Yeah, man, let's do it."

"Tell me what you got?" Booker asked.

"Five young boys, bout nineteen or twenty sellin' out of three houses, side by side." Mello leaned forward in the backseat.

The snitch definitely was ready to put work in, Malik thought.

"I can buy directly from the stash house where they're holding most of the drugs instead of from the runners," Mello continued.

"How you figure that?" Malik asked. He was really feeling it now.

"Cause I go by there and know the head man."

"How tough a bust will it be?" Booker now asked.

"They got the usual security. Plenty of young boys with walkie-talkies all up and down the street and hiding in the bushes. Or they just might be sittin' on the porches of other houses all along the block." Mello relaxed back in the seat. "When you do the raid you goin' have to hit 'em quick."

"Okay, let's check them out," Booker said. "Drive back behind that alley." He pointed to an alley near the spot where they were parked.

Malik pulled out, drove over to the alley and parked.

"You know the exercise," Booker said to Mello. "Out of the car."

All three men got out of the car, and Malik patted Mello down for drugs.

"He's clean," he said.

"Good," Booker said. "Now give us everything in your pockets. You go in there clean."

Mello emptied his pockets and gave all the contents to Malik, who then pulled out a twenty-dollar bill and gave it to the snitch.

"Let's go," Booker said.

They got back in the car and Malik drove back to within a couple blocks of the drug houses. Mello jumped out the back seat and hustled down the street to the drug house.

Malik and Booker watched Mello disappear around the corner heading toward the drug house. They waited fifteen minutes.

"Head over to Third Street. We'll pick him up over there," Booker said. "Don't drive pass the stash house. Go up a couple of blocks and then come back around."

"You got it," Malik followed instructions. He finally made it to Third Street, where Mello waited on the corner. He jumped in the backseat and Malik drove back to the alley and parked.

"What you got?" Booker asked while thrusting his open hand back toward Mello.

He put a small bag with a white rock like substance in Booker's hand.

"What's it like in there?" Booker asked as he put the bag in his jacket pocket.

"There are four young boys inside. The main one is a young brother they call Tech. His real name is Eric Johnson and he's about eighteen. It's his mamma's house, but she wasn't nowhere around. She works at night as a nurse's aid and she actually has a day care there during the day." Mello reared back and relaxed. "All them kids up in there during the day and their mamma's don't know right in that same house they running drugs at night.' He laughed as though it was funny and then continued. "When I went in Tech was sitting there cutting up a half key.

"Wait a minute," Malik interrupted. "You say it's his mamma's house and they run a daycare out of there during the day?"

"Yeah, that's right," Mello answered.

"You mean this fool is stashing and selling drugs right out of his mother's house with all those kids there during the day?"

"That's right," Mello said. "They all do it when they're that young and in the game. That's where they get started. Right under their mamma's eyes."

"You sure she wasn't in there?" Malik continued.

"No way. They do it during the hours their mamas are at work. When she gets home, they just close down the operation."

"You're telling me their mothers know nothing about what's going on?"

"They don't know until it's too late."

"There are no fathers?"

Mello broke out laughing. "Be serious. You all done already locked up the daddies. Then you do the sons. These boys think their daddies are heroes. You know like real men who took on the system."

"And lost."

"These boys don't see it that way. Prison is a rite of passage for them. Shows you're not afraid of the man's system and you'll take it on at all cost."

Malik now turned and looked at Booker.

"What'll happen to the mother after the bust?" he asked.

"Depends," Booker replied. "If she didn't know what was going on, nothing, but if we find out she was a part of it or even getting money from the sales, she could go down just like the rest of them." Booker paused for a moment, then turned his attention back to Mello. "Okay, let's wrap this up." He pulled out a fifty-dollar bill and handed it to Booker. "This is for your work."

"When you going to take them down?" Mello asked as he took the money and stuffed it in his pocket.

"Next two or three days, or when we know they just re-upped," Booker said. "I'll contact you. I want you to go down with the bust."

Malik stared over at Booker. "You want him to get busted, too?"

"Yeah," Booker answered. "We want him in the wagon so he can tell us what they talk about. That's the best time to catch them telling on each other and naming bigger fish to fry while they're scared about what's going to happen to them."

"I'll be ready," Mello said, opened the door and exited the car.

"What a piece of junk," Malik mumbled as he pulled back out into traffic.

"Don't be so hard on the brother," Booker said. "He's critical to our operation. Without him it'd be much harder to bust this riff-raff. Let's get back to the station, test this rock, and get our warrants ready for signature."

Malik and Booker rode in silence. As he followed the flow of traffic down Martin Luther King Boulevard, Malik's thoughts focused on the nature of the work he'd gotten himself into and the kind of people he'd be dealing with on a regular basis. Mello was a low-life, dirt bag with no value system and no morals at all. There were so many out there just like him that it disgusted Malik. There are two different worlds operating within the context of one America. There is that world operating above the surface of law and order. There are the millions of Americans who live what is considered a normal life. Then there is that world existing below the surface of legality, where nothing is considered normal except for those who live in it. Cheating, lying, stealing, and even murder is normal behavior to that America. Instead of going to college, they go to jail and instead of going to work, they go to court. Their boss is a judge who has total control over their lives. What frightened Malik is the fact that the world seemed to be winning the battle for the hearts and minds of young Blacks who admire drug dealers, because, according to their thinking, the dealer is getting over on the system. He is beating the man.

Malik shook his head as he pulled into the station's parking lot. He and Booker went straight to the evidence lab and had the rock tested. The results came back positive for crack cocaine.

"It's the real thing," Booker said. "Now all we have to do is execute the warrant and we'll put another group of these little punks away for a very long time."

"Yeah," Malik replied. "I'll catch up with you later," he said to Booker and headed to the restroom. He needed to clean up and get the filth off him. He needed to wash away the ugliness of what probably could never be washed clean.

A nervous Malik paced back and forth in the assembly area of headquarters. It had been a long day and now would be a very long night as all the SWAT teams assembled for the bust scheduled to go down at ten o'clock that night. Earlier in the day Mello called and told him that Tech received a big shipment of drugs that morning. He happened to be there when it arrived. Mello had really won the confidence of Tech to the point that he transacted his business right in front of him.

Once Malik received that tip, he notified Lieutenant Bronson, who in turn, organized the SWAT teams. He watched the men come into the room wearing all black army pants, black desert boots, black drug unit jackets with the words SWAT TEAM in bright orange on the back, and black Ninja masks. They carried nine millimeter Smith and Wesson semi-automatic pistols with two members armed with shot guns. He was awestruck at the overwhelming display of power. He felt ambivalent about what was about to happen. Young brothers who dabbled in the illicit drug business had to be brought down. At the least they were a menace to the community where they conducted their sick kind of business, and at most they killed people, either through the drugs or directly if they happened to get in their way. The other side of him harbored a deep-seated concern for the chaos and pain it caused the community in general and specifically the families of the boys who, once busted, would be forced to confront the prospect of a long time behind bars.

"Listen up," Bronson called out. "We got three houses to hit. Team one, you got twelve men and you'll be taking down the stash house, which is the place where they keep all the money and distribute the drugs. The main man will be in there. There'll probably be four other young men inside with him. Be careful and don't take any chances because they'll be armed with automatic weapons. Search and secure the premises." Bronson handed Malik a diagram of the house. He'd gotten the diagram to the insides of all three houses from a computer search. "This is a two-story house so make sure you search both floors thoroughly." Bronson paused for a second and smiled. "Do one of our patented re-decorating jobs on the interior."

Malik took the diagram and the other members of his team gathered around him to study it.

"Team two, you got twelve men and you'll take down the house to the left of the stash house. Team three you'll secure the house to the right. These are both distribution houses, and there'll be anywhere from four to six runners in there. Might be some crack heads inside buying drugs. Take everybody down. Afterwards we'll sort out who is who. That's not really our job. Let the District Attorney deal with that." He handed two more diagrams to the men in charge of the two teams. "Those are both one-story houses, but pretty much empty since they both are abandoned. Still search them thoroughly."

Finally, Bronson turned to team four. "You know your job. Take down and detain anyone out and about on the street. Hold them down until the area is secure and it can be determined they had no involvement with the drug activity from the targeted locations."

Bronson stopped for a couple minutes and allowed the teams to review the diagrams and talk.

"According to Malik's snitch they have lookouts up and down the street with walkie-talkies warning our targeted locations of any suspicious activity outside. To counter them we have to hit quick and fast. We'll jam the frequency they are believed to be using. To throw them off, we'll roll up on them in a U-Haul truck." Again Bronson paused and smiled. "We plan to haul something, but it ain't furniture. You'll deploy from the rear of the truck on signal from Sergeant Dowe who'll be your driver. Since we know they have weapons, we got a no-knock nighttime search warrant. When you get to the targets, take the doors off the hinges with a ram and swarm in like a pool of flesh eating fish. Make them sorry they ever dealt a drug or got up that morning. Put the fear of our awesome power in them. Let them know this is our world and this is a losing game. Any questions?"

Fifty men held their weapons high in the air and in unison shouted, "Yeah!"

An hour and a half after the SWAT teams left the station they pulled back in with their prisoners, including Mello who was busted right outside the stash house. Malik was impressed with how smoothly the bust went, with no glitches. Each team followed the game plan and those boys didn't know what hit them. They arrested Tech and four Black teenagers, along with $20,000, five handguns, and two kilo's of cocaine in the stash house. From the second and third houses, they secured six young men, all Black between the ages of fourteen and eighteen, five handguns and one ounce of cocaine. Ten Black men standing outside or around the houses were taken in for having crack cocaine in their possession and a couple had weapons. By any measurement criteria, Malik's first bust had been a success.

Along with four other men, Malik packaged and logged all the drugs and the money into evidence. For that moment, he was the hero, receiving accolades from every officer in the building.

"Malik, great job," one officer said and patted him on the back.

"Man, you sure learned the game fast," another said.

"Hey Malik, thanks for busting that bunch of trash. Too bad you didn't get a chance to take a few of them out," was the response from another man.

His words caused Malik to cringe. He actually wanted them to kill some of these young men. The thought sickened him. He had made a difference, but was it something to be proud of, he just didn't know. The images of those boys, heads bent and in cuffs, stayed with him. He had busted kids between the ages of fourteen and eighteen and now their lives were all but ruined. And as quickly as he took that bunch off the street, there would be another bunch to replace them. He finished logging the evidence in and had one more job to do before he could call it a night.

Mello had been removed and placed in a holding cell away from the others. Malik made it down to his cell, unlocked it and waved him out.

"Good bust," is all he could think to say to this man who he disliked.

"Yeah, and there'll be a lot more in the future," Mello said as he walked out of the cell.

Malik slammed it shut and the two of them walked back into the main area of the police headquarters. They headed outside and Malik handed Mello a package with $2,000 inside.

"For your efforts," Malik said.

"I appreciate your generosity," Mello replied and tucked the money in his pocket. "But let me get out of here. I don't want to push my luck cause ain't no tellin' who might be driving by here to see what they can find out. Every dealer out there know what went down by now and they'll be checking to see if they can put it all together. And I sure don't want them to find out I was the one."

"Makes sense," Malik said tersely. He really didn't like talking to this low life, but knew he had no choice. That was the nature of the business. "I'll be in touch."

"You do that." Mello put his hands in his pockets and strolled away.

Malik watched Mello as he disappeared around the corner. Instead of going back inside the building to get to the back parking lot, he decided to walk outside. He wasn't in the mood for any more accolades or "that-a-boys" and high fives. The energy rush he experienced during the preparation and during the actual bust right up to watching Mello put his hands in his pocket and turn the corner had dissipated and now Malik felt a bit depressed.

He made it to the back of the building and practically ran to his car. He didn't want to see any more policemen, he didn't want to see any more young Black kids, cuffed and heads bowed, a symbol of their demise, and he sure didn't want to see anyone like Mello at that time. Malik needed no reminders of the kind of people he was dealing with on a daily basis.

He looked at his watch. It read one o'clock and there were very few cars on the street. But there was one particular car that stayed a little distance behind him and it made him nervous. As he neared his home, he decided not to pull in the driveway, but instead kept going to the corner, made a right turn and went back on the expressway. He wanted to make sure the car wasn't following him. The driver did not turn; the car kept going straight. Malik smiled at the irony of it all. He was behaving in much the same manner as the drug dealers. Paranoia was settling in as he imagined every car behind him full of young thugs just waiting for the opportunity to put a bullet in his head. He needed to chill out. He grabbed his cell phone and dialed a number in Cleveland.

"Hey Dad."

"That you, Malik?"

"Yeah."

"How's it going son? Everything all right? Something gone wrong on the new assignment?"

"It's going. How are you and Mom?"

"We're fine, but you didn't call this time of night just to find out how we're doing. What's going on?"

"I'm not sure I like what I'm doing," Malik lowered his voice as if someone might be listening. His paranoia was kicking in again.

"You don't like doing that undercover stuff?"

"I have to admit I got mixed feelings about it and what some of those feelings are I don't like."

"What is it? Can you pinpoint it?" His dad's voice rose a bit.

"I like the power and prestige and I don't know if that is a good thing. I felt a surge of incredible power this evening when I participated in my first bust. But then when I saw the end result, which was about twenty young Black kids between the ages of fourteen and eighteen with their lives wrecked, I felt guilty." He paused but his dad said nothing. "Don't get me wrong, what these boys are doing is dead wrong and it has to be stopped. But they aren't anything but pawns for a much larger game organized at a level we'll probably never touch. I don't know if what I'm doing will really make a difference."

"It affected you that badly?"

"I think it's changing me. And I don't think the end justifies the means. A police raid is brutal, not only on the criminals, but the entire neighborhood."

"Son, don't lose your identity of who you are. Let the job become you, not you becoming the job. If you ever want a good laugh, Son, ask someone when you meet them who they are and the first thing they tell you is the title of their job." Now it was his father's turn to pause. Malik knew why. He was letting his advice sink in, something he'd done with Malik all his life. "You are someone who loves to help people--especially kids, you love family, and you're a humanitarian. You are someone who wants to make a difference. As long as you can remember that and never let them change you, then you'll survive this. You'll have to take tough but firm stands when confronted, but just remember it takes more courage for a man to be true to himself than for a soldier to fight on the battlefield."

"You're right, Dad."

"Just stay true to yourself, Son."

"I'll talk to you later, and I love you."

"Love you too, Son."

Over the next two weeks Malik was on a roll. Mello introduced him to five new players in the game and he was buying directly from them. Malik also had five new informants on the payroll and the number kept growing. The very ones that didn't seem like good prospects to snitch turned out to be the main ones. They were ready to set up friends and even family members in order to stay out of jail. His success had swollen his ego to the point that it had all but silenced his heart. He was on a high unlike any drug. And he was also developing the "us" against "them" mentality of the other members of the team, the one trait he'd disliked about the others.

Malik had been so good in such a short period of time that Lieutenant Bronson decided to send him into the most infected drug area of the city, Dupont Housing Project. It happened to be the area where he had originally been assigned when on police duty and where he wanted to do community service. Since he'd spent so much time in there before, he had to alter his looks even more than in the past. His beard grew thicker and longer, and he had dreadlocks. He wore a red, black, and green cap covering the back part of his head and the dreadlocks flowed out from under it. Knowing the area quite well, he knew his first task would be to establish a contact with someone so that he wouldn't appear suspicious. That neighborhood did not like outsiders just hanging around.

He pulled into the complex in his Maxima with the music blaring a Tupac rap song. About a half dozen young brothers standing on the corner eyeballed him and he knew what they were thinking. He needed to make contact with someone real quick. He spotted a young, slim lady, about five-feet-two and quite pretty. He rolled down the window and called out.

"Whuz up, baby girl?"

"What's up with you?" she replied. "Who you out here to see?"

"You, now." Malik smiled.

"Whatever, boy."

"For real, but you look like one of those heart breakers, so I don't think I should step to you."

"That's you playa."

Malik knew he was making good progress. "Come sit with ya boy and talk unless you got a man out here." He gestured for her to come around to the passenger side of the car.

She smiled and strolled around to the passenger side of the car, leaned down, and placed her arms on the car. "Myself, I'm living the single life."

"Well get in and let's see if I can win your heart."

She opened the door and slid into the passenger's seat.

Malik could now relax as the young men who had been watching his every action turned their attention away from him. They assumed that he was there to see the girl. He turned his attention back to her.

"What's your name, Shorty?"

"My friends call me Mae," she said with one of the prettiest smiles Malik had ever seen. This was one beautiful person.

"My name is Malik and I sure am glad I just happened to be driving down this street and saw you walking your fine self down it."

"Are you a playa or what?"

"Nah, baby girl. I'm just a hustler trying to make that money. You got a problem with that?"

"That's cool, whatever you got to do to make that money."

"I'm just trying to come up. You ain't in the game are you, baby girl?"

"Nah, but I know a lot brothahs out here that are. But they cool. I grew up with most of them."

"For real, cause I just got out here a few months ago and I need to make some contacts. But they have to be moving some weight, you know, no nickel and dime stuff."

"Ones I know are heavy hitters."

"Cool, that's what I'm talking about, a ride-and-die chick."

"Nah, I don't usually get down like that. But I think you're kind of cute, so I'll hook you up with them.

"At least I know these brothahs ain't going to try to rob me if they cool with you." Malik reached over and ran his hand along the contours of Mae's face. She didn't resist. "You eat yet?"

"Nah, you gonna treat me to something?"

"For sure. How about some Red Lobster?"

"That'll work for me. Let's go."

Malik pulled away from the curb and headed out of the projects. He pulled out his cell phone and called his surveillance team and pretended to be talking to his cousin.

"Yo, what up, cuz? Hey I met this shorty out at the Dupont and we about to go get some Red Lobster. After we eat and I drop her back off, I'll get up with you then. I'll holla at you later." He closed the phone, stuck it in his pocket, and turned his attention back to Mae. "You sure one fine sistah. How someone fine as you walking around without a man?"

"Cause these brothahs, they be trippin'. You know, tryin' too much to be possessive."

"Yeah, ain't nothin' worse than an insecure brothah. It's cool; ain't no pressure here. It's whatever day-by-day. I don't like all that drama myself. Life's too short for all that."

"Ain't it, though?"

Malik laughed. "I see we going to get along real good." Malik pulled into the Red Lobster parking lot, they got out and strolled into the restaurant.

They found a table near the window so they could look

out at the trees that lined the side of the building. The waitress approached them and put two menus on the table.

"How y'all doing this evening?" she asked as she pulled out her order pad and pencil. "You ready to order or do you need a little time?"

"I don't know about you, but I'm starving," Malik said as he picked up the menu and opened it.

"I know what I want," Mae said.

"And what is that?" Malik asked.

Mae looked up at the waitress. "I'll have the wood–grilled sirloin surf and turf with ice tea."

"Good choice," Malik said. "The lady has good taste." He looked up at the waitress. "The lobster lover's dream for me."

"What to drink?" the waitress asked.

"Raspberry lemonade," Malik answered.

"I'll bring your drinks right away and get your orders in also." The waitress turned and walked away.

They spent the next two hours talking and enjoying their meal. Malik constantly reminded Mae that he needed those introductions as soon as possible. She assured him it would happen and when they finished, he signaled the waitress over to his table. Malik pulled a large wad of money, peeled off a hundred dollar bill to cover the meal and another hundred dollars for the waitress.

"You ready to make a move, baby girl?"

"Yeah, but aren't you going to wait for your change?"

"What change?"

"Yo, you got it like that?" Mae said and smiled.

As they strolled out of the restaurant, Malik knew he'd made the kind of impression on Mae that would assure him of meeting those contacts.

Malik parked in front of Mae's apartment unit. No doubt she was attracted to him and this could go further. But at all cost, he had to avoid any kind of intimacy with her. He got out and walked her up to her apartment.

"Can I get that number?" he asked as she reached for her key.

"849-2016," she reeled it off quickly.

He knew Mae was waiting for him to ask to come in. She cracked the door open. He had to think fast. He grabbed his cell phone and faked dialing a number.

"Dre, what's up? I'm about to spend some time with a beautiful young lady. Anything I need to know?" He frowned, moved the phone from his ear acting like he just heard some terrible news. "What?" he shouted.

Just as Mae opened the door, he said. "Mae, I got to go. Something's happened to my cuz and I've got to get over there." He gave Mae a hug. "I'll call you later." He then ran to his car, swung the door open and jumped inside.

As he pulled out onto the street, he smiled. He was getting pretty good at this and it gave him quite a rush.

The next day Malik drove into the Dupont Projects and parked in front of Mae's apartment complex. Six young men stood around the outside of the apartments drinking and smoking.

"Wuz up, playas?" he shouted

"That's you, dawg. I can't call it," one of the men answered.

Malik laughed as he walked up to Mae's door and knocked.

"Who is it?"

"Malik, open the door."

The door swung open and Mae looked just as stunning as she had the day before.

"Come on in," she said softly. "I've been trying to study for my upcoming exams." She walked back over to a small dining room table covered with papers and books and sat down. He followed her over and sat across from her.

Seeing all those books stunned him. "Studying?" he asked. "Studying for what?"

"For my upcoming exams, silly."

"You go to school?"

"No, I go to college. I'm getting my degree in Business Management with a concentration in Information Management."

Malik was speechless. "How much time do you have before you get your degree?" he finally asked.

"One more year and I'll be graduating.'

"So you're trying to do something, huh?"

"Yeah, I'm definitely trying to get it together. I want to get up out of here," she said as she began to arrange the books and papers in front of her. "Malik, I'm from a family that's three generations in these projects. My mother lives in the building next door and my grandparents live two buildings down. Not to mention I've lost three cousins and two uncles to these projects. I just want a better life for me and my daughter."

"You got a daughter? How old is she?"

"She's going on three," Mae stopped moving papers and looked across at Malik. "She's at my mom's since I've been studying for my finals." She sat straight up in her chair and all her attention was on Malik. "I'm going to let you know that I'm going to introduce you to these dealers out there that I grew up with. But don't you ever bring that junk in my house or around me. It's just something about you I don't know what it is, but your eyes tell me you're really a good person. It's like you're out here hustlin' but it's not really you. I guess that's what I really like about you. Your eyes don't lie about who you are. They reveal your soul." She stopped and smiled.

The more she talked, the more Malik realized that he was getting in deeper than what was safe. He had to change the subject. One of the cardinal rules of his work was no personal attachment with the enemy and she, at that point, was the enemy.

"So what are my eyes saying now?" he asked as he looked up and down her.

She laughed. "Boy, you so silly. Can't you ever be serious?"

He was acting rather silly, but his mind was on a serious problem. Once Mae introduced him to her friends to buy drugs, she would become a conspirator and be locked up for conspiracy. It would be his fault. He would have used her and taken advantage of her need to find someone she could believe in and care for. It was so much easier to consider using Mae to infiltrate when he knew nothing about her. However, now it was too late to back off.

"Come on, let's walk across the way so I can introduce you to Kenny," Mae said interrupting his musing.

Yes, it was too late, he thought, as he followed her out of the apartment.

They walked across the yard into another apartment and started up the stairs to the second floor. As they started down the hall three young brothers came out of one of the apartments and walked toward them. The brother in the middle a very thin, tall brother seemed to be the leader.

"Hey Kenny, what's happening?" Mae greeted the brother in the middle. "I want to introduce you to my dude I told you about earlier this morning. He's my man and he's cool to deal with."

Kenny reached out and gave Malik daps. "Whuz up, what you need?" Kenny said.

"I'm cool for right now, but this weekend I'm gonna need to re-up," Malik replied.

"You're good, let me know when. My number's 883-2216," Kenny said. "Let me have yours."

"482-5611." Malik gave him the number that the police could listen in on. He then turned to Mae. "Thanks baby girl, I can take it from here. Don't you have to hit them books and study?"

"You right about that," Mae said. "I'll catch up with you later," she said then strolled back down the hall and down the stairs.

"So you brothahs get down on the basketball court?" Malik asked Kenny and the others.

"Yeah, we hit the court every once in a while. Why, do you ball?" Kenny asked.

"I got some game. Maybe sometime we can relax and play a little," Malik said.

"You got it brothah. In the meantime, I'll wait for that call."

"You got it." Malik held up his balled fist and this time gave Kenny dabs. "I'm out brothahs." Malik headed back down the stairs and out of the apartment building.

As he drove out of the complex he knew he was in. From this point on it would be pretty easy to set Kenny up for the fall. But in doing so, he was putting Mae in harm's way. There was a strong possibility that she would end up going to jail for just making the introduction. She would also be in harms way with Kenny if he found out it was Malik who would set him up. That could definitely mean her life. But unfortunately that was the game; take advantage of those who don't know any better and use them to get to key players. It had been so easy for him to get to Mae and use her and he didn't really know her that well.

The next day Malik went in early in order to brief Lieutenant Bronson and Ms. Laura Chante from the Attorney General's office. They met in the Lieutenant's office.

"I've pretty much made contact with Kenny Holloway." Malik sat across from Bronson and Chante at the conference table in the Lieutenant's office. They both had yellow legal pads and pens ready to jot down pertinent information from him. "I'll set up the direct buy from Kenny within the next few days. Yesterday I told him I was okay, but would need to re-up by the end of the week."

"He talked sells with you and he just met you?" Bronson asked.

"Yeah, only because Mae brought me to him. They've lived in those projects all their lives. In fact, they've been friends since elementary school. He trusts her and knows she wouldn't deliberately set him up for a bust."

"Well, that's exactly what she's done," Chante said while writing notes on the legal pad.

"Not really," Malik shot back. "I mean she hasn't deliberately betrayed their friendship."

"Well, she should've busted him a long time ago if she knew he was dealing drugs," Bronson added.

"Hey come on, Lieutenant, let's be fair. They're friendship is deeper than what he does for a living. They grew up together and even though she knows what he does is wrong, they're still friends."

"He's a drug dealer," Bronson's voice rose. "He's poisoning the neighborhood, killing kids and anyone else who gets hooked on that junk. What do you mean she shouldn't have blown the whistle on him? She's an enabler and all those people living in those projects are enablers to a crime cause they know what's going on and won't report it, and when asked they tell us they just don't know nothing."

"Maybe that's because they dislike us more than the dealers and what they're doing," Malik shot back at the lieutenant.

"Okay, okay, let's not fight over this," Chante intervened. "We got fish to fry and need to decide when it's going down."

"This weekend," Malik said. "I'll make the buy on Saturday, then with the warrant ready, we can go in that night."

" Kenny is the biggest dealer in Dupont. We bust him and we'll put a real dent in that operation for a while," Bronson said.

"I doubt that, but at least it will be a start," Malik demurred. "Chante, I want to ask a favor that we not arrest Mae. She--"

"What," Bronson scowled. "She's got to go down too if she's conspiring to the selling of drugs. She knows better and she knows it's a crime. She has to go to jail just like the rest of them."

"That's not necessarily so." Malik allowed a little pleading in his voice. "She only did it because she's attracted to me. She only knows these guys because of a forced living environment that she had no control over. This is not something she usually does."

"That's a bunch of crap," Bronson shouted. "I'm so sick and tired of these tired old excuses for that criminal element. The whole idea that she's just a victim of her circumstances doesn't fly with me. She's a criminal and should be treated like one."

"She really doesn't think she's doing anything wrong." Malik refused to back off.

"Does she know you want to buy drugs?" Bronson asked, this time in a lower voice.

"Yes," Malik answered. "I guess it's hard for you to understand unless you grew up in that kind of environment. I did and I understand how she could get caught up in it and not really be a part of it." He knew he was making no progress with Bronson so he turned his attention to Chante. "I'm asking for special consideration in this case."

"Malik has greater knowledge of the particulars because he's the one working the case," Chante said. "He knows what's going on and who the key players are. I think we should accept his recommendation."

"I can't believe this." Bronson abruptly stood up. "I need some air." He rushed out of his office and left Malik and Chante sitting at the table.

"He'll be all right," Chante said. "Give him a few minutes to cool off."

Malik wasn't concerned with Bronson. His entire concentration was to make sure that Mae didn't have to do any time. He wasn't sure how he would be able to live with himself if that happened.

"I need to be taken into custody and locked up with Kenny and his boys," he said.

"We can do that."

"And you just got to be careful and keep Mae's identity with me quiet."

"The only way to do that is if Kenny pleads. If the case doesn't go to trial then we won't have to bring you in to testify. That's the only way she won't be implicated." She stopped and put her notepad in the briefcase. "Given Kenny's past record he will probably want to work out a plea and given how crowded our dockets are that'll be what happens. He might end up being an informant."

"Not mine," Malik said emphatically as they made it back out into the general area. "Tomorrow's Friday and I'll call Kenny and set up the buy for Saturday morning."

"That'll work," Chante said. "Oh, and one more thing, Malik."

"Yeah what's that?"

"Don't forget who you're working with. Don't forget whose side you're on." Chante finished and walked away.

Malik was beginning to view this war on drugs as a contradiction. The true criminals get off by cutting deals and turning informant. Those that just happened to be in the wrong place and the wrong time and didn't know the rules of the game were the real victims. They were the ones being used in the game by both the police and the drug dealers. Malik thought the game was enormous and he didn't know if he was being played, and just one of the many pawns in the game. What was really clear, no one really wanted the drug game to end. The dealers thought they were winning by making money-selling drugs, but their cut amounted to pennies compared to the suppliers. Their major contribution to the total game was to destroy any normalcy in the Black community. They called crack "girl" for a reason. Black girls had a strong addiction to the drug to the point of abandoning their role in the Black family. Essentially you destroy the female and you have destroyed the foundation of the Black family. Even the police officers were being used with the poisoning of their minds about an entire community.

Malik didn't like the game, but knew there was nothing he could do about it at least not at that time. He vowed that when the opportunity presented itself, he was going to educate as many young minds as possible that the actions taken by them as socially acceptable within their peer group and community were against the law. He was sure that Mae never thought that she could get prison time for simply introducing him to Kenny. He knew education was the only way to make a difference. Some day he would proclaim loud and clear that it is all a game and we are being played.

****

"Kenny, wuz up fam?" Malik used his cell phone from his apartment. It was Saturday morning and everything was ready for the bust.

"Wuz up with you fam?" Kenny hollered back from the other end, also on a cell phone.

"I need to make that move."

"What you need?"

"I need a bird if the price is right."

"Twenty thousand," Kenny said.

"That'll work."

"Cool, give me a couple hours and call me back. I'll tell you where to meet me."

Malik hit the off button and then dialed Bronson's number at the station. The entire unit was on call for the bust.

"Lieutenant, it's a go," he said to Bronson on the other end.

"Good, I got people in place," Bronson replied. "We'll initiate the surveillance on Kenny."

"Don't blow it."

"We know what we're doing. You just take care of your part."

Malik knew he was alluding to Mae. Under these circumstances he couldn't dare go to her and tell her to leave the vicinity or go visit someone else. Even though he was quite sure she had no idea about the game, it might create some suspicion and cause her to warn Kenny. He had to bite his bottom lip and bare it.

Malik sat in the lieutenant's office at headquarters with Bronson and Ms. Chante listening to the report that had just come in from the surveillance team. "The prime target was spotted leaving his residence at 10 a.m. with three other men. They drove a dark colored Lexus registered to the prime target's mother. They were followed to a row house at 120 West 34th Street in the city. The four men entered the house and about fifteen minutes later two females exited the house, got in the Lexus and drove off. One of the vehicles with the surveillance team stayed behind to monitor the prime target's movement; the other team followed the two females."

While he listened his thoughts still were with Mae. She got up that morning, probably began studying for her exams with no idea that her entire life would be turned upside down if they arrested her. She could possibly do jail time and her dream of escaping the projects and building a better life for her daughter as well as herself would go up in smoke. And Malik would only have himself to blame. The surveillance team continued.

"The two females drove to an upscale part of town and parked in a cul-de-sac. They entered the residence at 4802 Big Rock Circle. They stayed in there only a short while and exited with four black duffle type bags. They drove back to the residence at 120 West 34th Street. The females were met by the prime target and the other men standing outside waiting for them. The prime target took the duffle bags back into the residence at 120 West 34th Street. Shortly thereafter, the prime target and the three men got back into the Lexus without the duffle bags and went back to the apartment in Dupont Projects. Surveillance teams were stationed at 4802 Big Rock Circle and 120 West 34th Street. Surveillance teams observed three other vehicles coming to 4802 Big Rock Circle and the same activity took place with females loading duffle bags from the residence to the trunk of their vehicles, and driving to different locations in the city."

"Add those addresses to the warrant list," Bronson said to one of the police officers in the room with them.

At 2:00 p.m. Malik received the call.

"Hey fam, come on over to the projects and meet me in the courtyard," Kenny instructed. He sounded all businesslike in his tone.

"No problem," Malik said. He turned to Bronson. "That's it. He's yours now."

"No, he's ours," Bronson corrected Malik.

"What about the girl?"

"Don't know. We might let her alone."

Malik and two other undercover detectives, who took the names of Dre and Devonte, left headquarters and headed for the place where the buy would take place. As he pulled off in the Maxima, Malik felt just a little nervous about Bronson's agreeing to leave Mae alone. It really didn't sound sincere.

Malik, Devonte, and Dre pulled into the projects where they spotted Kenny and his boys waiting in the courtyard. Malik backed the Maxima up next to Kenny's Lexus. They all three got out and walked over next to Kenny.

"These my cousins. They cool. I told you about them yesterday," Malik said as he greeted Kenny with the playa grip.

Kenny stared at Devonte and Dre for a minute then smiled and said, "Come on back here with me."

Malik followed him to the back of the car and Kenny popped the trunk. He grabbed a small duffle bag. "A brick," he said.

Malik opened the bag and checked out a solid brick of cocaine. He then strolled back over to his Maxima, popped the trunk and pulled out a briefcase. He opened it and peeled off twenty thousand dollars in hundred dollar bills.

Malik took the duffle bag and tossed it in the back of the Maxima. He and Kenny signaled to their boys that everything was cool. The two men gave each other the playa handshake and the three of them climbed back in the car.

"I'll be giving you a holla in a couple of days," Malik said and they drove out of the projects with the drugs.

Once out of the projects and off the main street, Malik pulled into a secure area where he pulled out a field test kit and checked the white substance. It tested positive for cocaine. Malik opened his cell phone and dialed Bronson's number.

"It tested positive so you can execute the warrants," he said.

The arrest went like clockwork. Two females were taken into custody at the West 34th Street residence and three kilos of cocaine were seized. Two males were arrested at Big Circle Drive along with ten kilo's. An additional raid took place at 1520 131st Street, where four men were taken into custody and five kilo's of cocaine were seized. Lieutenant Bronson and Agent Chante decided not to execute the warrant against Kenny and his boys at that same time, making it difficult to trace the bust to Malik and also implicate Mae. But it was coming.

Two days past and Malik had no contact with Mae. He just

couldn't do that knowing that her turn might be coming soon. She called a couple of times, but he put her off, hoping she'd get angry and not call him anymore. On the fourth day, it was time to move on Kenny and his gang. He placed a call to Kenny monitored by Lieutenant Bronson and Chante.

"Wuz up, fam," Kenny said, answering Malik's call on the third ring.

"Trying to get a couple of birds if you got them?"

"Nah, it's too hot right now. One of my main connections got popped so I'm laying low. I got a bird I'm sittin' on and that's about it."

"Do what you gotta do fam till it cools off and hit me up when you ready," Malik said.

"Cool, I got some peeps I can turn you onto. Let me holla at them and I'll get back with you."

"For sure fam, I'll holla at you later." Malik finished and turned off the phone, stuck it in his pocket and looked across the conference table at Bronson and Chante.

"I think we need to go after him now," Bronson said. "We don't want too much time to pass. Let's hit him while he's sitting on that one kilo."

"I agree," Chante said. "Since the warrant is in place we need to execute it. He'll think the folks from the bust the other day gave him away and that'll keep you out of it, Malik."

"You going to leave the girl alone?" Malik asked.

Bronson and Chante looked at each other but said nothing.

"What's the deal?" Malik pursued the question.

"Just leave that alone right now," Bronson snapped at Malik. "You got a job to do. We'll be ready in the next hour."

Malik knew not to push the issue. He could only hope that Bronson and Chante would exercise some discretion and leave Mae alone. He turned and hurried out of the room.

Malik, Dre, and Devonte sat waiting in a sub-station five blocks from headquarters. That's where they would be arrested and brought back into the headquarters, but it had to be after Kenny and his gang were brought in for booking. It had to appear that the police made a clean sweep and arrested Malik also so that the dealers wouldn't be able to pinpoint him as the agent. They had also waited the extra days so that it would appear that one of the dealers arrested during the original bust had cut a deal with the police and gave Kenny and his crew up for a lighter sentence.

Malik paced the floor unable to calm his nerves. He wasn't concerned about the arrest, but about Mae. They told him that she might not go down with this bust, but what if she did? How would that affect her and if it was happening just then, how did she feel? He knew she would be frightened to the extent of panicking. But why was he so worried about her? She was there to be used and he did what was necessary. The person he should be thinking and worrying about was Jonetta. Since he started this new job with the department they'd spent very little time together. Right after this bust he promised himself that he'd take a break and spend some time with her. She deserved it because she'd been very patient and understanding with the lack of attention she'd gotten from him. It was all good with her and he had to make sure it stayed that way.

His cell phone went off and he came back to reality. "Yeah, this is Malik."

"It's done," Bronson practically shouted in the phone. "We got them all, you can come on in now."

"We'll be there in less than thirty," Malik said. "It's done, cuff us and take us in," he said to the police officers waiting with them.

Malik, Dre, and Devonte were cuffed, put in the back of a police wagon and taken back to the station.   Still in cuffs, the police marched them into the booking area. As they marched in, Malik stopped right in the middle of the room.

Mae was sitting on the bench along the wall with Kenny and four other young men. Her head was down and he could tell she was crying. She looked up at him and the expression on her face told the whole story.

"Why?" she shouted at him. "Why did you do this to me. I told you no drugs or none of that mess in my place and now they think I had something to do with all this drug stuff. Malik you got to tell them I didn't have anything to do with it. You know what this is doing to my child, my mother, and now I won't be able to stay in school." She burst out crying and covered her face. "Why you do this to me? Why you wreck my life like this?"

"Shut up," Malik shouted at her. "Just shut up. They ain't got nothing on none of us. So just shut up." He moved over to the fingerprint station. Malik knew the worst reaction he could possibly have is to show any compassion for her. There was no way he could reveal any semblance of the real Malik because Kenny would pick it up and know he was the culprit. As long as he kept up the façade, he'd be all right and later could clear Mae. But it hurt to know that all the things she said to him were true, not for the reason she thought, but for a much more devious reason.

The sergeant on duty in the booking room pushed Malik up against the wall and said, "Get over there and shut up yourself." He pushed Malik over to the fingerprint station and took his prints. They then shoved him over to another station and took his picture. Through it all, he could hear Mae sobbing. God, if he could just go to her and let her know it would all be okay. If he could tell her he was undercover and would be able to clear her name and get her out of this mess. But there was no chance he could do that. It would mean his death and probably hers also. The time would come when he could make this all up to her, but then and there he had to play the game.

The sergeant grabbed him by the arm and took him out of the room. A couple other officers brought Dre and Devonte out also. Bronson and Chante waited for him on the other side of the station. He rushed Bronson and got right in his face.

"Why'd you arrest her? Why'd you go against your word?"

"We had to and you know it, even if we don't want to charge her. It had to look like we were after her also or her life wouldn't be worth two cents if Kenny thought she was involved in his bust. We'll charge her and get it reduced to a lower offense then let her go."

Malik backed off Bronson and sat in a chair to relax. He didn't know what to say to either Bronson or Chante, so instead he just stared at the floor.

"Malik, great bust, man," the policeman who arrested and brought him into the station said as he passed by where Malik had sat down.

"Congratulations, man, you're on your way to a great career. You're a natural for this work," another office said.

"Detective Malik Williams, you are an outstanding officer, and I'd like to recommend you to the DEA," Chante said. "We need more Black undercover agents to penetrate your communities.

Sometimes it's very difficult for the white agent. You have a knack with young Black dealers and they'll trust you. That's what we need. Great job," She finished and walked away.

Malik didn't look up while receiving accolades from his fellow officers or when Chante suggested that he go to work for the Fed's in undercover. He didn't acknowledge their compliments. He didn't feel good about himself. All along he thought he might make a difference being undercover and putting dealers in jail. Bottom line was that young brothers like Kenny didn't go to jail. They cut deals with the District Attorney and often got off on probation. They knew the system and understood every step of the way what they were doing. The Kennys of the Black community calculated their risks against the kind of lifestyle dealing drugs would provide them and they were willing to take a chance. But people like Mae didn't understand nor did they want to be in the game. They were the ones that often got trapped and their lives destroyed. Our communities may be home sweet home to most of our people, he thought, but in reality it's just a playground for drug dealers and cops. Malik couldn't do this anymore. He gave it a shot, but it hurt more than it made him feel good. He had to stay true to himself and not get caught up in this vicious game. He had locked up a drug dealer, but practically shattered Mae's life in the process.

He got up and slowly walked to the detective's locker room, all the time fighting back the tears. He looked in the mirror and no longer saw that man who, not long ago, told Jonetta that this work would be for only a short time, and that his heart was still set on community service. He had to make that happen and real soon. There was no way he could spend one more day as an undercover agent, giving him no fulfillment. In order to believe in himself he had to rediscover the love for himself. That could never happen doing work that ultimately would have the opposite effect.

He opened his locker and tore off the dreadlocks. Malik stripped down to his waist, strolled over to the washbasin and threw water all over his exposed body. He needed to wash away the filth, like cleansing his soul and purging it of the sordid kind of business he was now tied up in. He changed clothes and hurried out of that place, maybe for the last time. It now depended on whether the higher ups would make the transfer he knew must happen.

Whose Shoulders
Are You Standing On?

Toschia

An uncomfortable sense of anticipation overtook Dawani
Santiago when he first opened his eyes on Monday morning.
He wasn't ready for a new week to begin. He wished it were
still the day before when he had attended the First Freewill
Interdenominational Church with Grandma and Aunt Tasha. He
chuckled thinking about how Grandma had confronted a girl
named Kiara after church for writing him a sexually explicit letter.
Grandma had literally thrown blessed oil, which was nothing
more than Pompeian olive oil that Pastor Edwards had prayed
over, on Kiara. She walked right up to her, stuck her finger in the
bottle of oil and formed a cross on Kiara's head. Then, she dipped
her finger in the bottle of oil again, threw it on her and said loudly,
"Father, I bind this whorish, fast butt, 'lil' nasty Jezebel hussy,
concubine demon, in the name of Jesus."

It all started when his nosey Aunt Tasha smelled a stench
coming from his gym bag in his closet Friday afternoon. She was
lying, because it was impossible for her to smell his gym bag
located in the back of the closet. Her room was located on the
other side of the house making it virtually impossible for her to
smell anything that far away. Truth be told, she had just bolted
into his own space like a track star and started digging through his
personal belongings. He had forgotten about the gym bag being in
there, otherwise he would have tossed it long before the dragon
rushed in looking for anything that could get him into trouble.
Tasha constantly looked for an excuse to snoop. She didn't care
whether he was there to witness her sleuthing or not. When she
found the letter, she had to make something out of nothing.

111

Kiara, on the other hand, was crazy as all get out. Dawani had made it a point to avoid her and consistently thwarted her advances. She always craved attention because she wrote letters to just about every boy at school. Dawani felt embarrassed for her because her writing style was so elementary; it was comparable to that of a child who had just begun to write two syllable words. She would declare her love for whoever her latest male victim would be by writing them in her crude style. The guys would pass Kiara's letters around the locker room and get a good laugh.

Dawani was more ticked off that his Aunt Tasha would even fathom he would be interested in someone like Kiara. It was bad enough she was a freshman, but she was a stinky nasty "round the way girl." At the age of fifteen she already had two kids, who were just as ugly as she was. Word on the street was she had already burned half the junior varsity basketball, soccer, and football teams; luckily the nurse gave out free penicillin. If his nosey Aunt Tasha, the drama queen, had even bothered to ask him about the note he could have told her the real deal, which was he wouldn't be caught dead in public with that chicken head.

But, no, Aunt Tasha confiscated the letter and took great pleasure in reading it to Grandma, line by line, precept by precept. Dawani sat up trying to dismiss that nonsense from the day before. He didn't have time to think about that hot mess; he had more important things to ponder like the SAT test coming up in a week and the Emily Dickinson poem he would select for his final writing assignment in Advanced English. He liked several of her poems, or perhaps he could do a summary on Dickinson's writing style. The reason he didn't have time to waste on Aunt Tasha's nonsense was because school would be out in less than two months. They did have some snow days to make up which could keep them there until almost the Fourth of July, but still he hated to wait until the last minute to do his assignments.

Dawani swung his long legs out of the top bunk and yawned wishing he could sleep until noon. The sun shined into the room. His window didn't have any mini blinds so he got the full blast from the early morning rays. He sighed dreading the long week ahead. He then glanced over at the alarm clock. It displayed 7:15, which meant he was up early enough not to be late for school. The first class he had was English and his teacher Mrs. Wylan was a fire-breathing dragon. He couldn't afford to get another unexcused absence or he would face purgatory. He had to make a decision about the poem. He had narrowed it down to two. Despite the fact that most of her works centered on death, they were not as morbid as Edgar Allan Poe's works. Dickinson's poems, even though dealing with death, were more jovial. That woman had to be on crack or opium because she actually befriended death. That loon of a woman was actually flirting with death like they were on a date or something. He was happy that he was taking African American Literature his senior year because all those white poets he'd studied were crazy as hell. He experienced nightmares for weeks after reading "The Charge of the Light Brigade" by Alfred Lord Tennyson. He'd memorized some of the words and they reverberated in his mind.

Because I could not stop for death, he kindly stopped for me. Then there was the line, *I heard the fly buzz when I died.* The fly in that poem reminded him of his Aunt Tasha. The person couldn't even die in peace without some fly aggravating him. Then to make matters worse, the fly ended up gouging the lady's eyes out. His aunt was just like that fly with her annoying butt. He couldn't go to the bathroom without Aunt Tasha bothering him. She constantly harassed him, *"What you doing in the bathroom for so long? Open the door half-way so I can hear you pee and make sure you don't cheat on this at-home drug kit. What color is your pee? If it's brown you need to drink more water and stop drinking all those sodas and Capri suns because you are going to get diabetes and they will cut off your foot."*

Tasha knew how to piss him off. They had almost duked it out like two dogs in the street because he had been working on his science project in the bathroom and she accused him of playing in the water like he was six years old. He had chosen to compare and contrast the ph acidity level of the tap water in his apartment and the water in Lake Michigan. Tasha, the simpleton, picked the lock in the bathroom and accused him of making crack cocaine because she smelled vinegar. He was merely testing the ph levels in the water he had collected.

She needed a man or something because she was like his personal stalker. He wasn't surprised after testing the water on three different occasions that the data stayed the same. His hypothesis had been correct; the water in Lake Michigan was safer and more pure than the tap water in his home. No one cared about the poor people in his neighborhood. The people living there didn't even care about themselves because if they did, they would pick up the trash strewn all around the building.

Dawani jumped from the top bunk and his 6'2 frame hit the floor with a thud. The landing impact made his stomach feel like lead as a queasy feeling came over him. Probably just the cold pizza he had eaten at three o'clock in the morning. Or maybe it was a carry-over from Saturday night when his whole body got real tight and nervous when Homecoming Queen Leslie James asked him to dance. Whatever it was, it sure made him feel different. He had no reason to have butterflies. There was nothing going on at school, nothing outside of his normal mundane life as a junior in high school. Basketball season was over and his team had won the state championship, so that couldn't account for the nervousness.

As he got close to the bathroom, he began to gag from a stench coming in through the bottom of the door. He swung it open, hoping for fresh air, but that made the smell worse

"Uggh, Tasha, why you gotta use Clorox when you clean?" he asked. The entire bathroom reeked of bleach. He held his breath and tried to shut the door. Tasha pushed it back open so hard it almost knocked over the framed picture that was always crooked in the hallway. Dawani had painted that picture for his mother when he was in the third grade. It read, "God couldn't be everywhere; that's why he created mothers." No matter how many times they tried to center the picture it always leaned either right or left. After years of trying they had all unanimously concluded it would never hang straight and would be doomed to remain crooked. What an oxymoron, a sign about mothers that was always crooked. He hadn't seen his crooked, skeezing mama in almost a year.

"It's about time you got up; it's not your birthday. Ty already been up, ate breakfast, and caught the bus," Tasha scowled.

Ty was his six-year-old cousin who slept in the bottom bunk and always peed in the bed. Dawani hadn't even noticed that he was gone when he got out of the top bunk. He and Ty were both raised by Tasha's mother and his grandmother. Dawani's mother, who was Tasha's older sister, had dropped him off to visit with his grandmother eight years ago and just left him there. She would usually drop by once or twice a year, usually at Christmas, but would spend very little time with him. Ty's mother, his aunt, was a crackhead. Ty had been taken away from her by the state for negligence when he was two. His grandmother and Aunt Tasha agreed to raise both the boys. He knew Aunt Tasha had received a full scholarship to Columbia University but turned it down and instead enrolled at Chicago State in order to help raise her nephews. Dawani appreciated the sacrifice she made but that still didn't mean she wasn't a pain in the rear end. He rolled his eyes at her.

"Did I say it was my birthday?"

She glared right back at him and walked up in his face. "You need to brush your teeth with your stank breath."

Unbelievable, he thought. Tasha's hair was a hot mess and she had on a pair of daisy duke shorts that made her look just plain stank nasty. He couldn't believe she had the audacity to trip on him.

"Aw, heck no," he shrieked. "I know you ain't calling nobody stank with your codfish smelling behind. Smell like a doggone salamander."

"Boy, I'll knock you out," Tasha said and balled her fist. She was about to start her assault when the doorbell rang. She stopped and turned to look toward the door.

Dawani used that as his opportunity to scoot by her and rush to the bathroom. She had better be glad that the doorbell saved her because if she had hauled off and hit him, he wouldn't hit her back, but would give her a thorough shaking.

Tasha turned on her heels and strutted to the door. "Dawani, if it's one of your lil' friends, you need to tell them, unless they are walking with you to school, that is the only way you can leave here with them."

"Whatever!" He slammed the bathroom door and immediately heard his Grandmother's voice.

"I'm so sick of ya'll two with all that racket. Ty is the youngest one in this house, but he got more sense than both of ya'll put together." She began singing her favorite song by Mahalia Jackson. "Gonna move on up a little higher! Meet the lilly, lilly, lilly."

Dawani rarely had the chance to listen to his favorite contemporary gospel music even if he wanted to. Songs like, "I Don't Want no Peanut Butter and Jelly," by the Truthettes, "Hold my Mule," by Shirley Ceasar, and "Can't Nobody Do Me like Jesus," by James Cleveland were almost ritualistic songs his Grandmother absolutely loved and listened to all day long.

"Sorry, Grandma, but Aunt Tasha started it," he yelled..

Dawani prided himself in how fast he could get in and out of the bathroom. This morning was no different. He heard Aunt Tasha yelling as he came out and strolled across the hall to his room to get dressed.

"Why in the hell do you want to walk Dawani to school when you don't go yourself?" she asked.

Dawani laughed knowing exactly at whom she was hollering. It was his friend Mike Jones. His laughter was not due to his Aunt Tasha, but because Mike actually had people believing that he was the rapper Mike Jones from Texas. Mike had gotten more girls, props, and street "cred" until the real Mike Jones came to Chicago for a concert. There is a line in one of Mike Jones songs that says, "Who, Mike Jones?" so whenever someone said Mike's name they would always say "who?"

Tasha didn't like Mike because he'd dropped out of school and had too many run-ins with the law. Self-righteous people like his aunt never let him hear the end of it or gave him a chance to rehabilitate himself. Dawani grabbed his backpack and hurried into the kitchen. He walked over to the table where his grandma sat drinking a couple of coffee, leaned down, and kissed her on the cheek

"Bye, Grandma," he said

"Bye, baby, you be a good boy at school and make Grandma proud." She reached inside her bra and pulled out a few loose dollar bills. "Take this, baby, so you can have a little bit of spending money."

"Thanks, Grandma," Dawani said. He looked over at Mike. "Wassup?" he asked.

"You're not even going to eat breakfast?" Aunt Tasha rudely cut in on Dawani. She threw a pop tart, an apple, and bottled water into a brown paper bag and thrust it at him.

"I love you too, Tasha." Dawani laughed knowing his aunt was irked because his grandma always had his back.

Mike looked over at Tasha and his eyes begged for something to eat. She rolled her eyes pointing at Dawani.

"You need to get up and eat breakfast on time," she said, then turned toward Mike, "You need to go back to school."

Dawani and Mike headed out the door and onto the porch. They both skipped a few steps and cut across the grass onto the sidewalk.

Tasha walked out behind them. "Bring your sorry behind straight home after school," she scowled. "You gonna help clean up this house."

Three young boys wearing cut off shirts with their pants hanging down below their butts and a ton of tattoos up and down their arms walked toward the house to post on their favorite spots and wait for the next drug customer. They snickered, and one of them said, "Man, Tasha, you sho is fine."

She looked at them in disgust. "What the hell ya'll laughing for with your raggedy behinds? Ya'll lil' knuckleheads need to get your life together. And I know I'm fine, you lil' monkey."

Dawani rolled his eyes up in the air as he listened to his arrogant aunt. He really despised her. Just because she went to Chicago State and had an internship in the mayor's office she thought she was all that, but she wasn't. And he didn't like her ordering him to be home just like he was some kind of child. He was sixteen and knew how to take care of himself. It was his business if he wanted to stay out late after school.

Dawani and Mike walked in complete silence until they passed the housing projects. Mike finally broke the silence.

"Hey dawg, why don't you take a break from all this school stuff and hang out with me today. I know where we can go make some fast cash. School ain't going to call your Grandma if you miss one day. You got such a good record they ain't going to hassle your family."

"Are you crazy?" Dawani glared over at Mike. "You ain't gonna get me strung up. Aunt Tasha would probably send me to juvie for doing something like that."

"Come on D, man. You said you wanted that new Madden game didn't you? I know this old timer that's never home and he only lives two streets over."

"Mike you done bumped your head. Ain't nobody going to jail for no video game. I got too much to lose."

"Did I say anything about going to jail?" Mike shot back. "I know old Solomon cause he used to be sweet on my grandma. He got boocoo money. Old man is some army vet but keeps at least a couple of G's under his bed mattress."

"How you know that?" Dawani asked showing some interest. The two thousand dollars caught his attention.

"Cause I done hit him up twice! He never calls the police and he ain't never home."

Dawani could hear Aunt Tasha's voice resonating in his head, *"Show me your friends, and I'll show you your future."*

"Come on, we can be in and out of there in less than a half hour and we'll have over two thousand dollars," Mike continued prodding.

"We split the money even?"

"You know that, Dawg. You get one thousand and I get one."

"What if I stand outside and watch guard for you?" Dawani asked.

"Man, that ain't worth no half split," Mike said. "I'm taking all the risk."

They were nearing Marcus Garvey High School and Dawani had to decide what to do. Again Aunt Tasha's words, *"Show me your friends, and I'll show you your future."*

"Okay, fifty-fifty and I'll go in," Mike answered before Dawani could say anything more. Just make sure you signal me if you see an old bent over and crippled man heading up the street."

"I guess it won't make no real difference." Dawani knew his friend was right; the school wouldn't call his grandmother. He could easily get away with it this, one time.

"Now you talking, Dawg. Let's go make this money."

Instead of going up the steps and saying good-bye to his friend like he normally did, he kept going straight with him by the school. They walked towards Martin Luther King Boulevard.

"Yo, D, don't worry about a thing. You know I got your back."

Dawani didn't respond. That eerie feeling he experienced earlier had suddenly returned.

****

Solomon Reed sat on the old faded divan in his den with his 45 revolver in his right hand. Two upholstered chairs stood on a blue and red rug in front of an old wooden desk stacked with books. Top of the pile was a copy of *The Willie Lynch Letter to the Slaveholders of Virginia*. Periodically, the old man would pull out his copy of this instruction to slave owners on how to keep their slaves passive and humble for service to the owners. He read it because he saw that it had worked, not only two hundred years ago, but right on the streets of the South Side of Chicago today. Ceiling-high shelves, also filled with books stacked neatly on each shelf, were to the left of the desk. The den was a small space with a window right in front of where Solomon sat. His place had been broken into twice in the last few months. The rage he felt as a result of some punk robbing him, as hard as he had worked his whole life, was enough to make him want to snap their necks like twigs. He spent every available moment that he could between errands and daily activities perched at the same spot awaiting the day the scum would return. Criminals were creatures of habit and three times was always a charm. He had grown up in that neighborhood, and as a child he remembered sitting on the front porch with his parents while they listened to the Boss of Chicago, McKinley Morganfield better known as Muddy Waters. His mom's best friend was the daughter of the great blues man Pinetop Perkins. The five and dime store around the corner was the source of all activity. As youngsters they would race to the store to get penny cookies and candy when they received their allowance.

During the summer he and his friends would run under the water sprinklers to cool off. The same neighborhood that was now virtually void of culture had been in the past the Mecca of Chicago. Blacks in the South would have killed to be on the South Side back then. It wasn't just Chicago that had gone to hell in a hand basket, but virtually every major city in the country was overrun with gangbangers, crackheads, and prostitutes. But whoever stole from him had another thing coming cause they had messed with the wrong one this time. Since he was seventy-two, they thought they could just run over him; break in, and take whatever they needed. Hell no! Not him.

The main reason why they could break into his home was because he refused to put bars around his window. He never thought he would see the day when elderly blacks had to put bars on their windows. He wasn't going to live like a prisoner in his own home. Every house on his street had bars with the exception of his. He had been a prisoner of war in Vietnam and although the Vietnamese treated him a lot better than the three white soldiers also captured from his platoon, he had to seek counseling for years afterwards due to the nightmares about being imprisoned and the bars that barely allowed him to see sunlight. He hated bars and would rather die before he put them on his house. That's why he sat there everyday and waited. And he'd sit there everyday and wait for those bastards to return until they put him in the grave.

Somebody had to put a stop to this nonsense. It made no sense for Blacks to have fought white oppression all those years just to turn around and feel trapped by a kind of Black oppressive system. Solomon knew the punk who stole his money would be back and this time he had a real surprise for him.

That morning, he had fixed himself a bowl of homemade Quaker oatmeal and added plump raisins, butter, and milk. Since he was a child, oatmeal had been one of his favorite foods. He could eat it morning, noon, or night without his wife nagging him to eat a healthy meal. He gulped down the last of the oatmeal, got up, and took the bowl into the kitchen. Just as he was rinsing it out, the telephone rang.

He dropped the bowl in the sink, huuried into the living room and looked at the caller i.d. His wife was on the other end. He snatched the phone from its cradle.

"Baby, I'm sorry I didn't call you to make sure you made it to Washington without any problems, but the car broke down," he said beating her to the punch before she began scolding him. His youngest daughter, Gabriella, was defending her dissertation in Molecular Biology at Georgetown University. His wife had flown to the East Coast, along with his other children, to join in the celebration. He refused to go and watch her be put through the rigors associated with the Doctorate Degree, but promised he would be there for the graduation ceremony in December.

"Solomon, you know I didn't expect for you to call. I know how forgetful you are," Shirley said. His wife of fifty years would always call to remind him to say his prayers at night and to not watch senseless television. She had worked for thirty years as a school principal; unfortunately the nurturing nature of her personality didn't retire with her.

"How's Gabriella? Is she real nervous?"

"Wouldn't you be if your future was in the hands of four old gray-haired white men and one gray-haired Black woman."

"At least there's some color. Dr. Rivers will have her back."

"Don't you sit up there half the night watching television," Shirley said, conveniently changing the subject. "And don't forget to pray before you go to bed."

"I ain't going to forget to pray and I don't even have the television on." He smiled thinking she'd probably prefer he watch television instead of what he was watching.

"Gabriella stepped out but she should be back in here any minute," Shirley said.

"That's okay; tell her I said good luck," Solomon shot back. "I got to go and I'll talk to you tomorrow." He quickly hung up the phone before Shirley could even say good-bye. He hurried back into the den and sat back down on the divan. He did not want to talk to Gabriella because it always ended up in an argument. She did things just to get him angry, like the time she showed up at the New Year's Eve dinner with some Iranian looking man. Why would she bring a man who might be connected to terrorism when she knew exactly how he felt about people like that. Solomon was not a prejudiced man, and they had taught their five children to judge people by the content of their character and not the color of their skin, but an Iranian. That was a different matter. Yes, his baby girl knew how to pick at his last nerve.

Solomon could smile now as he recalled her first boyfriend years ago. He was from West Virginia and had the gall to have a Confederate flag displayed on the front bumper of his truck. She claimed he wasn't a racist, but only took pride in his heritage, a strong symbol of Southern pride. Bullcrap! In spite of the fact that he had retired as a Sergeant Major in the Army serving his country for well over thirty years, he knew that systemic racism was inculcated in the American psyche. While stationed in Germany he lived right next door to Russian soldiers, had dinner and made life-long friends with lots of Europeans. The white people outside of the U.S. were actually A-OK. In fact, he was very encouraged with the people of all nationalities that he had encountered over the years.

He took his eyes off the window long enough to glare over at the family portrait. His other four children were all respected members of society. His three sons were members of his fraternity, following in the tradition of their father, as well as Dr. Martin Luther King Jr. and Adam Clayton Powell, all men wearing the black and gold. His oldest son was a professor at Duke University, his second a high school teacher, and the third boy had just graduated from University of Chicago Law School last year and was working for a large prestigious firm in New York. He looked at the smiling face of his oldest daughter who, at the time the picture was taken, was still at MeHarry Medical School. Now she was a pediatrician on the South Side of Chicago. She was the one who was most dedicated to her people and felt a duty to serve young pregnant girls so that at least they would have healthy babies, even if they were poor. Gabriella, on the other hand, was the assimilationist in the family. But he was proud of her as she was about to get her Ph.D. Solomon looked up at the ceiling and whispered, "Thank you, Lord, for blessing our family."

His eyes were getting heavy and he really wanted to take a nap, but didn't dare leave his post. He was confident that those punks would show up today since his car was not in the driveway. On the way back from the airport he'd stopped to get gas and when he got back in the car it wouldn't turn over. He'd asked a young man who was also pumping gas to give him a jump. He did, and it failed. Solomon ended up calling a tow truck. In a way, the car's failure to start was a blessing. There would be no car in his driveway, offering even greater incentive for those hoodlums to try and break in that morning. Just the thought of someone invading his private space that way sent his blood pressure up.

He had bought that house for his wife and himself when their first child was born over fifty years ago. He'd gone off to many assignments during his twenty-five years in the United States Army and left her there with the kids. All four of his children had gotten married in that house, and most of their holidays were spent in the kitchen fixing Thanksgiving and Christmas dinners, and in the living room opening presents under the Christmas tree.

The old man stared out the window onto Martin Luther King Avenue in utter disgust. He didn't know if the debris strewn along the street or the young Black boys with their pants hanging down below their butts caused him more anger or empathy. He was perplexed because one of the nicest original Black neighborhoods in all of Chicago had gone to hell in a handbag. Apathy was pervasive and he couldn't believe what had happened. He and his wife's family had moved to Chicago from Mississippi during the great Black migration from the South to the North in the 1930s. Back then and while he was growing up there, Black folks took care of each other. The old saying, "It takes a village to raise a child," was put into practice. You didn't sass your teacher and you'd better mind all the grown ups or they'd tear your butt up. Then you'd get another whipping when you got home. Back then before the war, them people loved and watched out for each other. They didn't have a whole lot of money but they had plenty of integrity and a lot of morality. Now, these little drug dealers had the cars, the money, and the girls, but absolutely no morals. The only way to deal with this new breed of Blacks was the same way they taught him to deal with the Vietcong and that is with a bullet. They'd be back, and he'd be right there waiting for them.

Solomon rested the gun in his lap and rubbed his eyes. He usually didn't think of getting out of bed until after seven. He was sleepy and could feel himself nodding a little. He quickly snapped his head back up and leaned forward in the chair. His thoughts briefly returned to the tow truck driver who gave him a ride home after dropping his car off at his friend's garage. Solomon had called William and left a message to call him when he found the problem. It could only be one or two things, the alternator or starter.

The red-headed young man arrived no more than fifteen minutes after Solomon had called it in. The driver's name was Greg. Solomon was instantly impressed with his demeanor He watched as Greg loaded his vintage Mercedes Benz onto the trailer bed. Once they were both in the cab of the truck, Solomon noticed the young man staring momentarily at Solomon's tattoo on his right arm, which was a symbol for his service in the 2nd Cavalry.

"What you know about the 2nd Cavalry Division?" Solomon asked.

"My Grandpa had been a member of the 2nd Cavalry Division down at Fort Hood back in 1962. He used to tell me some great stories about being in that division," the young driver answered proudly. Not too many young men impressed Solomon these days, but Greg did. He had such a keen sense of history, knowing that his ancestors had fought in the Civil War for the Union. Solomon was certain there were many young blacks whose grandparents had served in the military but their grandkids probably didn't know it. In fact, many young people didn't know about their grandparents' struggles and the sacrifices they had made for the next generation. What did they get for it? Nothing but disrespect.

Solomon had stopped going to the American Legion and the VFW except when they had fish fries. He only went because they fried good ole fish with the bones and the head still left on them. Colored folks done got so uppity that they mutilate the fish now; they cut the heads and the tails off. There wasn't anything closer to heaven than a tasty hot fish sandwich, especially the crunchy tail, with some Mustard, hot sauce, and two slices of white bread. But as much as he liked the fish he had to give himself a pep talk before going in because the young people were so disrespectful and he knew he was trigger-happy. A lot of the old-timers would try to rap with the young bucks about life, but them disrespectful knuckleheads would resort to cursing out their elders.

Solomon laughed out loud remembering the look on Greg's face that morning as they drove closer to his neighborhood. He looked nervous. Hell Solomon didn't blame him. The South Side had become the home of savages, ingrates, and hood rats. He convinced Greg that it was safe to drop him off at the Chevron station a few streets away from his home.

When they reached the station, Greg handed him a business card and asked Solomon to call so they could do lunch sometimes. Their brief conversation had made him feel closer to his grandfather who had recently passed away from cancer.

Solomon agreed to call him and got out. He cut through the back of the station and took the back way home. He had walked those streets many times sneaking to see a sweet young filly named Lila, his high school sweetheart. Everyone knew they were sure to marry but as soon as he went off to boot camp she married another boy, Josephus Russell, the town loser. When he returned from his advanced course training she already had a child. Lila was one smart girl but she never got out of the cycle of apathy and poverty. All she wanted to do was live vicariously through a man. He wondered what ole Lila was up to now. He'd heard she had about six or seven kids. Some were dead, others in jail and on drugs.

As he walked past her house he thought he saw a silhouette of a young woman reading a book. As he kept walking, he heard some young punk yell.

"Booh." A young boy with dreadlocks, sagging pants, and a dirty pull over sweater threw his hands up in the air indicating he was packing.

Solomon opened up his jacket pocket and pulled out his 45 revolver from its holster,

Whose Shoulders are you Standing On?

"Booh back, you punk."

The young boy took off running. Solomon swore lightly as he watched the boy disappear around a building. He picked up his pace and walked quietly until he reached his basement steps. He was disgusted with the vandalism that had taken over his neighborhood. He loved his house like he loved his family and knew whoever had broken in before would see his car not in the driveway and would try to come back. He almost did a somersault because his wife wouldn't be around to stop him.

****

Dawani began to have second thoughts. Why did he let Mike talk him into skipping school and then, of all things, agree to rob some pathetic old man? If Mike had already hit this old guy twice, he'd probably taken some kind of precautionary steps to make sure it didn't happen again. And Mike probably got all the money the other two times. After all, this wasn't Hyde Park. Folks in that neighborhood didn't walk around with thousands of dollars just tucked away and available to be taken from them.

They finally turned onto Martin Luther King Boulevard and Mike quickened his pace.

"Slow down," Dawani scowled. "Why you in such a hurry?"

Mike pointed to a house and said, "Cause that's the old man's place and his car ain't in the driveway so he ain't home."

"How you know? Maybe his car's in the garage."

"Where you from? Ain't no garages in this neighborhood," Mike said. "Come on let's get this money and get out of here. This is perfect."

Mike and Dawani sauntered to the side of Solomon's house, opened the gate, and headed to the back.

"Last time I hit this old bastard, I went through a back window he'd left unlocked. You know how old folks are, always forgetting something," Mike said as they came close to the window and he prepared to be the first to crawl through the window and inside the house.

That eerie sense of anticipation again troubled Dawani as he followed close behind Mike. He knew he should be in Mrs. Wylan's class listening to her carry on about the virtues of poetry instead of carrying out an act that had no virtue at all.

****

Dawani awakened to a throbbing pain at the back of his head and his sight was blurred. He tried to focus but felt like he'd been drugged. His neck ached and his eyes fluttered He blinked profusely trying to grasp the reality of the situation. Then he tried moving his hands but they were tied tightly behind him. He looked down and saw that his legs were bound at the ankles. He slowly turned his head slightly to the right and saw Mike with his head bowed, still unconscious. He was also bound at the hands and feet. Dawani closed his eyes hoping that would make all this go away.

"Ain't you Josie Mitchell's grandson," Solomon asked as he got up from the chair he had been sitting in, sauntered over and stood right in front of Dawani.

Dawani tried to nod his head yes, but any movement increased the pain.

"That's all right," Solomon said. "I know you are." He took the 45 revolver and placed it right at the temple of Dawani's head. "So y'all thought you'd rob the old man for a third time. I ought to blow your young, dumb, stupid brains out." He grabbed Dawani under the chin and turned his head looking up at him. "If you weren't Josie's Grandbaby I would, but I couldn't do that to her. Couldn't put her through that kind of pain." Solomon released his grip and said, "Understand what you owe her and that's your life."

He then moved over next to Mike whose head was still bowed. He put the gun right under his chin. "But this one is a different story. I believe he'll meet his Master today. Less you can give me a good reason why I shouldn't shoot his sorry little butt. If you can't he's leaving this world this morning."

Suddenly Dawani's pain dissipated. This man couldn't be serious, he thought. Would he really shoot Mike for just breaking into his house? And how could he save Mike's life? He didn't know what to say or better still he had no idea what this man wanted to hear.

"How you know my Grandma?" was all he could think to say. "I ain't never seen you on our street."

Solomon turned away from Mike who was still out cold. "We grew up on these streets when there was a lot less of us. We knew each other. Not like now, no one really knows anyone else. If they did, you boys wouldn't be doing this crazy stuff. Robbing your own and hurting each other."

"You really going to kill Mike?" Dawani asked, again not knowing anything else to say to this man.

"Shouldn't I?" Solomon asked, but didn't wait for an answer. "Why does he need to live? What good does he do?"

"Don't everybody have a right to live?"

"No, sometimes you lose that right. And what you know about rights?" Solomon's voice rose. "You brought your sorry self in my house with full intentions of robbing me, didn't you?"

"Misterr I am sorry," Dawani whispered. "I knew this was a mistake, but I still went through with it. But I wasn't involved in the other two." He thought that rationalization would work with the old man.

"We much too easy on you young punks," Solomon said totally ignoring Dawani's apology. "You too scared to go on the other side of town and try to rob people got money cause you know they'll definitely kill you. So you run around here, robbing people ain't got enough to even rob. And sometimes you end up killing people." Solomon rushed up on Dawani and held his revolver up like he was going to use it to hit him. "What sick bastards you all are. You rob the very people that made it possible for you to be here. Everybody know there ain't no race of people that rob and kill their old." Solomon's hand began to shake as though he was fighting the temptation to bring the butt of the gun down across Dawani's head. "You're disgusting."

He finished and again moved over to Mike. "And this one, yeah, this one, we all know what he does." Solomon shook Mike real hard and he began to stir. "You ain't hurt much as you should be so wake on up."

Mike jerked his head up and began fighting to get loose. He tried to stand up even though he was tightly bound to the chair.

Solomon pushed him back down. "Sit your little ass down," he scowled. "Where you think you going?"

"Let me out of this chair. Cut me loose you old bastard," Mike shouted. He tried to get up and fell back with the chair crashing to the floor. "You better let me go. My boys know where I was going and if I ain't back with them, they going to come looking for me."

"Good," Solomon shot back at him. "I got plenty of room and plenty of rope."

Mike shot a glance over at Dawani. "Hey, dawg, why you didn't warn me?" he asked. "You were supposed to be looking out for me."

"He got me by surprise. Then I guess he got you," Dawani said. "I just don't know cause it happened so fast. Anyway, you the one said he wasn't home. You the blame for this. So don't talk no mess to me. You got me into this situation anyway."

"Don't act like you so innocent," Mike retorted. "Ain't nobody twisted your arm and made you come along. And don't forget, you the one asked for a fifty/fifty split.

"The little rats gone to fighting each other now they done got caught," Solomon said. "You know I could help you little rats out by putting a bullet in both of you. I believe I would be justified in doing that since you invaded my private home with the intention of doing harm to me. But I think I'm going to let you cowards decide who should live." He paused and stared at the two boys. "Dawani, which of the two of you deserve to live and who should die?" He asked as he glared at Dawani.

Dawani was silent for a moment and finally said, "Sir, I think we both should live. I know what we did was a bad thing, and we got to get some kind of punishment. But taking our life doesn't equate to breaking in to your house and robbing you. You can always get property back, but not a life."

"You're a bright young boy to be so dumb," Solomon answered. "Okay, you think both of you should live. How about you?" He turned and faced Mike. "Who you think should live?"

"Me," Mike said with no hesitation. "Let me go and I can pay you."

"Pay me with what? Blood money? Money you stole or money you made from selling dope to children?"

"I don't sell dope to--"

"Shaddup, you do too and everybody know you do including the police," Solomon interrupted. "And you was probably the one that robbed me before."

"No I didn't; it was Dawani. He was the one who told me to come with him this time and how easy it would be to rob you. He checked to see if your car was in the driveway and when it wasn't, he convinced me to do this with him."

"You liar," Dawani shouted. He struggled to free himself. "If I could get out these ropes, I'd beat your--"

"Both y'all just shaddup." This time Solomon interrupted Dawani.

Solomon moved back away from both of them. "Is this what we have to look forward to in our race?" He asked rhetorically shaking his head. "You two are pathetic excuses for Black men. You exactly what Willie Lynch said we would be." He paused to look for some reaction from the two. He got none. "Do either of you know about the Willie Lynch Letter?"

There was silence. Irritated, Solomon put the gun right under Mike's chin. "Do you know who Willie Lynch was?"

"No," Mike shrieked.

Solomon put the gun to Dawani's head. "How about you?

"No," Dawani said more subdued in his answer.

Solomon hurried to his bookshelf and pulled out a thin booklet that was tucked between two larger books. He leafed through it until he found what he was looking for. He then placed it right in front of Dawani.

"Read the second line from the top?" he said. He then turned toward Mike. "I would've asked you to read it but I doubt you can even read. But you can listen and you damn well better or you going to be the first of you two to leave out of here and not on your feet.

"In this bag here I have a fool proof method to control your slaves," Dawani read in a very low voice.

"Speak up," Solomon ordered.

"I guarantee every one of you that if installed correctly it will control the slaves for at least three hundred years."

"Stop there," Solomon again ordered. He pulled the pamphlet away from Dawani. Willie Lynch was a white slave owner from the Islands who came to Virginia to teach the slave owners there how to make their slaves behave and become submissive to them. He again thrust the book in front of Dawani, "Read."

"You must pitch the old Black slave against the young Black male and the young Black male against the old Black male. You must use the dark-skinned slave against the light-skinned slave, and the light-skinned against the dark-skinned. You must use the

129

female against the male, and the male against the female--"

"Stop," Solomon snatched the pamphlet away from Dawani. "In the year 2012, it will be the three hundred years since Lynch made that prediction and look at the two of you, breaking into an old man's home to rob him. You making his prediction come true." He paused and placed the gun right at Mike's heart. "That makes you his slave. And that makes all the rest of you young fools running around in the ghetto acting like clowns with your pants down below your butts, smoking that junk, spending time on the street corner instead of in the classroom, and talking trash his slaves also."

"I ain't nobody's slave," Mike shrieked.

"You idiot, that man told white folks how to make us hate each other, how to hurt our elderly, cheat our young, and disrespect our women almost three hundred years ago, and we still doing it. And you sit here with your ignorant self and say you ain't nobody's slave." Solomon took his right hand and squeezed Mikes face. "I ought to kill you cause you really are a menace to our race. You still that man's slave and you trying to help him make all the rest of us slaves."

Mike struggled to free his face from Solomon's grip. The old man finally released his hold on him.

"Slavery ended long time ago," Mike shouted.

"Boy you sure are dumb. You a slave. Yes, you are. Dawani knows what I'm talking about, don't you boy?" Solomon now pointed the gun at Dawani. "Tell your robbing friend what I'm talking about. You supposed to be smart."

Dawani struggled to turn his body all the way to the side to better see Mike. "He means what we tried to do to him comes from a dependent mentality which is just like being a slave. We are slaves to greed because what we did was a greedy act."

"Now you're talking, young man," Solomon interjected. He stood back to allow Dawani to continue without the gun in his face. "Carry on soldier," he said.

Dawani took in a deep breath and slowly released it. "We slaves to ignorance cause we ain't in school trying to learn. We slaves to racial self-hatred cause we go around calling each other niggah and dawg."

"This boy here got it together," Solomon added. "Give me one more and I might let you go."

"We slaves to irresponsibility cause we don't take our responsibility to our family, our race, and our culture serious."

"Now the question is, which of the two of you is the biggest slave?" Solomon said as he looked at Dawani and then over at Mike. "If you are a slave then you pretty much belong to Willie Lynch and he already done told the world he know how to keep his slaves in order. All you got to do is have them turn against their own people."

"Let me out of here," Mike suddenly began screaming. "Let me out of here, you old bastard."

He tried to get up but Solomon took his free left hand and shoved him back down in the chair.

"Shaddup and sit still," Solomon also raised his voice. "You don't seem to understand the danger you're in. I can shoot you and won't nobody know to search for you here. So you need to just shaddup and hope like hell that I don't decide to kill you."

"You won't get away with it," Mike continued screaming. "My boys will get even, and you'll be toast, old man."

"But you'll be dead, so what good will that do you," Solomon replied. "At eighteen, you'll be dead, and maybe I will be too, but at least I'm seventy-two. You sure giving up a whole lot more than me. Whichever way you look at it, you sure got the short end of the deal, so it's best for you to just shaddup." He brought the gun back like he was going to hit Mike, but stopped before he delivered the blow. He now turned his attention back to Dawani. "I sure hate this position you all done put me in. We ain't suppose to be killing each other, but we ain't suppose to be robbing each other. If I let you all go, then nothing ain't been resolved, and I'll be doing a disservice to the next person you rob. I got the power to stop at least two of you criminals."

"Really, Mister, I'm not a criminal," Dawani pleaded. "I made a terrible mistake and I got weak to temptation. But I don't want to die. Please Mister, I don't want to die."

"You should've thought about that before you came crawling your little narrow butt through my window," Solomon shot back. "Let me ask you something, and I want the truth; if I hadn't been here and you found a pile of money, would you have taken it, not knowing what I might need that money for?"

"Hell yeah, he would've taken it," Mike shouted.

"I told you to shaddup." Solomon smacked Mike on the side of his head with his bare hand. "We know you would've taken it. In fact, I'm pretty sure you're the one that robbed me before. Believe me, I'm going to deal with you."

He then turned back to Dawani. "Answer me, would you have kept that money, not knowing what I might need it for. And not knowing how long and how hard I had to work to get it."

With head bowed, Dawani whispered, "Yes."

"At least you got one good virtue and that is you're honest." Solomon hurried back over to his bookshelf, found an old crumpled newspaper and put it in front of Dawani. "Do you know who Maya Angelou is?"

"Yes," Dawani answered. "She's a great Black poet. We read some of her poetry in my English class. My teacher loves her poetry.

"Good, then read that article." Solomon pointed to an article written by Maya Angelou.

"In these bloody days and frightful nights when an urban warrior can find no face more despicable than his own, no ammunition more deadly than self-hate, and no target more deserving of his true aim than his brother, we must wonder how we come so late and lonely to this place."

Dawani ended and looked up at Solomon. "I'm truly sorry, sir, I'm so sorry."

Solomon stared intently at Dawani. He then tucked his revolver down into his pocket. He began to loosen the ropes binding Dawani. "Next time you decide you want to do harm to a fellow warrior trying to do nothing more than survive in this jungle of life, remember Willie Lynch and don't do it. And remember those words you just read and then look at yourself in the mirror and decide if you going to be that urban warrior who hates himself and hates his race or you going to be a different kind of warrior. You're getting a second chance, but I promise you, there won't be a third chance. Next time you going to go down just like this boy over here." He pointed at Mike.

Freed from the ropes, Dawani jumped out of the chair. "You going to kill Mike?" he asked.

"No, I ain't going to kill him cause I am not that warrior that Ms. Angelou described in that article. As much as I detest him and dislike young brothers just like him, I don't have it in me to kill. I saw enough killing in Vietnam and on our streets here in Chicago." He pulled his revolver back out and pointed it at Dawani. "When you walk out that door, I want you to think of whose shoulders you going to stand on. Are you going to be a slave for Willie Lynch or you going to be a warrior, carrying out the work of Frederick Douglass, Malcolm X, and Dr. King? Now get out of here before I change my mind."

Dawani hurried out the back door and made it to the front of the house. He started up Martin Luther King Boulevard. He wasn't sure if he would ever see Mike again in life. But the old man said he wouldn't kill him. The one thing he did know is that he would never make the same mistake again, and tomorrow at school he would be more than willing to take his punishment for today's indiscretion.

He'd walked a couple blocks when he heard the police siren and two police cars sped right by him. He turned and watched as they stopped with red lights blinking right in front of the old man's house.

A Time Remembered

Leslie Perry

The elderly Black man with dark, rough skin and short Afro styled gray hair proudly strolls out of his small apartment and up the street to the school where he will help make history. He is from another generation that seems so long ago. When he was a boy, show fare was twelve cents and bus fare only a nickel. He was eyewitness to air raids and sugar rations during the big war. His family was too poor to buy war bonds, but he remembers the time when fund raising would take place in movie theaters and he would put his pennies in the collection plate when it passed by him.

He also remembers that Black folks lived on one side of town and whites on the other. And the side where the whites lived was so much better than where the Blacks lived. And he remembers when television came on the scene and how mesmerized he and his family were with this new entertainment regardless of the fact that all the faces on the screen were white.

Some of his fondest memories were of Joe Louis, the Brown Bomber, battling it out in the boxing ring for race and country. He reflects back on his family glued to the radio flinching at every blow that Joe took and the rejoicing when he came out the victor. Everyone in the house and the neighborhood celebrated. He thinks about Jackie Robinson breaking into the major leagues and how proud the entire Black race was because of one man's accomplishments. He thinks about the time the first Black face appeared on television. Was it the "Beulah Show?" He's pretty sure it was.

He stops at the corner for a red light and watches as a car full of teenagers race by him. He thinks back to his teenage days.

135

The terrible picture in *Jet* magazine of Emmett Till lying in the casket after being brutally murdered by some sadistic racist in the South appears in his mind. It brings back memories of the Civil Rights Movement. He didn't really get involved, but his heart and mind was with those who did. He flashes back on the Lincoln Monument and thousands of black and white faces standing on the Mall waiting for the one prophet of the time to speak. Even as a young man he was glued to his television that historic day in August 1963 when Dr. Martin Luther King Jr. told the world of his dream.

The light turns green and he continues across the street with a big smile. A major part of Dr. King's dream was about to happen today and he would be an active participant. But then the smile dissipates as he recalls the tragic event only a few weeks after Dr. King's speech. The entire Black world and a great many whites cried and mourned the loss of four beautiful Black girls and two brave Black boys who were tragically killed again by a bunch of animalistic racists when the Sixteenth Street Baptist Church in Birmingham, Ala., was bombed. On that tragic Sunday he almost lost faith in mankind. But his better senses calmed him down and made him realize that evil is always going to make one last desperate attempt to destroy change for the better. Through Dr. King's work and the work of millions of other Americans, and especially the young brave Black children throughout the South, segregation was tumbling down just like the walls of Jericho.

He sees the school only a block away, and he is only a block away from helping achieve the dream. As he passes by an old white house where he lived back in 1957, he thinks of Little Rock, Ark. He recalls that day in September when nine brave Black boys and girls boldly crossed over the wedge of segregation and walked into Central High School, defying the mob and the racist Governor. All these events that now race through his mind like a thoroughbred horse racing to the finish line at the Kentucky Derby were necessary in order to make this day a reality.

He cried when he heard the news that Dr. King had been assassinated. He also felt hurt when two months later Bobby Kennedy met the same fate. He thought at that time, "What is happening in this country? Have our people all gone insane?"

He didn't' agree with the Vietnam War, but didn't protest, he didn't march, and didn't demonstrate. In a way he wished he had.

He knew some boys his age that didn't come back.

It took time before he adjusted to the natural hairstyle, dashiki, and the Black power slogans. It also took him some time before he stopped using the word Negro and started using Black. It was James Brown's song, "Say it Loud, I'm Black and I'm Proud" that changed him. He remembers very clearly how uncomfortable some of his white friends were with the Black and proud feeling among his people. When the whites became uncomfortable, he became comfortable. He even got his hair cut into a natural. He also had a girlfriend at the time that wore her hair in a natural. She was beautiful, proud, and smart. You had better not call her out of her name as happens today with young men and women. They even sing insulting songs to our sisters, something that never would have happened in the past.

He saunters onto the school grounds and heads toward the open double doors leading into the building. As he enters the building he thinks about the time when Jesse Jackson ran for president. He voted for him in the primaries in 1984 and again in "88." Even gave contributions to his campaign in both races. He also went to hear Jackson speak when he was in town. Jackson made him think about Dr. King when he spoke. But he also thinks about Shirley Chisholm who made a run for the presidency almost twenty years before Jackson. Very few give her credit for being bold, Black, and beautiful, taking such a step when her opposition was so strong.

He enters the auditorium and stands in line. It is a long line and it will take a while before they get to him. He doesn't care because this line stretches back over three hundred years and the wait is now about over. These are his thoughts as he waits to get a ballot, and these are his thoughts as he enters the voting booth and pulls the lever associated with the name Barack Obama for President.

PASSING THE TORCH

Margaret Richardson and Lenton Collins

On the day of the funeral, Maximillan Massai Warner III stood at the foot of the hill and watched the sun come up over the pond below him. He felt the cool breeze tickle across his face. Massai, as family and friends called him, was dressed in a black three-piece suit, vest and all, with patent leather Stacy Adams. Grandpa had always told him that it was important to always look your best, especially at church.

"Starting the day," Grandpa said in his deep voice, "and dressing your best, even when the clothes are safety pinned together, always seems to put a little extra spring in your step."

Especially, on this particular day, Massai made sure that he looked his best. And he did look handsome, with his high cheekbones and dimples in both cheeks. His suit was perfectly cut for his broad shoulders and long legs. His wildly swirled purple and black tie was a perfect fit. Grandpa had given him the watch snuggly fitting on his wrist seven years ago and he wore it everyday. Grandpa was not one for a lot of jewelry, just his watch and wedding band. All dressed and ready to go, Massai looked like his father and Grandpa before him, proud, dignified and strong.

He slowly strolled down the hill and sat at the bank of the pond. He picked up a rock, skipped it across the water and smiled, thinking back to the day that Grandpa taught him the art of skipping rocks across the pond. Grandpa was a pro, slinging the rock so that it would literally walk on its way to the bottom. With no more than a flick of the wrist and twist of his hand, he made aquatic art and Massai could never quite emulate that same fluid movement.

Coming to this spot always made him feel at home. Sitting

there, he couldn't keep the tears from freely flowing down his face. He was at his favorite place in the world, alone and missing the one person who loved the pond more than he did. Massai had spent many a day at that very place with Grandpa fishing and just chewing the fat.

Grandpa always had a story to tell, always long and always about learning a lesson. Massai listened and paid close attention; indeed he had no other choice. The one time he fell asleep and started snoring, Grandpa slapped him upside his head with his big hands that covered one entire side of his face. The slap was so loud Massai swore he heard an echo. He smiled and touched the spot where he had been slapped and awakened from his slumber.

"Black people always caught short and forever complaining about something, but always sleeping when they should be listening," Grandpa said after waking him up. "Never let anyone catch you sleeping. Always pay attention because you never know when something might happen that can be used to your advantage."

After that, Massai never fell asleep around him again.

One day while they were fishing, Grandpa told Massai about a similar trip he made down to the pond with Massai's daddy, Max, when he was only fourteen years old. Max hated fishing and complained every time Grandpa started toward the pond. He grumbled and muttered under his breath that, "Dad must not have anything else to do."

Grandpa just smiled and grabbed his rod and reel and a bag of sandwiches.

"Get the bait, the cooler, and tackle box," Grandpa said. They made it to the pond just as the sun was going down.

After setting up camp, Grandpa baited the hook with an earthworm and threw out his reel. Max didn't want to use live bait because he hated the way the earthworm wiggled in his hands. He threw his line out into the water without bait.

"Get that line in and bait your hook," Grandpa scowled when he saw what Max had done.

Max knew better than to cross Grandpa when he spoke. He obeyed and pulled his line back, baited his hook, and recast it, all the time grumbling under his breath. He was miserable and reasoned that if he looked miserable, surely his father would see it and release him from the hell he suffered out there.

But his father knew exactly what he was doing and couldn't have cared less. They were going to spend some time together if it killed them and he wasn't about to let Max spoil his fun. Grandpa started whistling "April in Paris." He nodded his head and moved his feet in time with the song, reaching the climax and starting it all over again. He finished the second time with a smile on his face. Grandpa looked at Max and said.

"That was Count Basie, one of the greats." He paused, glanced at his son and changed the subject. "School's almost out. What you planning on doing for the summer?" He worried about Max because his attitude was changing with age. He was always sullen, talked back, and generally got on everyone's nerves, even his mother.

"I'm hoping that I'll get that fellowship for the summer to study piano." Max was a gifted pianist and spent every minute of his spare time practicing. In fact, he'd rather be practicing right then instead of trying to catch fish. A frown crossed his face as he watched his father pull in his third fish.

Grandpa caught that frown. "You got to give the fish something they can catch on to," he instructed his son. "They like live bait. They snatch it up like lightning."

Max reasoned that fish couldn't move that fast, but he didn't care. He was, however, smart enough not to debate his father on the merits of using live bait.

Grandpa continued, "Once you cast the line, you'll have to wait a bit before the fish feels frisky enough to play. Take your time and wait it out. You have all the time in the world."

Max didn't care about all that and tried not to think about catching a fish, even though he'd never actually caught one before.

Suddenly, the line bucked a bit, bringing Max out of his musing. The line kept bucking and the reel almost slipped from his hand.

Grandpa looked over at him, and with his line still out in the water, calmly walked Max through reeling in the fish.

"Reel it in. Pull back a little," he said. "But not too much. Reel it in. Don't let go. Don't let go. Ride with it, Max." He was now shouting. He helped his son with the reel and smiled as Max began laughing at his success.

After getting the fish out of the water, Max watched as it

bucked back and forth, trying to free itself from the hook. In spite of himself, Max was proud because he gave the fish the fight of its life and won.

Grandpa looked on with pride as Max celebrated his victory.

"Congratulations, Warrior, you have won a good fight," he said.

Max smiled at Grandpa and he smiled back at Max and, for a time, the unhappiness Max felt earlier had faded away. He handed Grandpa the fish who then dropped it in the water cooler.

Grandpa sat down and rested for a minute, setting the fishing rod down next to him. "How you feel after all of that action you went through to catch your first fish?"

Max stuck his chest out. "I feel good, strong, and fearless," he answered. Even though he had only caught a fish, he felt like he was a conqueror. Max couldn't keep the smile off his face.

Grandpa studied his son's reaction.

"And you did it all on your own," he said.

"I had help."

"But you didn't give up."

Grandpa closed his eyes and started whistling "April in Paris" again. He stopped momentarily. "Can you play 'April in Paris?'" he asked his son knowing that he could.

"Yes," Max answered with pride.

"Can you play 'Flying Home?'"

"No, but Lionel Hampton never played it on the piano," Max said.

Grandpa smiled. "A good musician can find a way to play a song on an instrument he had like that crazy Hendrix guy. Didn't he play the national anthem on his guitar?" He paused to let his knowledge sink in with his son. "It sounded like a bunch of noise, but I could tell the parts that mattered most. Now can you play 'Flying Home' on the piano?"

"No, I can't," Max replied more emphatically.

"Maybe you ought to learn. Maybe you'll pick it up while you're at camp this summer. That is, if you feel like going."

Max couldn't believe his ears. He looked at his father but couldn't say anything. He wanted to go to camp but wasn't sure if

Grandpa would let him.

Grandpa smiled and after a long silence asked, "You think you'll be able to learn to play that song?"

Max, with a grin across his face, shook his head yes.

"I know one thing," Grandpa said. "I must really want to hear you play 'Flying Home,' because you sure don't deserve to go to that camp, not after your behavior before we came out here."

Max looked on in wonder because he didn't think his father had heard his remarks about going fishing.

"Yes, I heard you this time, the last time, every time you utter something you shouldn't, I hear it. I don't say anything about it because I hope that you'll see and understand that your behavior hurts me and your mama when it shouldn't."

With his head bowed Max asked, "Why you letting me go if I don't deserve it?"

"Maybe you need a rest from us and we need a rest from you."

"Is that how you feel?"

"Not really, but me and your mama know something got to change with your attitude. Maybe going to summer camp will give you a chance to find yourself and stop sulking all the time." Grandpa stared intently into his son's face hoping that his words would register with him. "And besides that I want to hear you play 'Flying Home' for me and your mama when you get back."

Unable to hold back his emotions, tears filled Max's eyes. "I promise you."

"And it better be good just like you better be good. Next time you show out, I'll take you to the Marine recruiter myself, I don't care if you are under age, you'll be in the Marines and then let's see you act up."

They both sat back and laughed, luxuriating in the peace between them.

Grandpa told Massai a million times about how he and Max bonded on that fishing trip. Massai thought about his father and how he often treated him that very same way. He could see pieces of Grandpa in his father as well as in himself. He knew that they were all spades of the same color and it amazed him that Grandpa could tell exactly what Massai was thinking, even before he could get it out. Massai's son, Max IV, acted just like those before him, both hardheaded and stubborn. But what tickled Massai was that he would be able to tease his father about stories Grandpa used to tell him about how Max grew up.

Sharing the pond was the best gift of all. It was a family treasure that stayed with them at Grandpa's insistence. One time when Dad talked about possibly selling or leasing the land out, Grandpa would assert his right of possession. It was Grandpa's land and he intended that it be passed down through generations. No one was to break this inheritance, and he worked doggedly to make sure that the land was well cared for and the pond always full of fish. Max and Massai came to love the pond as much as Grandpa wished and Massai hoped that his son would love it as well.

Massai glanced at his watch. He still had some time before he had to do what he most dreaded in life. A petal glowing on a lily caught his attention. Calla lilies—beautiful colors of fuchsia, sunshine, and magenta mixed with the greenery of the lush grass and sparkling turquoise of the pond. Massai closed his eyes and listened to the birds singing with the breeze lifting hair on their throat. Right there at that moment, Massai felt as if he were in paradise. The day was shaping up to be a beautiful one, even though Massai dreaded what he would be doing. Having a funeral on a day like this one saddened him and took some of his joy away.

He continued thinking about the many times Grandpa talked with him at the pond. Grandpa always had stories to tell, some good, some bad, but always life changing in some way. The few stories Massai told always brought a laugh from Grandpa. He laughed because Massai's stories always bordered on the outrageous and strange like something from a science fiction movie. One time Grandpa tried to verify one of Massai's stories with Max, who would just shake his head and apologize for his son's large imagination. Max thought of some of the humdingers he used to tell and wondered why Grandpa always laughed, even when he knew that many of them were made up.

Massai understood then that just like Grandpa could read his mind, he could also see right into his soul. Grandpa knew when Massai was telling the truth, pulling a fast one or riding the fence. And maybe he felt a little sorry for Massai and made up stories when just talking about life was always more interesting.

The funeral would take place in a couple of hours. The family was still getting up, eating breakfast, and dressing. The funeral director would pick up the family, and Massai hoped that the pastor wouldn't be late. He was habitually late for everything, funerals, weddings, and all other events at the church. He always had a reason, though, but no one cared enough to challenge the validity of his excuses. Maybe the pastor was putting his stories together like Massai used to do, but he couldn't imagine someone as old as him still watching the Saturday morning cartoons. In any case, Massai knew that he had time before he needed to be back at the house, so there was no need to rush.

He stood up and took a flower off the stem. He twirled it in his fingers and looked intently at the flower as if searching for an answer to one of life's mysteries. Massai brought it up to his nose to catch the familiar fragrance it held within its pedals. As he took it in he thought back two years ago when his Grandma died. That was a bad time for the family. As much as Grandpa was the spiritual head of the family, Grandma was its backbone, and she held Grandpa's heart in the palm of her hand. She had been sick for a while but no one knew about it until just before she took to her bed in the final days.

Grandma was a big woman, six feet tall, over two hundred pounds with big feet and big hands. She had deep brown eyes, caramel skin, and a smile that lit up the room. Grandpa fell in love with her at first sight, but she couldn't stand the sight of him. Grandma could be intense. She was a serious person and more mature than her years. Her parents died early, leaving her to raise her younger sister and brother. She worked the farm by herself all day while still going to school. She struggled with her siblings for two years before her uncle popped up out of nowhere and took custody of her brother, who died a year later. No one was ever sure of the circumstances, only to say that John didn't want to be with Uncle Oliver in the first place.

Grandma was very close to her younger sister and had just sent her off to college when Grandpa came into her life. She was at a college dance and he asked her to dance. She said no, but Grandpa was the only one who could make Grandma smile. He was naturally good-humored, intelligent with a wonderful personality and eventually he grew on her. He would ask her to dance again at another school event, and this time she accepted. Grandpa couldn't dance a step but she let him lead and they eventually began to date. Grandma held him at bay long enough to see how serious he was about building a life with her. Once she was convinced that he was serious, the marriage took place and they spent the next fifty-two years dancing together.

The first sign that something was wrong with Grandma happened during a family reunion. She was preparing a huge pot of chicken and dumplings. She sat the pot on the stove and turned to put the pan of cornbread on the table. The other women in the kitchen thought that she simply lost her footing and fell against the stove. Maybe she was just tired. After all, she had also finished the potato salad, the broccoli and rice casserole, the cornbread stuffing, home made rolls, pumpkin bread, two lemon meringue pies, a German chocolate cake, a red velvet cake, and a big bowl of banana pudding.

Grandpa said that she was doing too much and needed to rest. She wasn't hurt, but this had never happened before. One only had to know Grandma to understand that she moved deliberately and methodically, never wasting unnecessary steps.

Grandma did manage to get some rest but she never could get her footing right after her little accident. Anytime she was asked what was wrong she joked that old Arthur had finally caught up to her. The kids wanted to know who old Arthur was, but everyone over the age of thirty knew. Arthritis was an acquaintance that always seemed to drop in on people when they least needed to see him. And so it was with Grandma that she let people believe old Arthur had found a home with her. But it was a lie, a merciful lie.

Grandpa knew something was wrong and took her to the doctor after she fell again. Kicking and scratching all the way, Grandma complained and cursed Grandpa the whole way back. Grandpa just looked at her and said,

"I love you more than life itself. I cannot and will not stand by and watch you fade away without knowing what's going on. So you'll just have to complain. It's worth it to me to make sure you're okay."

She stopped complaining and turned away from him, but not before she saw the tears fall from his eyes.

Cancer. It's an ugly word with an ugly meaning. In those days of cancer treatment, the destination was always the same and it was a painful ride all the way. Grandma had it in her blood and it caused her to get weaker and weaker. She tried to keep pace, working as she always did, taking care of her family, and watching her grandchildren grow up. She took care of Grandpa and helped him take care of the pond. But her steps grew slower, her handshake grew weaker, her smile waned, and the light slowly faded from her eyes. She could no longer stay at the pond with Grandpa because the breeze would drift right through her.

Grandpa did what he could to comfort her, but he looked on with increasing despair. He was slowly losing his wife. The knowledge that she was fading away pained him more than he let on. He tried to keep her spirits up and keep her laughing. He told some of the weirdest jokes, always acting out the parts so that she could see the punch line. She did laugh, but not because the jokes were funny. The jokes were stale, but Grandpa worked so hard to entertain her that she laughed just to see him smile.

Grandma held on for two years. She was in a lot of pain and there was nothing that could be done. Everyone knew that her condition was serious but she never let on just how serious it was. She didn't want people feeling sorry for her or looking at her with pity. She'd decided that she had lived her life as she wanted to and had no regrets. She didn't like the pain she had to endure, but she was ready for whenever God called her home.

One night she set her hair, now completely gray and thinning. She put on a gown and set out a suit for Grandpa to wear. On top of the suit was a note, asking for his attendance to a private dance, to begin as soon as he was present. She gingerly walked to the living room and found one of her favorite pieces, "Moonlight Serenade." Then she changed her mind when she came across "It Had to be You." She sat down and waited for her groom to arrive.

Grandpa went to the bedroom and instead of finding Grandma, he found the suit on his bed with the note. He followed the instructions and went to the living room to see what would happen. When he got there, he found Grandma on the love seat waiting for him. He couldn't believe his eyes. She was a vision in her lavender gown with her silver hair coiffed beautifully. She had a bit of rouge on and held a calla lily in her hand. He smiled his biggest smile and couldn't hold back the tears that flowed.

When Grandma saw Grandpa standing in the doorway, she also smiled.

"Come and sit with me," she said in a low, weak voice.

He strolled over to the love seat and sat close to her.

"You look so handsome," she said.

"And you are as beautiful as that first day I saw you at the school dance."

She blushed. "Thank you. Would you dance with me?"

His voice choked, "It would be my pleasure." He stood up and reached for her hand. He pulled her up and walked her to the middle of the room.

He held her and they danced for the first time in years. They stayed close and reminisced about their life. They joked, laughed, and danced, enjoying their time together.

Finally they walked to the pond and sat under the moonlight. When it grew too cold, Grandpa wrapped his suit jacket around her and they snuggled like they used to do. After a time, they walked back to the house and went to bed. Laying there, holding her close and still feeling good from the night's activities, Grandpa started whistling "April in Paris."

Grandpa still held her the next morning. He kissed her cheek and tried to wake her but she didn't move. She'd slipped away during the early morning without a shake or shudder. She was at peace, her face showing no pain or stress, quiet in the arms of the one she loved most. Grandpa embraced her with all his energy and love, then started to cry. He stayed there with her alone for a very long time, but finally realized their time on this side of the mountain was over.

He alerted Max, and Grandma was taken away. But Grandpa remained in their bedroom and held on to her pillow still fresh with the scent of her perfume. It was clear from all who saw him from that moment on he had just lost his best friend. Friends and family began to gather around him and everyone paid their condolences as best they could. The days before her funeral were a blur, but everyone agreed that Grandpa and Grandma had a love story that few will ever know. Grandpa was silent throughout, never uttering more than a couple of words for hours.

Grandma's sister, Olivia, sat with him. Olivia and Massai were the only two Grandpa wanted near him. Max and his brothers, Mitchell and Matthew, took care of the arrangements while his sisters, Marguerite and Marie Rose, took care of the guests.

Maureen May Oliver Warner was put away beautifully and

laid to rest next to her parents and her brother John.

After everyone left the house, Grandpa walked to the pond. He had been there for over three hours by the time Massai finally caught up with him. Like everyone else, Massai was worried about Grandpa.

"How you holding up?" he asked.

Grandpa remained silent for a long moment. In fact, he was too quiet for too long.

"Grandpa you all right?"

Grandpa smiled and looked at his grandson. "Yeah, I'm okay."

Massai knew better. There was no way he felt all right, not after just burying the most important person in the world to him.

Grandpa must have been reading Massai's thoughts. "Yes, your grandmother has passed on. She is no longer of this world and I miss her more than you will ever know. But I am humbled by what we shared, this life one earth and everything that came with it, both the good and the bad."

Grandpa picked up a stone and tossed it across the top of the water as only he could do.

"She was my earth, wind, and fire. She was all of the elements I needed to survive and my life will never be the same without her." A tear rolled down his cheek, but still he smiled. He wanted to remember his dance of fifty-two years with the love of his life rather than to focus on the slow pain his beloved endured to the end.

Grandma's passing was a while ago, seven years and six months exactly. Massai couldn't know how much Grandpa hurt every day since then. To begin the next day after your beloved has departed is rough, especially if you were together for what seemed like an eternity. Massai yearned to help Grandpa, but hoped that one day he would know of the special love that his grandparents obviously shared together. He was always amazed at how Grandpa could see a blessing in any circumstance or misery. He also wondered how Grandpa lived out his last days missing Grandma as much as he did. He would always say, "You live each day as it comes, one minute at a time. It makes no sense to try and predict what will happen or if something might happen. All you can do is to live each moment as if it were your last. You do that and you won't have so much to worry about." It sounded like good advice so

Massai followed it, making it his own code of survival.

Massai checked his watch again. It was time to join the family inside. He walked from the pond back to the house where his wife, Malia, waited for him.

"You okay?" she asked as she took his hand and held it tightly.

"Yes."

"What were you doing down at the pond all this time?"

"I was with Grandpa."

They walked hand in hand over to Max and Max IV. Malia took her son's hand and walked away while Massai hugged his father. Max was now elevated as the patriarch of the family and his shoulders were heavy with bereavement for the loss. He was without his mother or father and felt like an orphan, even at his age. He and his son headed out of the house and to the limousines waiting to take the family to the church.

On the way to the church, they all sat still, caught in the maze of their own emotions. The only time they laughed was when Max IV grabbed himself and said,

"Mommy, I got to potty."

"Hold on for just a few more minutes and we'll be at the church," Malia whispered.

He was able to hold on until they reached the church, and Malia rushed him to the restroom while the rest of the family assembled in the foyer. Once the family was all gathered, they walked into the sanctuary, strolled by the open casket and paid their respects to Maxmillan Massai Warner Senior, the man they knew as Dad and Grandpa. The family took their seats and waited for Pastor Washington to get the service started.

Massai wished they'd gotten someone other than Pastor Washington to officiate over Grandpa's home going service. The good pastor was all right enough, Massai supposed. But he drank like a fish and felt the need to get up in your face to say something. You always needed to wipe off after a conversation with him and also ask if he wanted a tic-tac. Besides that, Pastor Washington tended to be nosy, and if you weren't paying close attention, you'd think he nodded off during his sermons. Massai remembered one time when Pastor Washington went into a rant about something he accused Max of doing. Max explained that the circumstance was a misunderstanding, but Pastor Washington wouldn't let it go. Everyone got the message, but not Pastor Washington. After losing his patience over Washington asking the same question, Max snapped, got right in the minister's face, and shouted.

"Are you stupid or just ignorant?"

Pastor Washington didn't know how to respond, but it shut him up. Needless to say, he never messed with Max again. Massai laughed at the memory and looked at Max, winking his eye at him as they saw Pastor Washington coming in.

The service began with the pastor reading "Psalms 23" and then offering a ten-minute prayer. Grandpa would have said that it was too long—that God didn't need to hear all of that if the prayer was genuine. Mitchell and Marie Rose did a duet, "In the Upper Room." Grandpa loved that song and asked his children to do it right.

Next, Matthew gave his remembrance of Grandpa. He told stories about how Grandpa grew up as an only child, how he met his wife, and was the kind of father that his children admired and looked up to.

"As a father, Dad put the fear of God into us early because we were some bad children," Matthew said. "He wanted to make sure that we remembered that anytime God is put into the equation, the outcome will always be what you need it to be." Matthew finished up as Marguerite came up.

Before Marguerite reached the pulpit, Pastor Washington was on his feet offering another prayer and started to sing, but Marguerite politely asked him to sit down. She thanked Pastor Washington for his heartfelt friendship during her family's time of loss. She reminisced that what Grandpa always talked about was how involved Pastor Washington was in the lives of his members and how much the good pastor meant to the community. Massai could hear people snickering and he started to laugh as well because they were well aware how Grandpa felt about the good pastor.

Marguerite got so carried away that she had to catch herself from calling Pastor Washington Reverend Such and Such. Grandpa had given him that nickname after the good pastor came over to the house, ate up most of the food, and interfered in Grandpa's business once too often. Marguerite wrapped up her remarks and sat down, smiling all the while.

Massai finally got up to do the eulogy. He didn't know what he could say that might do the man he called his best friend justice.

"We come together today to bury our beloved father, grandfather, and friend, Maxmillan Massai Warner Senior. He was a God-fearing man who took care of his family, took care of his community, and tried to be the best he could be." Massai didn't know how to say the rest. He looked at his father who sent him looks of encouragement. "Grandpa was the man we all looked up to. He was our role model, our leader, our teacher, and our friend. He taught us that to be a good Black man, you didn't have to wear it on your sleeve. To be a good Black man, you didn't have to beat up anyone or yourself to prove that you were a man. You didn't have to prove anything except to yourself. You owe it to yourself to be the best that you can be. Take care of your responsibilities, always stay around to finish the job you started, and accept no less." Massai took in a deep breath to keep from choking up. "He taught us to always give as much as you receive and you never let anyone say that you are worthless. My grandfather gave me the self-worth of understanding that I am a warrior, not a thug, not an animal, but a human being." This time Massai paused to look directly at his father and force a smile. "Through my father, my grandfather let me know that I am priceless and valuable as a human being, as a Black man, and as one of God's children. If I am half the man my grandfather was, I'll consider it a victory for which he deserves the credit."

Massai grabbed the sides of the pulpit to help keep him up. His legs wobbled because with every word he spoke he realized just how important Grandpa had been to him and the overwhelming magnitude of their loss. He also knew that all over the country, services were being conducted just like this one, and he could only pray that the person who was being eulogized meant just as much to his or her family as Grandpa meant to the Warner family. He continued:

"Our lives were enriched through Grandpa's presence. We were all made richer because we saw the example he set with his children, his grandchildren, and all the people he loved. He wasn't afraid of hard work. He wasn't afraid of saying no when you hoped he'd say yes. And he wasn't afraid of saying yes when he should have said no. He protected us, taught us, and wasn't afraid to discipline us when we needed it. He pushed us, cheered for us, and wasn't afraid to cry with us when we cried. I said earlier that we have come together to bury our loved one, but I was wrong. We have come together to celebrate a life that touched us all, a life as precious as the earth, wind, and fire it took to help him survive. All our lives have been made better for the dues he paid and the road he paved for us to travel along. I know that he loved us as much as we loved him.

"Lastly, I say to my grandpa, my best friend, Maximillan Massai Warner Senior, well done my beloved warrior. God knows that you have fought the good fight, won your victory, and deserve your reward. We love you."

Massai walked from the pulpit down to where Max sat and hugged him. Massai never noticed until just then how much his father resembled Grandpa in looks, spirit, and temperament, although Max was a lot quieter than Grandpa was.

Max got up and strolled up to his father's casket, stopped, and placed his hand on the side. He then continued over to the piano. Max took a deep breath and placed his hands on the keys. He always did that when he was about to begin. He closed his eyes and touched the keys to one of his father's favorites, "Mary Don't You Weep," bringing the congregation to their feet. Max truly had a precious instrument in his voice although the piano was slightly out of key. It didn't matter because Max knew what he was doing. He played the piano like a virtuoso. No one was even aware that the piano was off key. He opened his eyes as he finished the song, but couldn't get up.

Max sat there, thinking he needed to do something else. He looked back at the casket and said under his breath, "Dad, this is for you." He played "Flying Home" just as his father had once asked him to do. He'd never gotten the opportunity to play it once he returned from the summer camp. He and Grandpa had forgotten about the request, at least he had. Maybe Grandpa had been waiting for him to live up to his promise. He never would have asked him because he shouldn't have to. Max decided that even if he were doing it a little late, his father would get his request filled. The tears continued to flow as he worked his way through the song. He cried because he knew somewhere his father was smiling. He was right, Max could play "Flying Home" on the piano, just like Grandpa thought he could all of those years before.

Max finished and bowed his head still sitting at the piano. His brothers, sisters, and his son Massai hurried up to the piano and hugged him. They all walked back to the pew together. Pastor Washington tried to say another prayer, but Mitchell stopped him. The service came to an end and they marched out to the limousines preparing for the ride to the cemetery. Pastor offered to ride in the lead car with Max and his family, but they pushed him up to ride with the funeral director in the hearse.

When they arrived at the cemetery, Mitchell, Max, Matthew, Massai, Massai's brother Michael, and cousin Deacon carried the casket to its final resting place. After placing the casket on the hoist for lowering into the ground, the boys took their place along side Marguerite and Marie Rose and waited for Pastor Washington to catch up. The pastor said another prayer, but kept it short this time after Mitchell warned that he would not get paid for officiating the service if he didn't. The family together recited the Lord's Prayer quietly, and the pallbearers took turns throwing their roses into the grave.

Max sauntered over to his mother's grave. He whispered:

"Okay, Mom, you're together again. Dad's ready but you'll have to lead. Enjoy your dance." Max turned and walked back to the limousine where the family waited for him.

The procession returned to the main house. Max IV was given free reign to play since he'd been so good all day. He somehow managed to charm great Aunt Olivia and they became friends. Some church members came over and helped take care of the guests. There was enough food given to the family for three funerals and everyone filled up fast except Pastor Washington who seemed to have a bottomless pit for a stomach. In the end, the leftovers were given to Pastor Washington.

Massai slipped out and sauntered down to the pond. It was the first place Grandpa and his father took him and the only place in the world he felt secure. He sat down at the bank and took off his shoes and socks, letting his toes play at the edge of the water. He loosened his tie and rolled up his sleeves to get even more comfortable.

"Grandpa, I know you hear me," he whispered. "Did you hear Dad play? He was amazing. Everyone was awesome except Pastor Washington. Aunt Marguerite almost called him Reverend Such and Such when she was speaking." Massai started laughing hard.

"Washington is a piece of work," he continued. "I'm glad I don't have to deal with him. We gave him the rest of the leftovers. I hope he enjoys them." Massai was now rambling, but he had to do this because he didn't want to let go.

He remained quiet for a minute, then got up and reached for a calla lily. Taking one of the stems, he played with it in his fingers. He began again.

"You would have been proud of us today. We were a family. We leaned on each other just like you knew we would. We weren't afraid to cry." Massai looked around like he was waiting for Grandpa to walk up. He stared at the flower and said, "I know you told us that we're supposed to live each day as it comes, one minute at a time. I know that I can do the best I can and be the man I was raised to be. I want to make you proud of me. I'm going to be a good father to my son. I promise I won't be like other Black men, donating sperm to whatever girl they fancy for the moment."

Again he paused to gather his thoughts. What he said was so important and he had to say it right. "I'm going to do so much for him and spend so much time with him that he'll get tired of looking at me. But however tired Max IV gets, he'll never be able to say that his father didn't love him or want him around."

Massai stood up as it all suddenly came together for him. He knew what he had to do and it amazed him that it took so long to see what was obvious. He laughed, shook his head, and said,

"Okay, Grandpa, I gotcha. I'll be right back." He went back to the house and got Max IV.

Massai brought Max IV back to the pond he'd fallen in love with long ago. He let his son run around and after Max IV sat down, Massai joined him. He took off his son's shoes and socks and let him splash in the water. Massai told Max IV that he was very young also when his father first took him to the pond. And his father was brought there by his father, renewing the cycle of a father sharing with his son a rich heritage and culture that was passed down from generation to generation.

Massai looked at his son, smiled, and hugged him. He released Max IV, promising to be the role model his son needed, just like his father and grandfather had been for him.

One Boy's Quest for Knowledge

D. L. Grant

The woman at the massive oak desk looked up unsmiling when the little boy walked into the building. Usually, it was her job to smile, answer questions, and help people find books. Standing outside the building, the boy observed her manner through the glass pane in the door as she interacted with two young girls who did not look like him. She smiled while dealing with the two girls.

She was still smiling when he first walked into the building, but when she looked into his brown eyes and at his dark skin her smile dissipated. It was replaced with a smirk and it caused the boy's stomach to tighten and his blood to rush to the top of his head causing him to feel dizzy. He had walked a long way to reach this place. He wanted to reach out and hold on to one of the two massive columns that led through the foyer and into the building. He started to extend his hand but thought better of it. Somehow that single act seemed as though it would be worse, more intrusive than stepping all the way inside the building.

You don't have to touch. Not right now. One day you will.

Stepping inside the building, the place smelled different than any place he had ever visited. He could not describe it but it was not unpleasant. Then it hit him. It was the smell of books. His excitement nearly overtook him. He made a tentative step in the direction of the reading room off to the left but decided against it. He took one step back. Better not look too familiar. He knew he wasn't supposed to be there. The woman who stopped smiling knew it, too. More than a hundred years of history, culture, and tradition screamed that he was not welcome inside. Then he remembered himself. He swallowed hard but did not turn and head for the door. His heart couldn't possibly beat any faster than

157

it already was, but he had gone too far, sacrificed too much. The minute he set foot in the building he had been marked. He was already the little darkie that came into the library. Hatred would not lessen. The threshold had been sullied, compromised. Maybe they would burn the place down, start all over again. He felt other eyes on him and their stares were as cold and steely as the woman at the desk.

"I..." he stammered. "I..."

"May I help you?" Her voice was insistent. Her manner was meant to send him running.

He had endured the hateful eye from whites his entire young life. He knew it well. It shocked and it stunned, but it did not kill. It was not the look that did the killing. The look was the warning. It was a cautionary measure.

"Boy, do you want something? You can't have any water. And you know you can't use the bathroom."

Still, he said nothing. People stared up from their newspapers and books. Eyes peered from around the book stacks. His heart continued racing, and he was certain he could not have spoken a complete sentence if a script had been placed in his hands.

"No ma'am," he managed to stammer.

He stood his ground and looked around at the people whispering none too quietly. He could pick up snatches of conversation. Familiar words such as uppity, nigger, darkie pelted his back. Insults were of no consequences.

The boy stared up at the ceiling. It was high and vaulted. He drank in the sheer magnificence of the craftsmanship that was evident in the dark wood that framed the tall windows that seemed to go on forever. Painstaking artistry was everywhere, in the molding and carvings that adorned every wall within view, even in the portraits of old bearded men that hung here and there and sweeping landscapes that captured scenes of the state's past. It was the grandest place he had ever seen. It was like something he saw in the movies whenever he had a nickel to see one. And the books! Books were everywhere. The place was just as magnificent as he had imagined it must be and he had passed by it many times. He began to imagine the words and the images that must be contained in those books that were close enough for him to touch.

Finally, he glared back at her, no longer oblivious to the gentle echoes of hard shoes on the tiled floor. Their eyes met and seemed to communicate. Words unspoken passed between them. He was certain she knew what he was thinking. Like Adam in the Garden, his eyes became opened. Now he knew things. Unlike Adam he was not embarrassed. There was no apology in his eyes. He was not sorry for being there. Instead, he understood fully, as she did that an apology was owed to him because she had loved the books all along. She had to love them in order to come into a magnificent place like this day in and day out. But to not share them—and this building—with all the people was a sin of the most unconscionable kind!

The slightest hint of crimson tinged her hard face. Her back stiffened, she sniffed, pushed her glasses back up on her nose, and looked away. He had made his point and she knew it. A victory! He had scored one for every colored face she had turned away from the building. Still, she rallied. All she had was her hatred, and how would that serve her at judgment? Now, she meant to put him back in his place.

"I don't know why you're here. Are you lost? She asked defiantly. "There's nothing here for you." She realized the foolishness of her words. *Nothing here for you.*

The young boy regarded her again whispering to himself, *"Why does anyone come into a library?"*

She folded her arms and looked away impatient with his stubbornness.

He turned and walked out of the building. Head bent down, the boy headed home. He lifted his head to look over his shoulder now and again, wondering if anyone was following him.

That evening he sat down to a meal of beans, cornbread, and leftover collards. He was silent at the dinner table and the rest of the evening. His days were the stuff of the secret life of boys. There was, after all, the life of children that parents know and the life that they don't. Beyond the watchful gaze of parental eyes were old abandoned buildings that cried out to be explored, creeks to play in, and railroads to be followed in bare feet. This too he would keep to himself.

The next morning he did not return to the library. He awoke, marveling to himself that the house had not burnt down while his family slept inside. Sunlight crept gently across the floor of the room he shared with his older brother. He was alive and had not received a beating from his father for…well, what could he be punished for? For quietly insisting that people give him something he knew he had a right to? Intellectually, he could not quite frame the thing that so occupied him. But what was as clear to him as his own name was the fact that no one should have access to something he could not have. Not if he could help it.

The following two days he did return to the library, stood in that same spot and received the identical stern stares from the lady as if warning him to do not dare enter. With each day his anger became more intense, his determination more dogged. Finally on the fourth day he returned and received those same disapproving stares and heard the same whispers. It was this way the next day and the next. The woman, he figured, was the librarian in charge. She was the one who still asked in an impatient voice if she could help him. He never ventured very far away from the entrance. He would arrive, stay a few moments, then leave, careful to make sure no one was following him as he made his way home. Each night on those occasions he frequented the library, he sat nervously back at home eating dinner and wondering if anyone might ask about his clandestine visits to the library. When asked how he spent his day, he delivered his stock response, "Nothing much."

That summer of 1963, he didn't bother to read newspapers and was unaware of the demonstrations at segregated facilities upstate that resulted in numerous beatings and, in a couple of instances, deaths of colored folks who were demanding the same rights he sought at the library. Still, at some level, he perceived there could be danger in what he was determined to do. But he had come too far to give up what he had started. He was so close. So close. He was certain that he could change people's minds. He would help them to see that colored people were as good as other people. A boy reasons this way, believes he can change minds and erase boundaries long established, however unfair, by merely being good. For all his pluck, he still saw things the way a boy did. He did not understand that what was at stake was a way of life that now seemed threatened. *You give 'em the right to access, what would they ask for next?* He was unaware that the simple act of taking a seat in the all-white library was another blow to years of tradition.

He had returned to that library every day for a week and now on a scalding hot Friday, the first day of August, he decided it was going to be a day of action. Actually, the deal had been sealed the night before when he'd laid down his head to go to sleep. When he awoke that morning, he found that he was too excited to eat so he bypassed the plate of breakfast food prepared for him and now was sitting on top of the kitchen stove. He dawdled around the house, waiting for his older brother to leave, also headed to points unknown. Then he made his own move.

The young boy with frayed nerves was out of the house and down the street, headed toward the place where he would make his demand known and would in doing so force justice to be tested. Destiny awaited him. Maybe it was cockiness. Maybe it was impatience. Maybe still it was the incredulity of the situation—denying colored people the right to use the library. Whatever it was, the time had come for the ultimate act of defiance, and it had to be today. He had tired of walking the long distance to the library, just to turn and walk away. The people should be used to him by now. They should know that he was not going to cause problems or make a mess. He could sit quietly and behave just like all of the others who used the library. Indeed, today was the day he would make the ultimate demand. He would have a seat in the white man's library, open a book, and read.

Small balls of sweat rolled down his face as he walked up the ten steps that led into the building. He was hot but it didn't matter. All that mattered waited on him inside the pillars of the building. The boy strolled with pride inside the building and instantly locked eyes with the woman at the desk. By now he was certain that she was the person in charge. Whereas once he thought he might have sensed a hint of resignation, he now saw a decided look of determination in her hard blue eyes. Perhaps she had awakened with the same sense of purpose as he. It was strange the way it seemed she could read his mind and determine his motive. He swallowed hard. Yes, here I am again, he thought. His eyes fixed on hers, he stepped gingerly in the direction of the nearby reading room.

In an instant the woman came around her desk and blocked his path. Calmly, he started around her but she moved to block him again. He again attempted to make his way to the reading room. They just looked at each other.

"Don't you know anything?" Her voice was but a whisper and he was not certain if he had heard her correctly. She was almost pleading with him. "Leave now."

He was trying to figure out what to do next when he was given a hard shove from the back.

"You really don't know what kind of danger you are in, do you, boy?" A harsh, deep voice said suddenly, catching him off guard.

He had not heard the man approach. The nearness and forcefulness of his voice made the boy jump. He turned to confront a red-faced man with angry gray eyes.

"Otherwise you wouldn't be in here where you are not wanted. Where you don't belong," the man continued.

The boy was too afraid to move.

The man removed the belt from around his waist and held it close to the boy's countenance.

"You see this, boy? I could wrap this belt around your neck and drag your nigger behind out of this building and hang you from that tree over yonder. No one would care." The man bent close to the boy and spoke softly. "You know what they're doing to uppity negras like you up in Shuler County? Do you want to hang from that tree?"

Still, the boy could not speak or move. But he was aware that some customers had begun to rise from their tables and were looking on. He could hear the scrapings of oak chairs as still others vacated their seats to see what was going on. Suddenly, no plot in any book was as compelling as what was taking place right before their eyes.

He had never seen this man in the library before. Though he was a stranger to the boy, there was no mystery about him. The sight of a little colored boy trying to break customs much older than he, customs that had been necessary to maintain the proper relationship between superior and inferior human beings, evidently repulsed the man, and the boy knew he meant to do harm to him.

For the first time the boy felt doubt and the doubt was mixed with fear. Had he overplayed his hand in his demand to have access to books? Before he could respond the man snatched him off his feet and lifted him a couple feet off the floor.

"Put me down," he cried. "Put me down!" Tears flooded his eyes as he struggled and kicked. He clutched at his neck and gasped for air.

The man was quite strong and his anger seemed to increase his strength. His knuckles dug into the boy's neck and limited his air supply.

"Put him down!" a woman's voice shouted. "Put him down!" The voice belonged to the woman who each day glared at him and who moments before had barred him from entering the reading room. "You will not harm a hair on his head. I will not allow you to disgrace this building with your brutish behavior. It's not right. This is not Shuler County."

The man stood his ground with the boy still hoisted in the air. He glared at the woman and she glared right back at him. She wasn't about to back down, not when the dignity of the library was at stake. It represented something greater than the Southern tradition, the Southern ways. It represented civilization for hundreds of years and that had to be protected from this uncivilized intrusion.

The man finally dropped the boy back to the floor. The thrust forced him to his knees, but he quickly jumped back up.

The lady with the steely blue eyes and the hard stare, took his hand and walked him to an office, leaving the man huffing and puffing where he stood. The boy watched as the lady sat at a desk and inserted a small card into the roller of an old manual typewriter. Instead of typing anything on the card she looked down at the keys and then at him. She then took his hands in both of hers.

He stared into her eyes. She was older than he thought at first. Her blue eyes now seemed tired instead of hard.

"I want to tell you something," she said, words no longer harsh but soft and gentle. "I knew this day was coming. I just didn't know when or how or with what fanfare. I suppose I should thank you. North of town, over in Shuler County, people are being beaten and killed for attempting the same thing you were doing." For the first time since their confrontations, she smiled. "I love this library and no library should be a place where people fight and die. Seeing you here has made me know that the time has come. I am very sorry about what happened to you today." She squeezed his hands and then released them.

"You know all this time I haven't known your name, but now I must so that I can issue you a library card."

"Levi," the boy whispered still somewhat in shock.

"Your full name must be on your library card." She emphasized the "your."

"Levi Flood, ma'am."

She typed his name and said, "I don't know if I will have a job here tomorrow or if I will be asked to resign from my church. But I would like to give you something." She rolled the card out of the typewriter and handed him a library card that read La Fleur County Library with his name "Levi Flood" typed out below it.

"Well, Levi Flood, let's go back inside and find those books that you like best."

THREE SHORT TALES AS TOLD BY

GRIOT LESLIE PERRY

The Door of No Return

People called her crazy. Her husband left her and took their three children with him. He took another woman as his wife and had two more children with her.

The woman the villagers called crazy lived just outside the village. Why they called her crazy was because of the things she said. She talked about being kidnapped and taken aboard a great ship. She talked about being rescued by a magical fish.

There was a time when she was a young teenage girl no different than any other girl in the village. But then one day she disappeared. Her father went hunting for her. Other men of the village joined him. They hunted several days, but could not find her. Her father never stopped hunting.

Months went by and her entire family, as well as the other members of the village, were heart broken. They had lost one of their own and they suffered as a family, just as when the occasion presented itself, they celebrated as a family. The occasion to celebrate came one day when the young girl suddenly appeared in the village. But she was different. Much more quiet and refused to talk with anyone. She only said that she was taken away. She did not say who took her or where she went.

A few years after she had returned she was married. She gave birth to three children. Sometime after the birth of her last child, she began to tell a strange story that no one believed. And that is when her husband and other villagers began to call her crazy.

Because of her strange story she was forced to live alone in a small hut outside the village. Life has taken a toll on her and she looks much older than her actual age. It has been a long time since she first began to tell her strange story and now all three children are grown and have children of their own.

One day as Maleka, for that is her name, is cleaning her hut she looks up and there standing outside her doorway is a young girl.

"Hello," Maleka says.

The young girl says nothing

"I know who you are and I believe I know why you have come."

The young girl still does not speak.

"Come closer. I will not harm you, for you are my granddaughter."

How do you know who I am?"

"I have seen your mother and I have seen you with your mother. But I would know you anywhere. You carry my likeness with you."

"People say you are crazy," the little girl says.

"There are people who say that," Maleka agrees. "But I think it is best to learn on your own. Don't you think it is better to learn on your own…to really know things, and not believe what others have said?"

The young girl says nothing, but just stares directly into Maleka's eyes.

"Shall I tell you a story—the story some people don't believe— the story that some people think makes me crazy?"

Maleka detects some curiosity in the young girl's stare. She extends her hand and waves her into the hut.

"You can come a little closer if you wish."

The little girl stands her position and still does not speak.

Her stand-off nature does not deter Maleka. The time has finally come to tell her granddaughter what happened to her. Maybe she will also think Maleka is crazy, but the little girl has to know. Hopefully, it might make her a bit more cautious when wandering outside the safety and comfort of the village.

"It began a day like this." Maleka steps outside the doorway to be closer to her granddaughter. "I was just a few years older than you. I was getting wood for the fireplace. Do you sometimes get wood for your mother when she is cooking?" Maleka pauses hoping the little girl will open up to her. She does not and Maleka continues. "Well that is what I was doing.

"I wandered a little too far from my village and I saw people from another tribe coming at me. There were warnings among the elders of my village that some tribesmen from other villages would kidnap children. So as soon as I saw them I started running. I could hear them behind me, and gaining on me. I could run fast as a young girl, but they still caught me. When they did, they bound me with rope and led me away—away from my village, away from my mother and father, away from all my friends." She pauses as tears well up in her eyes remembering that dreadful day.

"Several hours later I was taken to a place where there were other people who were also bound by ropes. They were bound around their wrists and necks and with ropes connecting one person to the next. I was bound together with this group of people.

"None of us said anything. The people who bound us spoke a language I had never heard before. But I knew what they were saying by their shouts and gestures was not good for me."

Her granddaughter moves a step closer to Maleka and allows her to place a hand on her shoulder. It is the first time she has ever touched this little girl who means so much to her. She feels a chill.

"The first night we slept on the ground in the night air. We were not given any food or any water. Early in the morning we were led away. I do not remember how long we walked or how far, but it seemed that we walked forever.

"Finally we came to a dungeon. Men with a strange skin color—a color I had never seen before, met us. They looked us over very carefully. Then we were taken into the dark, damp, and cold dungeon. Once we were inside the ropes were taken off and we were all chained together." Maleka stretches out both arms and cuffs her hands simulating the manner in which they were chained. It is all very difficult for her to do, but it has to be done so that her granddaughter will understand. All the children of the village need to hear her story, but they think she is crazy.

"Do you know what chains are?" she continues. "They serve the same purpose as ropes. Only you can't cut them and you can't break them."

Maleka feels the young girl warming up to her so she leads her into the hut. She sits on a stool inside. Telling this story and recalling all the horror tires her out. The little girl sits on the floor near her.

"I cried many tears in that place. Oh, how I cried. We stayed there for many days. The food we ate was not like the fresh food that comes from the earth or the fruits that come from the trees or the fish from the rivers. The food we ate had a strange smell and a strange taste and that made it hard to swallow." Maleka simulates swallowing to demonstrate.

"At night I could hear the lapping sounds of water hitting the walls of the dungeon. Sometimes I smelled water—a great body of water. And then one day a door opened that had never been opened before. And each of us were led out of that door."

Maleka smiles. She really loves this child, her granddaughter.

"Where did the door go to?"

"To a world of no return," Maleka says. "Actually we boarded a boat. A very large boat. But we had to go down into the belly of the boat. And we were forced to lie down like slabs of wood, one person lying down next to the other with barely enough room to twist or turn around and no room to lift up our heads because the ceiling was only inches from our faces. Each of us was chained to the person next to us."

"Did you have to sleep that way?" the young girl questions..

Maleka's smile broadens. Her granddaughter is talking with her asking questions, unlike the adults in the village who call her crazy. "Would you mind if I call you granddaughter?"

The young girl nods her head. "You can call me granddaughter."

"To answer your question, Granddaughter, that's how we had to stay at all times, lying side by side, day after miserable day. For a short time each day, we would be unchained and marched up to the top of the boat. Drums would be beaten and we would be forced to jump around as if we were dancing to the drums. Then we would be marched down again to the belly of the boat, to the foul smell and the darkness, always the darkness." She pauses to catch her breath. A feeling comes over her similar to the feelings she had in the darkness.

"One night a person lying not far from me stopped breathing. He lay there all night and in the morning one of the men on the boat unchained him and dragged his body away. He was buried in the waters." Maleka's body trembles all over. Her voice cracks. "One night, or day, I don't remember, I was unchained and taken to a room where the man in charge of the boat stayed. He did something to me that hurt very badly. The next day or night I was taken to this room again. And the next night and many nights after that."

"What did he do to you?"

"Very terrible things that children shouldn't know about," Maleka answers abruptly. She doesn't mean to be short with her granddaughter, especially since the child is opening up to her, but what happened in that room night after night shouldn't be told to a child.

She changes the subject. "During my days on that boat I had seen some poor souls jump into the water. They were not jumping to swim to safety. We were too far from land to do that. They were jumping for another reason."

"To die?"

"Yes, to die," Maleka answers in a subdued tone. "And I decided to do the same if I had to opportunity. And I knew that I would have the opportunity, Granddaughter, because every time I was taken to that room I was unchained. The people who jumped into the water were also unchained. When they would take us to the top of the boat to jump around like we were dancing, we were unchained. That's when these poor souls jumped knowing when they did that the man-eating fish were following the boat."

Maleka looks fondly at her granddaughter. "Would you like something to drink? I have some fresh goats milk?"

The girl shakes her head no. She then cups her hands together and rests her face, constantly staring at Maleka.

She continues. "Now, this is the part of my story that your grandfather did not believe, and when he began to tell me I was out of my mind. This is the part of the story that people say was not true. They say I made it up. That it didn't happen." Maleka leans forward in order to be a little closer to the little girl. "For a long time I did not remember what happened. I did not know how I made it back to the shore of my homeland." Again she pauses to draw in a deep breath and slowly release it.

"But after your mother's birth, the horror of what happened came to me in a dream. Every night I was filled with the same terrible dream. Every night! Every night! Soon I was filled with every living moment of what took place." Tears fill Maleka's eyes

171

and her voice chokes up. "I can understand why your grandfather left me, but he hurt me terribly when he took your mother and my other two children from me. That was more painful than to be called crazy." She pauses to gain her composure. She doesn't want the child to see her cry.

She needs a break from telling the story. "You look a lot like your mother. Does she know you're here?"

The little girl nods her head no.

"Do you want me to tell you the rest of the story?"

She now nods yes.

"Every time I went to that dreadful room, a man would walk with me. He would usually walk a little behind me always pushing me along. To get to the room we had to go to the top of the boat, then go down to a cleaner, fresher part of the boat. For a brief moment I could see the water all around and the far away sky above. One night when they were taking me to this terrible man, I decided to jump when we got to that opening." She smiles.

"Finally, the time was right and I jumped. I felt like I was reaching for the sky as I soared through the air. The next thing I knew I was swallowed by the water, going down, down, down! And then I came up. It was pitch black down there and there was nothing but water all around. I was not afraid. I felt relieved even though I knew I was going to die. But I knew that my soul would remain in Africa if I died that close to the homeland."

Once again Maleka pauses, cups her hands together and holds them up high in the air. For a moment she closes her eyes. She then brings them down and looks back at her granddaughter.

"I couldn't swim. I had never learned how. The boat was moving off and I was kicking and splashing the water with my arms. I felt I was about to drown."

Maleka flings her arms high in the air.

"And then it happened. A barking fish came up to me and I calmed down. I don't know why, I just did. The fish seemed to tell me to get on its back. At first I kept sliding off, but somehow I managed to climb on. The fish swam off with me holding on. For days that fish carried me over the waters. Every so often, the fish would make its barking sound as if it were talking to me. Telling me everything was all right. Everything was just fine." She finally brings her arms back down and relaxes on the stool.

"When the villagers found me on the shore I was later told that there was a great big fish in the shallow part of the water. They said they caught it and had a great feast. I was saddened when the fish was eaten. That was my miracle fish. Every night I pray blessings to it. That fish saved my life."

Maleka is absorbed in her own emotional rush. She remains silent for a few moments and then says. "That is how I came back. When I finally remembered what happened to me, I told your grandfather. And I told other villagers. I told anyone willing to listen. No one believed me, but that is the truth."

Maleka looks closely at her granddaughter. "Do you believe my story?"

"I think so," her granddaughter says. "Yes, I believe your story."

"Do you think I'm crazy?"

The little girl shakes her head no.

"Will you come back to visit me again?"

She smiles, nods her head yes, then jumps up, and runs out the door.

Maleka also smiles as the young girl runs off. It was the warmest smile she has received in years.

Sunshine and the Gummy Man

Sunshine was a slave. Now you might wonder why Sunshine was called Sunshine. Well, he was called Sunshine because he was happy all the time. No, he wasn't happy because he was a slave. He would love to be a free man. Who wouldn't? To be a free man was his greatest wish, his deepest hope, and his most powerful dream. No. Sunshine wasn't happy because he was a slave. He was happy because he didn't do any work.

You see, he was always trickafyin,' always goofadoin.' When old master would say, "Sunshine, go hitch up the mule to the plow, we goin' to do some plowin' today."

Sunshine would go to the barn and come back without the mule and without the plow and tell old master, "Can't hitch up the mule to the plow. The mule is sick and the plow is broke." He was always trickafyin,' always goofadoin.'

Another time old master would say, "Sunshine, go get the cotton sacks. We goin' to pick some cotton today."

Sunshine would go to the barn and get the cotton sacks and show them to old master.

"Can't do no cotton pickin' with these sacks. Some rats chewed the bottoms out of all the sacks." He was always trickafyin,' always goofadoin.'

On another time old master would say, "Sunshine, go get the hoe. We goin' cut the weeds from around the collard greens."

Sunshine would go to the barn, bring back the hoe and show it to old master and say, "Can't do no hoin' with this hoe. The handle is broke." He was always trickafyin,' always goofadoin.'

Master got tired of Sunshine getting out of work all the time. So one fine sunny day he went over to the general store and bought

175

some brand new cotton sacks. Ten brand new cotton sacks! And then he hid them in the big house. And the next morning, before the first crack of day, he went over to the slave quarters to wake up Sunshine.

"Sunshine, get up! We goin' to do some work today or your back side is goin' to be mine with this bull whip."

Sunshine put on his clothes and followed old master out to the cotton field.

"Sunshine, I want you to pick all that cotton before noon or I'm goin' to lay you out with this bull whip."

Sunshine looked at all the rows of cotton. There were a hundred rows and each row was a hundred yards long.

"Master," Sunshine said. "If I got to pick all that cotton before noon, I'm goin' to need some help."

"Sing!" Master scowled. "That'll help you."

"I can't," Sunshine replied.

"Why can't you?" Old master asked.

"Cause a crook got caught in my throat lookin' at all that work," Sunshine said, trying to make old master smile. "Master, if I make you smile, would you give me the day off?" he asked.

"If you make me smile, I'll give you two days off," Master said.

"What would you do if I made you laugh?" Sunshine displayed a broad smile across his face.

"I'd give you three days off."

"Master, you might as well set me free as to give me three days off. Think about how the other slaves would feel lookin' at me takin' life as easy as a blue jay, sittin' under a shade tree, and drinkin' a mint julep. They would get so mad and jealous they might start an insurrection, maybe start a civil war."

"Well, you ain't made me smile and you sure ain't made me laugh," master said.

"I was just about to do that. But first I got to tell you somethin.' You is the handsomous man I ever did see."

"I'm sorry, Sunshine, but I can't say the same thing about you."

"You could if you told a big lie like I just did." Sunshine broke out laughing. He laughed so hard his sides begin to hurt.

176

He laughed so hard his stomach begin to ache. He laughed so hard tears came out of his eyes.

Old master didn't laugh. He didn't even smile.

The truth about old master was that he never smiled before in his life. Some folks claimed that a boll weevil bit him on his lip and got his jaws locked. And if he laughed, he probably would get a heart attack.

Master went back to the big house to get a nap since he woke up so early to get Sunshine up. So there was Sunshine looking at all those rows of cotton. And he started talking to himself.

"Self."

"What?"

"You don't want to do no work today, do you?"

"Sure don't."

"Self."

"What?"

"Why don't you run away? Run away to Canada."

"You know old master will be lookin' out the window of the big house and see I'm gone and then send the blood hounds after me. You know that."

"Self."

"What?"

"Why don't you make a dummy, set him in the middle of the cotton field and when master look out the window of the big house, he'll see the dummy and think it's you. But you'll be on your way to Canada."

"Good idea!"

So Sunshine made a gummy man from the gummy tree. It didn't look like him, but he knew old master wouldn't know the difference. And he high tailed it to Canada.

Long about noon, old master came out of the big house to see how the work was fairing. He walked up to the gummy man thinking it was Sunshine.

"Sunshine, what are you doing standing here? Get back to work!"

Of course the gummy man don't say anything.

"If you don't get back to work, I'm going to bust you side the jaw."

Of course the gummy man don't say anything.

"I'll give you the count of three." And the old master starts counting. "One…two…three!" Then throws his fist upside gummy man's head and he gets stuck.

"Let me go!"

Of course the gummy man don't say anything.

"I'll give you the count of one. One!"

Master kicks the gummy man and he is stuck for sure. He is stuck for sure.

Meanwhile Sunshine is running fast and running fast. He's running fast on the side of the road at the edge of the woods. He's running fast and he's running fast. He figures if he runs in the middle of the road, he might get caught and if he runs in the woods, he might get lost. He's running fast and he's running fast.

Suddenly he hears a voice.

"Hello there, Sunshine. Hello there, Sunshine."

Sunshine stopped in his tracks. He looked around, but he didn't see anyone. "Who called out my name?"

"Me. I called out your name," the voice said.

"I don't see anyone," Sunshine said. "Where are you? Show yourself. Let me see you."

"I can't show myself. Not until nighttime. I'm the North Star. When darkness falls, you'll see me. And I'll guide you to freedom land."

"How do I know you the North Star? Stars don't talk. Least I never heard of one talkin'."

"Now you have and I'm going to take you to freedom land. But you got to do what I tell you. You got to go in the woods. Don't worry you won't get lost. Just follow the sound of the blue birds. They will guide you in the daytime and my beacon light will guide you in the nighttime. So do what I tell you. Go into the woods."

So Sunshine went into the woods. He was running fast and he was running fast. When darkness fell, he saw the North Star and he knew he was going in the right direction.

"Hello there, Sunshine. Hello there, Sunshine."

Sunshine stopped running. "I'm listening," Sunshine said.

"You're going to come to a river. You're going to see a man standing next to a boat. Don't be afraid. Don't be afraid."

After a while, Sunshine did come to a river and he did see a man standing next to a boat.

"Hello there, Sunshine," the man said.

"How did you know my name?" Sunshine asked.

"The North Star told me your name."

"Who are you?" Sunshine asked.

"I'm a Quaker, and that's my religion. I'm a conductor of the Underground Railroad. That's my job. Get in the boat. I'm going to take you to freedom land."

Sunshine got in the boat. The man rowed the boat down the river for a few miles. Then he pulled up to the bank on the other side of the river.

"See that house over yonder on the hill with the light beaming in the window?"

Sunshine nodded his head.

"Go and knock on the door. There's a lady waiting for you. She's going to help you on your way to freedom land."

Sunshine got out of the boat. He quickly stepped up to the house and knocked on the door.

A tall woman with a stern look on her face opened the door.

"Hello there, Sunshine," the woman said.

"How do you know my name?"

"The North Star told me your name."

"And who are you?" Sunshine asked.

"I'm a Quaker, and I'm a conductor of the Underground Railroad. Come in the house. I got some food for you to eat and a nice comfortable bed to lay your head on."

Sunshine went into the house and there on the table was a fine spread of food. There were collard greens, black eye peas, and mashed potatoes. There was corn, fried chicken, hush puppies, and sweet potato pie. Dishes were set out to eat on and utensils to eat with and a big glass of milk to wash the food down. It was a spread worthy of a king, and Sunshine was having his royal moment.

After he finished eating, Sunshine went into a bedroom and laid his head down for a nice restful sleep on a nice comfortable bed. Before he knew it, he was fast asleep. Before he knew it, he was being awakened.

"Sunshine, time to get up. There's a man outside sitting on a wagon with two horses raring to go. They're going to take you on to your next step to freedom land."

Sunshine got up, but just before he was about to leave, the woman stopped him.

"Take this blanket with you. You're going to need it on those cold chilly nights."

Sunshine took the blanket. It was a patch quilt blanket. Once outside, Sunshine saw the man sitting on a wagon with two horses raring to go.

"Hello there, Sunshine," the man said. "Get in the wagon and under the straw. We got some traveling to do."

Sunshine got in the wagon, under the straw and the man got those two horses moving. They traveled for two whole days, just stopping long enough for Sunshine to stretch his legs and get a bit of food and drink of water.

After two whole days the man said, "All right, Sunshine, you can get out."

Sunshine got out of the wagon.

The man continued, "Go in those woods yonder. You're going to see a clearing and you're going to see some people like yourself and some women and children."

Sunshine went into the woods and saw a clearing filled with people. They were sitting on the grassy ground with their meager belongings. Sunshine joined them.

After an hour they heard some singing.

"Steal away, steal away, steal away to Jesus." The singing came from inside the woods. "Ain't got long to be here."

Out of the woods came a woman. She was a stout woman. She really wasn't stout; she just looked stout. She was a big woman. She really wasn't big; she just looked big.

"Come on children," the woman said. "We're going to freedom land."

The people gathered their meager belongings and followed behind the woman. She led them back into the woods. They soon came to a stream and the woman started walking in the water. The people followed behind. They all began to sing together.

"Wade in the water. Wade in the water, children. God's going to trouble these waters."

They came to the other side and kept on walking. Hour after hour they followed behind the woman. Just before dusk, the woman stopped and said, "We're going to rest here."

The people pulled out their blankets. Sunshine was about to lay out his patch quilt when he glanced over at the woman. She was staring at what appeared to be a patched quilt with some peculiar designs. She seemed to be studying it like it was a great puzzle. He glanced over her shoulders at the patch quilt. It had designs looking like farmhouses and forest areas and bridges with long stretches of rivers running under them. High up in a corner of the quilt was a yellow star.

Sunshine wasn't able to make much sense of her quilt, so he lay down on his patch quilt and went to sleep on it. Soon after, the woman awakened him.

"Get your things. We on our way," she said.

In the night, the folks got their things together searching in the dark. Sunshine looked up at the stars. There was that star that talked to him earlier in his escape. The woman walked in the direction of the star. The people followed behind. Sunshine knew they were going in the right direction.

They traveled for ten days and nights. Sometimes they would crawl through cotton fields, sometimes they hid in old abandoned barns, and sometimes they slept under bridges. But they kept on going and going on.

Finally, after all the hiding and all the walking, the woman stopped. She looked at all the people and said.

"You all is in freedom land now. If you go in that direction, you'll go to Michigan. If you go to Battle Creek, Michigan, you might see Sojourner Truth. If you see Sojourner Truth, tell her Harriet Tubman said hello. If you go in that direction you might go to New York. If you go to New York, you might go to Albany and if you go to Albany, New York, you might see Frederick Douglass. Tell him Harriett Tubman said hello. If you go in that direction, you might go to Canada. If you go over to Windsor, Canada, tell old Henry Bibb hello and that we still fighting the good fight down here in the South.

Canada is the direction that Sunshine went. And when he got to Canada, he went to a private school taught by Mary E. Bibb, and he met a fine young lady and got married. They had ten children, eighteen grand children, forty-seven great grand children, ninety-five great, great grandchildren, and no telling how many great, great, great grandchildren. And all those greats and great, greats and great, great greats spread all across this land and became our ancestors.

Stone Gumbo Soup

The Civil War was over and three Black soldiers were on their way home. They were traveling through Georgia on their way to Louisiana. The three men were tired and hungry and they hadn't had a restful sleep in weeks. The only food they had eaten were apples from an apple tree earlier in the day.

But they were happy because the war had ended and they were heading on home. They had walked for hours through cotton fields, through thick trees and brushes and across a river. They finally saw a plantation mansion through a clearing in front of them.

"Look there," one of the men said. "Finally, a place where we can get some real food and maybe a bed or at least some hay where we can get a decent night's rest."

They quickened their steps as they hurried up to the mansion.

Now the only people on the plantation were ex-slaves. The master and the mistress had left when the Union soldiers came. Now these ex-slaves weren't greedy people and they weren't selfish people. But when they saw these three soldiers coming, they thought of when the Union soldiers first came.

When those Union soldiers showed up they said, "We come to help you people." But all they did was help themselves to the people's food.

Then the Confederate soldiers came and they said, "We've come to help you people." All they did was help themselves to more of the people's food.

Naturally, when these poor folks saw these three soldiers, it wasn't a welcome sight. They didn't know if there was a small regiment or an entire army coming up behind them. They decided to be cautious. They decided to hide their food. They hid their onions, celery, carrots, corn, okra, tomatoes, and what little meat they had. They hid their food in croak-a-sacks, under blankets, in bushel baskets, and in old buckets. They hid their food as best they could. And after they hid all their food, they came out to meet the three soldiers.

"How do, good people," one soldier said. "We wonder if you good folks might have some food to share. We've been walking a lot of miles and we got a lot a miles to go and we sure are hungry."

"We don't have any food," the people said in unison. "The army came by and ate all the food we had. There's a town up the road. Maybe the town folks can give you some food."

"How far is this town?" the soldier asked.

"Oh, about thirty or forty miles," the people said in unison.

"We can't walk that far," the soldier sighed. "We're plumb worn out. We can't walk another half mile of a half mile."

One of the other soldiers spoke up. "I know what we can do. We can make some stone gumbo soup."

"Stone gumbo soup," the people said in unison. "What's that?"

"That's gumbo soup made out of stones," the soldier told them. "All we need is a big cooking pot. Anyone know where there's a big, big cooking pot?"

An old lady bent over, with gray hair and wrinkled tired skin, stepped forward and spoke up. "I know where there's a big, big cooking pot. In the plantation house. I used to cook out of it for the master and mistress when they gave their big hoop-de-do get together. I'll get my husband to help me bring it out."

The old lady and her husband, also bent over and bow legged, with sun cracked skin and only blotches of hair left, went into the plantation house and brought out the big, big cooking pot. They set it right in front of the soldiers.

"Now all we need is some kindlin' to put under the pot. Anyone know where we can get some kindlin'?"

"I got some kindlin' leaning against my shack," another old man said. "I'll go get it for you."

The old man, who walked with a severe limp, headed to his shack, got the wood, and brought it back and placed it under the pot. Placed it under the pot.

"Now what we need are some nice round, smooth stones to put

in the pot," the soldier said. "Does anyone know where there are some nice round smooth stones?"

"I know where there's some nice round, smooth stones over by the creek. I'll get my little brother and we'll get them for you."

The young boy and his brother went over to the lake, got some nice round, smooth stones and put them in the pot. Put them in the pot.

"Now," the soldier said. "What we need is a bucket of water."

Another old man said. "I got a bucket of water in my shack. I'll go get it."

The old man got the bucket of water and poured it in the pot. Poured it in the pot.

"Now it's time to light the kindlin," the soldier said. And so they did.

Soon the wood was burning. Soon the water was boiling.

"Mmm mmh!" the first soldier said. "Smelling good. Smelling good."

"Mmm mmh!" the second soldier said. "Smelling good. Smelling good."

"Mmm mmh!" the third soldier said. "Smelling good. Smelling good. But it needs something else. It needs something else. It needs some salt and pepper. Salt and pepper sure will bring out the flavor, don't you all agree? Now I know you are some poor folks and you don't have any food to share, but I wonder if someone has some salt and pepper?"

"I have some salt and pepper," a little old lady said. And away she went to her shack. She came back with the salt and pepper.

"Mmm. mmh!" the first soldier said. "Smelling good. Smelling good."

"Mmm, mmh!" the second soldier said. "Smelling good. Smelling good."

"Mmm, mmh!" the third soldier said. "Smelling good. Smelling good. But it needs something else. It needs something else. It needs some onions. Onions sure would bring out the flavor, don't y'all agree? Now I know you some poor folks and don't have any food to share, but I wonder if someone might have some onions?"

"I got some onions," a young and beautiful Black girl said. And away she went to her shack, got those onions and came back with them, peeled and cut them, then tossed those onions into the pot. Put them in the pot.

"Mmm, mmh!" the first soldier said. "Smelling good. Smelling good."

"Mmm, mmh!" the second soldier said. "Smelling good. Smelling good."

"Mmm, mmh!" the third soldier said. "Smelling good. Smelling good. But it needs something else. It needs something else. It needs some celery. Yes, it needs some celery. Celery sure would give this stone gumbo soup some flavor. Don't y'all agree? I wonder if any of you poor folks got some celery?"

"I got some celery," a woman with very high spirits said. And away that woman went. She got that celery and brought it back, cut it up, and put it in the pot. Put it in the pot.

"Mmm, mmh," the first soldier said. "Smelling good. Smelling good."

"Mmm, mmh," the second soldier said. "Smelling good. Smelling good."

"Mmm, mmh," the third soldier said. "Smelling good. Smelling good, but it needs something else, it needs something else. It needs some carrots. And it needs some corn too. Anybody here got some carrots and some corn?"

"Me and my wife," an old man with his wife standing next to him and the two looking much alike said. "We got some carrots and we got some corn. We'll go get it for you." Those two old folks, in unison turned and hurried off to their shack, got those carrots and got that corn and cut them up and put them in the pot. Put them in the pot.

"Mmm, Mmh!" the first soldier said. "Smelling good. Smelling good."

"Mmm, Mmh!" the second soldier said. "Smelling good. Smelling good."

"Mmm, Mmh!" the third soldier said. "Smelling good. Smelling good, but you know what?"

"It needs something else," a large lady wearing a red bandana said.

"You right," the soldier said. "It needs something else. It needs some okra. Can't make stone gumbo soup without okra."

"No you can't," the same lady said. "And I know where there's some okra." She hurried inside the big house, got that okra, cut it up, and put it in the pot. Put it in the pot.

"Mmm, Mmh!" the first soldier said. "Smelling good. Smelling good."

"Mmm, Mmh!" the second soldier said. "Smelling good. Smelling good."

"Mmm, Mmh!" the third soldier said. "Smelling good. Smelling good, but oh, it needs something else. It needs something else."

"What about some tomatoes?" a young girl no older than ten, said.

"That'll be fine," the soldier said.

So the little girl, and her little sister went to where their mamma had hidden the tomatoes and brought them back, and then some of the grown-ups cut them up and put them in the pot. Put them in the pot.

"Mmm, Mmh!" the first soldier said. "Smelling like that stone gumbo soup we made a while back for General Ulysses S. Grant."

The people looked at each other and said, "They cooked for a General?"

"Mmm, Mmh!" the second soldier said. "Smelling like that stone gumbo soup we made for President Abraham Lincoln."

The people looked at each other again and said, "They cooked for the President?"

"Mmm, Mmh!" the third soldier said. "Smelling good. Smelling good, but it needs something else. It needs something else."

"I know what it needs," the old man whose wife worked in the plantation house said. "It needs some meat."

"Sure do," the soldier said.

"What about some chicken," the old man said.

"That'll help a whole lot," the second soldier said.

"And some ham hocks and some sausage," another old man said.

187

"Very good!" the first soldier said.

"How about some fish? We got some fresh fish just straight out of that lake over yonder," the oldest of all the old men said. He pointed toward the woods.

"Great!" the third soldier said.

So those old men got the fish and the meat and brought it all back. And with the help of the women cut it in small pieces and put it in the pot. Put it in the pot.

That food cooked and cooked. The smell filled the air. And the folks took turns stirring the pot. The young folks stirred and the old folks stirred.

After an hour's time one of the old folks said, "I think it's cooked enough. I think it's ready."

The first soldier asked, "Is there a place where we can all go and eat this food together?"

The lady who worked in the plantation house said, "There sure is. In the big house. There's a giant size-eating table in the grand hall. And it's big enough for everybody here. There sure is. And I know where the mistress hid the dishes and silverware. I sure do. And some of these lady folks can help me set things up."

So all those slaves who had worked the cotton fields for years, and those soldiers who fought a war to help get them out of the cotton fields proudly strutted inside the plantation house and sat at that banquet table. They ate that stone gumbo soup together, eating from dishes and with silverware they only dreamed of using when in the cotton field. They ate till they were well fed.

After they finished eating, the old men came out with their musical instruments. They came out with their banjos, fiddles, and harmonicas. And for the first time in their lives, played music they could enjoy for themselves because there were no more cotton fields. And they danced and sang; they shouted and clapped their hands; they celebrated because there were no more masters and mistresses and no more cotton fields.

They celebrated, oh how they celebrated! They celebrated freedom! Yes, they celebrated freedom! They celebrated Frederick Douglass and Harriet Tubman and Sojourner Truth and John Brown and all the people who fought for freedom. Oh how they celebrated.

They celebrated the coming generations. They didn't know we were coming, but they celebrated just the same. They celebrated Malcolm X and Martin Luther King, Jr., and Rosa Parks, and all the people who stood up for freedom. Oh, how they celebrated. They didn't know we were coming, but they celebrated just the same.

They celebrated Paul Robeson, Langston Hughes, and Barak Obama. Oh, how they celebrated. They didn't know we were coming, but they celebrated just the same. Yes, they celebrated just the same.

They celebrated and they celebrated. And finally they decided to rest their bodies. And each of those good folks went off to their shacks, leaving the three soldiers in the plantation house. And those three soldiers rested their bodies also. They slept in the master's bedroom.

The next morning the soldiers were on their way to Louisiana. As they were leaving, they heard all the people call out to them, "Good bye! Good-bye! And thanks for the stone gumbo soup."

PART TWO

SHORT AUTOBIOGRAPHIES AND ESSAYS

Coming Of Age To Manhood

Dr. Loren Alves

The final weekend in January 1963 will burn deeply and be etched in my memory for the remainder of my life. Events out of my control had a profound effect on me. At age twelve, I wasn't sure if I would ever recover from the sorrow and trauma I experienced that weekend. I did, and that is why I am sharing that short period of my life with you. I want to reveal what happened to me as living proof that we can overcome most obstacles placed in our pathway to a successful and happy life.

Levi Cobb was my closest friend. He had moved into a house right down the street from the DeSoto Bass Courts, the projects where I lived with my mother, two sisters, and three brothers. Every year we walked to Miami Chapel Elementary School together. We would be punching, shoving, heckling each other, as all young friends do at that age. We went from the third grade to the seventh together, and had just begun our second semester when everything fell apart.

In the seventh grade, our favorite teacher was Mrs. Mesmer. Although she was a white teacher from the other side of town, she instilled discipline, respect, and friendship in her teaching methods. She had also been my older brother and sister's teacher when they were in seventh grade. They had told me I would have fun learning from her, and I did.

Our last class that Friday in January 1963 was Home Economics. Our other close friend Harvey was in that class with us. We all joked about how poorly we had stitched our aprons and then argued whether Jim Brown, the star running back for the Cleveland Browns and our hero, would rush for over one hundred yards that Sunday.

We also agreed to meet after school and play a couple games of "scrambled eggs," at the field near my apartment in the projects.

I had also become one of the school's patrolmen. Now, instead of waiting around for Levi in the morning and walking home with him in the evening as I had done for years I needed to get to my post two blocks from the school.

That final Friday in January leading into the fatal weekend, right at 3:25, five minutes before school dismissal, I hurried out of the classroom, picked up my pace as I rushed down the hallway and finally out of the building. As soon as I stepped outside the cold wind slapped me right in the face and my nose turned red instantly. I could see my breath every time I breathed out. Cold chills shot through my body as the wind penetrated through my coat and other clothes I was wearing. But it didn't deter me from my safety patrol post a couple blocks from the school. I took my job as a patrolman seriously. It made me feel real important, wearing my bright orange safety patrol strap. There was a silver badge attached to it in a spot right over my heart. I proudly held a stop flag attached to a six-foot pole always in my right hand.

Exactly at 3:30, I heard the bell ring and like a herd of cattle the students ran out of the building and headed to the corner where I stood in control. They rushed up to me, but I stood firm, with arms extended, stopping them from running out into the street.

"Look at Mr. Important," a young skinny kid in my class said.

"Yeah, we should all rush him at the same time and then see how he can stop us," another young boy who liked to act tough scowled.

Every day was a repeat performance. They threatened to overtake me, but never did. They just loved to tease me. Ignoring their taunts, when traffic cleared I raised the stop flag pole in the air and shouted.

"All clear traffic, you can now cross the street."

The kids ran into the street with Levi and Harvey in the last wave of students to cross over. As they shot by me, Levi got in one last taunt.

"Hey, Mr. Policeman, I guess you going to grow up and put us all in jail," he shouted.

"Yeah, he ain't going to be able to hang with us anymore, cause he's going to be trying to arrest us," Harvey shrieked in his high-pitched voice. "Probably won't even show up for our game of scrambled eggs today." He reached out and tried to knock my stick out of my hand. He missed and kept on running.

"We'll see you at the field in an hour," Levi shouted from the other side of the street and headed up the block.

I stayed at my post until 4:00 and then ran all the way to our apartment. I rushed through the front door and tossed my bags on the couch.

"Why you in such a hurry and running around all crazy?" my older brother, Donald, shouted at me. He sat on the couch with my other brother, Ronald, watching television. Barbara, my sister hadn't gotten home yet. Delores, the oldest of us all was never home. She was the only one who had a different father. Mama had been married prior to marrying my dad, Big Raymond. Even though some would say we were only half sister and brother, we all looked at her as one of us.

"Got to get out to the field and kick some butt," I answered and went into the bedroom I shared with my brothers. Clothes were scattered everywhere and the beds were half made up. I quickly got out of my school clothes and changed into jeans. I grabbed my heavy Cleveland Brown's Jersey, slid it over my head pulling it down tight. Then I slipped into my old gym shoes and shot out of the bedroom. Without saying anything to my brothers, who both gave me a hard stare, I ran out the door and headed towards the park.

When I arrived, the other boys were already there, with the exception of Levi. I found that strange because he never missed the opportunity to show off his speed and agility.

"Where's Levi?" I asked, rubbing my freezing hands together to keep warm.

"Don't know," Harvey replied. "He'll probably show up. Let's get this game going. It's cold and we need to move around to keep warm."

"We're not going to wait on him?" I asked still concerned that Levi wasn't there.

"No, we going to get started before it gets too dark," Larry said. He was a friend of ours but a year older than the rest of us. He loved to show off his physical superiority.

"You right, he's probably babysitting his little sister or

his mamma got him doing chores. She always got him doing something," I chimed in.

Being the smallest in the group I don't know why I even played the game of scrambled eggs, which simply was a game where one of the players would catch the ball and run like crazy from everybody else. It was a test of brute strength and endurance. My disadvantage was quite apparent, but in my neighborhood you never backed down or showed any signs of being afraid. Knowing those were the rules of the projects, I lined up in a circle with the other five boys and Harvey tossed the ball in the air.

Larry caught it before it hit the ground. He then took off running towards the line barely legible in the frozen turf. Gregory tried tackling him around his shoulders but with no luck. John and Bernard both grabbed a leg and I tried to get my arms around his waist. Larry was so much stronger and he just dragged us along with him to the goal line. Once he crossed the line, he shook us loose and I voluntarily released my grip on him. Harvey threw the ball in the air four times and each time Larry would grab it punishing the rest of us. I wasn't about to go for the ball and get pummeled by all those boys bigger than me. I figured my punishment was minimal if I limited my involvement to reaching out and grabbing at Larry. After four games we decided to call it quits. In the heat of the battle we forgot about Levi.

Exhausted from our game, we found an icy park bench and sat on it. Larry stood in front of us tossing the ball up in the air. The temperature had dropped, but we were so heated we paid no attention to the cold. Instead, the conversation turned to Sunday's football game. The Browns would be playing the New York Giants for first place in the Eastern Division of the National Football League. It was the last game of the season and the winner would go on to play the Los Angeles Rams for the championship.

"We going to beat their butts, you know." Harvey said. "Ain't no way the Giants can beat Cleveland at home, not with Jim Brown running the ball."

"I'll bet he goes for 125 yards." Bernard said. "He's going to run over that sorry linebacker Sam Huff for the Giants."

"Yeah, just like I ran all over you all." Larry bragged with his chest stuck out.

"Where is Levi?" I asked again. It was really bothering me that he hadn't showed up. I didn't quite accept the earlier explanation. I had a weird feeling about him not being there.

"Who knows," Larry said with a little attitude in his voice. Evidently he didn't like me changing the subject about his defeat over us. "If you're concerned why don't you go over to his house and find out."

"No, I'll call him later." I said. "Let's bet on how many yards Jim Brown's going to get. I bet my Pay Day candy bar he goes for 130."

"You got a bet!" Gregory chimed in for the first time. He was always quiet until it came time for betting. He always thought he might beat someone out of something. "I'll bet my Baby Ruth against your Pay Day."

"You're on," I said.

After placing a couple more bets on the game, we finally broke up and headed home.

The next morning it felt good to sleep in late. The temperature had dropped and it was snowing. It was Saturday and I didn't have to go out in the freezing cold. But I had a strong urge to run over to Levi's house and make sure he was okay. Instead, I picked up the phone and dialed his number. I had to get his bets for tomorrow's big game.

"Hello, Mrs. Cobb," I said when his mother answered the phone. "Is Levi home? We missed him yesterday and we all made our bets for tomorrow's game. I wanted to find out if he was going to take the Browns?"

There was a long silence and I could hear heavy breathing. It frightened me. For the first time I considered the possibility that something had happened to my best friend.

"Mrs. Cobb, is Levi all right?" I asked with a lot of anxiety in my voice.

"Loren, Levi was in an accident last night and he's in the hospital." she shouted into the phone.

"Is he all right?" I asked.

Again a long hesitation and finally she said, "yes," in a very faint voice.

We hung up and I nervously called Harvey and the other guys and repeated what Mrs. Cobb had just told me. We decided to stay in touch in case one of us heard anything about Levi's condition.

On Sunday morning I got the answer, as did the entire neighborhood. I sat at the breakfast table, while my brothers and sisters sat in the living room watching television when the station cut it to bring a special announcement. I couldn't believe what I heard.

"Friday evening a twelve-year-old Negro boy, Levi Cobb, was accidentally shot and killed by his uncle while trying to break up a fight between his father and his uncle. Police are still investigating the incident. No one has been arrested as of yet."

I dropped my fork, jumped from the table and ran to my bedroom, slamming the door behind me. I didn't want to talk to anyone. The television reporter was lying. My best friend was not dead. I had just seen him Friday and he was alive, laughing, and enjoying his youth. This couldn't happen to us. It couldn't happen to my best friend because those kinds of things didn't happen to a twelve-year-old. I was ready to go right back out there and confront that reporter on the television and insist that she admit to everyone she was lying and that nothing as vicious and ugly as the murder of my best friend had actually occurred. But I was afraid because in all reality nothing would change. The reporter wasn't lying and I was trying to stop time and go back to Friday. I wanted to say good-bye to my best friend and tell him I'd see him in the park in a couple hours to play scrambled eggs. But Levi hadn't shown up, and his mother told me he had been hurt. Finally, the lady on the television told me he was dead. My best friend was dead at twelve years old. I was forced to confront a reality of inner city life. Death seemed to be a constant companion to being poor, Black, and trapped in deplorable conditions that no person, young or old, should have to confront.

The next few days at school were the saddest of our lives. We didn't talk about Jim Brown running for 135 yards and the Cleveland Browns beating the New York Giants. In fact, no one remembered the bets. Suddenly none of that mattered. We all viewed life from a different lens. Being quite young we thought life was forever; we were invincible and nothing could happen to us. We talked about football, girls, and sometimes school but never about death. But sitting in Ms. Messmer's class waiting for her we were silent for the first time. I believe all our thoughts were similar: Levi wasn't there. Where was he? Was he in Heaven or could there be a place that young kids went because they were still too young to die? We just didn't know and because we didn't we sat silently waiting for our teacher to help make sense out of it all. Finally, she strolled into the classroom with a sense of authority as if she knew what had to be done.

"I know you all are feeling a lot of pain today," she started. "We all are. It is so difficult when we lose someone so young but it happens and we must learn how to go on. You all must learn how to go on for Levi. That's exactly how he would want it and it's exactly what you all must do."

Ms. Messmer's words were soothing and made me feel better. They didn't quite take away my pain and depression but helped considerably.

"Now we do have some work that must be done so let's try to concentrate on that for right now," she continued.

We all tried to concentrate, at least I did, but my mind kept wandering back to Friday. I could picture Levi running across the street and disappearing around the corner. He had waved with his back to me. If I had any idea what would happen later that evening I would have shouted out to him to turn around so that my last memory would have been of his face. I couldn't hold the tears. I tried my best to hide them from the other boys. They probably were all crying as well.

That week seemed to drag on forever. We went through our usual routine. I manned my post at the corner. However, there was very little teasing from the other boys. They didn't even run up to the corner. No one yelled and laughter was totally subdued. By Friday I was exhausted, but knew on Saturday I would have to conjure up enough strength to attend Levi's funeral.

I was up and about early the next morning. All night I'd tossed and turned knowing I would have to look at my closest friend lying in a casket. With the sun shining through the bedroom window I jumped up, tossed on my pants and a shirt, and hurried into the kitchen, being careful not to wake my brothers. I sat alone at the kitchen table staring out the window. It was a clear day and the sky was a radiant blue. Because there were no clouds, I knew it would be awfully cold. The sun helped to lift my spirits. Mama began to move around in her bedroom and I knew real soon she would come out dressed and would be ready to go to McLin's Funeral Home. A nervous energy invaded my body and I could hardly put the spoon of cereal up to my mouth. My mind began to wander. I could visualize Levi as an angel singing and praising God. At least that's what they taught us in Sunday School classes. I would look around the church and think that everyone with gray hair, slumped over bodies, or walking with canes had to worry about those things. Death didn't come visit young boys; we were immune to its invasion.

But death knew no age, race, or gender and when it was ready for you, it just came and took you out of here the way it did Levi. As Mama came out of her room dressed and ready to go, I knew attending the funeral would age me more that what I was ready for. Mama and I walked out of the apartment and got into her old Oldsmobile that we called the "Beast" and headed for my first experience at growing up.

McLin's Funeral Parlor was one block from Levi's house and I stared at his front porch as we drove by. I tried to will Levi to walk out that door and run down the front steps as I had watched him do so many times. But I knew the house was empty and a dark ambiance surrounded it. I wondered as we drove by how people can make happy sounds in such a sad time? How can they express joy when there is so much pain? Why did God have to create death? At that moment it made more sense to me that we should live forever. All of us boys were happy going to school, playing scrambled eggs, and betting whether or not Jim Brown would run for over one hundred yards. We were content with this life; why did we need the other one?

Mama pulled into the parking lot at the funeral home. She turned off the car and opened her door. I did not move. I felt paralyzed like some terrible disease had taken over my body, and I could only sit there. I would have preferred that much more than going inside that place.

Mama sensed my hesitancy. "Kind of hard to do, isn't it?" she asked in a very mellow tone.

I didn't answer. Instead I stared out the window.

"Come on, Loren, you'll be all right," she said. "Just remember that Levi is with Jesus and he is happy."

Mama's voice was reassuring and her words gave me strength. Most importantly, I knew she would be with me. I opened my door, got out, and we hurried inside.

I practically came to a stop when I looked to the front of the church and saw Levi in the silver casket. He was so quiet and still with his hands crossed in front of him. We found seats in the same row with Larry, Gregory, Bernard, and Harvey, all sitting with their parents. No one spoke; we were all fixated on Levi's still body. It was an awful feeling seeing someone whom you had known as a friend, always energetic, admirably funny, spastic at times, yes, even bothersome, but now, lifeless, motionless, eerie, and lying there in what could only be described as his last resting place on this side of the universe. We sat there in disbelief, each of us trying not to express emotions, shed tears, or make eye contact, showing our fear of the moment.

Throughout the entire service my mind was oblivious to the funeral proceedings taking place right in front of me. I disappeared into my own world. My mind drifted from place to place and also to nothing with real relevance or significance. I tried desperately to look away from the casket. But, I still knew Levi was lying there, not moving. I looked up into the ceiling lights. I stared at the windows and read different scripture passages above the pulpit. However, my eyes would wander back to that silver casket and tears flowed freely from them. I didn't want to cry but every once in a while it all got the best of me, and I would give in to the emotions.

Mama decided that we would not go to the burial site. When the funeral was over we expressed our condolences to Levi's family, climbed into the Beast and headed home. I tried to make my mind wander to anyplace far from the funeral home and my friend's body. As we drove by Levi's house, I didn't look over at it. After seeing him lying in the casket, I knew for sure there was no chance he would come bouncing out the front door ever again. I vowed to never go to another funeral; they were just too depressing. Even at that age I knew there was something wrong with how we buried our loved ones. Everyone was so sad. It seemed like we were cheating Levi of his right to leave here on a happy note. I wished they had sung "Oh Happy Day" in celebration. The songs they sang sounded real good, but they left me feeling depressed and wanting to cry more when the choir finished.

I glanced over at Mama; she hadn't uttered a word since leaving the funeral parlor. Maybe she was grieving in her own way or maybe she was just giving me some space to deal with loosing my best friend. Suddenly, she gripped the steering wheel tightly with both hands and the car began swerving and pulling to the right. I heard a loud flapping noise coming from outside. Taking my lead from Mama I gripped the armrest on the door.

"What happened?" I asked as calmly as possible.

"We just had a blow out." Mama shrieked.

She managed to steer the car over to the curb bringing the "Beast" to a stop.

"I need to find a phone booth so I can call your brother to come and change it," she said.

A couple times while riding my bicycle I had stopped and watched two men change flat tires on their cars. I was a quick learner and from observing them I figured I could change our flat. I had to act like a man in this situation.

"I think I can change it Mama," I said. "You don't have to call Raymond. I can handle it." I opened the door and headed to the back of the car.

"Boy, you can't change that tire. Now get back in the car and I'll find a phone booth and call your brother," she scowled at me.

"Mama I can do this!" I said with more determination than before. "I watched a whole lot of people change flat tires." I exaggerated but figured it was necessary in order to convince Mama I could do this.

"You trying to show Mama that you're grown," she said smiling. "Go ahead but be real careful, that stuff is heavy." She put the emergency brake on and got out of the car.

Mama stood off to the side as I opened the trunk. I didn't know if what we needed to change a tire was all in the trunk, but as I began my search I found the jack, the jack stand, the handle and the lug wrench. They were all so heavy, and I struggled to get them out and put them on the side of the car. After lining all the tools up in an orderly fashion, I grabbed the spare tire. With one strong effort I lifted it out of the trunk and placed it next to the tools. I was beginning to gain confidence that I could actually change a tire.

I removed the hubcap and loosened the lug nuts on the wheel. Then, I placed the jack setup on the rear bumper and hoisted the car up. I was proud of myself and shot a quick glance over at Mama. She was beautiful with a slight smile and a look of amazement that enveloped her face.

"Look at my man. You're doing just fine, Loren, just fine."

Finally, I got the rear end jacked up just enough to get the tire off the ground. I finished removing the lug nuts from the wheel then I removed the flat tire, grabbed the spare, and then struggled to get the tire onto the frame, but it wouldn't work.

"Loren you have to jack the car up a little more. Remember, the tire you just removed was flat and you have to lift the car a little higher to get the other one on." Mama said reassuringly.

I dropped the tire on the ground and hurried back to the jack. "Oh yeah, I knew that," I proudly proclaimed.

I lifted the car a little higher, got the spare tire on, tightened the nuts and put the hubcap back. After loading everything into the trunk I jumped in the front seat with my chest sticking out a mile. For a few minutes I had forgotten that I was depressed because of the funeral. Proving to my mother that I was man enough to change a flat tire had given me sufficient joy to temporarily replace my sadness. But what happened next deflated my positive feelings and shocked me to no end.

"How old are you Sonny Boy?" Mama asked.

What a strange question I thought. "I'm almost a teenager," I said.

"Precisely." she said without hesitation. "That's why I think I can tell you about who your father really is."

Stunned by what Mama said made my eyes widen. My mouth tightened and I looked straight ahead. At that moment I wished I was driving the car so I could just slam on the brakes and shout, "What did you just say?" Instead, all I could do was stare at the front windshield as if I were a deer fixated on the headlights of the Beast.

"Loren, I was truly astonished today. I watched your coming of age to manhood," Mama continued. She reached over and touched my leg as reassurance. "You boys showed a great deal of courage today at the funeral. I am not sure I could have been as strong as you all were if it had been someone as close to me as Levi was to you all. And the way you handled changing the tire for your Mama. You are growing up on me."

I heard Mama's words but they really didn't register. I wanted her to get back to the subject of my Father.

"Mama what do you mean, my real Father?" I asked, with my voice cracking. "Isn't Big Raymond my real Father? You mean I'm just like Dolores? I have a different Father from everyone else?" I began to feel lost and out of place.

We pulled back into the parking lot at the DeSoto Bass Courts. She began looking for a parking space and gestured with her finger for me to stop asking questions. I turned my body away from her in protest. When she parked I jumped out of the car and not waiting for her rushed into the apartment. She followed closely behind me.

Mama closed the door and motioned for me to have a seat at the kitchen table. We were the only two in the apartment. She sat right across from me and folded her hands on the kitchen table. She had a look on her face that I had never seen before and it made me nervous. What exactly did she have to tell me that caused such concern on her face?

"Before watching you today, Loren, I still looked upon you as my little baby boy," she started in. "I asked you how old you were because your behavior today seemed much beyond your age and I figured that it was time." She hesitated and stared at me. I assumed she was allowing me time to take it all in. "I knew someday I would have to tell you the truth, but I didn't know it would come so quickly. The funeral also made me aware of my life. If something were to happen to me then you would never have known the real truth about your father and that wouldn't be fair to you."

"What real truth, Mama? What are you talking about?" I was getting anxious and wanted her to cut through all this other talk and get right to the facts.

"After the divorce from Big Raymond times were hard," she said. Her words were hard and tough. "I had to do domestic work just to try and make ends meet. I wasn't getting any help from Dolores' father or from Big Raymond. Taking care of your brothers and sisters fell on my shoulders. I met a real good man who helped us out. He put food on our table and paid some of my bills." Again she paused, looked up at the ceiling and then back at me. "I felt obligated to give him what would make him happy since he was helping me and my kids. In the process I got pregnant with you."

"Where is he now?" I asked not really wanting to hear the rest.

"Let me finish telling you the whole truth." Mama got up and poured herself a glass of water. She sat back down and continued. "I figured the people I worked for would fire me if they knew I was pregnant and not married. So, I didn't eat well to try and stay thin and hide my condition. I never ate the foods I should have for your nourishment. You were born in the middle of one of the worst blizzards in Dayton history. Because of your father's insistence I was able to have you at Miami Valley Hospital. But you were extremely underweight and terribly undernourished. At eighteen months old you suffered from a terrible vitamin D deficiency (Rickets) that caused you to have knocked knees and missing teeth. With the help of welfare, I was able to get you braces to straighten your legs and special care.

"Where is he now?" I insisted.

"Loren, your Father is dead. He was killed in a car accident."

"So I never saw my Father and now I never will?"

"Yes you did meet him. You remember the man who used to come by here and would give you a dollar every time he left."

"Yeah." I said vaguely recalling a man who would come by and sometimes bring groceries and would always give me some money.

"That was your Daddy," she said. "When he died, they notified me that he had left you part of his insurance money but I refused it. You are an Alves and that money was not going to set you apart from the other children, so I turned it down."

It made me feel good knowing that my real Father had left me part of his inheritance. Big Raymond did nothing for any of us. It didn't make me feel good knowing that Mama had turned the money down but I understood why.

Mama stood up from the table. "Loren, you are man enough now to handle the truth. Don't let it stop you from believing that you can accomplish anything you put your mind to. Just like you made it through Levi's funeral and you changed that flat tire for your Mama, you can do anything. You can handle what I just told you and not allow it to stop you from becoming the man I know you will be." She turned and walked away.

I followed her every move until she finally disappeared up the stairs and out of sight. Her final words resonated with me. At twelve years old I was mature enough to handle the death of my father who once in a while stopped by our apartment and dropped off some money for Mama and was now dead. That was my unofficial welcome to the projects and to poverty.

As time passed, Mama had been right all along. I handled all those issues well. I accepted the challenge to overcome the obstacles placed in my way. The ill health, death of Levi, and never knowing my real father would not stop me. In the eighth grade I advanced to the A-classroom. In fact, I did so well I was qualified to apply for admission to Patterson Cooperative Vocational High School, comparable to a magnet school today. I finished the ninth grade at Paul Laurence Dunbar High School and then entered Patterson in the tenth grade. I pursued three years of auto mechanics and was fortunate to land a job at Delco Moraine, a division of General Motors during my junior year of high school. The cooperative partnership the school district had with Delco allowed us to work for two weeks and then attend school the other two weeks. This was a year-round program.

Having graduated Top Senior Mechanic, I was offered a full time job with the Vehicle Test Laboratory Department at Delco Moraine in the summer of 1969. At eighteen I was convinced I had found the career and job for the rest of my life. But when Delco began to lay off workers, I knew that would be the end for me since I was the employee with the least amount of seniority. Although I didn't get laid off, that incident made me understand and realize the importance of an education. What looked tempting at eighteen may not be as inviting and might not be available at age forty. I needed more security and began to look around for other opportunities.

God has a mysterious way of living up to his promises to us. All I could think of then was what Mama would say to me all the time, "and this too shall come to pass." I was in the right place at the right time when my neighbor, Phyllis Dillon, heard from my brother, Donald, that I was interested in dentistry. She looked me straight in the eyes and said, "You can pursue the answer to your missing teeth if you want to know it bad enough get busy and serious.

I was nineteen and afraid to give up a great job with General Motors but certainly was influenced by her challenge. Mrs. Dillon invited me out to her job at Wright-Patterson Air Force Base Oral Maxillofacial Prosthodontics' Dental Department to get a taste of the workplace. I was totally awe struck and needless to say blown away with what I learned about the science of missing teeth and the opportunity for a career in dentistry.

Feeling the need to get busy and serious about my future, I enrolled in Sinclair Community College in Dayton, Ohio. On a tip from my brother Donald I enrolled at Bowling Green State University in the fall of 1970. During the two years I spent there I became a dormitory resident advisor. After that, I then transferred to Central State University in Wilberforce, Ohio. That summer I also married my high school sweetheart, Phyllis Arnold. In 1975 I graduated from Central State with honors. I was now married, a college graduate, but definitely wanted to continue my education.

Because of my missing teeth, my dream had always been to become a dentist. So when I received the opportunity to enroll in an eight-week summer program at MeHarry Medical School in Nashville, Tenn. I didn't hesitate. This was an opportunity of a lifetime! I would be assured a seat in their fall dental school class if I finished among the top five in the summer program. When I was into my sixth week of the program, Phyllis called me from our home in Dayton and told me that Washington University in St. Louis, Mo., assured me a place in their fall dental school class as well. I jumped at the opportunity. MeHarry still hadn't offered me a place in their class. As a firm believer in the saying, "A bird in the hand is worth two in the bush," I dropped out of the eight-week program at Meharry. I hurried back to Dayton to pack up my belongings. Phyllis and I headed straight to St. Louis where we spent the next four years. I finally graduated and passed the dental examination. Following dental school I was commissioned as a Captain in the United States Dental Corps and served my country for twenty-one-and-a-half years. I retired as a full Colonel with a specialty in pediatric dentistry and now serve my Eastside minority community, currently as the first and only Board Certified Black Pediatric Dentist in San Antonio, Texas.

There were many obstacles I confronted growing up in the projects in Dayton, Ohio. I lost my best friend at twelve years old and struggled throughout childhood without my biological father, but I made it. It wasn't easy, but no one is promised an easy life. Some are born with privilege and others, like me and many of my fellow young Black men in the real world, are not. I refused to allow my circumstances to stop me. To all you young men out there, do not let anything prevent you from fighting for your dreams. As the old song goes, "You can make it if you try." I did and so can you.

Even now, many years later, I am eternally grateful for that time in life that afforded me the opportunity to mature right before my mother's eyes. I am especially grateful to my brother, Donald, for referring me to his Vietnam War friend at Bowling Green University in 1970, where I learned how qualified and ambitious, but poor young men and women could get into college. I will always remember my neighbor, Mrs. Phyllis Dillon, who challenged me to "get busy and serious" about my goal to become a dentist.

And finally, I am unequivocally thankful to my wife Phyllis for taking the call from Washington University School of Dental Medicine at a time when I was away from home, and getting the message to me, which ultimately led to my career as a dentist.

I Have Overcome

Alexis Williams

All I can remember of my childhood is pain and suffering. I don't have memories filled with love from my family. Instead, I only envision the pain inflicted on me at a very early age, which led me down a path of destruction. I grew up in a single parent home. My mother had her first child when she was fourteen years old growing up in Detroit, Mich. By the time she was twenty-one she had four girls and one boy, all living in the inner city with no father in our lives. We moved from Detroit to San Antonio, Tx. when I was four. And my nightmare began when I was nine years old. It was a nightmare no young child should have to endure.

That Friday in the spring of 2001 began like any other day, but would end in a nightmare. After school my two cousins and I hurried over to Aunt Marie's house. I ran through the front door, threw my backpack off, and headed for the backyard. My cousins and I played so much that time flew past like ice cream melting on a hot day. Just as it began to get dark we went back into the house, settled on the couch and began to watch cartoons on television. My Uncle Edward was stretched out on the other couch on the far side of the room. We could hear him snoring. It was early evening and we knew he was already drunk.

After about an hour of watching television, Aunt Marie came out of her bedroom and stood at the entrance to the living room.

"All right, kids, time for bed," she said and pointed her finger toward the bedroom.

My cousins bounced off the couch and hurried into the bedroom. For some reason I decided not to go to bed but instead remained sitting there. Once my cousins got up and headed towards their room, I stretched out, propped my head up on the armrest and continued watching cartoons. I could still hear Uncle Edward snoring. Aunt Marie disappeared back into her bedroom so there were only the two of us in the living room.

About a half hour later my eyes got heavy and I drifted off to sleep. I don't know how long I had been sleeping but I was awakened as I felt and smelled smoke in my face. I opened my eyes and was startled to see Uncle Edward standing above me with a stare on his face that frightened me. He put his fingers up to his mouth like my teacher would do when we were being too loud in the library. Not knowing what to do, I sat up, and he plopped down next to me.

I tried to move away but he grabbed my arm with one hand and began to stroke it with his free hand. His hands felt heavy and rough, and every time his palms cuffed my shoulders he squeezed them.

Filled with fear, I began to cry. I wanted him to stop. He finally got up and I prayed that he would go away. I closed my eyes tightly trying to wipe this all away by not looking at him. But I could hear his belt buckle hit the floor. I opened my eyes and he began to undress.

"Oh, God," I gasped. It wasn't over.

He came closer and stood over me with parts of his body exposed.

"Don't! Please leave me alone," I cried out. I pulled the covers tightly against my body. I even pulled them up over my head.

I felt the covers being pulled away from me and then my spandex shorts were lifted from the front. I began to shake all over. My fear was so strong I thought I would faint. He began to stroke my exposed body and it felt terrible. A man had never touched me before. I was so scared I felt chills throughout my body. He hovered over me and finally dropped his body down on top of mine practically smothering me. I could hardly breath. I felt like a mat under the weight of his body pressed against mine. I didn't know how to defend myself. I just lay there, unable to move or to cry. I held both arms, with balled fists, in front of my body. He grabbed both my arms and forced my hands open. He tried to force me to rub him in certain places, but I refused. Fear had totally engulfed me and I knew I would die. The pain was excruciating, and his sweaty face against mine with his alcoholic breath made me sick. I wanted to vomit. But I couldn't do a thing because my body was paralyzed.

After he finished I felt numb all over. He slid off me, grabbed his clothes and headed for his bedroom. But before he left, he again placed his fingers to his lips as an indication that I should keep this quiet. I could not contain the tears as they flowed freely down my face. I feared what would happen next. Would he decide to come back and do the same thing all over again? Or would he come back out there and hurt me to make sure I didn't tell anyone what happened? I felt cold and began to shiver. The darkness seemed darker than usual. I didn't dare move and I couldn't sleep. I tossed from one side to the other always looking at that door for fear he would walk back out. With every little sound I jumped straight up. I imagined he was back on the couch across from me, and any minute would get up and attack me again. I needed my mother, but I was afraid to get up and dial her number to come get me. The night took forever to end, and I felt some relief when the sunrays crept through the cracks in the blinds.

The house was quiet as everybody still slept in their rooms. I had to get out of there before he got up and I would have to face him. I finally mustered up enough strength and courage to get off the couch. I rushed over to the phone sitting on the end table across the room. I looked back at his door fearful that it would swing open any minute and he would attack me again. I dialed my mother's number. Every number I pressed sounded like a car's horn as it echoed throughout the phone.

Suddenly, my aunt's door slowly opened. My eyes widened in fear. They were riveted on that door waiting to see who opened it. I put the phone down and frantically ran back to the couch. My heartbeat sped up as I watched my aunt's cat run out of her room and into the kitchen. I took a deep breath and headed back to the telephone. I dialed mother's number a second time and listened as it rang. She had to pick up. This is one time I didn't want to hear the answering machine. She had to come and get me before this animal of a man could attack me for a second time.

Again, my heartbeat quickened as my mother's voice began to flow on the answering machine.

"I'm sorry I can't come to the phone right now. Please leave a message."

Fear and disbelief shot through my body. She hadn't answered and I needed her. "Mama come and get me," I said in a whisper. I managed not to cry. "I wanna go home." I placed the phone back down, crept back over to the couch and sat there with my legs crossed tightly staring at the wall.

It seemed like I sat there for an eternity with all kinds of frightening thoughts rushing through my head. Was I a terrible person because my own uncle had violated me? Was it my fault since I didn't go to bed when Aunt Marie told me to? Did God hate me? Would boys never want to talk to me?

Finally Mama came through the front door and she immediately knew something was wrong with me.

"What's the matter?" she asked

I started crying. "Nothing, Mama, I just wanna' go home."

"Where's your Aunt Marie?" She looked around in confusion.

"They're all still sleep." I answered meekly.

"Let me wake her up and let her know we're gone." She headed towards my aunt's bedroom door.

"No!" I shouted.

"What's wrong with you, girl?" She stopped dead in her tracks.

"Nothing, Mama. Can we just go home? Don't wake anybody."

A frown crossed Mama's forehead. She stood there for a couple seconds staring at me. She then turned and started for the door.

"Okay, then let's go," she scowled. "But I'm sure going to call your Aunt Marie later this morning and find out what happened. Why were you the only one up and nobody else was? Something strange is going on." She finished and we walked outside.

We both got in the car and she drove off. I wanted to hurry up and get home so I could hide in my bedroom. On the drive home the usual scenery that would have normally excited me, like the sky, trees, and flowers looked different. Nature's beauty that once used to catch my eye now looked dull and unattractive.

We pulled in the driveway at our house and I jumped out of the car and ran straight to my bedroom, slamming the door closed behind me. Feelings of an intense sense of guilt overtook me. I crawled into my bed and pulled the covers over my head. I mourned for what happened to me. I knew that the assault would change my life forever. Suddenly, I became angry with myself. Why hadn't I told my mother right away what happened to me?

And how could I possibly tell anyone that my uncle had raped me?

Since the age of seven I always loved to write. I had pages and pages of writings about my feelings. When I was depressed, when I hated the world, and when I felt unhappy, I wrote. It was my therapy. Writing made everything all right. With that in mind, I jumped out of the bed, grabbed some paper along with my pencil and began to write what happened. I wrote two identical accounts of the rape and addressed one to my favorite teacher, Ms. Marie, and the other to my physical education teacher, Mr. Welch. Convinced this was the right approach to handle my crisis, I climbed back in bed and would stay there until Monday morning when it was time to go to school.

The rest of the weekend, Mama never asked what happened and left me alone in my room. I only came out to eat and use the bathroom. Sunday flew by fast and then Monday morning came and it was time for school. I climbed out of bed dressing in pants and a shirt. I pledged to never wear a dress again. I would never let anyone see my legs or my developing body. It was the reason I was abused and to prevent it from ever happening again I wouldn't expose any of my body ever again. I was dragging that morning as I thought about the day ahead of me. I clung tightly to my two letters.

I arrived at school just before the tardy bell rang. As I walked into my first class all the kids looked at me like they knew I had something to hide. I lowered my head and sat at my desk. The bell sounded signaling the beginning of class. Ms. Marie strolled into the room and took her place behind the desk in front of the class.

"Get into your groups," Ms. Marie said.

I raised my hand.

"Yes Alexis, come up front," she said.

Trying to keep my balance and not fall over from nervousness, I hurried up to her desk, placed the letter in front of her, and walked back to my seat. It wasn't unusual that I gave her a note to start her day. I did it all the time, but this was different and I am sure she noticed my unusual demeanor. I watched from my desk as she read my letter. She smiled as she opened it, probably assuming that it would be another positive and sweet message from me to her. But her smile disappeared as she read the contents. A solemn expression came over her face. I began to cry. I could tell she wanted to as well because her nose had turned red.

The bell ending class sounded off like a fire truck siren. I let everyone get up and leave class. I didn't want them to see me crying. Finally, I got up and walked slowly out of the classroom.

"Alexis, wait a minute," Ms. Marie said.

I turned around and slowly walked toward her. My emotions were now out of control. I didn't know how to feel. I started crying again.

"Don't cry, honey," she said softly and reassuringly. Her warmth toward me made the tears continue to flow. "I will handle this for you. You just go on to your next class and it will be all right."

The warmth in her voice gave me the courage I needed to make it to my next class.

That class was physical education, and it was the fun class for the day. When I walked into the gym I handed Mr. Welch the other letter and hurried to my assigned seat. He stared at the paper and then stuffed it into his pocket. Before he could say anything to the class, the intercom came on.

"Coach, can you have Alexis Williams please come down to the nurse's office?" the female voice carried throughout the gym.

Mr. Welch looked at me, and before he said anything I got up and walked out of the gym. As I hurried down the hallway I felt relieved and afraid. I was relieved because I knew the only reason I would be called to the nurse's station was because Ms. Marie shared my letter with the principal. I was afraid because everyone now knew that I was involved in something bad, and I figured they might blame me. Often times Mama would blame me for things I didn't do. They would probably do the same.

As I walked into the nurse's office, Mama and her boyfriend were the first two I saw. The nurse took me by the hand and led me into a private room. She asked me to tell what had happened. I didn't understand why I had to do that? It was all in the letter I wrote to Ms. Marie. But I managed to recall for her, every detail of what my uncle did to me.

"Get this poor child to Methodist Hospital quick," the nurse said. She handed my mother some papers. "Doctors and nurses will be waiting for you there."

We rushed out of the school building and into Mama's boyfriend's car. He took off speeding out of the parking lot and onto the main street. I curled up in the corner of the car with my body resting against the door. My head was bowed and I felt drained.

"Is there anyplace you want to go that would make you feel better?" Mama asked looking back at me against the door.

"McDonald's," I answered in a timid and low voice.

Mama smiled and James made a quick left turn and headed to the McDonald's only three blocks away. He pulled into the driveway and headed to the drive-up window.

"What do you want baby?" Mama asked.

"Big Mac and a coke."

She ordered my food and James pulled up to the window. They grabbed the hamburger and coke and handed them back to me.

I took one bite and felt sick. I wanted to throw-up. I laid the Big Mac, still wrapped, on the seat and held the drink in my hand. I drifted off to sleep but did not spill the drink. I must have dozed off for a good fifteen minutes and was jolted back awake when the car came to an abrupt stop.

"Where are we?" I asked still clinging to the coke. I stared up at the giant building in front of me and again fear took over. I didn't want to go in there.

"The hospital, baby," Mama said. "We have to see if anything is wrong with your body." She sounded convincing and I felt relieved.

We walked through the double doors and two policemen, two doctors, and a nurse greeted us.

"You must be Alexis?" one of the doctors asked as we approached them.

I nodded and the nurse took my hand. She guided me into a small room with white walls, a thin bed, and a table with shiny metal objects on it. There were a number of chairs and my mother took one. James was not allowed to go back with us.

The nurse lifted me on to the bed with my legs hanging over.

"Are you comfortable enough to put a gown on for us?" the doctor asked.

215

"No!" I blurted out. The thought of my bare body being exposed and examined frightened me. I clinched my clothes tight against my body.

My mother got up and walked over to the bed. She took my hand.

"If you put the gown on we can get out of the hospital faster." She knew how to persuade me to do things I did not want to do.

Mama took my clinched fists, released them and loosened my clothes. I changed into the gown.

"I need you to lay on your side facing me," the doctor said.

I shifted my body to the left side. The bed was cold and I just wanted to get up and run out of there.

"I'm going to examine your lower body," the doctor said as she separated my legs. She began to press and pull my inner thighs.

I clamped my legs together. "That really hurts." My voice was weary and tired.

The doctor pulled out a small device and again pried my legs open.

"What is that?" I asked.

"It's a tiny camera, the size of an ant," she said as she hooked it onto a long tube-like stick. "What I'm going to do is examine the inside of your body. The camera can see places where there might be damage that my eye cannot see."

As she inserted the instrument into my private area, my face tightened and I began to cry. "It's hurting me," I shouted.

"It's okay, honey," the doctor whispered. "It'll all be over in a couple minutes."

She finally pulled the small device out of my body. I put my clothes back on and ran over to Mama.

We walked back out into the waiting area. The doctor rushed over to the two policemen and said something to them. I couldn't hear them talking but whatever she told them, they hurried out of the hospital. She walked back over to us.

"She has internal tearing along the walls of her private area," she said. "I can tell something happened to her, but to make sure I will contact you when the results are in."

"Thank you, doctor," Mama said. She took my hand and we

walked back into the foyer and out of the hospital.

Later that day we received word that Uncle Edward had been arrested and was in jail. The court also notified Mama that his trial for molestation of a juvenile would begin that following Monday. This ordeal was tearing our family apart. My brother wanted to get a gun and kill Uncle Edward. Mama and Aunt Marie had a verbal fight over the incident. Aunt Marie claimed it never happened. Mama told her that she would make sure he went to prison. And the fight continued for the entire week before the trial.

Mama was able to convince the principal at my school that it would be best that I not return until after the trial. She arranged to get all my homework for the next week and helped me with it at home. The rest of the week dragged on forever. I stayed in my room most of the time. I was depressed because I began to feel I was to blame for our family falling apart. If I had just kept my mouth shut and said nothing then none of this would be happening. I wished it would all go away. But I knew it couldn't. We had to see this through. No matter how difficult it might be for me in court, I had to make sure my uncle didn't get away with his vicious act. He stole my innocence and he had to pay. By Sunday night I was a nervous wreck. I wondered what would happen in court and would I have to see my uncle, a person I really didn't ever want to see again in life?

"Get up, Lexi Pooh, it's time to go to court," Mama said as she walked into my room.

I wasn't ready for the day to start. I really wanted to pull the covers up over my head and just go back to sleep. In fact, at that point in my life, I wanted to sleep forever. But Mama went over to my closet and chose the clothes for me to wear.

"A dress!" I shrieked. I threw it under my bed along with the sparkly shoes she had laid out for me. I couldn't believe she picked that hideous dress. My feeling about girly clothes was changed forever. I rummaged through my closet and found my favorite pair of jeans and my football jersey.

"You're not going to wear that, are you?" Mama asked.

"Yes, Mama, all I want is pants and a shirt." I was still upset that she would suggest I wear a dress.

Mama didn't argue with me or force me to wear a dress. She understood that my rejection with anything female had to do with

217

the incident. She shook her head and walked out of the room.

This time it was just Mama and I. James did not go with us. I sat in the front seat staring out the window as she drove toward the court building.

"Now remember, Alexis, it is important that you tell the truth. Just let the judge know what happened and everything will work out just fine," she preached.

"Yes, Mama," I kept repeating to her. She told me everything would be just fine, but I was not convinced. Everything wasn't fine. Our family had fallen apart and now I was about to send my aunt's husband to prison. That would cause an even greater rift within our family.

We pulled into the parking lot at the courthouse, quickly found a space, and then hurried through the huge wooden doors into the building.

"Right this way, ma'am," the officer said as he guided us through the metal detector.

We then headed into the courtroom filled with many people, some I knew and others were just faces. A very tall man, whom I didn't know, guided me through a small swinging door and to a table.

"Alexis, I am the District Attorney," he said to me in a mellow tone so as not to frighten me.

My tiny body sat at that large table in a big chair and looked up at this woman sitting high above us and dressed all in black. An overwhelming feeling of helplessness took over and I felt intimidated by it all. My body began to shake when they brought my uncle into the room and sat him at a table to the left of me. It was the first time I'd seen him since that frightful night and I just wanted to get out of there. At that point I needed someone but as I looked around I couldn't trust anyone, not even Mama. I was alone. Where was my father who should have been there to protect me? He was only not in court, but where was he when I was attacked? Where was that male figure with the strength to make me feel secure?

"This court is now in session?" a man in a police uniform called out.

The first few witnesses were the nurse from school and the doctor who had examined me. One of the police officers that arrested my uncle also got in the witness chair and talked about the arrest. By that time I was so light headed I didn't hear anything being said.

Finally I heard the district attorney call my name.

"Alexis Williams," he said, "I need you to come up here so we can ask you some questions."

The walk up to the witness chair took forever. I saw Uncle Edward out of the corner of my eye. He frightened me, but Mama and the district attorney told me not to be afraid because he could no longer bother me. With their words echoing in my ear I sat in the chair. The judge turned to look at me.

"You comfortable?" she asked.

"Yes," I said in a low whisper. My head was bowed. I refused to look up because if I did I would see Uncle Edward.

With my head bowed I could still see the District Attorney and Uncle Edward's attorney talking with a lady who I recognized from Child Protective Services. They huddled for about three minutes and then the lady opened the railings and approached me. She had a doll in her hand.

"Are you okay?" she asked

"Yes," again I whispered. Why were all these people asking me if I was comfortable and was I okay? I thought. No, I wasn't comfortable or okay.

The lady held the doll out toward me. "Alexis, I want you to take this doll and point to where on your body you were touched?"

I didn't want to do it. I held my fist tightly clenched next to my body. I could feel my emotions building up and knew any minute I would cry. I kept my head bowed.

"Alexis, honey, you have to do this," the lady coaxed me. "If you don't, we can't continue. Don't you want the man to pay for what he did to you?"

When she said "man" I shot a quick glimpse over at Uncle Edward. He looked so ugly and ominous to me. I just knew he was going to come out of that chair and attack. But Mama and the District Attorney assured me it would be all right. Without raising my head and with my hands shaking, I reached out and took the doll. I placed my finger on the doll's lower parts. It sickened me and I wanted to vomit.

I tried to relax back in the chair. Now that I had done it, I felt it was over. But it wasn't.

"Can you point to the man who did those things?" the lady asked.

I couldn't hold it any longer. The tears flowed freely down my cheeks as I remembered Uncle Edward's fingers in front of his mouth as a warning that I shouldn't holler out. I felt traumatized. Why was this happening and why would they ask me to point him out? Why wasn't he the one that was being questioned, after all I was only nine years old? They placed the responsibility to prove him guilty on my shoulders, and that didn't seem fair to me. I started hyperventilating and momentarily felt paralyzed. I couldn't raise my arm to point him out. I was overwhelmed as my body began to shut down.

I could feel all their eyes were on me as I now cried hysterically. I looked at Mama and she was also crying.

"Please take her down," the judge said. "We will take an hour recess and then see if she is able to continue."

The lady took my hand and helped me down from the witness chair. I ran to the railing. My mother jumped out her seat and met me at the railing, taking my hand. We followed the lady to a small room right outside the courtroom. They called it a children's playroom. Mama sat me in a chair carved into a giraffe's head.

The lady gave me some blocks to play with, and I built a house while she watched. I calmed down as I stacked the blocks on top of one another.

"Do I have to go back in there?" I asked the lady.

"No you don't," she answered.

I took my fist and crashed the house I had built with the blocks. I then laid my head on the table and closed my eyes wishing everything, the incident, and the people would all go away. I must have lain there for a good hour and then another lady woke me, picked me up and carried me out of the room. Mama was waiting right outside. The lady handed me over to Mama and said.

"Time to go home, young lady, all your worries will be gone now."

Holding my hand tightly, Mama and I walked out of the courtroom. I thought it was all over. I thought I would be able to put it all behind me and forget what happened. But it wasn't going to be that easy. I had lost all respect for everyone. Why hadn't Mama done something to this man and where was my father? In fact where was any man that would protect and take care of me? I began to believe that, at nine years old, the burden of my existence rested on my shoulders. I had become a statistic, just a number. I was nothing more than a young girl who had the terrible unfortunate luck to be raped. My first experience with a part of life that should have come much later, came much too early and what should be a beautiful experience was an ugly ordeal. I turned against the world and for the next five years became labeled as a juvenile delinquent.

I did nothing but sleep for the next two days after the trial. We got word back from the court that Uncle Edward was found guilty and given a three-year prison sentence. My Uncle Edward's violation of my innocence and the short sentence of only three years for such a dastardly act set my brother off. I was awakened on Wednesday morning to the sound of loud voices in the kitchen. I heard the rattling of silverware and the slamming of a drawer closed.

"Put down that knife, Jeremy," Mama shouted.

"No, I'm going to kill him," Jeremy said. "They only gave him three years and Alexis is going to have to live with this for the rest of her life. Someone got to act like a man around here."

"Jeremy, if you do something stupid, then this family will have suffered twice. First Alexis being abused, then Edward going to prison, and your cousins losing their father. If you do something to him, then you'll be gone also.

"I don't care, Mama," Jeremy said. "He shouldn't have hurt my sister. I'm the only man around here and someone's got to protect her."

"She'll be all right," Mama said. "She'll recover and get on with growing up."

I ran back and got in my bed. I pulled the covers over my head. How could Mama excuse it so easily? I was hurting badly. But I was so tired I felt like never getting up again. It didn't take me long to drift off to sleep only to be awakened by two loud voices.

"Your husband is a sick man, and he needs to stay locked up for a long time. Only consolation we have is that he'll be labeled as a child abuser for the rest of his life," Mama said.

"You don't really believe Edward raped Alexis do you?" It was my Aunt Marie's voice. "She lied and you know she did. She ain't nothing but a problem child anyway." There was a moment of silence. "Edward told me he was just looking for his lighter he'd left on that couch earlier in the evening."

"A lighter in my daughter's pants," Mama shot back. "Give me a break."

"Well you need to know that Alexis just broke up my family when she sent my husband and my children's father to prison," Aunt Marie said.

"That's where the sick bastard belongs," Mama shouted.

"I'm out of here," Aunt Marie now shouted. "Your daughter is tearing this family apart. She is the one who needs help."

I heard the door slam and then silence. My aunt and mother had fallen out and I felt guilty for that happening. But I hadn't lied. Uncle Edward had raped me and the damage to my body proved I was telling the truth. Why didn't my Aunt Marie believe me? Did she love that man so much she would question something so obvious it was beyond doubt?

Days went by and my aunt, who usually came by our house all the time, didn't call or come over. My cousins didn't come over either and I had no contact with them. Our family had now fallen apart and I blamed myself.

Carrying the burden of responsibility for the break-up of our family weighed heavily on me. I felt fear all the time. I withdrew and didn't want communication with anyone, not even Mama. Returning to school was difficult because I told myself, "If you let your guard down, bad things will happen." My body was developing into that of a teenager and I wanted to hide it from sight. I felt comfortable with my clothes hanging off my body. I walked around with my head down unable to look others in the face because I knew deep inside I couldn't trust anyone. I was unable to let the hurt go, but as long as I kept it in my heart and on my mind, I was only hurting myself.

Trouble arose like a match striking the ground. My outlook on life became increasingly negative and belligerent with each passing day. Small things that happened sent me into a rage. I fought everyone who got in my way or I thought had crossed me, including Mama. Our home was dysfunctional with Mama's drinking and the number of men in and out of her life, all of them looking at me with that Uncle Edward gaze. By age thirteen, my battles with Mama were so vicious that we actually exchanged blows. Fights eventually landed me in a juvenile detention center.

My run-in with the authorities started in 2005 when I entered Roosevelt High School. One of the girls in my class made what I considered a derogatory comment about me and I attacked her. That fight earned me a trip to alternative school. I was fourteen years old at the time. Once in alternative school my problems escalated.

One morning while walking to school with a friend, who also attended alternative school, the boy slipped some prescription drugs into my backpack. During first period, the authorities did a random search and they found the drugs. I didn't tell them my friend put them in my backpack. A cardinal rule among teenagers was that you never told the authorities on each other. I had to take the hit for the drugs alone.

Once again I was in court, but not as a witness or victim. I was the defendant. The judge sentenced me to six months in a Juvenile Justice Academy, which essentially is a prison for young people. Being locked up like a prisoner was an excruciating experience. The girls in that place were tough and in order to survive I had to become a much tougher person than I was before going inside.

After six months I was finally released and put on twelve months probation. The authorities did give me a choice of going back to alternative school or I could attend a charter school if I could find one that would accept me. I did not want to go back to alternative school because they are merely breeding grounds for more trouble. I wanted a new start away from all the negative influences that had invaded my life. I had a couple weeks to get accepted so I put all my energy into researching the possible schools that were available to me. I chose George Gervin School on the east side of San Antonio, close to my neighborhood. I had found a new kind of joy knowing I would now go to a good school named after a great basketball hero who had played for the local pro team, the San Antonio Spurs. Little did I know, but would soon discover, that this great hero's school did not think much of kids like me. I went to the school and did everything they asked of me. I filled out all the necessary paperwork and went home to

223

wait for their answer.

A week later I got it. A big fat NO! They did not want young people who had drug convictions. They didn't give me the opportunity to discuss that conviction with them. If they had I could have explained what happened. But they judged me by the conviction. The George Gervin school administration didn't even take the time to call and interview me in order to determine if I was deserving of an opportunity for a better life. It was obvious that they wanted only what they considered to be good kids. I did not fit into that category so I got that big fat NO and went back to alternative school.

I was now fifteen and convinced I had dug a hole that I would never be able to get out of. Life for me might as well have ended because I had no future. George Gervin School had told me I had no place in their world. Since the "good" world did not want me, the only option was the world of "trouble."

Mama and I had grown increasingly confrontational with each other. We argued all the time and often it came close to blows. When she was inebriated, which was all the time, her boyfriends would look at me in ways that made me uncomfortable. Mama fought with them all the time, but not because they were seductively looking at me. One day she was in a real battle with her boyfriend. He had blackened her eye and left heavy red marks around her neck. I watched in horror as he grabbed her and threw her across the coffee table. She crashed to the floor. He turned and ran out the door. I'd had enough. I ran to my room and packed a few things I owned into an old duffle bag. I hurried back out of my room and raced for the front door.

Mama stepped in my way and started shouting at me.

"Where do you think you're going?"

"I don't want to be here anymore. I'm leaving," I shouted back at her.

"You're not going anywhere. Get back to your room."

"Move Mama. I'm leaving." I tried to get around her but she kept blocking my way. I ran to the patio door, but she beat me there and blocked my exit.

While standing there she opened her cell phone and called the police. "Emergency," she shouted into the phone, "please help me, my daughter has attacked me and I need help." She hesitated for a moment and then continued. "My address is 1630 Copper Road, hurry I need your help."

My efforts to leave were now in vain. I fell back on the couch and waited for the police to arrive.

Within fifteen minutes they knocked at the front door. Mama told them that my probation required that I not leave the house without her permission and I had jumped her and given her the black eye and bruises on her body in an attempt to leave. They believed her lies and the next day I found myself back in Juvenile Detention Center. The charge against me was assault and attempt to violate probation. Once again the courts were not interested in listening to my version of the incident. I did not inflict those bruises or the black eye on my mother, but they believed her.

I stayed in Juvenile Detention for three months and was released, but I received eight more months' probation. This time I did not go back and live with Mama, but moved in with my older sister. Mama didn't object because I really don't think she wanted me back in her home. Somehow she had gotten this crazy idea that all her problems were caused by me. I began to doubt that she really believed I had been raped. She also knew that her sick boyfriend had actually tried to molest me also, but she turned a blind eye to that reality. She had gotten to the point that she preferred to believe I was not telling the truth than accept the truth that her boyfriends were sick perverts.

Again, I was given the choice of going back to alternative school or seeking out a charter school just like before. This time I didn't even bother applying at George Gervin, but did apply and was accepted at Southwest Preparatory School. Living with a sister only two years older than me and her boyfriend only three years older, was not the perfect arrangement, but it was better than Juvenile and living with Mama. I had to try and make the best of a less than perfect situation. It had been six years since the rape, and I felt like I was adjusting well to being back in school and then trouble struck again.

On January 18, 2008, I had made plans to attend the King Holiday march with some friends. I was going to take my younger sister with me. The march started at ten that morning, so she was supposed to meet us at our apartment at nine. She was two hours late and the two of us got into an argument. That argument turned into a fight. During our struggle, I damaged the outside mirror on the passenger's side of a friend's car. She became irate and insisted that I pay her immediately for the damage. I had no money so there was no way I could pay for the damage. The entire day turned out to be a disaster.

That evening, I stopped by Mama's house to explain to her why I had tried to whip my baby sister and how she had fought me. Mama wasn't about to listen to anything I had to say. She went into a tantrum, and started hitting me. About that time, the friend whose car mirror I had damaged showed up at Mama's house and insisted on me paying for the damage. Before I knew what was happening, everything seemed to fall apart and again I found myself in the backseat of a police car.

The charges this time were assault and damage to another person's property. Again, no one cared to hear my side of the story. And again I found myself in Juvenile Detention Center. My sentence was for three months and I served two. I was given six months probation. During those two months in Detention, I was under the supervision of a guard named Noel. She was in her early thirties and took a strong interest in me. She noticed that I loved to write. Throughout all of my ordeals I would always write. When I was raped I wrote about it, when sent to Juvenile the other two times, I wrote about it, and when refused admission to George Gervin School, I wrote about it. This time, while in Juvenile I began to write nonstop. I let Noel read some of my writings and she was surprised at the depth and clarity of my thoughts. One day I told her of the tragic events that I had suffered over the years and she encouraged me to always fight back and never give up. She was the first person to ever appreciate me as a person. I no longer felt like some kind of object to be abused by anyone who felt compelled to do so. Because of Noel, I finally believed that I could be somebody. More than anything in the world, that somebody I wanted to become was a writer. Noel was the first positive female, someone who could serve as a role model for me, that I ever had in my life. She started me on my journey to turn my life around. It only took one additional person to make the change complete. That happened once I got out of Juvenile Detention, finished the semester at Southwest Preparatory, and was finally admitted back into public schools.

First Sergeant Donald Halford, who is in charge of the ROTC program at Sam Houston High School, was the first positive male role model in my life. I was sixteen and every man whom I had dealt with over the years left me practically hating all men. I didn't know my father at all since we left Detroit when I was very young. I believe he was in jail when we left. Mama's male friends, who were all Black, had either made lewd gestures or tried to molest me. So when I first walked into First Sergeant Halford's ROTC class I knew I would confront the same kind of Black man once again. It fills my heart with joy to admit I was wrong.

My second semester at Sam Houston High School, I was assigned to ROTC. I had very little interest in the military, but if it made the counselors at the school happy I agreed to it. First Sergeant Halford was a no-nonsense man who conducted his classes just like we all were in the military. I quickly ascertained that this was a man that could be instrumental in helping me change my life. I became very active and volunteered to carry out specific assignments whenever possible. Sergeant Halford noticed my enthusiasm and began to nurture my growth and development. He instinctively knew I carried a lot of troubled baggage and began to spend time talking with me and giving me encouragement. I needed a great deal of help because I still suffered from low self-esteem. But with Sergeant Halford and Noel I began to gain confidence in myself.

During the spring of 2009, I was chosen to participate in a cross-country bus ride sponsored by an organization called God Parents Youth Organization. Even though it was an all-expense paid trip, I still needed additional clothes and money for myself. Sergeant Halford provided me with the funds that I needed. I went on the trip that started in Los Angeles and visited over thirty cities in thirty days, taking us across the country. We visited a number of Historical Black Colleges and Ivy-League institutions also. We visited Washington, D.C. and went up to New York and Boston, finally making our way back to Los Angeles thirty days later.

As of the writing of this essay, I am planning to graduate from Sam Houston High School within the next month. I had once thought I would join the United States Air Force, but since I was given the opportunity to participate in this anthology, I have decided to attend college. I want to pursue a writing career. I am not sure in what genre, but I do know I want to write. I believe the many encounters, mostly bad but a few good, have prepared me for my mission in life, and that is to continue my writing in order to share with other young people. I want to share with others who have also been abused to let them know that there is hope for them. I want to encourage them to never give up. During those dark days, I never dreamt or could even imagine that I might be given the opportunity to participate in an anthology with such outstanding writers. I know I am blessed and look forward to a future filled with rewarding opportunities that will help eradicate all the negatives that dominated me for the first sixteen years of my life.

Beating the Odds and Winning the Battle

David Floyd

According to statistics I should be either strung out on drugs, in prison, or dead. The so-called experts on human behavior categorize Black men based on their sociological/economical criteria. I was a young Black boy who his entire life battled the pathologies that are destroying the Black communities all over this country. I grew up in the middle of a vice-ridden Black neighborhood. It was the east end of Freeport, Texas, sitting right at the banks of the river where the shrimp boats docked for the summer. After being out to sea for up to three weeks, the shrimpers got off those boats ready to party and party they did, right in my neighborhood. Heavy drinking, prostitution, gambling, and every once in a while, a murder took place all around my brothers, my childhood friends, and me.

My family was not immune from the effects of those vices. For most Black families, survival was their goal and they were determined to do that by any means necessary. Mama understood that struggle and all the games associated with it. We survived because Mama knew how to manipulate around the many pitfalls waiting to swallow up those too weak to fight back. I guess I got my no-quit attitude from Mama. The more obstacles that were placed in my way, the more determined I was to defeat them.

My battles began from the first grade on when it became quite apparent that I could not read. At six-years-old I couldn't understand why I was unable to do what all the other students had no trouble doing, and that was to read passages from a beginner's book. I began to believe something was wrong with me, and my teacher, Mrs. McWilliams, did nothing to dispel my fears. I dreaded eleven o'clock because that was the time we had to read out loud while the rest of the class listened. I sat there hoping that somehow the words would come to me. As the rest of the class took turns, I tried to figure out exactly what I would be called upon to read. Sometimes I asked the little girl sitting next to me to tell me the words with the hope of memorizing and simply reciting them when my turn came around. That always led to a paddling from Mrs. McWilliams because she claimed I badgered the other students. She called me to the front of the room, paddled me, and sent me back to my seat, hurt and embarrassed.

I could associate certain words with objects such as the word dog placed below or next to the picture of a dog. Same for cat, cow, house, and tree. I did just fine with those words, but others that had no association with objects baffled me. It made me angry and frightened at the same time. To add to my consternation, Mrs. McWilliams would actually taunt me.

"Come on, David, we don't have all day," she would scowl. "David, these words are easy. A kindergartener could read this. I believe you are just being lazy."

Her attacks made it much more difficult. I could feel all the other children staring and just waiting for me to mess up so they could laugh. That was the most difficult part of all, the others staring and laughing. If I stuttered or failed to pronounce a word correctly, they laughed and it reverberated like an echo chamber over and over again. The laughter increased the longer I stood there with that book in my hand. Readings, stories, and words seemed deliberately designed to humiliate me. They gave others a reason to look down on me, and that gave me a reason to fight them. After a while, I no longer cared about reading and I only wanted revenge. I wanted to hit and hurt the ones who laughed, and through the power of my fists let them know it was no fun not being able to read.

The real tragedy is that Mrs. McWilliams simply gave up on me. She conveniently placed the blame for my failure on Mama. Many times she would shout, "If your mother or someone in your family would only come to one of the parent meetings, they'd know you can't read." If she had taken the time to contact Mama and tell her of my problem, then that would have been enough to let her know I needed help. But no one did a thing and with each week I became angrier and much more violent, because the other students could read, and I couldn't.

Whippings by the principal of the school and Mrs. McWilliams became practically an everyday occurrence for me throughout that entire year, and I was only six years old. After a while, I don't believe Mrs. McWilliams needed a reason to whip me, she just assumed I did something wrong. I was the target of her wrath. My teacher and I had a confrontational relationship. I no longer cared about my behavior in the classroom. I talked all the time, laughed at the other students, played tricks on Mrs. McWilliams, and sometimes threw a punch or two. The whippings would continue throughout elementary school because my defiance grew with each year that I fell further behind the other students in reading.

By third grade I had really come to hate school because I was such a failure. My teacher, Mrs. Brown, was no different than Mrs. McWilliams in that she was relentless in her demands that I read.

"David, take your time and concentrate on each word," she said.

I would tightly grip the book, stare at the words, but nothing registered.

Her patience was short. "Don't you want to pass third grade?" she scowled.

"Yes ma'am."

"Well read for me."

"Jjjjohhhnnn lllliked tttto." As I stuttered the others laughed. "Leave me alone," I shouted. "Leave me alone." I threw the book on the floor and ran out with tears flowing down my face.

Mrs. Brown caught me in the hall, grabbed my arms, and jerked me all the way to the principal's office.

"Why did you throw your book down and run out of the class?" Mr. Waniack, the principal, asked, even though he knew why. I did it so many times over the years it seemed rather ridiculous for him to ask. Before I would cry and tell him that no matter how hard I tried, the words just wouldn't come out. And when the others laughed I couldn't stand there and let that happen. But he never heard me.

Mr. Waniack did not feel my pain and embarrassment. He didn't understand that I wanted to read the words in that book more than anything else. Or maybe he just didn't care. His response never changed. He'd simply grab his paddle and say.

"Bend over."

I must hold the record for bending over and getting paddled at O. A. Fleming Elementary School. After a while I became immune to the whippings since they happened practically everyday. Mr. Waniack never considered the possibility that something was wrong with their teaching methods. Or possibly, they really didn't try to understand. The teachers at that school humiliated me every day for five years, but still passed me on to the next grade, knowing that I could not read. How could they possibly not know that I wanted to desperately overcome my handicap?

Mama never knew I couldn't read. She assumed, that since I was passed from one grade to the next, all my learning skills were developing as expected. I was too ashamed to tell her and the other kids knew they had better not. So Mama was in the dark. I compensated for my failure with an extremely competitive spirit in other subjects. While in the third grade, we had a math contest. The student who knew their multiplication tables best would win a Baby Ruth candy bar. Mrs. Brown actually tried to convince me not to compete. With reading she badgered me to do something I couldn't; with math she discouraged me from doing something I could do. I won that contest and it was the proudest moment in all my elementary years. I really enjoyed that Baby Ruth.

My three years at Freeport Intermediate School were just as traumatic for me as were the previous years. My reading worsened, my behavior worsened, and the paddling continued. Not only did I get paddled regularly, I also received in-school suspensions. They bused the students at our school to another intermediate school to serve out the suspension. We were housed in a separate room away from all the other students and marched like prisoners to the cafeteria for lunch where we ate at separate tables. We stayed at that school the entire day in a room without windows, and then were bused back to our school. Students at both schools stared at us like we were prisoners. They might as well have put a big X across our foreheads. Our schoolmates viewed us as being different. Just as students scorned me because I couldn't read, here was a second time I faced the same kind of embarrassment.

The teachers at Freeport Intermediate knew I could not read; however, just like at O. A. Fleming, they passed me on to the next grade. It made no sense, but I didn't complain. I sure didn't want to spend any more time there than necessary. My teachers did not want me for another year and the feeling was mutual. It worked best for all of us. What I didn't realize was that, in the long run, I would be the only one to suffer.

David Floyd, the boy who could not comprehend a kindergarten reader, was now in high school. They assigned me to developmental classes, including developmental English. I would be called on in that class to read orally from different books, but I no longer feared my failure because all the other students in the class could not read much better than me and had no right to laugh. The school system had categorized us for the entire student body to recognize as slow learners or non-learners.

I had no illusions about learning to read at all in my life. But somehow I would make it just as I did in the past. It became clear that the school officials did not care if a Black child couldn't read, do math, or any of the subjects you were asked to pass in order to graduate. Many young Blacks in my condition had graduated with no chance of success, and many of them were stuck in prison with no future. That's how I felt at that time in my life. Eventually I would come to realize that my attitude was self-destructive and sometimes used as an excuse not to learn. I was doing exactly what they wanted and that was failing.

Basketball saved me during my three years at Brazosport High. I eventually became one of the star players and the teachers passed me because of that reason. My friends and I also concocted an ironclad scheme for cheating. When we had exams, they would find a way to get me the answers to the test. It worked quite well in all my classes and now as I look back on it, the teachers probably knew all along what was happening. They didn't care; they just wanted to get me out of their class.

At that time I didn't think anything was wrong with cheating. It was survival for me, and without cheating I never would have graduated. Ultimately, it served me well. If I had failed to graduate from high school, my will power to achieve may have been broken and I never would have learned to read. I inevitably would have become one of those statistics assigned to me by society.

When I graduated from Brazosport High School I was literally reading at the second grade level. With hopes of winning a basketball scholarship to San Angelo State University, I took the ACT examination as part of the requirements for admission to the school. I scored a nine on the exam and five points were given to you for just signing your name on the exam. There was no way I could read and comprehend the questions on the exam. This time there was no one to help me. My reading disability had finally caught up with me. All my life I had depended on my basketball skills to compensate for my inadequacies. I knew someday I would be in the National Basketball Association and reading would be inconsequential. But when I received that nine I then realized the consequence of not reading.

I still refused to give up. I recognized and accepted the fact that I would never make it to the NBA. That's when I decided I would never lean on any other crutch for a balance. I would confront the problem and win the battle. I had no idea how I would do that, I just knew I would. It was two wonderful men and one beautiful lady who showed me the way.

I will always be grateful to the late Mr. Maceo Smedley, one of the few Black administrators at Brazosport High School. He helped me identify the college that would be willing to help a young Black man who lacked the ability to compete at the college level, but had all the determination to succeed. I will never forget my meeting with him in his office.

He sat and listened as I explained my intentions to him. Every once in a while he smiled, especially when I expressed my determination not to be stopped by anything or anyone.

"So you want to get a Ph.D. in accounting?" he asked.

"Yes, sir, no doubt I will get a Ph.D., not I want to."

"You can't read, David." He gave me a hard stare. "How you going to go from an eighteen-year-old boy who probably shouldn't have graduated from high school to a Ph.D.?" he continued, not being mean but realistic.

"With great will power and your help," I said. "Please help me pick the right school."

Mr. Smedley presented me with three choices. The first was Texas College in Tyler, Texas, the second Paul Quinn in Dallas, and the third was Huston-Tillotson in Austin Texas, all historical Black Colleges.

I choose Huston-Tillotson and it turned out to be the very best choice I could have made. It was there that I met the other two people responsible for my overcoming my reading disability.

With the exception of fighting and playing basketball my skills were limited. I had very little knowledge of the world outside of Freeport, but as I walked onto the Huston-Tillotson campus in January 1987, failure was not on my mind. I was entering a new world I know very little about; however, I did know I must not fail or my life would, as Langston Hughes poetically put it, "fester like a sore and dry up."

It didn't take long for me to find out just how little I knew about the world beyond Freeport or for that matter how little I knew about something as simple as getting admitted into college. The depths of my naiveté became quite visible as I stood in front of the registrar's desk with my application all filled out.

"Your name," he asked without looking up. A notebook of green bar computer paper loaded with names sat on the table in front of him.

"David Floyd," I said almost in a whisper.

I watched as he leafed through the pages looking for my name. He turned a page and then the next, doing that a couple of times.

"That's interesting," he mumbled. He spent another half-minute studying those pages. "Did you attend Huston-Tillotson last semester?"

"No sir, I didn't."

"So you're a second-semester transfer?"

"What's that mean?"

The registrar stared up at me with a slight frown. "It means you're entering college in the spring semester and not the fall when most students enter."

"Yes sir, I guess so. Is something wrong with that?"

The man continued staring at me now with a frown on his face. "Most students start in the fall, but no, there is nothing wrong with it," he answered. "But there is a problem because I don't have you listed as a registered student." He looked back down at the names on the computer sheet. "When did you send in your application for admission and when did you receive your acceptance letter?"

"I have my application with me and it's all filled out," I said.

"You didn't submit your application for admission earlier?"

"No I didn't. I thought I could do that when I came up here. I do have my approval for financial aid."

"That's only half the procedure, young man. Financial aid means nothing without first being admitted to an institution."

"So what does that mean?" I asked.

"It means you are not admitted to the college and you'll have to wait until the fall semester to be admitted."

My knees weakened under me and I almost fell to the ground. This man had just told me I couldn't attend Huston-Tillotson when classes began in a couple days. I had to get into college right then because there were no other options open to me. I didn't even have enough money to get back to Freeport. I knew no one in Austin and had no place to stay. There was no way I could go back to Freeport. There was nothing there for me but trouble.

"Sir, you have to let me register," I pleaded. "You see I can't go back home. In fact, I don't even have enough money to get back home and no place to stay here."

"There is nothing I can do," he said. "I have no record of you and as far as the school is concerned, you just don't exist. I'm sorry." He sounded sincere. "The only person with the authority to admit you now is the president."

"Where is he?" I asked.

The man pointed to a large white building across the grassy mall. "In that building. When you get inside turn left and you can't miss his office."

What happened next is a wonderful testimony to our Black colleges and the kind of care most teachers and administrators show toward their students. Dr. Joseph T. McMillan Jr. did not have to help me when I showed up in his office. After all, I should have known that my application had to be submitted to the university before the semester began, and most importantly I had to be accepted as a student. Dr. McMillan could have easily taken the attitude that anyone who didn't know the basic procedures for admission had no business going to college. He could have turned his back on me and forced me to give up my dream at that moment to go to college. He didn't do any of those things; instead he took a chance on me. I wasn't the smartest applicant, but he sensed my determination. He invited me to come into his office and in doing so, opened the door to my successful pursuit of a dream.

"How can I help you, young man?" he asked as he removed his glasses and stared across his big oak desk at me.

"I need your permission to register for classes." I felt nervous energy burning through me. I was actually talking with the president of a college. "The man outside at the registrar's desk told me the only way I can get into college is if I see you. He said something about I didn't apply ahead of time and that only you could let me in." I was beginning to feel foolish having to reveal me naiveté again.

"Why didn't you apply?" he asked in a very somber tone.

"Honest, sir, I didn't know I had to. I applied for my financial aid and got approved. That's all I thought I needed." I showed him the financial aid papers. "See, sir, I got them right here."

He took the papers, glanced at them and handed them back to me. We stared at each other and that's when I broke down. Tears flowed freely down my face. Again, my legs buckled and I placed my hand on the edge of the chair in front of the desk to keep from falling.

"Sir, you got to let me in. I can't go back home because there is nothing good for me there." I paused to wipe the tears. "I don't want to end up as just another statistic, either in jail like a lot of my friends or dead."

Dr. McMillan just kept staring at me and I knew he was not touched by my story. Why should he be, and did I think he would care for a boy who didn't have enough sense to get admitted to the school before showing up to register? He must have thought I was some kind of ghetto fool.

Assuming I had failed, I prepared to leave.

"I'm going to admit you on a special provision," Dr. McMillan said. He pulled some papers from inside his desk drawer.

Stunned, I stood there while he filled them out and handed them to me.

"Take these to the registration desk. They'll have to schedule you to take some tests in order to determine what classes you should take. We need to test your skills in reading, writing, and math." He stood up and glared at me. "You said you wanted a new life and a new start. This is your chance. Huston-Tillotson is giving you that opportunity. Don't let the university or me down."

"Thank you, sir," I said in a choked voice. "I'll never let you or the university down. I promise you that." I turned and hurried out of his office.

I meant exactly what I said. There was no way I would disappoint him or the university, for in doing so, I would disappoint myself. I knew the real battle was just beginning, after all, I still couldn't read, and that would surely be reflected in my test scores. It did and I was assigned to remedial reading and writing classes. It was in the remedial reading class that the other individual to whom I owe so much of my success came into my life.

The second week of classes Mrs. Roder, the remedial reading instructor, called on me to read a paragraph from a fourth grade reader.

"Tttttthhhhe bbbbbboy wwwwwho…,"

"That's okay, David," Mrs. Roder stopped me. "We'll come back to you. Relax and realize we are all friends."

But we weren't all friends. My reading level was the very lowest and when I tried to read, just as it happened in elementary and intermediate school, college students laughed. The irony was that they were also in remedial reading class.

After a few weeks of the laughing and teasing, I decided to sit down with Mrs. Roder and discuss the problem. Unlike most of my teachers throughout elementary, intermediate, and high school, Mrs. Roder really cared. She was Black and I believe that was the difference.

"What is it, David?" she asked as I took a seat in her office. "What's bothering you?"

"It's the reading exercises in class," I said.

"I know. It's the laughing and snickering isn't it? I try to control it as best I can, but they're so immature."

"Mrs. Roder, there was a time in my life when I would've fought every one of them laughing. I would've come out swinging, but I've matured beyond that point."

"That's good, David. That makes you a better person." She walked from behind her desk and took a seat next to me. "How do you want to handle this? I don't want you to be uncomfortable in class. You'll never learn to read that way."

"What if you don't call on me in class?"

"David, you have to do the reading exercises. That's the only way you'll learn to read."

"Could I do it privately with you?"

Mrs. Roder sat there silently for a moment, obviously thinking about the situation. I prayed that she would allow me to meet after class and read to her privately. I almost got what I prayed for.

"I tell you what we'll do," she finally said. "Instead of meeting with me after class, you'll meet with Ms. Phillips, my assistant, and read to her. You still must come to class and please do not miss any of your scheduled meetings with her."

I choked up and again tears welled up in my eyes. The faculty at Huston-Tillotson was becoming my best friend.

"Mrs. Roder, that is something you'll never have to worry about," I said. "I will be here on time and ready to learn."

"Good, David. I know you will." She smiled at me as I turned and walked out of her office.

Over the next four years, I never missed a scheduled meeting with Ms. Phillips who became a very special person to me. She was that third person I mentioned earlier responsible for my success.

We began our sessions with a kindergarten reader, *Buttermilk Bill and the Train.* It was the same book my teachers at O.A. Fleming tried to force me to read and I was never successful. But this time the circumstances were different. I felt like I was with a friend and for that reason I knew I would win this battle. I asked Ms. Phillips if we could start all over whenever I stumbled over a word. She agreed and we started over many times. But I finally mastered it, and we moved on to other books at a higher-grade level. Because of Ms. Phillips' incredible patience and her outstanding teaching techniques, my reading skills increased quite rapidly. With each threshold I met my pride grew. Despite a full load of classes, I always found additional time to practice reading. After a while, I would catch the bus and go over to the library at the University of Texas. There, I spent endless hours reading all kinds of books and especially ones dealing with history.

Due to just sheer determination, I graduated with a Bachelors Degree from Huston-Tillotson in three years. Also, because of sheer determination, I was accepted into the Masters of Science program with a major in Accounting at Bentley University in Boston, Mass. Bentley is recognized as one of the top business colleges in the country. David Floyd, who grew up in a dysfunctional community, dysfunctional family, and dysfunctional school system, competed in a graduate program with students from Harvard, Massachusetts

Institute of Technology, and many other elite Ivy League universities and succeeded in getting a Masters Degree.

I am now a full time professor of Accounting at Austin Community College and will receive my Doctorate Degree in the next two years. I have authored an autobiography that chronicles my struggles and determination. There are a million other young Black boys who have experienced the same hardships as me, and hopefully my story will serve as the inspiration they need to never give up. My determination never wavered, and my hope never died. No one could destroy the burning flame that lit my spirit and drove me to succeed. For all the young brothers and sisters who read this and then my autobiography, please remember that in many ways you are the captain of your soul and the master of your fate. Always be encouraged by the words in a song by Sly and the Family Stone and that is, *"You can make it if you try."*

The Forty-Yard Dash in 4.2 Seconds

Anthony Prior

In the pursuit of a dream there are people who defy the odds and push through life's obstacles. My dream was to play professional football, and I refused to allow all the pitfalls, problems, and disappointments that are a part of life's journey, prevent me from accomplishing my goal. When fans watch the athlete perform, they are often mesmerized by the effortless talent, but fail to realize the long hours and years of development it took to get to that point. And that is exactly what it took for me, beginning at the age of eight to achieve my goal.

Ask any football player in the world what question his peers ask him most often and he will tell you, "How fast can you run the forty?" Most of the time athletes will exaggerate their speed. If any player says speed doesn't matter, usually they never possessed any. Over half my life has been based on forty yards, the most important length in considering any athlete's potential in sports. I have one of the fastest times recorded in history for the forty-yard dash, having run it in 4.2 seconds on a consistent basis. The forty yards sprint has motivated and inspired me much of my life. I dedicated my time and all my efforts to achieving and maintaining that speed. I recall training four hours a day, six days a week for five solid months to reach that plateau. Those 4.2 seconds would take me away from family and friends, but that is how we elevate towards greatness. We must be willing to sacrifice for those things we believe are important to our success. Let me assure you that I didn't always have that kind of speed. It took time to develop it once I found out I did have the potential to be a standout runner and football player. I was ready for the long journey to the NFL.

241

As a teenager in high school all I heard my father and brothers talk about when it came to playing football was their speed in the forty-yard dash. My brothers were pretty fast, often racing against each other in the streets of our neighborhood. Since I was the youngest, it was my job to line them up and holler, "Go" when they raced against each other. It usually took several tries to get them off to a fair race because one of them would always jump the gun and take off early. I stood at the finish line, waving my arms frantically as they argued over who won the race. They never took my word for it because the finish was always very close.

I stood in awe of my brothers and never thought I would ever become a fast runner. I struggled with my speed when I first entered high school. I had no technique, but had a strong desire to win. My first year in track was a learning experience. I finished last in the one hundred yard dash. I never wanted my parents to come to any of my track meets. I was finishing last, sometimes third place or fourth, but never first. But I would come home and tell them that I took first place.

After my first track season, the following fall I tried out for the football team. I became so frustrated, I was ready to quit, but for some reason decided to stay the course. That decision changed my entire life because the next day the coach put the team through some speed drills. He explained and demonstrated to us the art of running with higher knees. As I began to implement what he showed us, I immediately experienced a difference in my running ability. My speed and my confidence kicked in like a cowboy riding a hungry bull. After practice I began to have visions of doing great things with my speed, from playing college football to going to the National Football League.

This new speed revelation was somewhat of a phenomenon for me. I was so fast and was able to cover so much ground with every stride just from the lifting of my knees, all I wanted to do was test my speed over and over again. Each time I would sprint it was like discovering something new within myself. This gift and talent was an unstoppable force of inspiration. I had ballistic speed. At that point I really didn't care about playing football; I had my sights on track. I wanted revenge for all those times I had been beaten badly by others on the track team.

When the football season ended, I refused to take time off and began preparing for the upcoming track season. There was a hundred-yard dirt trail on the side of my parent's house. I cleared out all the rocks and debris to make sure there was nothing in my way that could slow me down or cause an injury. My brother Stanley used to watch me and was amazed as he noticed my speed increasing with practically every practice. I ran the forty as a training exercise for football and the one hundred for track. I concentrated on all aspects of the art including the start, acceleration, duration, form, breathing, footing, posture, and confidence. Every day after school I would run up and down that trail until I was too tired to run anymore. I would always run full speed and walk back. I was at the point that I believed I could beat my brother. He was still faster than me, but I was closing in fast like a cheetah on its prey.

One day I hit a gear like none I ever felt. The weather was perfect for running. It was about 102 degrees outside and my brother Stanley and I started off jogging at first. After we reached the starting point we thrust into full speed simultaneously. I felt myself reaching with my knees, and it was effortless. My brother was even amazed. At first I thought he let me win, so I tested his manhood and told him the next time we sprint together I would give him a two-yard head start. The next day when we lined up to race, with him two yards in front, his facial expression said I was a little too ambitious to be challenging him. We began to jog and for some reason his jogging was faster than usual. Before I could say, "hold up,' there were two explosions one after another. I saw my brother's feet and elbows take off in front of me. But his progress seemed to come to a halt as I began to accelerate. With controlled but relaxed anger I saw my knees reaching beyond him, and before I could blink twice I was running alone on a trail leading to something greater than myself.

When track season finally arrived I was running varsity. That same spring, my brother stopped running with me. He proudly admitted that I was faster than him and he wanted me to go all the way to the NFL. "If you have to rely on your speed, ride it all the way to the top," he said. "Anthony, run so fast the coaches will have to make a spot for you." My brother and I never owned a stopwatch. We ran strictly on instinct, technique, and feelings. The first time I was clocked running the forty-yard dash was my junior year during spring football drills. I ran a 4.3 and everyone was saying, "Wow, did you see that?" They asked me to run it again for verification and I proved my speed was legitimate. They loved my form because when I run I loved to look good.

I had gotten so fast and good at football I received a scholarship to Washington State University. The coaches there told me I had a lot of potential, but what they were really telling me was that I was so fast they would take their time with me and see if I could develop into a good player. My problem was, even with my speed, they didn't know where to put me. I didn't catch well enough to play as a receiver and didn't cover well enough to be a corner back. They let me know that without my speed I wouldn't have a scholarship. I began to take the attitude that I would see just how far my speed could take me. At that point in my life, all things revolved around my speed, whether I was studying for a test, on the track, or in bed asleep. I meditated on those forty yards day and night because I knew if I wanted to be great at anything, then I had to master it and get rid of all distractions. I had what I call, "Positive Tunnel Vision."

My speed was the result of what many fail to do and that is prepare themselves as best they can. My purpose was to distinguish myself from everybody else. My determination kept me out of the box of mediocrity. To elevate I understood there must be less talk and more action leading to my objective. My brothers and friends watched me practice and perfect my craft in many different ways, whether lifting weights or running in the rain. I became isolated and alone, as they were not willing to make the same kind of sacrifices I made. When they were going to parties, drinking, staying up all night, I was by myself.

Three weeks before the National Football League scouts were coming to Washington State University to test players in the forty-yard dash and other drills, my roommate decided to throw a party. About ten o'clock that evening, many of the guys on the team were partying and they asked me to relax and just party with them.

"Are you crazy?" I said. "The scouts will be here in a few weeks. I need to train."

"What are you going to do, run the hill outside?" my roommate asked.

"Exactly," I replied.

I took my roommate's truck, and turned on the bright lights so they could illuminate the hill. I walked up to the top and ran down so fast I fell and scarred my knees and elbows. While stretched out on the ground that voice of distraction spoke to me, telling me to quit this nonsense, go into the party, and allow life's alleged pleasures to get in the way of my destiny. I ignored that temptation, got back up, and ran with a passion between anger and inspiration. I could see people going into my apartment, drunk, talking, and laughing essentially about nothing. I enjoyed listening to the music coming from the building while I ran. My brother's words filled my mind, "Let your speed take you where you want to go."

The following few weeks flew by and on March 13, 1991, the NFL scouts witnessed a record-setting time in the forty-yard dash ever recorded at Washington State University. I ran it in 4.21 seconds. The men who were partying that night made their own choices; we all do. However, at that young age I had a vision and my joy at setting the record far exceeded any pleasure I may have experienced at that party.

I did not become a starter on the football team until my senior year when I played free safety. I could not cover that well, but the coaches saw in me, a kid who was not afraid to hit and could run like a deer. I am thankful for my coach, Mike Zimmer, who recognized my ability and gave me a chance to shine. During one game we were playing against the University of Southern California, always a powerhouse in the Pac 12, he put me on kickoff returns. Because of his confidence in me, I was determined to prove that he had made the right decision. I caught the kickoff three yards deep in the end zone and took off. I saw an opening to the left and shifted to high gear. To this date, I cannot recall my feet ever touching the ground I was moving so fast. Before I knew what was happening I had an open field in front of me. I knew at that point I would record the longest kick-off return in Washington State history because no one could catch me. I was also aware that this feat would create an interest in my potential among the NFL scouts. That is all the inspiration I needed to look beyond the present challenges and consciously focus on greatness.

After my senior year, I was invited to the NFL combine in Indianapolis, Ind. It was a dream come true. All I had to do was run the fastest forty and I knew I would have a chance to go to the big show, the NFL. At the combine I did not run the fastest; I ran very average. I felt like a pigeon in the pack with the others. I thought, when it came to the forty, I would be an eagle. Usually I soar alone—there is me and then there is everyone else. But for some odd reason I don't know what happened to me that day. The forty is all I had going for me. I wasn't one of those players who had four great seasons all through college to fall back on. My only stronghold was my speed, and it disappeared that afternoon.

That evening in the hotel lobby I sat with a professional scout named Sutherland. He bought me a coke. At first he asked me if I wanted a beer, and I initially said, "yeah," to a professional scout. I quickly caught my error and said I would take a coke.

He said, "You ran pretty well out there."

Average is what he really meant.

I said, "I'm way faster than that."

"I know," he replied. "I'm coming out to Washington State in a couple weeks to check out your time again."

His words were like magic to my ears. When I returned to school that Monday, I broke up with my girlfriend and started living with friends. I began a relentless regimen of training and couldn't afford any distractions. One fact that most young athletes fail to recognize is that involvement, especially sexual, is one of the greatest distractions they can face, and one of the greatest temptations. I loved and cared dearly for my girlfriend, but quite honestly it was a love I couldn't afford at that time. My concentration was totally on working out the problems I faced in Indianapolis with my speed. The great Nelson Mandela's words were my inspiration; "The glory in living does not lie in never failing, but in rising every time we fail." I had to rise to this perceived failure and nothing would stand in my way.

One morning, about 5:00 am, my roommate heard me getting cleaned up in the bathroom and shouted.

"Man, don't you ever sleep?"

I replied, "I have to train because the NFL scouts will be here next week. Sleeping is a distraction just like sex and drinking. I have to find my 4.2 speed again and I have to do it fast.

He got up, walked, and stood at the entrance to my bedroom. "What will you do if football doesn't work out for you?"

I turned and glared at him with sheer determination in my voice. "It will work out. Greatness is always around the corner, and it depends on whether or not you have enough of what it takes to go and look for it." I paused for a moment to gather my thoughts. "We can always look for the negative things in life. But I have looked for great things and, with that attitude, I will do great things." With those words I hurried out of the apartment and up the hill to work on regaining my speed.

The scouts did return to Washington State University and I did redeem myself by running a 4.26 in the forty. Even though it was a cloudy day, I knew that somewhere behind all those clouds was sunshine. That is how I lived my life. I felt really good about what I did that day; the scouts and Sutherland seemed to be impressed. I was fortunate to have the New York Giants draft me because I ran such a great forty-yard dash that day.

The night I was drafted, I cried and laughed out loud at the same time. Turning my head from side to side my thoughts took me back to the days when it all started, running with my brother on the side of my parent's home. I thought of Stanley who inspired and encouraged me every step of the way. I didn't get a million dollar contract. I wasn't even on ESPN, and there were no major endorsements coming my way, but the reality of setting a goal, putting a dream in motion, and actually watching it come true right in front of me was beyond expression. Along the road of inspiration, there are always those who want to bring you down to mediocrity. There were people who were full of doubt in the beginning and envious of my accomplishments, because I was living my dream. The great long distance runner Roger Bannister said, "The man who can drive himself further, once the effort gets painful, is the man who will win."

I left Washington State and went home to California for a month before leaving for New York. I trained with my brother Stanley for the entire time, running on the side of my parent's house. It was such a special time because it took me back to where the dream started. When I left for New York, I was ready for the new challenge in my life, playing football at the highest level.

On my arrival in New York, all the other rookies talked about their college stats and accolades. While they bragged on past accomplishments, my thoughts were firmly on the next day when we all had to run the forty. That next morning, the rookies had a big workout, doing drills and running the forty. I had tunnel vision. I didn't care how well I did in the other workouts; my specialty was running. Everywhere I have traveled I have always been the fastest. My drills were okay, but I was the very best in the forty and I was not going to give that up. And yes, I wore the crown once again, this time on the east coast.

However, after a long, tough, grueling training camp I was

cut. I was devastated. I figured I was playing pretty darn good, making good plays, hitting hard, but in the end I came up short. I called my parents and then my agent and gave them the bad news. I then started my long drive back to Washington. As I drove across country, I would do a little stretching every time I stopped for gas because my agent told me that I could get called anytime and needed to keep in shape. I stopped at a rest area in North Dakota to do some drills and sprints in the grass. People were looking at me like I was crazy. I didn't care because I was on this journey they call chasing a dream. When you are truly motivated by something, you often look like a fool to other people. I guess that is the cost of greatness. Sometimes you have to look silly, but strangers can't see the passion that takes over when you are in between chasing a dream. Because failure is not an option.

I finally arrived back in Washington and stayed with some friends. I was so excited that night I couldn't sleep. It was snowing and I didn't care. I got up, went outside and marked off forty yards in the snowy night. I started running back and forth. I felt like I was cheating myself because I couldn't go full speed in the snow. Next morning, I went to the gym and spent the entire day running the forty yards. While running I thought of another quote to keep me motivated. It kept going around in my mind. Winston Churchill once said, "Success is going from failure to failure without losing enthusiasm." Even though I had experienced a major setback, I was still motivated and enthused about my prospects for success. When I got back to the apartment, my agent called to tell me that the New York Jets wanted to work me out as soon as possible. I knew this time something good was going to happen, and once again, it would be determined by my performance in the forty-yard dash. I was ready to fly to New York the following morning.

That next morning, I woke up late and the airport was all the way to Spokane, about seventy miles east, an hour and a half drive. My plane was leaving at a quarter to nine and I woke up twenty minutes before eight. I jumped out of bed like a wild animal frightened by the night.

"Oh, my God," I shouted. "I'm going to miss my plane."

I ran to the car with my bag, jumped in my Porsche, and was speeding the entire way. I didn't care; I had to be on that plane. This was my opportunity to show the Jets what I could do. But I missed the plane. I called the Jets coaches and told them there had been a mix-up at the airport. I wasn't about to tell them I overslept. They accepted my explanation and put me on a later flight leaving at ten that morning. When I arrived in New York, the man who picked me up told me what was expected that next morning, eight o'clock wake up and nine o'clock workout.

That night I left the hotel and asked a taxi driver to take me to the Jet's facility. He dropped me off and I jumped the fence about ten o'clock at night. I walked along the turf where I knew I would probably be running the forty-yard dash. I walked every inch of that stretch of turf, closed my eyes, and thought about that dirt trail along the side of mom and dad's house. The Jets facility was close to the hotel so I walked back. I slept that night knowing in my heart this time that I wasn't going home.

The next morning, with the scouts watching on in awe, I ran the forty so fast they didn't bother telling me my time, nor did they ask me to run a second time. One of the scouts excitedly said.

"I'll be right back."

He hustled up a few of the coaches and brought them back over to where I had just run the fastest forty they had ever seen. They put me through a few drills and I signed my first professional contract with the New York Jets that afternoon. At that time in my life, I was leaning on one thing, my speed. There comes a time in life when, for a moment, the things you do make sense, and I was having one of those moments. I thought about forty yards and realized this was a relationship that had no end in sight.

Being a New York Jet was a lifetime fulfillment. It felt great. I was a professional football player, something millions dream about, thousands sacrifice for, and only a few accomplish. It gave me the opportunity to play with one of the men I most admired as a football player. Before I arrived at Washington State University, James Hasty held all of the running and lifting records. I had never met him until I became a Jet. He would eventually help further my career and make me a better football player.

My joy was short lived, because half way through the season I was cut. They told me it was because of a numbers game. I prepared to fly back to Washington and when I arrived my car, which had been parked there for months, had two flat tires. I just laughed it off because sometimes you laugh to keep from crying. When I got home that evening, I started running and after my work out, my agent called and said that the Canadian Football League (CFL) was interested in me. I agreed to fly up there and the next morning I was on a plane to Calgary, Canada. I wasn't very excited about going to Canada because it was not the NFL, just CFL.

I flew into Calgary and was supposed to work out the next day. I had convinced myself that I didn't like the place at all. I didn't like the guys around me and I didn't like the food or the hotel. I had decided that my forty was in a class all by itself, and all I wanted to do was embarrass the other players. I didn't want their times to be even close to mine. Just as I did in New York, that night I went to the stadium and walked every inch of the field where I would be running the next morning. I walked every corner and meditated, reaching back to the dirt trails where it all began, and embraced the moment.

The next morning I ran the fastest forty in the team history and they asked me to sign a contract right then. I said no thanks. The general manager asked why I refused to sign with them and I told him because it was not the NFL. He laughed and said they didn't want me, but I responded that I'd take my chances.

The next day I went back to Washington. I spent the next month complaining as I watched the NFL season come to an end. I told myself over and over that I should be on an NFL team because nobody could run as fast as me. I was still young and had to make darn sure that my aspirations to play in the NFL didn't fade away. I wanted to keep that dream strong and fresh in my mind. I immediately started training for the next year. That same year I watched as the Calgary Stampeders won the Grey Cup Championship, and said, darn, maybe I should have signed that contract.

A few weeks later during the cold winter, I decided to run in a track meet in Cheney, Washington. It was a 50-meter dash and I won it easily. I called the New York Jets and told them. Several weeks later I was back in New York preparing for mini-camp with the team. This time I was determined to regain the respect of the players by running the forty so fast there would be no way they could ignore me. All I concentrated on was that forty-yard dash. The team's strength and conditioning coach asked if I wanted to do some cornerback drills and I told him no. All my energy was focused on the four seconds that would bring me fame, not those football drills. Besides, no one ever got recognition for their skills by doing drills. On the other hand, you get noticed for your speed.

The Forty-Yard Dash in 4.2 Seconds

The night before I was to run the forty I had a sore ankle, but that was not going to slow me down. As usual I took my ten o'clock walk and meditated. The next day, I ran a 4.2 forty and that got everyone's attention. I made the team for the second time and this go round I would be there for four years.

As the years went by I began to develop into a pretty good football player. The Jets had a few coaching changes within those four years, bringing in different personalities, with new philosophies. I managed to weather the storm with each change. However, there are some storms in life, no matter how well you are prepared, those rare slips can eventually turn into a fall. In life there are some things we have no control over and so one spring morning after four years with the Jets, I got a call telling me I had been cut again. I grabbed my running shoes and started sprinting that night with a rage..

A week after returning home, I received a call from the Cincinnati Bengals. They told me they would honor my contract I had with the Jets. I was excited. They sent me a schedule of their mini camps. My excitement grew stronger when I found out at mini camp everyone would be required to run the forty at least two times. I called my brother Stanley and told him.

"Man, I'm going to show that organization who is the king when it comes to running the forty."

I didn't care about football drills; all I could think about were those four seconds that had been so good to me. I began to view the forty as my specialty to sustainability.

I arrived in Cincinnati pumped and ready to go. When I got to the hotel I waited until about ten at night, called a cab and went to the training facilities. As I had done in the past, I walked along the turf reminiscing about where my journey began, the dirt trail on the side of my parent's home. I got in the cab and headed back to the hotel. Perhaps, the driver thought I was a little weird, but when you are on a mission, you do what needs to be done.

Back in the hotel, I smiled confidently at myself in the mirror. I slept well knowing in the morning I again would catch the attention of not only the coaching staff, but also all the media there covering the practice as well. The following morning, I thought if anyone in Cincinnati didn't know who I was, they were going to get to know me in about three and a half hours. And they did. I ran the fastest time in Bengal history. I made the six o'clock news that night and once again those forty yards brought me back to the place I wanted to be. I couldn't wait to get home and tell my friends and family about my success. My enthusiasm was destroyed two days before training was to begin. I received a call from the Bengals' management informing me that I had been cut because of salary cap problems. I was stunned because teams already had their rosters together for training camps. Once again, I found myself left out.

Days passed and I finally got a call from the San Francisco 49ers. The following day I flew to their training camp in Sacramento, Calif. I was a late addition and knew I faced an uphill battle. When I arrived they told me I would be working out the following morning and that the workout would be on grass. That evening I walked along the grass with my eyes closed and thought only of my beginnings and that dirt trail.

The next morning I warmed up and was ready to run. However, they surprised me and told me they were going to put me through some drills and that would be all.

"Don't you want me to run the forty?" I asked.

"No, just drills," the coach said.

Even though they signed me that morning, I was disappointed. I wanted the chance to wear the crown as the fastest man on the team. I wanted to run that forty. In the football world, word spreads fast, and we often make a name for ourselves if we are able to do something outstanding. The 49ers already knew of my speed so they were concerned with my agility and football skills.

I played my rear end off and had a great camp. I made big plays, hit hard, but despite all of that, I came up short and was cut before the regular season began. I drove back home to Riverside, Calif., about a seven-hour drive. I got there about nine in the morning and by noon was at the local high school training again for another shot at running the forty. I trained alone for the next two months.

There were no calls from teams or from my agent; then one day out of the blue, the Denver Broncos called. I was thrilled because at the time they were the hottest team in the NFL. When I arrived in Denver, it was extremely cold, but that didn't matter. Once again I would have the opportunity to wear the crown of the fastest man on another team. I ran that morning on wet grass and I was so fast they had me wait for four hours at their practice facility while they tried to work out a deal. But I came up short once again. They told me that they were not going to release anyone or make any changes at that time. I was crushed. My reliance on my speed had failed me this time. I spent the next day in a state of confusion. But like a warrior, I returned home to California and began believing in those forty yards once again.

The following week the Minnesota Vikings called and asked if I was in shape. Was I ever in shape! They flew me to Minnesota the very next day. When I arrived I was a little tired, but still had enough gas in the tank to feel good about everything. When I arrived at the Viking facility, I was told by a coach, "Head coach Dennis Green doesn't like to wait so be ready to run as soon as he opens those double doors." He pointed to a set of doors in the facility. "You'll have about one minute to get to the starting line and run."

I stared anxiously at those doors and when he opened them, I threw my hands up in the air and said, "Let's do this right now."

I had nothing to fear. "I'm not only good at the forty, I'm great," I declared to everyone within range of my words, "I am speed." At that moment, I transcended into something greater than myself. I ran a sensational forty. They originally wanted me to run two times, but after the first time all they could say was, "Wow, let's do some drills."

I did some drills and that afternoon I signed with the Vikings. That year I played in my first career playoff game. Forty yards had delivered for me once again.

I spent two seasons with the Vikings, and again I was a free agent. That spring I went to the Carolina Panthers for a free agent work out. I blazed in the forty, but they did not sign me. I wasn't disappointed because it was early in the year and I had plenty of time to sign with a team. A week later my agent called and said the Kansas City Chiefs wanted to work me out. I was excited because James Hasty was now playing for them. I called him and told him that I would be working out with the team. He wished me the best and told me he would love to have me as a teammate once again.

I arrived in Kansas City with an old teammate from the Vikings who was also trying out. The personnel director and coach said they wanted to offer me a contract. I called my agent while they were working out a deal. I waited in the hotel thinking about forty yards, not the contract. This time I wanted to get a substantial signing bonus. I believed if I ran an awesome forty the next morning I would get that bonus. I didn't sleep that night and all I could think about were those forty yards. Once again I was placing all my trust in four seconds.

The following morning I ran those forty yards so fast the Kansas City Chiefs gave me a signing bonus that was better than I had imagined. While riding back to the hotel, all I could think about was that I could have run a little faster. There are gifts we all carry around. Some discover their craft and master it, and some die with it, never knowing what ability they possessed. That day I figured I was actually living and mastering my gift. Forty yards once again came up big for me, and before I knew it, I was in training camp.

I was actually having a great training camp, and then I hurt my lower abdominal muscle. I was forced to miss a week of practice. I played average in the last pre-season game and was cut the following morning. I flew home to California and that evening once again was at the local high school training for the forty.

After a month and a half of inactivity, a few of my friends called pretending to be NFL scouts. I got all excited only to find out it was a joke. Shortly after that, the Oakland Raiders called. I thought my friends were again playing a trick on me, but came to find out it was the real thing. Later that evening I was on a plane to Oakland again ready to showcase my speed. However, this time I was somewhat intimidated. The Raiders were known for always having the fastest players in the NFL. We all knew of Davis Love's speed, but then it hit me they hadn't seen speed like mine. When I landed in Oakland, the words of the famous tennis player, Arthur Ashe, struck me. "One important key to success is self-confidence. An important key to self-confidence is preparation." If his words were applicable to any athlete, it was me.

I packed a lot of clothes because I knew I would be staying. I reminded myself that I train for moments like this; it was my time to shine. The following morning when I warmed up, a good sized crowd and a number of players stood there in anticipation of my performance. It was a cold day and the grass was wet, but it didn't slow me down. They timed me and were shocked at my speed. I was put in the category with all the other world-class forty-yard dash sprinters.

The Raiders signed me and by the following Sunday afternoon,

I was playing on the field. I played that 1998 season with the Raiders, but was not signed the following year.

The next call of interest was the San Diego Chargers. They brought me in for a workout in early 1999. I knew my speed would again get me through the initial workout. When I arrived on the field, I noticed that the finish line was very close to a brick wall. I pointed this out to General Manager Bobby Bethard. I asked if we could back up a little because there was not enough room for me to slow down. He smiled and said, "Okay."

As I had done time and time again, I shot out like a canon and ran, some say, the fastest or one of the fastest times in Charger history. Because of my speed, they offered to sign me, but I turned it down. I didn't feel the signing bonus was as large as it should have been. Often when we get good at something, we expect the same commitment from others as we have committed to ourselves. But life does not work that way. I failed to realize I was not being paid to run a forty, but to play football. I ended up not playing for any team that year.

That spring, I hurt my hamstring one morning and had to turn down a work out with the Carolina Panthers after the San Diego Chargers in 1999. I ended up sitting out the whole season of 2000. No phone calls, no opportunity to show my talent. No thrills. Even though I didn't play football that season, I trained as if I was going to get a call at a moment's notice. I had decided to always be prepared so that when the call came I would be ready. I was in shape to run the forty, but no one was calling. I reluctantly concluded that I had run the last leg and put my gear away.

That night I sat outside staring at the millions of twinkling stars and a full bright moon. I was sending my thoughts to God. I was not praying, but listening for the voice of reason and I began to look back over my career and counted the many times I had been rejected. When I reached the number seven, I couldn't believe I was still motivated. I had so much confidence in my speed I overlooked my weaknesses. I stared up at the moon one more time and then went back into the house. I sat on the couch feeling desperate for answers. In desperation I picked up my Bible and randomly searched for a passage that would give me some relief. Would you believe I opened it up and I looked down immediately and found in Proverbs Chapter 24, verse 16. "A righteous person may fall seven times, but he gets up again. However, in a disaster wicked people fall." For some reason those words from the Bible inspired me. I changed my clothes, put on my running shoes and took off outside to do sprints at 10:30 that night. I ran past midnight.

The next week I found out that the pro scouts would be at UCLA so I drove to the campus because they were having timing events. I showed up like a thief in the night with only my running shoes in hand. At first, they weren't going to let me run. Then I found the athletic director of football operations. He must have seen the desperation and hunger in my eyes when I explained to him that I needed to do this. He spoke with the scouts to make sure it was all right for me to run. They agreed and I blew everyone away in the forty and in the overall workout. But still there was no call.

That next week the scouts were at San Diego State. Again, I blazed in the forty. My problem, however, was that I needed to run in front of a general manager of an NFL franchise, and not scouts. My greatest concern that I might not ever be able to play in the NFL again was growing but I wasn't concerned about my ability to run the forty. I knew that covenant was secure because I owned it, and established it long ago. There are certain things we all possess and the forty was my secret weapon, my angel, my expertise, my mastery, and my life.

Several weeks later, the Calgary Stampeders from the Canadian Football Leaague called. Remember them from earlier? They were holding a big workout in Los Angeles, right in my backyard, and no one could outdo me on my own turf. During the warm-up, I glared at the other guys trying out. They didn't stand a chance. I thought about every individual there, and how they all had a dream like I did. We were going to run the forty and they had no chance at all. However, I had now come to a new realization that the forty couldn't knock down doors. It couldn't be used as a sledgehammer to get what I wanted. Yes, I wanted to be back in the NFL but sometimes a person has to let the past go so they can make room in their heart for new adventures and new memories. I was ready for this moment and this time running the forty became a new starting point for my life.

As I ran the forty a strange silence came over me, it was an unexplainable peace that can only come when a person embraces their destiny. After I ran, I spoke with the head coach, Wally

Buono. He was blown away because the coach standing at the finish line said he didn't hear my feet hit the ground. A few days later, I signed a contract to play in the Canadian Football League. I rationalized at that point it shouldn't matter where you do your best, and a bird in the hand beats two in the bush. I packed my bags and headed north to play Canadian football.

I played one season with the British Columbia Lions. I also played with the Calgary Stampeders for two seasons, and helped my team win a Grey Cup championship.

Testing Positive:
What I Did to Have Sex with Her

Chris Cannon

Friday night at about eight-thirty in downtown Detroit was when it always happened. The sounds of the hottest music, the sight of the finest women, and the confidence of knowing twenty-two other young men had my back if anything jumped off that night was reassuring. Although we had each other's back, we also were in a competitive battle that could have caused anyone of us to abandon the friendships if necessary in order to win.

As we prepared that night for our weekly ritual of excitement and testing our ability to win, each boy bragged that he would get the most telephone numbers or end up leaving with the best looking girl. For me, I always went for the very finest girl because it proved that I had the most confidence in my ability to score and, of course, I held that title. Later that night, I knew, even if I didn't get the finest one, somebody was going to get lucky enough to have sex with me. It was scary how confident I felt, knowing I could have sex with someone who I hadn't even met. I used young ladies to build my confidence, enhance street credibility among the brothers, and most important, to prove my manhood.

That one particular night as I began to work my magic, my life changed because I recognized something then that I wasn't aware of before. All of the young ladies I met on the streets of Detroit who were willing to grant me access to their most prized possession had one thing in common: none of them had a relationship with their father. I didn't care about their personal lives, but it came out in general conversation and I viewed it as a great opening to score.

259

When I made this connection with young girls and their fatherless lives, it took my game to a whole new level. I began to seek out girls without active fathers in their lives because they were easier to manipulate than those who did have fathers living with them or taking time to be involved with them. In the process I also recognized something about me and the other brothers hanging out in down town Detroit every weekend: we were all trying to fill some kind of void in our lives to compensate for our fathers not being around.

It soon became clear that every girl willing so easily to have sex with me was only looking to find in me what she never received from her father. And conversely, what I was receiving from them was validation of my manhood. The reality is that we all were trying to establish our identities, find someone to appreciate us, make us feel good, love us, and care for us in a way that made us feel special, even if it was temporary.

The greatest fear young men must confront is the fear of failure and their greatest need is for respect. That is why young men use young girls for competition. We are programmed to believe conquest of the female will gain us that respect because we have conquered the coveted prize that most young women don't realize is their greatest asset. On the other hand, a young girl's greatest need is security and their greatest fear is abandonment. The primary reason why she might have sex is not because the guy is the man like I thought I was, but in most cases her fear of being alone. When I finally understood this, it crushed my ego because I believed I was special, not ever realizing what they were offering me was probably offered to others also.

The reality is girls use sex to get love, and guys use love to get sex. Think about it, a guy might tell a girl anything he thinks she wants to hear just to have sex with her, and she might have sex with him just to get that security she never received from her father. The fear of abandonment in young ladies and the fear of failure in young men cause them to reject truth and rationalize having unhealthy relationships. My action toward females was strictly driven by fear. It wasn't love, respect, or commitment. The fact that my friends were watching what I did is what influenced my behavior because my identity as a man was based on what they thought of me. Honestly, I was so insecure I had to use girls to build my confidence and make me feel good about myself. It wasn't only me, but all those young men standing on the street corner every Friday night in downtown Detroit.

However, what I never took into consideration were the consequences for my actions. What I have since learned about life is that you can do anything you want to get short-term pleasure and fulfillment, but what you can't do is chose the long-term consequences that come with the lifestyle you may chose. When dealing with the consequences, people act like they don't know how it happened. All things have a process that leads up to the outcome. Out of all the crazy things my eyes have witnessed, I have never seen two naked people skipping down the street and the man accidentally slips and falls on top of the woman and gets her pregnant. Besides that, there are some diseases out there that will cause your testicles to swell to the size of grapefruits. I know some people would probably like that, looking down on their stuff saying, "Now that's what I'm talking about; I'm the man, I'm the man, BIG BOYYY." They may be thinking that the fairy God penis delivered them the big one, not realizing they have a sexually transmitted disease.

All right, seriously, I know I don't have to lecture you about disease or pregnancy; you already know about those things. And, no, I am not going to tell you to just use a condom either, because a condom cannot protect you from a female who has gone flip crazy because her emotions were played with and now she's looking to hurt someone for REAL! Condoms also will not solve the issues young men have that make them depend on sex to feel good about themselves and to help cover up their insecurities because their fathers never taught them about being a man. Besides, condoms only cover 1% of your body. Yeah only 1%. A real man relies on self control, not birth control and treats a lady with honor and respect, two words that are foreign when it comes to how we should treat females, but they can become common, starting with you.

I fully understand the beauty and pleasure derived from sex, but without knowing you, I do know that you have dreams and goals that you want to accomplish in life. Never trade what you want most out of life for what you want at the moment. I promise you, it is never worth it. So many young people have future goals and dreams just like you. But they never accomplish them because they rationalize that they'll just have fun for now and come back to their goals later. Right at that moment they are just going to do their thing, never realizing the price they must pay later on in life.

261

It is necessary therefore, to make your expectations greater than your temptations, because your behavior is the true measure of the success you claim you want.

Your desire to become sexually active is natural. However, sex is just like a fire. Let me explain what I mean. In my home, my wife and I have a fireplace. At times we might just sit and talk or have a nice romantic dinner in front of a crackling fire. We even use fire to cook the food we like. If we took that same fire and put it on the carpet in front of the fireplace what do you think would happen? Quite naturally, the carpet would burn. Not only the carpet, but the furniture and possibly the entire house would burn down. Tell me this: Did the fire change? No, the fire did not change. The only thing that changed was where the fire was placed. When the fire was kept in its proper place, it was warm, romantic, and helped to cook our food. But when it was taken out of its boundaries, it was very destructive and could have possibly killed someone. Always remember, boundaries keep good things in and bad things out. Sex is just like that fire. When it is kept in its proper place, it is a great thing, but when it is not, it can be destructive and possibly take someone's life just like that fire. If you have already let the lion out of the cage, no worries. My job is not to judge or look down on you. I want to encourage you to choose and live the best life you can.

I now wish that I could have told my wife that I was man enough to wait to have sex until I married her, but I couldn't because I was weak and tried to live my life for others. I understand now that a wish changes nothing, but a decision changes everything. Make every decision as if a generation is depending on it, because everything you do in life will have a positive or negative impact on someone else's life. Think for a minute about someone who did something that impacted your life and how it affected you. If it was good, I am sure you feel good about that person. If it was bad, I am also sure that both persons regret it, especially if they are aware of how it made you feel. Never put yourself in a situation where you cause someone else pain that you will grow later to regret. If you don't remember anything else, always remember there are two major pains in life, the pain of reward or the pain of regret. With every choice you make, always ask yourself is the risk worth the reward? If you have to think about it for more than a few seconds, the answer is NO.

You may be the kind of young person who claims that this isn't really relevant to your life because you never plan to marry. I totally understand because I felt the same way. During the earlier years of my life I was against marriage and thought it stupid because of what I saw from the people around me. The one married couple I saw on a daily basis didn't even like each other. Usually when I saw them, she was upstairs, he was downstairs. When she was in the kitchen, he was in the garage, and when she was in the living room, he was in the basement. They did everything in their power to stay away from each other. As I watched them evade each other, I surmised that if this is what marriage is like, I don't ever want to get married. I also pledged to always be faithful—to three different girls. Sounds crazy, I know, but when I was in high school I had three girlfriends and I constantly stressed that I wasn't going to be with anyone else outside of the three. Keep in mind they didn't know each other. This was all Chris Cannon trying to make himself feel more like a man in order to hide his insecurities.

As I mentioned earlier, I always went after the best looking girl in the school or neighborhood. My senior year I decided to jet on the three. I had to go after the prettiest young lady in my senior class. She looked so good I would brush my teeth before calling her on the phone. When we got home after being with each other all day at school we would call each other ten minutes after we parted company. Sometimes we wouldn't say anything, just listen to each other breathe into the phone. We used to go out to eat, go to the movies, have sex, and we even went out of town a few times together. She and I dated for two years before she went off to college. I thought I was in love and wanted to spend the rest of my life with her. About three months before she graduated, I didn't eat lunch for two of those months and saved up all my lunch money and bought her an engagement ring just before her graduation night. I remember going to the mall with a few twenties, a whole lot of dollar bills, quarters, nickels, dimes, and, yes, pennies.

The night she graduated, I got down on my knees, grabbed her hand, and asked her to marry me. The question I have for you is did I really love her? Before you answer, keep in mind we spent all of our time together, and we had a lot of sex. Now, I'll ask the question again, do you think I loved her? You would think the answer to that question is obvious because not many people would sacrifice lunch to buy an engagement ring. Right? If you think I loved her, I have to disagree with you. The reason is because I knew she wanted to graduate from college and be a psychologist. Every time we had sex my actions proved that I was more concerned about my sex interest than her best interest, and that is not love. When true love is not understood, people use sex to prove their love for another. The act of sex only lasts as long as it takes to perform, but love lasts a lifetime. Sex is what many people build their relationships on and when it is removed they have absolutely nothing left, which was the mistake I made. Sex should never be used to define a relationship; it should only be used to celebrate the commitment of it. Think about if my girlfriend had gotten pregnant, it would have made it that much more difficult to finish college.

After only three weeks of dating, I told my girlfriend that I loved her almost every day. That experience taught me that communication without demonstration is manipulation. If you are not demonstrating what you are communicating then you are manipulating someone. That is exactly what I did because when I told her that I loved her, what I was really saying is I love me, and I love you for what you can do for me. When you love someone you want what is best for them and you put their needs before your desires. A real man understands that you have to control your desires, not satisfy them, especially at the expense of jeopardizing your own future or the future of someone else's. Just like oil and water do not mix, sex and manhood do not mix either unless marriage is in the center of it. The primary role of manhood is to protect and to provide, and having sex before marriage will only jeopardize your future and go against EVERYTHING that manhood represents.

As young men you must acknowledge that marriage itself is not the problem; it is always the people within it. Let's look at college basketball as an example. The team that won more championship titles than any other in the history of the game is UCLA. There was a time when they were winning championships back to back and other teams didn't want to play them for fear of getting embarrassed. Why were they so successful? Did they always have the best players? The answer is no. What made them successful were the principles they lived by, their discipline, sacrifice, and work ethic. But recently, they had their worse season ever. They lost 19 out of 29 games. That meant every time they won a game, they lost two. What happened that this team once considered the king of the court went from winning almost every game to losing so many? Was it the college? Was it the team? No, it was the players and the coaches that made up the team. Those players and coaches moved away from the morals, values, discipline, and work ethic that built their success. They tried doing things their way instead of following what had worked years before they arrived. Marriage and sex is just like the players on the team both the winners and losers, based on their decision to stay disciplined and follow the proven plan or try to go against what has always worked.

I have experienced the adventure of having sex with multiple females, especially in college, and can tell you from experience that it never brings fulfillment. After sex, I felt empty, lost, scared, depressed, insecure, and even contemplated suicide. That kind of sex never solved my problems or filled the void that was in my life. The insecurity I felt always led me to seek out more sexual partners. With each conquest I would brag to my friends trying to impress them and find manhood, the further it took me into depression, insecurity and confusion. I did not trust or respect the females who were willing participants in my sexual escapades because I knew my confusion and thought they were stupid for being involved with someone like me. I never considered them marriage material. I didn't trust them with money, my secrets, and definitely not my heart. Let me make it quite clear: The problem was not them it was me. I didn't trust myself, and my insecurities caused me to accuse them of being as promiscuous as I was. Without trust, all relationships are worthless, especially when they are built on sex only. When a young man has sex with a young lady, it brings out his insecurities in most cases because he starts to think about her having sex with somebody else. Why? It's because in the back of his mind, he knows that having sex with her is only to satisfy his insecurities and lack of self-control.

A real man understands it is better to have one woman one thousand different ways than one thousand different women. When I graduated from being a grown boy to a grown man, I stopped trying to convince myself that I did not want to get married. There was nothing wrong with marriage; there was something wrong with my thinking. By not getting married, I could reconcile having sex with as many ladies as possible. However, the concentration on sex interfered with concentrating on those things that could provide me with a more productive life. I remember while in college studying for an exam I had to take the very next day. In the middle of my studies, a young lady called me and asked, "Are you busy?" I said no, what's up? To this day, I do not remember her name, but

I can tell you she was not worth the time and money it cost me having to repeat that course because I failed that exam. Distraction and lack of focus will always be the case when sex is taken out of its proper context and the desire for it exceeds the importance of priorities and purpose for one's life. As young people, I want you to make the best possible decisions when you set priorities for your life. I know that you have goals, dreams, and immense gifts to offer future generations that can positively impact them. Believe in yourself! You can do it. I can assure you that people who do not expect anything out of life will jeopardize your future also if given the chance because they don't feel they have anything to lose or anything to offer outside sex. You are different, though, because your talents, skills, and abilities are the solutions to someone's problem and the answer to somebody's question. Believe it or not, you are the model for others to follow. Children younger than you are looking to you right now for direction, and your choices will have a positive or negative influence on their lives.

More than anything I want to advise you to wait and have sex with your wife, because she is going to be the best thing that ever happens in your life, besides the birth of your children. You will be able to accomplish things with her that were never possible without her. We all need someone in our lives to show us how to be better than we know how to be and this is what a wife will do for you. This is why I appreciate my wife so much, because she's brought freshness to my life that was never there before, so that I cannot imagine living without her. She knows my thoughts before I think them, my words before I say them, and my needs before I need them; it's a beautiful thing! I get emotional just thinking about my wife at times, because what we have together cannot be explained; it can only be experienced.

Marriage is the greatest gift ever given two people to express their love for one another. Before I ever had sex with my wife, I knew it would be different because she was different and I had to be different also. When it came to sex with my wife I knew that foreplay for us involved a wedding ring. The man that I needed to be and the man that she desired was what I was practicing to be, long before we connected. Just like you, I was told that practice makes perfect, but that is not true. Do you think all the practice I had with the different females in high school and college prepared me to have a perfect relationship later in life? Of course not. The truth is practice makes permanent. Whatever lifestyle you practice will permanently be your experience.

I knew I wanted better and different so I began to change my lifestyle to meet the desire of my heart, which was for someone to love, honor, and respect me as a man. The reality is most people marry someone who is of equal quality, which is why you want to start now on being the best that you can be for that special young lady later. There is a famous saying, "Give and it shall be given back to you." So you definitely want to give the best to your future wife so you can receive the best in return. With all the mistakes I made I can tell you I was an exception and feel very fortunate to have married my wife. There is no doubt in my mind that if I hadn't changed my lifestyle early to a better model of true manhood, I never would have married my wife. Avoid the same mistakes most men make by thinking they will start making better choices later in life, when the time is NOW. Anyone who disrespects young ladies and risks their future for three minutes of pleasure, or uses women to cover up their insecurities can always continue that lifestyle, but they also have to do one thing, drop the title because they are not men!

Remember this, future generations of young people are depending on you. Here is my last question, I promise. When others from your generation or generations to come are looking for direction and examples on how to respect themselves and how to treat a young lady, or how they should be treated as young ladies, will you test positive? I am not talking about STDs or being someone's baby daddy either. Will you test positive for the identity of manhood that they need to see in YOU?

Making History
with the King Holiday Legislation

Frederick Williams

When Senator Edward Kennedy invited my boss Senator Birch Bayh and me to his office in order to discuss the feasibility of introducing legisltation to make Dr. Martin Luther King Jr.'s birthday a national holiday we immediately recognized the overwhelming task that would be. As I strolled into the Senator's office on the fourth floor of the Russell Senate Building and saw Coretta Scott King and Congressman John Conyers sitting there I knew I was about to be a part of making hsitory. Peter Parham, who was my couterpart on Kennedy's staff, was also there.

As early as 1968, only four months after King's assasination on April 4, Conyers had considered the possibility of designating King's birthday as a national holiday. Since he first floated the idea in Congress he had confronted relentless Southern opposition in the House of Representatives. The Southern coalition still dominated the House side of Congress and they were determined there would never be a holiday named for a Black man or woman. Despite the efforts of the Congressional Black Caucus they still were unable to make any progress so Mrs. King and Conyers decided to ask Kennedy, as Chair of the Judiciary Committee, to introduce the legislation on the Senate side. Since Bayh was the ranking Democrat on the committee he was invited to participate during the initial stages of the process. Knowing my boss quite well, there was no doubt in my mind that he would gladly join in. Even though Bayh was from a very conservative state, which it still is, he could always be counted on to support legislation beneficial to the Black community. Black America credits Kennedy as being their best friend in the United States Senate but Bayh deserves a place in the hearts of Black America also.In the years I worked for him I can not recall one time when he didn't support legislation beneficial to our communities.

As chairman of the committee, Kennedy agreed to introduce the Bayh Bill, S. 25 which was identical to the Conyers measure on the House side, H.R. 15., and hold a two day hearing. That marked the beginning of a four year struggle to get the legislation passed into law. It would also be one of the first times in the history of the United States Senate that two Black American staffers organized a hearing on a major piece of legislation. Working closely with Mrs. King and Conyers, Peter and I identified those leaders who would be invited to testify in support of the legislation. We placed notice of the public hearing in the record and then had to set the time for the opposition to testify.

One of the most important functions of a staffer is to write the floor statement for their boss. This is read into the Congressional Record when the bill is first introduced. The tone of that statement will also dictate the tone of the hearing. It was important that Kennedy and Bayh's statements reflect exactly why Dr. King was deserving of a national holiday in his name. That was a critical strategic consideration and we knew that the statement had to reflect the universal nature of King's work. It could not be limited to civil rights but had to encompass human rights. The speech with the best expression of universal love was that portion of Dr. King's 1963 delivery at the Lincoln Monument that has now become famous as his "I Have a Dream," vision. No one could possibly find fault with the message in those words. I also included King's message in his "Letter from a Birmingham Jail." The "I Have a Dream" talks about a world where color is no longer a factor, but instead God's love rules. The "Letter from a Birmingham Jail" speaks of the importance of justice over laws. Since laws are simply the will of the majority at the expense often of the minority, they must always be subordinate to justice, which is God's laws. I would have loved to include the earlier message in Dr. King's speech at the Lincoln Monument when he scolded America for their failure to live up to its promises to Black America. I would have also been thrilled to include a mention of his 1967 Riverside Church speech when he valiantly spoke out against the Vietnam War. But our goal was to pass the legislation and all other considerations had to take a back seat to that fact.

As we prepared for the hearings we knew the first obstacle we would confront was the tremendous amount of opposition from the Southern Senators both on the Judiciary Committee and within the full body of the Senate. We were not disappointed. After the elected officials who were in support of the legislation testified, they were followed by Senators Strom Thurmond, a Republican from South Carolina and Jesse Helms, also a Republican from North Carolina. They were the two leaders of the opposition within the Senate. The leader on the House side was Congressman Larry McDonald, a Democrat from Georgia. The key opposition outside the Congress was the Liberty Lobby and its spokespersons StanleyRittenhouse and Julia Brown.

After Kennedy and Bayh read their opening statements they were followed by a number of the thirty-seven Senators who had signed onto Bayh's "Letter of Support." At the beginning of the hearing it appeared that we were very close to the fifty-one votes needed to pass the legislation on the Senate side. After a number of the Senators testified in support they were followed by many of the members of the Congressional Black Caucus, to include Conyers. Then many of the Black leaders spoke in favor, to include Mrs. King and Joseph Lowrey, President of the Southern Christian Leadership Conference. Mrs. King made a very passionate plea to the Senate to pass this legislation as a tribute to a man who had sacrificed all his life to help make the United States a better place for all its citizens. She told the Senators that more than any other man, King was committed to achieving the words set out in the Declaration of Independence, and that is all men are created equal with certain inalienable rights to include a pursuit of happiness through liberty. Lowrey's testimony was in support of Mrs.King.

Unfortunately, Mrs. King's words did not convince Thurmond, Helms, McDonald and the entire contingent of congresspeople opposed to the legislation. Thurmond was the first to testify against the bill. He argued from a cost perspective. His assertion was that it would be too expensive to the taxpayers to have another paid holiday for government workers so close after the Christmas and New Year holidays. His compromise was to have a recognition day on every Sunday before January 15, the actual day of King's birth. He argued that since King was a minister and that Blacks were an extemely religious people why not just have a special day for King on that Sunday. Kennedy and Bayh immediately requested a cost benefit analysis from the Congressional Budget Office (CBO). The results of that study indicated that the money spent on that holiday would bring in quite a bit of tax revenue for the government and easily offset the money lost in salaries to the employees. With the CBO figures we were able to dispel Thurmond's claim of the cost and that effectively quieted his opposition.

Jesse Helms and Larry McDonald's opposition was based on their assertion that King was influenced by Communist and may have been a Communist himself. This argument was a "no-brainer" to defeat. We simply asked them to prove that King had ever attended a Communist meeting, had professed any allegiance to the Communist doctrine and to reconcile how an ordained minister could possibly be a Communist, which is an ideology that essentially denies the existence of God. They were unable to support their position.

However, Helms and McDonald did not give up the battle. Instead, they turned to Stanley Rittenhouse, chief lobbyist for Liberty Lobby, and Julia Brown, a Black woman who had been an undercover agent for the Federal Bureau of Investigation in Cleveland, Ohio. My most disgusting experience while listening to their testimony was having to sit by and listen to Brown state that she couldn't say for sure that King was a Communist, but in conducting her undercover investigation, "she knew him to be closely connected with the Communist Party." However, her testimony could not withstand the scrutiny of questioning from Kennedy and Bayh, and fell apart right at its core. Her strongest argument was that Stanley Levinson and Bayard Rustin, both advisors to King at different times, had Communist affiliation. What they implied was guilt by association and it was a dismal failure.

Finally, Helms tried to bring up a morals charge against King. Helms was relentless in his attempt, actually passing around a file to other Senators with alleged information about King. Senator Daniel Patrick Moynihan was sickened by this attempt to attack King's reputation. "The Congress of the United States has never been so sick as it could be today," Moynihan said on the Senate floor, "if few were to pay attention to the filth in this brown binder that has been passed around the chamber today." He then tossed the binder onto the floor and walked away.

Despite the inordinate personal attacks on King and the

tremendous opposition to the legislation (there had never been a bill passed through Congress honoring a civilian with a national hoiday), supporters for the King holiday never gave up. Even though our initial S. 25 was tabled in the Senate it did open the door for debate. We were able to place it on the congressional agenda and facilitate discussion. Once it was before a committee, we only had to listen to the opposition and one by one destroy their arguments against the holiday.

Mrs. King then initiated a massive lobbying effort facilitated by the King Center for Non-violence. The spokesperson for the holiday was Stevie Wonder. He woud lead the rally at the Capitol every year on King's birthday and released the song "Happy Birthday to You," in King's honor. After a four year up and down battle, the legislation finally passed in the House of Representatives by a 338 to 90 vote and in the U. S. Senate by a 78 to 22 vote in 1983. It all got started that day in March when Senators Kennedy and Bayh introduced the idea of a national holiday in the Senate. A great deal of credit must be given to those two champions of causes supported by Black Americans in this country, to include the King legislation.

When Reagan finally signed the bill into law on November 2, 1983, he made the following statement. "Dr. King had awakened something strong and true, a sense that true justice must be color blind and that among Black Americans, their destiny is tied up with our destiny and their freedom is inextricably bound to our freedom; we cannot walk alone." This represented a very strong statement committing our country to a destiny tied toegether from a man who did so much to drive us apart.

However, the most important remarks were uttered by Mrs. King right after Reagan spoke. She summed up the importance of Dr. King to this country stating that, "In his own life's example, he symbolized what was right about America, what was noblest and best, what human beings have pursued since the beginning of history. He loved unconditionally. He was in constant pursuit of truth, and when he discovered it, he embraced it."

The Authentic American Culture

Calvin Thomas

As I look back over my life as a Black man in America, one fact is certain: During all those years of growing up I never paid much attention to the whole notion of culture. I never gave much thought to its meaning or importance in my life. So, with that in mind, let's first define culture so the young people who are now like I once was, can be in the same place I am today. The word culture is often confused with the words myth, folklore, and legend.

A myth is a traditional story of a people or group with unknown origins. It is usually told in support of some phenomenon about the group that is beyond human comprehension and fills its members with wonder and awe. Folklore has sayings like, "Davy Crockett was born on a mountaintop in Tennessee, the greenest state in the land of the free, raised in the woods where he knew every tree, and killed him a bear when he was only three." That George Washington never told a lie is also folklore. Legends are tales such as the exploits of Billy the Kid, Jesse and Frank James, the Younger Brothers, Buffalo Bill, Daniel Boone, and Wyatt Earp. Even though these were real characters, their exploits were exaggerated.

Culture can be viewed as the total development, improvement, and refinement of the intellectual abilities, humanitarian contributions, and all art forms associated with a particular race of people. Their ways of thinking, communicating, acting, their ideas, artistic abilities, and customs are transferred or passed along to succeeding generations and can only be associated with that group of people. Our definition suggests that the most authentic culture in this country is the one that evolves from the African.

We must understand when referring to our history and

culture, as it relates to being the descendants of Africans from the continent of Africa, that our ancestors were a stolen people, taken by force, from the land of their birth, brought to America, and forced into slavery. Slaves weren't allowed to openly practice any of their original culture and/or traditions. They were separated by many degrees, scattered throughout this country for the purpose of completely removing them from any reminders of their African past. They were denied the right to speak their original language, taught to speak a language foreign to them, fed a foreign food, and forced to practice many different forms of Christianity.

Although physically removed from all things remotely close to their original African cultures, the spiritual connection remained intact. Based on their natural spirituality, and the need to survive, they created, cultivated, and established here in America an incredible history and one of the most fascinating rich cultures, unparalleled by any modern civilization known to humanity.

The Black culture came about as a result of the need to survive the tyranny of slavery. Our proud ancestors never accepted slavery and fought against it every opportunity they had. Nat Turner, inspired by a vision from God, led a rebellion that was a warning of events to come; he preceded the Civil War. Harriett Tubman, by anyone's measure, had to be one of the bravest women to ever live. She not only struck out for her own freedom, but went back down into the South thirty-nine times and brought other slaves to the promise land. The last trip she made was to get her mother and father out of bondage.

Referring to that natural spirituality of the Black race, Ms. Tubman, in interviews later in life, claimed that God directed her and he safely protected her from any harm. She tells of the time when she received a vision from the Lord that she should not take her usual route out of the South. She altered her route and safely made it back up into New York. She later found out that a patrol of slave hunters had been lying in wait for her along that original trail.

Sojourner Truth, another strong Black woman, was guided by her faith in God as she spoke out against the evils of slavery. We must also recognize the thousands of brave Black men and women who risked their lives working the many routes of the Underground Railroad that guided escaping slaves to freedom. Frederick Douglass, the greatest spokesman of the Nineteenth

Century could mesmerize a crowd with his riveting stories about the de-humanizing nature of being property of another individual.

Finally, among these early Black heroes, there is a man that you will never read about in the history books and that is David Walker. As young students reading about the American Revolution and those men who spoke out for freedom, you will inevitably be introduced to Patrick Henry. All of us read his fiery speech that ends with his ultimatum to the British, "Give me liberty or give me death." But when in our same history classes did we get the opportunity to read from *David Walker's Appeal,* a much stronger statement about freedom than Henry? In his *Appeal*, Walker argued for the active resistance to slavery. He advocated for Black pride, unity, collective action, and liberation "by any means necessary." Walker concluded his *Appeal* with the bold words of warning:

I speak Americans for your good. We must and shall be free I say, in spite of you. You may do your best to keep us in wretchedness and misery, to enrich you and your children; but God will deliver us from under you. And woe, woe will be to you if we have to obtain our freedom by fighting.

Every child in America should have the opportunity to read of this man and his appeal for freedom, not only for one group of people, but for everyone. Walker was a true American who believed in the basic democratic principles articulated in the Constitution.

Tubman, Douglass, Truth, and Walker expressed their unique abilities as outstanding speakers and writers. Blacks also used the spiritual as a way to relieve their suffering and stay in touch with their spirituality. They created songs to work by, songs that kept them connected with their roots, and songs for happy times. They had songs that were codes loaded with hidden messages. Songs like "Swing Low Sweet Chariot," "Kam ba yah, Come By Here," "Nobody Knows the Trouble I've Seen," "Run Mary Run," "Steal Away to Jesus," "In the Great Getting Up Morning," and many more. These spirituals emanated right out of the slave fields and are as much American as any other form of music. As such, they represent the roots of American culture.

By the turn of the Nineteenth Century, and under harsh Jim Crow Laws, the Black culture rose to one of its highest peaks of survival. A culture born out of slavery was now responsible for creating new art forms and popularizing many genres of music. In spite of being denied the proper education, we also became outstanding entrepreneurs, entertainers, inventors, doctors, lawyers, and teachers.

Our forebears were leading land surveyors, and did work in the scientific fields of astronomy, mathematics, engineering, and electronics. A Black man invented the cotton gin that brought the South an economic boom in cotton. We developed the filament which ignites the light bulb, and developed the mechanical oil lubricating device which extends the life of the perpetual engines. It was a Black man who designed the first three-way traffic device. A Black also invented the air conditioning unit we now enjoy on hot summer days in our homes and cars; and refrigeration that preserves the nutritious value and life of perishable items. A Black scientist developed the method to preserve blood and made the process of transfusions more efficient by separating the red blood cells from the white cells.

George Washington Carver produced over three-hundred products from the peanut, sixty from the pecan, and one hundred-and-seventy five from the sweet potato; extracted blue, purple, and red pigments from the red clay soil in Alabama; and created the process by which stains and shades of textile dyes are extracted from paint. From the short time span of thirty-five years, 1865 to 1900, our ancestors, the ex-slaves, were singularly most responsible for America's emergence onto the global sphere as the most powerful nation on earth.

This talent all sprang out of the Black culture that was not visible because the dominant group kept it marginalized. Instead of allowing us to build the image of the great and magnificent people we were at that time, the dominant culture found it necessary to tear us down. For the first one-hundred years after slavery and during slavery, white America dictated those images and identities of Black Americans and they were all negative. Culture is about image building. All races have built their images based on positive identification. We never had that opportunity until now. For the first time in our history, we can be in total control of portraying our heroes and heroines in a positive image, the way it should always have been done. When I was a young man, I never had the opportunity to read about the many great Black Americans who did so much to make this a great country. Young Black Americans are privileged to have that opportunity, but it is up to them to take advantage of what is before them.

Sports are another field in which Blacks have excelled. The Black athlete's ability and talent, as early as 1889 through the various Negro Leagues, was on display and often drew very large crowds. These athletes increased the level of excellence in all sports, the first being baseball with Jackie Robinson. Once he was called up to play for the Brooklyn Dodgers, the manner in which the game would be played was changed forever. Prior to Jackie, the game stressed only power, but with him it began to shift to base running, bunting, and other aspects of the game. Blacks had the same impact on basketball.

Before we were allowed to play in the National Basketball League (NBA), the game was extremely slow and the winning scores were twenty to seventeen and even eleven to seven. When a team managed to score fifty points, it was the shot heard around the world. The Black player's ability to run faster and jump higher gave rise to the jump shot and dunking. It took the game to a new level of finesse, excitement, and entertainment. In 1951, because of the superior athletic ability of the Black basketball player, the NBA took away the big man and the speed advantage by widening the lane from six feet to twelve feet.

Blacks also excelled in horse racing as early as the nineteenth century. In 1896, Monkey Simon, a Black jockey rode at Clover Bottom Race Track near Nashville, Tenn. In 1870, Ed Brown, another Black jockey, won the fourth running of the Belmont Stakes. On May 17, 1875, in the running of the first Kentucky Derby, fifteen of the seventeen jockeys were Black. Among them was Oliver Lewis, whose winning horse, "Aristides," was trained by a Black trainer, Ansell Williamson. Over the span of twenty-eight years, eleven Black jockeys won fifteen Derbies. Between 1893 and 1898, Willie Simms, won in different years, all three legs of the Triple Crown, the Kentucky Derby, the Preakness, and the Belmont Stakes. Because of their incredible success in the sport of horse racing, Blacks were barred from riding in any of the three major races for seventy-nine years, from 1921 to 2000. However, in 2000, Marlon St. Julian broke the drought by riding in the Kentucky Derby. In that same year, a gentleman named DeWayne Minor became the first Black to ride in the distinguished gentleman's sport of harness racing.

Black Americans have also had a historical presence in rodeo shows. In 1911, fifteen percent of all rodeo cowboys were Black. In that same year, William "Bill" M. Pickett, performed all over the country and in Europe. His rodeo event was called "Bulldogging," also known as steer wrestling. Because of his distinct and unique technique, he was called by two different names, "The Dusky Demon" and the "Bull Dogger." Many have referred to him as the greatest cowboy ever to perform in the bulldogging event. In 1982, another Black cowboy, Charlie Sampson, became the national bull-riding champion.

I could easily write a book highlighting the positive impact of the Black athlete on the world of sports in this country. Blacks have become so dominant in major sports that a 1997 study conducted by Northeastern University Center for Sports in Society found that seventeen percent of Major League baseball players were Black, sixty-seven percent of football players and eighty percent of the NBA's players were Black.

In spite of all the problems that we as Blacks confront on a daily basis, the longer I live the more I appreciate my race, and I am totally mesmerized and incredibly proud of my culture. I make a sincere effort every day to look within myself and search for ways to be deserving of the struggles, sacrifices, and contributions of my ancestors to our culture. My drive for living is to do something of benefit for our youth in honor of those who have gone before us, and have given so much of themselves.

Our culture will always represent change for the good of all humanity. I want every young Black man and woman to experience this fire within my soul about my race and culture. Always remember that we Blacks, although still not considered by the dominant group as full American citizens, are as American as the old proverbial saying "Apple Pie." I titled this paper "The Authentic American Culture" because that is exactly what Black culture is. It is a fact that the majority never wanted to accept the Black race as equals in this country, but did embrace our music, art forms, dress styles, and even the slang. The most blatant theft came in the field of music. The pioneer rhythm and blues singers had their style stolen by whites, who didn't want to use the same name, so they changed it to rock and roll. Elvis Presley readily admitted to stealing dance routines from Chuck Berry. The popular song, "My Babe" was specifically written for Little Walter, but Elvis Presley made millions with his version.

It is also the Black culture that helps to give America genuine humanitarian standards of decency recognized by other countries.

The Authentic American Culture

When President Barack Obama was elected, this country's negatives went down within the international world of public opinion. In fact the world embraced him more than many members of this nation. His first mission, once sworn in as president, was to travel to other countries and renew their trust in us. He has been quite successful in doing that to the chagrin of his enemies.

Over the decades, Black entertainers have served as ambassadors of good will to other countries. Louis Armstrong was considered the ambassador of music, Muddy Waters was well received in London, and Michael Jackson was loved all over the world. In the late 1970's it irked many from the white political structure when the Rev. Jesse Jackson was able to obtain the release of white hostages being held in countries at odds with the United States. Even President Obama was surprised when he received the Nobel Peace Prize. If any one statesman has the ability to bring permanent peace between Israel and the Palestinians, it is Obama.

During the past century, Black athletes always represented America on the diplomatic front. For years the greatest ambassadors of humanitarianism were the Harlem Globetrotters. They traveled all over the world, showcasing their outstanding basketball skills to the world. Young people today know very little about the Globetrotters since the great players now have been integrated into the NBA. In 1947 and 1948, the Globetrotters beat the Minneapolis Lakers, with George Mikan, considered the best player in the professional ranks, in exhibition games. Reece Goose Tatum, Marques Haynes, George "Meadowlark" Lemon, Albert "Runt" Phillips, and Inman Jackson were players who easily would have dominated the NBA if not for segregation. Just imagine the line-up the Globetrotters would have today if all the dominating players in the NBA were forced to play for the Globetrotters.

In all aspects of American life, Blacks, when finally allowed to participate, have dominated. No wonder the dominant group attempted for over one hundred years after slavery to limit our participation. The government and media supported their racist customs and laws. The government at all levels condoned segregation and the media distorted our perception and importance in books, magazines, movies, and finally on television. Minstrel shows were an abomination against Blacks, and *The Birth of the Nation* was the greatest lie ever told and projected in a movie.

However, this exclusion could only last so long and with the successes of the Civil Rights Movement, Blacks were finally welcomed under the Big Tent of Integration. Blacks relished this newly acquired equality, and the more they experienced it, the greater their appetite and hunger for it became. Blinded by the prospects of inclusion into the ruling class, Blacks never realized that as a free people their culture is the only thing about the Black race of interest to whites. They stole from the culture and then marginalized us as a people. However, as a result of integration, Black communities as they existed during the segregated period, are all but extinct. At one time in our history we adhered to the belief that it takes a village to raise the children. In other words, the family structure stretched throughout the entire community. Ms. Henrietta, who lived at the end of the block in my neighborhood, would chastise me if she caught me doing something wrong. She would then tell Mamma who would whip me for the fact that Ms. Henrietta caught me being bad.

During our years prior to integration, the "n" word was forbidden in most homes, and there was always a high level of respect for ladies, from mothers to sisters, aunts, and cousins. Today the "n" word has been made into some kind of distorted term of endearment. How is it possible that a word that carries with it so much tragic history for our race, can be considered a loving term. Young men refer to each other as "dawg" which is rather strange to me. A dog is a pet and is considered part of the animal life below that of man. Why would they deliberately put themselves in that category when for so many years we fought whites for trying to do the same thing? It seems rather incomprehensible to me. You turn on BET network during a Saturday when our children are home and you see video tapes of women half dressed and in fact there was one specific tape that only showed the back ends of young Black girls keeping rhythm to some rap song. There was also the tape where a rap singer swipes a credit card between the cracks of a young female's rear end, I guess as some kind of indication that she could be bought.

I recall one incident back in 2007 when some white man on television referred to the beautiful Black sisters playing for the Rutgers University basketball team as "nappy headed whores." He was rightfully fired from his job with MSNBC. But when asked to comment on his derogatory description of these smart, talented, and beautiful Black sisters on *The View*, a Black comedian hesitated for a minute and slowly repeated the descriptions, "nappy headed whores," and then said, "Yes, they are." There were no repercussions against this so-called Black comedian. Another Black comedian, on one of the late night shows, said that, "they (the Rutgers Basketball players) may not be nappy-headed whores, but they were sure some ugly women." Have we become that callous and insensitive to our own image that we would allow this to happen without the greatest of uproars and complaints?

What would be the response if this had been done against any other racial group? I wonder how many times a day do our children hear the "n" word or the saying "my 'n,'" my dawg, my O.G., my Hoe, or the "B" word on television, radio, or from the mouths of people who look like them? Just whom do they think of when they hear these words? How many Blacks have ever heard or know the meaning of words such as "Hymie", "Kike", "Sheeny," "Shylock," "Heeb," and "Yid"? My guess is none, and that is a good thing.

However, if they have heard them it probably was not on television or radio. If so, they were used in some historical contexts making reference to the Jewish Holocaust, and were not meant to be understood as terms of endearment or as a joke. The Jewish people do not use or direct those terms and words toward one another. Jewish people consider it a desecration when the word Holocaust is associated on any level with the Black struggle. In all reality, Holocaust is a sacred word used for the exclusive purpose of distinguishing the historical suffering of the Jewish people. Now, that is power.

Unfortunately, Black people as a collective group have very little control over how they are portrayed through the print, audio, and visual media in news and entertainment. However, that is beginning to change. There are a few Blacks today with the clout necessary to give the green light to some television shows and movies that have made positive statements and expressions of our people. Immediately, what comes to mind is the movie *The Great Debaters*. This movie is not about sports figures, but about thinkers, scholars, and great speakers. It highlights historically Black Wiley College, which before the movie, very few people even knew existed. It is a historically true story. Wiley College did debate University of Southern California and defeated them, giving more credence to my earlier point that when we break the racial barriers and compete against the opposite race, we are usually victorious.

I have written a lot, but nothing will exceed what I am about to address to the beautiful young Black men and women, the flowers of our wonderful Black race and culture. Know that you are the descendants of an African people who were brought to this country against their will. Your heritage evolves from a people who suffered immeasurable brutalities and then forgave the people who committed such horrendous crimes. Your ancestors made them see the errors of their ways, and brought forth the changes that have made this a better country.

The insistence and determination of your people to be free, ultimately made freedom an attainable dream for every oppressed person in the world. The spirit and faith, along with the resilient nature of your people, brought forth the Civil Rights and Women Rights Movements in this country.

The Black race has made so many unselfish contributions toward humanity that I could write for the remainder of my life and not be able to convey the real compassionate nature of your race and culture. I can only plead and encourage each and every one of you to read and study the accomplishments of your race. You should listen to the stories of the elderly members of your family and community and research the Internet to learn more.

Your beautiful history and rich culture stem from one of the most extraordinary civilizations in the world.. Look around at yourselves and appreciate that you are one important component of the universe of races.

Realize that everything about you is beautiful. Your hair, nose, lips, and skin tone are made in the image of God. Recognize that the negative words you may hear are false manifestations of what some may want you to believe about your race. Remember your presence among some is a constant reminder of the wrongs they and their fathers have committed against you and your fathers. Some cannot forget the debt they owe you, yet they refuse to pay it. They know they are wrong, yet their nature just won't allow them to make atonement for their indiscretions.

Understand that in the nearly three hundred years of building America, we have never done anything or committed any aggression against the ruling class on any level that comes remotely close to what was done to us. They know that at some point in the future, world opinion will force them to do the right thing and atone for their many sins. I am sure they are well aware of this possibility and plan to do everything within their power to rid themselves of the burden of having to pay reparations, a debt they have no intentions of paying. I say to young Black men and women that no matter what happens, short of total destruction of the United States, they will not be successful in their attempts. Atonement must be made; the debt has to be paid if this country wants to remain the leader of the free world.

You must also recognize that the ruling class of this country does not like you. Not because of who you are, but rather for who they are not, yet want to be. I plead with you, young Black men and women, to have no fear in embracing your blackness, and the legacies and enslavement of your ancestors, their sacrifices, suffering, and losses. Stand up tall, look around you, and say boldly to yourselves aloud, "I am the sum total of those who came before me. I am and I represent their pain. I am their cry for freedom, the whelps on their backs left from the oppressors' whips. I am everything they ever were and yet more as a result of them. I am standing tall, representing the great attributes of a great culture and a mighty race of people. I will continue to build upon their legacy, for the good of mankind and the greatness of the God that lives within our hearts

I respectfully submit to you, young people, to fill up on the accomplishments of your people and your culture, speed off to self-determination, self-reliance, independence, and a renewed sense of self, created for the purpose of assisting people who look like us.

Recognizing Your Foundation

Michael Booker

While standing at the fifty yard line in the Orange Bowl, I knew there were young Black men, like my brother, crowded into small rooms to watch the Superbowl game on a prison television. So many memories flooded my mind on that late Sunday afternoon on January 31, 1999, when I put on my helmet and ran out to my position as cornerback for the Atlanta Falcons in the Thirty-eighth Super Bowl game in Miami, Fla. At that very moment, as I heard the roar of over one-hundred-thousand football fans and knew they were looking down at me and my teammates, I recognized just how fortunate I was to be standing there. I thought about Cheryl Johnson whose death at the young age of fifteen had helped get me to this place in my life. Before her tragic death, my future could have gone another way. The other key component to my standing before a stadium full of football fans and being watched by millions all over the country was my mother, who was my foundation, my strength, and my guide to making the right turns in life. My trip to that cornerback position for the Falcons took many bumps on the road to getting there and many times I wasn't sure I would make it. But there I was shadowing a wide receiver for the Denver Broncos and determined that the first pass from John Elway would not be caught against me. It was that same determination I want to now share with young people all over this country, and especially those who will never put on the uniform of a National Football League team or any professional sports team.

My journey began in Oceanside, Calif., the third largest city in San Diego County. Like most cities in this country, Oceanside is divided between the haves and the have-nots. The disparity between the rich and poor is enormous. One side of the city was riddled with gangs, while on the other side were the rich who drove the Bentley's. Even though we weren't poor, we still lived on the gang-side of town. I was introduced to that lifestyle at an early age

I grew up in a house with four siblings, and there was never a dull moment. Damaris was the oldest, I was the middle boy, and Dion the youngest son. Then there were the twins, Adria and Andria. Damaris was always the serious one, assuming the role of protector of us all. I was the jokester, and Dion was the real athlete. Our two sisters were the beautiful princesses of the family. We were very close growing up because Mama insisted on that. Dad, a Marine, was often away protecting the country so Mama became the primary mover and shaker in the family. I don't, however, want to give the impression that Dad was a silent, passive man. He was just the opposite when he was around. He enforced an old-style Marine discipline on all of us. And he did it with very little compassion. If you were looking for love, you'd better look somewhere else, and that was always to Mama.

The burden of raising five children fell on Mama's shoulders and she did the best she could. Sometimes the peer group forces were just too strong for her to overcome. That was the case with Damaris and, to a certain degree, me also. The problem was the gangs. Damaris fell prey to them and joined the Crips. He became a big-time player with the members and gained their respect. Respect from the Crips, unfortunately, meant no respect from the police. Mama was constantly responding to something Damaris did to get locked up.

After a number of arrests by the local police, Damaris finally committed a crime that landed him in prison. That had a tremendous impact on me and I resolved to never do anything that could send me to prison also. My older brother was the only one out of the siblings to end up in prison. There was a time before Damaris was sent away, when it seemed that I was also on my way. I admired his lifestyle, hanging out and going to "gangsta" parties. What I didn't realize is just how dangerous those parties could be and how hanging out with gang members could be detrimental to my well-being.

When I entered El Camino High School as a freshman, I was "chasing the thug." I wore the sagging pants and had no idea as to how ridiculous it looks for someone to have his pants hanging down below his waist with his underwear showing. I also wore my hair in braids. I had no interest in football or in school. The only reason I went was to chase the girls. Lunch period was my favorite time of day. I tried out for the football team my freshman year, but quit in the middle of the season. It took too much effort and time from what I was interested in doing at the time. Then the drive-by killing happened. I wasn't there, but word spread fast that Cheryl Johnson had been shot down outside the apartment where she lived. She wasn't the original target but happened to be in the way. There is something about the finality of death when the person gone is only fifteen years old. The young people who have been in gangs and experienced the death of someone close to them understand exactly what I am saying. She lost her life in a useless and senseless battle between gangs that own nothing but lack respect for each other as human beings. Cheryl wasn't supposed to die. Instead she should have gone on to college, graduated, married, become a mother and lived to see her children grow up. The highest rate of death among young Blacks is murder. There is something quite pathological about that statistic. If our children die young and go to prison, what does that say for the future of our race?

Cheryl's death made me realize that I was not invincible. The same fate could await me. Damaris' conviction and sentence to prison made me also realize that if death wasn't waiting patiently for me as a gang member, then prison was. It was at that time that Mama stepped up and helped me to get back on the right track in life. She encouraged me to find something of interest and to pursue it with a determined goal and a clear vision for success. I turned to football. Don Coleman, who was the coach of the junior varsity team when I quit, had recognized my talents early on and suggested that I get back into the game. That is exactly what I did.

My sophomore year I excelled on the junior varsity team. In the middle of the season I was promoted to the varsity. I was a natural fit for the game and became a star in high school. I enjoyed all the privileges that come with being a standout on the football field. One of those privileges was passing from one grade to the next without having to study and learn the subject material. I did just enough to pass. That would come back to haunt me as major universities began to recruit me for their programs. My junior and senior years I was inundated with coaches from all the major universities coming to my games, watching my tapes, and trying to get me to play for them. I could have gone to any school in the country but I did not have the grade point average to get into them. However, the National Collegiate Athletic Association (NCAA) had adopted new rules for eligibility that made it possible for me to move on, even though under normal circumstances there was no way I would have been admitted to a major university in this country.

The new rule passed by the NCAA was Proposition Forty-eight. It was designed to get outstanding high school athletes, with poor academic performance, into the major collegiate athletic programs. I fit that category. The rules were as follows: If a student failed to score at least a seven-hundred out of a possible sixteen-hundred on the SAT or seventeen out of a possible thirty-six on the ACT, then the student would not be allowed to play or practice with a college team his or her freshman year. The athlete could be recruited, but would not be eligible for athletic scholarship money and would have to pay the full tuition, as well as room and board their freshman year. If at the end of the first year, the student had passed all the required remedial courses, he or she would then be eligible to receive an athletic scholarship and be able to compete. Under the conditions of Proposition Forty-eight, I was admitted to the University of Nebraska. As I prepared to enter college, I knew that, because of my lackadaisical behavior in high school, I had to pay a price. With the strong support of my mother and father, I was willing to take on this challenge and make it through that first year. My foundation, which had always been there, was strong and gave me the strength to overcome this first obstacle on my trip up the road to success.

In July of 1993, I prepared to leave for a strange place somewhere up North. I was leaving my support system for the first time, that is my familiar surroundings, my family, and especially Mama. I left a month early because I had to find a job to help pay my tuition. Since I was not eligible to live in the dormitories on campus, Coach Tom Osbourne had arranged for me to live with Danta Jones, the outside linebacker for the team. He lived in an apartment off campus. For the entire first year, I had to sleep on his couch in the living room of his apartment. Coach Osbourne also helped me get a job at a local grocery store, bagging groceries every day after classes, in order to help pay for my tuition. My parents also helped with my tuition that first year, for which I will always be grateful. During my high school years I had made a major mistake. I didn't take care of business in the classroom.

I had been an athlete instead of a student/athlete with studies as my number one priority. To make matters worse, the car my parents had given me broke down and I was forced to ride the bus everywhere I went.

That first year on campus I felt estranged, not part of the campus life at all. I made very few friends and stayed to myself. Despite my feelings of alienation, I was determined to meet the academic requirements so that I could play football the next year. At that point in life I viewed myself as a loser. Despite how well I could perform on the football field, I was not performing well in life. The test would be passing all my classes and moving from the category of practically an illiterate to a functional citizen of society. If I couldn't accomplish that, then football would be meaningless. I did not want my only accomplishment in life to be able to beat up on the opponent on a football field. That required more physical than mental ability, and I wanted a balance between the two, with a greater emphasis on the mental. Thank God for my foundation back in Oceanside. Mama constantly encouraged and helped convince me that I could do it in the classroom, just as I did on the football field.

That very first year I fulfilled all of the Proposition Forty-eight requirements for eligibility to play football. Becoming academically eligible to attend a major university was one of my proudest accomplishments. I was a naturally gifted athlete, but academically I was challenged. The fact that I could take on that challenge and win the battle meant more to me than preventing a wide receiver from catching a pass or sacking a quarterback on a blitz. Those years that I was practically flunking out of school and also out of life, I could have easily given up as so many young brothers do when they face obstacles. Instead, those early mornings and late nights when I struggled with English and mathematics, I thought about my foundation back in Oceanside and knew I could never let her down. Mama had already lost her oldest son to the system, and if I had quit and returned to Oceanside, she would have been terrified at the thought of losing me also. There was no way I could do that to the one person who sacrificed so much to help me get to where I was in life.

In the fall of 1994 I moved on campus, living in the dorm with the other football players. I felt as though I was sandwiched between two classes. The sophomores who were on the team the previous year should have been my class. But since I couldn't practice or have any dealing with the team I wasn't really a part of that class. And then there was the freshman group, all one year behind me. I wasn't quite sure where I belonged. It took me a while to adjust, but once I did, I became an outstanding defensive back on three outstanding University of Nebraska football teams. In 1994, we were undefeated with a 13-0 record. We beat the University of Miami in the Orange Bowl, 24-17 and were crowned the National Collegiate Champions for that year. In 1995, we were also undefeated and beat the number two-ranked team, University of Florida, in the Fiesta Bowl by the outrageous score of 62-24, and I was the Defensive Most Valuable Player of the game, having returned an interception for a touchdown. Again, that year we were the National Collegiate Football Champions. According to a *USA Today* computer ranking, our 1995 team was considered the best team in contemporary collegiate football history (post 1956). My final year at Nebraska we lost only two games. Our twenty-six-game winning streak was broken the second game of the season by Arizona State. That same season we went back to the Orange Bowl and beat Virginia Tech, 41-21. In the winter of 1997, I was invited to play in the Senior Bowl and the Hula Bowl. That spring I was drafted number eleven by the Atlanta Falcons.

I played a total of five years in the National Football League, three with the Atlanta Falcons and two with the Tennessee Titans. My last year with the Falcons in 1999, we made it to the Super Bowl. It is every professional football player's dream to play in the Super Bowl. As a player and a team, you strive to be the very best, and making it to the grand game of them all is confirmation that you and your teammates have accomplished that goal.

I am very much aware of the success I have enjoyed as an athlete. But I must never lose sight that it was God's gift to me as an athlete that made it possible for me to enjoy those victories. However, my real challenge came when I had to succeed academically. It took a great deal of work that first year at the University of Nebraska to get my grade point average above the "C" level threshold. I was able to do that because I finally believed that I possessed the ability to be a successful student. That confidence was drilled into me by my mother and now I am determined to pass that same kind of belief to as many young Black men and women as possible. I want to help them find their foundation that will give them the strength necessary to build a successful future. It begins with an understanding of who they are and the culture they represent.

You Can Learn a Lot from Dead People

Toschia

One of the most disheartening problems I have witnessed working as a child advocate is the lack of understanding of history with regards to young people, especially in African-American children. There tends to be a great disconnect or rift between both old and young, rich and poor, and the other silly, trivial socio-economic barriers that people contrive to not work together. Many of the young people that I come across do not think that they can make a difference in the world.

They, like many adults, think the average minority young person isn't capable of much beyond hanging on the corner, having babies, or over populating the prison system. I think that people in general must understand that YOU have the power to change the world! It starts with YOU! The list goes on and on with things that are wrong in our communities: homelessness, apathy, lack of education, crime, hunger, AIDS. We usually look at these problems and decide they're too big for us to do anything about. Thus, by our lack of effort to even try to evoke change we are assisting in creating a permanent social underclass. Many young people think they will make a difference "one day" or "someday." We think things will be better when we get out of middle school and go to high school. Or it will be better the next grading period, or it'll be easier when we get to the next grade. Or we would be happier if we had a two-parent household or if we had more money. But we should live for today! Carpe diem; seize the day! Do the right thing today so that you will have a better tomorrow.

Many dead people changed the world when they were young just like you! Think about David from the Bible. He was just a teenager when he made a major accomplishment. He simply didn't fit in! He was too young to sit at the kids' table but too old to sit at the adult table. David was probably around the age of an eighth grader, which is a time when you really don't fit in anywhere. But that same boy, David who probably had pimples, smelly armpits, and trouble fitting in, was used by God to slay a GIANT! Can you imagine that?

Another example of a courageous youth was Mary, the mother of Jesus. She was just a teenager when she was chosen to bear the long-awaited savior. God could have chosen her cousin Elizabeth; certainly she would have been more qualified. She was much older and she actually *wanted* a baby. I'm sure all the messy, gossipy women that sit on the front porches with nothing to do probably judged Mary because she was an unwed mom. They probably thought Elizabeth was more qualified to be the mother of Jesus. I'm sure Mary wasn't from the suburbs but from the hood. She probably had the equivalent of Payless BOGO (buy one, get one half-off) shoes and not Nike or Jordan's. Nonetheless, God chose Mary, the teenager from the equivalent of the projects. Imagine that? Kids have always taken the lead in world change because young people rock! The Civil Rights Movement was just one of the many movements by young people that changed the course of history.

So if you're thinking "someday," think again. You can take the initiative to make sure your pants are pulled up, young men, and influence others to do so. If you don't take yourself seriously, no one else will. Young women can take the lead by not engaging in sex! Make a young man respect you and your body. Many of the young men who will pursue you are suffering from their own personal demons and use sex as a way to dominate women. They go from girl to girl and as soon as they are gratified sexually they won't call you or take you to the prom, and many will cause you to be an unwed mother. It's not worth it. Young men, do not allow a conniving young woman to get you caught up in their games by pitting you against another young man. She isn't worth it. I have seen one too many young men die over a silly girl! Sex is a deadly weapon, literally and figuratively! Most teenage parents end up dropping out of school and end up on welfare. Life doesn't have to be hard if you listen! Sex is not all it's cracked up to be but it's a great responsibility between two people that give themselves to one another, understanding that they are giving the very fiber of their soul. Believe me, it's worth the wait because it's complicated. Many young men sleep around because they have indirectly come to hate women and have never seen their father's love or cherish their own mothers. Subconsciously they use women for their physical fantasies. And like a candy wrapper, they get thrown away once they have been eaten. Many young women are looking for the love they never got from their fathers so that five minutes of touching that they receive from a man is a substitute for something greater. Sex is too complicated and emotional so just leave it alone! So many young people are rushing to grow up. For what? To pay bills, bills, bills.

Enjoy your childhood while you can.

Take your extra energy and put it into making good grades, making changes, being unique, and becoming a leader. All young people have the potential to be leaders! *You* can take the lead by speaking up when someone in your school is being mistreated or picked on. Or choose to remain silent before saying something derogatory to someone (I'm still working on that one in my thirties). You can take the lead by befriending kids that are having a bad time in school, or by not getting involved in cliques that look down on other people. It has taken me awhile to learn the qualities of a good leader, so I will pass these qualities on to you so that you can be successful in all that you do.

I'm no expert on leadership, but these few traits have helped me. They are discernment, which is knowing when enough is enough, wisdom (applying truth to everyday situations), and finally confidence (not arrogance or cockiness) and determination (sticking to something). You don't have to be a certain age to be a leader or change the world. I'm sure David wasn't carded to make sure he was of age or asked to show ID as he walked away after killing Goliath. There is one important ingredient necessary for success and change, and that is the ability to listen to those who have achieved success before you. It is imperative that you listen to your elders and respect them. Listening to those who have experienced what you are going through will save you a lot of heartache and pain. Life does not have to be hard, and a lot of issues that young people face can be alleviated by just listening to their parents, teachers, mentors, or clergy. Then, you can help lead a new generation one day as well.

Remember that we all stand on the shoulders of giants that

fought for freedom. There was a time when our people were killed for even thinking of picking up a book, yet when the yellow school bus (free…I might add) comes and stops directly in front of our home, some choose not to get on and take the magic bus ride to school. The magic bus that will drop us off to the magic kingdom that is public school. The magic kingdom has the key to end poverty, apathy, and a lot of the myriad generational curses that can help lead our people to the promised land.

See, in that magic kingdom there is a sacred place called the library, where we can enter the supernatural realm and come face to face with our ancestors by using the enchanted and clairvoyant tool called a book. Once you enter the magic zone, there are so many different historical figures that will give you a different outlook on life and help you prepare to change the world. In the magic kingdom you have the privilege of learning from DEAD PEOPLE!!

When you learn from dead people, your life will seem mundane and very boring compared to those who have come before you. Sometimes young people feel like they are having a bad day because friends are gossiping about them or something happened in English class. Or it might be their football game is rained out or their parents don't allow them to play the Wii game on the plasma TV in their room, even though their grades are mediocre.

Once you enter the magic kingdom, you will learn from the dead that a truly bad day is when you are awakened to the sound of your slave owner yelling at you, telling you to get to work. Imagine every muscle in your body throbbing in excruciating pain as you hurriedly get off the hard ground you slept on. You grimace in pain as the fresh wounds from the night before sting from the sweat on your body. Quickly you wash the dust off yourself and try to hold down your breakfast of hard grits and dirty water. You try to remove the particles of dirt in the water with your fingertips. Next you dig out a few ants and a roach out of the bowl, praying it doesn't make you ill. You rush to make it to the field on time; you don't have a watch so you have to rely on the sun. You take several slow breaths to avoid having a panic attack because you know if you are late you will be beaten again. Your wounds are dripping blood and each drop of sweat that enters the cuts evokes horrific pain.

You hurriedly make it to your destination and crouch on the

floor with the other slaves, your backs pressed up against the wall in a dark, dusty, smelly room. You pray that everyone in your family stays together and no one is sold today. After reading about tales of adversity and triumph from other dead people, I promise your bad day won't seem so bad. I know some people suffer greatly; I do not mean to minimize that. Some kids have to endure the loss of someone they love, the divorce of parents, not having money for adequate clothing, and sadly experience some abuse. But some of the petty things that bug us don't seem to matter as much once we visit the DEAD PEOPLE! One thing that I've learned from the dead people is that in life we have to face challenges. If you read practically any respected leader, you will find that he or she at some point faced some significant challenges.

Reading autobiographies can change your life! They can motivate you to try to change the world; they can help you garner intellectual arrogance. After reading a few autobiographies you will feel compelled to graduate high school, go to college and not just receive the basic bachelors degree, but also seek more education. Heck, anybody can get a bachelors degree! But leaders, movers, shakers, and those on a mission know that you can't just stop at the minimum for, you see, education is one of the tools that you need to slay those dragons of poverty, apathy, and despair. For those of you who, in lieu of college, chose a technical trade, be the best that you can be! Receive as many certifications to propel you to be the best auto mechanic, barber, or any other trade you choose. If you are seeking a career in the military, move up through the ranks as quickly as you can. Be the best soldier in the U.S. military. If you are a cake decorator or baker, take it to the next level; take a business class and open up a bakery.

By reading autobiographies you will feel empowered to move your butt! Empower others! Think outside the box and if you have to do it alone, you aren't scared because you know that others accomplished great feats before you, when the chips were down. They overcame and you will as well. Many young people throughout history from Paul Revere to Mother Teresa found ways to overcome and excel.

In the Bible, the book of Jeremiah 29:11 reads, "For I know the plans I have for you. Plans to prosper and not harm you, plans to give you hope and a future." Sometimes the obstacles we have to overcome can make us stronger, helping us to achieve our goal in life.

A lesson that you will also learn from dead people is that they made sacrifices in order to get to the next level in life, as will you if you want to succeed. A sacrifice can be as simple as taking the extra time to complete extra homework assignments in order to qualify for college scholarships. Sacrifices require laying aside something that matters to you. It might be television, video games, or hanging out with friends. Successful leaders like Dr. Martin Luther King Jr. and Malcolm X made sacrifices for equality. The biggest sacrifice of all was the death of Jesus Christ for our sins. These people were passionate and steadfast in their quest to change the world and they sacrificed with their lives. No one expects anyone to give their life for a cause. But I'm afraid there aren't enough people making basic sacrifices, like volunteering at a soup kitchen, mentoring others or even volunteering to help out the elderly.

Young people, you have the gifts of zeal, youth, and innocence on your side. So just do it! Young people who only talk the talk can eventually become adults that talk but aren't willing to work to make their dreams a reality. I come across a lot of adults who want to make changes. There are countless organizations and people that are allegedly trying to help our youth. Some have failed because of their inability to listen, dive in, get "dirty," or follow up and talk to young people to see how they feel.

Life is not pretty for many, but that can't deter you from being the best that you can be. Are you willing to make sacrifices in life to help other people? Many Americans have a hard time understanding what a sacrifice is. In our comfortable world, we don't take advantage of the opportunities to sacrifice for others. If possible, travel and see the world while you are young so that you can be a better, productive adult. If you can't afford to physically travel, that is still no excuse because your mind can travel within the magic kingdom--the library. As you travel and read you will be amazed at those that can guide you. Jesus Christ is the most spectacular because Harry Potter's wizardry has nothing on the man who sacrificed his life and rose from a tomb after being dead for three days! That same man would put Harry Houdini or David Copperfield's magic tricks to shame. Jesus turned water into wine. He performed all types of outstanding miracles. Then his haters killed him, but guess what? He let them hurt him but he got the last laugh. He rose from the grave and became the Prince of Peace and the ruler of the whole world. Talk about a sci-fi story, Jesus was the bomb.com. I'm telling you that once you start to study the DEAD PEOPLE, now, you will be armed, fired up, and ready to go change the world. These dead people are going to give you the keys to success. Eleanor Roosevelt, Jesse Owens, Harriet Tubman, Louis Braille, Clara Barton, Marian Anderson, Fannie Lou Hamer, and so many more that have changed the world for the better. These people, along with contemporaries in your life, like positive adults, can help you gain strength, courage, and confidence. You will be changed by every dead person you meet which will help you look fear in the face. Some dead people like Shakespeare have even written books, poems, and short stories to enlighten, entertain and sharpen your imagination. The books by Dr. Seuss, the poetry of Robert Frost or Gwendolyn Brooks, and a personal hero of mine Mary Shelley are others who have made changes.

Mary Shelley was a young teenage writer who lived in an era when women had no rights and were expected to write only about love. She defied the odds and said, "Anything boys can write, girls can write better." Yes, she was a young girl that scared the "bageebies" out of everyone with the very first horror tale, *Frankenstein!* Subsequently other women like George Eliot stopped writing under male psuedonyms to sell books. Dorothy Wordsworth stopped writing her brother William's stuff and wrote her own *Grassmere Journals*. African American and Asian American writers like Alice Walker and Amy Tan exploded on the literary scene. See what one teenager did? Mary Shelley, Phyllis Wheatley, Dorothy Wordsworth all started a precedent of women writers that transcended race and literary era, and even stretched across continents. Mary Shelley proved that she could scare the heck out of you just as well or better than any boy! Talk about courage? Eleanor Roosevelt said, "You gain strength, courage, and confidence by every experience in which you stop to look fear in the face. You must do the very thing you think you cannot."

Courage is not the absence of fear. Courage is when you choose to acknowledge your fear and look it dead in the face! Many people, young and old alike, are afraid of failure. They are afraid of what people will think if they get an "F," afraid of people making fun of them if they found out their family was on welfare, or that their father hits their mom. Or if one of their parents was an alcoholic or went to jail. Always remember that it doesn't matter where you come from; it's where you are going! All that we experience in life is merely preparing us for the greatness that is to come. So the next time you feel abandoned because you are in state protective custody, write about it. How do you feel? What do you want for your future?

The next time your parents are fighting and you put the pillow over your head to block out the noise and fear that you feel, pull out paper and pen and write about it. If you have a child out of wedlock as a teenager and people look down on you, write about it. If you have the misfortune to read this from behind bars, write about it. Remember all that is for your good is coming! You must always remember that a good leader shows others how to lead. So when you write your feelings, emotions, and experiences down you must share them with others. You never know who could benefit from your experience or who can rely on your words as strength to overcome, just as you will. Write, share, and write! God doesn't allow you to go through circumstances and overcome obstacles to be so selfish as to not share with others. Just as we learn from dead people we want others to learn from us.

Please utilize the magic kingdom. Read fiction, nonfiction, and magazines anything you can get your hands on and write as well. It may not look cool to be caught reading and you may even be called a geek. But take it from me and many people who have done pretty well in life; always remember we learned a lot from dead people and you will too.   You can still play video games, participate in sports and have fun. In addition to your daily routine, try to incorporate the "secret place" called the library into it. I promise you will be better for it; you will lead a better life and will be able to affect others in a positive manner as well.

The Seat of Knowledge

Rosalind Patton Brown

Large wooden rocking chairs and a wooden swing attached to the ceiling by heavy chain link on an L-shaped porch of our home in Spartansburg, S. C., afforded family elders and young listening ears the opportunity to rock into the education of a lifetime. All the neighborhood kids gathered on the porch for fun, discussions, snacks, stories, and good old fashioned advice. One of the earliest lessons we young folks learned from the elders was the beauty of the universe that God created. Watching the sunset, gazing into the stars at night, making a wish while grabbing a lightening bug and putting it in a jar brought joy beyond belief.

The boys had to sit on one side of the porch and girls on the other, unless of course, it was just my brother and me. Grandmother would say a million times, it seemed, "Stop giggling. Cover your knees, put your knees together, and sit like a lady. Don't hit your sister, never put your hands on a girl, and men don't hit women. Sit up straight. Always say please and thank you. Say 'yes, Miss, Mr., or Mrs. So and So. Look people in the eyes when you are talking to them. Have you read your Sunday School lesson? Make sure you brush your teeth every day; nobody wants to look at your yellow teeth! What did you learn today in school? Have you completed your chores? You know I'm going to check them." These instructions went on, day after day, while we sat swinging and rocking into oblivion.

Thank goodness for the social skills, religious teachings, stories of family heritage, and the closeness of loving family and friends who shared a wealth of knowledge with me while I just enjoyed the simple pleasure of rocking! Sometimes, however, I viewed the porch time with Grandma as sheer torture. In a heartbeat, the porch could change from the place of comfort and solace to the

301

den of punishment.

"I told you not to leave this yard," she would say.

"But I just went next door to Ms. Amy's house..."

"You just sit in that chair until I tell you to move."

The unwanted directive was delivered right in the middle of my explanation.

"You sit in that chair until you learn to do as you are told. If it means sitting until the basket weave chair bottoms are deeply imprinted on the back of your thighs or until your feet and legs are numb, you had better not move again without permission."

Grandma's admonition to stay put until told to move was harsh and sweet at the same time. Her tone may have been stern, but what she demanded that I do was filled with unrelenting love for me. Her goal was never to punish but to teach. And teach she did, as millions of grandmothers have done over generations since our ancestors first arrived on these shores. You see the heroes of yesteryear are not necessarily like those playing on the ball fields, fighting in the wars, producing movies, or rapping their hearts out. They were the persons who took the time and interest to instill in us moral value, pride, quest for knowledge, and the desire to become somebody. They realized that their mission was to develop and empower young people to become leaders of tomorrow.

Countless stories of injustices of slavery, and obvious disparities in the overall treatment of deeply hued Americans gave impetus to our forefathers who were determined to pave the way for a better life in our now native country, America.

One of the most difficult obstacles many of us had to work through is the hostility and dislike of persons in our race who had no choice in the color of their skin. You see, the marvelous tones of complexion donned by the Americans of color were not chosen. It is what the times delivered by virtue of the fact that as slaves, our women were at the whim of the slave owner. This was not meant to divide us as a people...though it does so even today. The late Reverend Dr. Martin Luther King Jr. has yet to have the dream fulfilled of judging, "not by the color of one's skin, but by the content of one's character." There is no question, we have made remarkable strides, but, even today, we continue to be judged by the color of our skin.

When we look at the accomplishments of our ancestors, we

must ask, "Where did the 'means' come from?" Limited resources, low paying jobs served as no obstacle for the past generation of heroes. They found work and saved their earnings. They planted crops to provide food, education, and clothing. They prayed hard and were tenacious in every pursuit. My grandmother wanted to be a teacher, but the only way she could achieve her goal was to attend ten consecutive summer sessions at South Carolina State College in order to earn a Bachelor's degree. It had to be done this way so that she could continue to work as a teacher during the school year. How many of us would have been willing to make such a sacrifice for ten consecutive summers?

Not only were we taught through verbal instruction, we had persons whom we could emulate. Most little girls wanted to be just like their teachers. For the boys, there weren't that many male teachers, but there were preachers, deacons, and a sprinkling of lawyers and other professionals who appeared quite well to do.

Among our black youths, I see great things evolving. I also see a decline in morality and religious conviction. Having trod rocky roads, studied from worn hand-me-down textbooks, worn consignment clothes before they became in vogue, entered the movie theatre through a side door, and given a seat in the "colored balcony section," checked out books to read from the USO (neighborhood center) because we couldn't go to the public library, and countless other discriminatory acts, I think the words penned by Maya Angelou "...And still I rise," still ring true.

It is my personal appeal to our young people to reach higher and higher. Black on Black crime must end! The use of illegal substances, sale and consumption, must be halted. Respect yourself, and give the world the best that you have. Continue to make strides in these United States of America.

To our parents, take charge of your children, know where they are, oversee homework, attend church with them, and teach them that in order to gain respect, they must give respect. Continue to hold your heads high and make your ancestors proud for the many sacrifices they have made. We must take back our high moral teaching and reestablish high standards. Our youth can become the epitome of the "American Dream." Do not accept the use of non-standard English. Reestablish dress codes for our young people. Expect and foster the highest expectations, create your own "seat of knowledge."

I was born in Spartanburg, a textile town full of obstacles for Black Americans. But the strong Black men and women who lived there had the will and determination to not only succeed but to provide the young people with as many opportunities as possible, so that they would grow up to be independent, self-supporting citizens, leaders of the future. I always heard the term "across the tracks" when referring to Black neighborhoods. Honestly, I was dead in the middle, for the train track ran straight down the middle of the street where we lived. Our house was on the corner, and Blacks also occupied the three houses below us. The paved street stopped at the corner, just where my house began. Up the street, we only had white neighbors; they respected us and we respected them.

Mom broke down and bought a television for us because one lady came out every evening and would yell, "Rozzie, Joey, it's time for Howdy Doody, come on." Just to keep us home, Mom bought us our own television. Our first television was a RCA Victor Table Top, black and white (circa, 1952.)

To this very day, I value the friends that were made on East Henry. Black and white, we were a little family. I have had the opportunity to travel to several countries: England, Scotland, Italy, Germany, Austria, and Switzerland. Although these places were beautiful and exciting, I love Spartansburg...my home.

In many ways, Grandma, along with the endless other grandmothers, was tagged with a very difficult task. The years I am writing about were very difficult ones for Black people and the fact that they survived is worth all the praise and honor that we can bestow on them. There are countless stories of injustices during slavery and the years following the Emancipation Proclamation. Despite all the inequalities heaped on them, our ancestors were still determined to pave the way for a better life for us in our own country. They had to survive through the hostility and dislike of our race by individuals who viewed our color as a badge of inferiority.

My brother and I were fortunate to be brought up in a three-parent home, Mom, Dad and Grandma. Joseph and Fordham Patton and Ada Bagwell Foster (maternal grandmother) did all they could to lead us in the right direction. My brother, Joey, and I attempted to conform to their teachings. We were not perfect; we veered off from time to time, but those voices of reprimand heard on the front porch continue to ring in our ears today. My brother and I attended grades one through eight in the public school system. In ninth grade we were sent to boarding school. Joey attended St. Emma Academy in Powhatan, Va. I began ninth grade at St. Francis De Sales High School in the same town, but when my brother left, my parents felt that it was too far for me to travel alone. I transferred to Allen High School in Asheville, N. C. where I completed high school. Some of the people in my town resented the fact that we were able to go away to school. It was not our decision but that of our parents. After rearing two teenagers, I decided that mother knew best, having us away surely took the stress off parenting for her! The one thing no one ever considered is the extreme sacrifice that was made to send us to these schools.

My dad was self-employed as a barber and that created some independence for him and us. We were not at the mercy of the whites for our survival. Grandmother and Mother taught school during the regular school year. In later years, during summer vacation my grandmother worked in the Black public schools, repairing outdated torn textbooks so that the Black students could use them the next year.

Most of the time, the books had already gone through the hands of the white students. Mother always managed to get employment for the summer. She taught teacher-training workshops at Fort Valley State College, Fort Valley, Ga., and Florida A&M University, Tallahassee, Fla., in order to pay our school tuition.

The sacrifices, as I look back, were supreme. How grateful we are for tenacity of our parents, and many parents like them who paved the way for us. They are the real "Unsung Heroes and Heroines" of my generation. They set the example and we must see to it that our young people know not only what needs to be done, but also how to do it.

It is an honor and a privilege to have been asked to share a little of my life as an American citizen with the younger generations, for you must know how far we have come in order to realize how far we must go. The journey rests on your shoulders. Black heroes/ heroines aren't necessarily the ones recorded in the annals of time, read about in slave narratives, written in history books. They are the loving, devoted, determined parents and grandparents who provided, "The Seat of Knowledge."

May they all rest in love and peace.

KKK: The Real Boogeyman
By Jayme L. Bradford

Growing up, I was always afraid of the boogeyman. But for me, the boogeyman wasn't Michael from the movie Halloween, or Jason from *Friday the 13th* or even *Freddie Krueger,* the charismatic dream slasher from Nightmare on Elm Street.

My boogeyman wore a white robe and hood. He could be a neighbor, businessman, or even my teacher. He was a member of the Ku Klux Klan. I knew that he hated the thought of me just because I am African American. My character and intelligence didn't matter, simply because of the color of my dark skin.

One of my earliest childhood memories was that of a 19 year-old boy named Michael Donald, who was lynched in my peaceful hometown of Mobile, Ala., in 1981. This incident had a major impact on my life and changed my perception of race relations. Donald was the target of a Ku Klux Klan initiation. Randomly chosen, he was abducted while on his way to the gas station to purchase a pack of cigarettes. Two Klansmen Henry Francis Hays and James "Tiger" Knowles, Jr. beat the teenager unconscious with a tree limb.   Then they slipped a noose around his neck and strangled him. Hays slashed his throat three times to ensure that he was dead *(Jet,* Dec. 26, 1983). They later hung him in a tree near downtown for the entire community to see. Those pictures continue to haunt me.

My family had recently moved back to Alabama after living in Atlanta. We left the big city in part because of the Atlanta Child Murders, which took the lives of 28 African American youth. My parents were very concerned about raising three young children under those conditions, so they decided to move back home to

307

Mobile, where they thought their children would be safe. Despite Wayne Williams, a young African American male being convicted for the serial murders, the African American community thought otherwise. We believed that it was the work of the Klan.

Then, everything changed. When Donald was lynched, I realized that my parents did not have the power to protect me. The boogeyman was real, and he could kill me and get away with it if he wanted too. Even as a child, I was outraged. I wanted the people to do something, but I failed to realize that they were frightened too. If it could happen to Donald, it could happen to anyone.

I remember participating in my first protest march with my father, who taught me to be politically active at an early age. It was a big deal because two local attorneys, Michael and Thomas Figures, were taking the lead and the Rev. Jesse Jackson, a civil rights leader who later ran for president of the United States, came to town. I recognized him because my father proudly hung his large portrait in the den.

In 1984, Hays and Knowles were found guilty of murder/ lynching and sentenced to death and life imprisonment respectively. Frank Cox, Hays' brother-in-law was sentenced to 99 years in prison for providing the rope to hang Donald. Hay's father, Bennie Jack Hays, was also charged in the murder, but died before his trial. I believe that God judged him accordingly.

In 1997, the year I finished graduate school at the University of West Florida, Henry Hays was executed. I had never favored the death penalty until then. I wanted to go to the prison the night of his execution, but my father thought it was too dangerous. I listened to him and monitored the local news for updates.

The Exalted Cyclops was 42 years old when he died. His death was significant in the state of Alabama because he was the first white man to be executed for killing a black man in 84 years. His death proved that white men could no longer lynch African Americans for sport without just punishment.

That same year Beulah Mae Donald, Donald's 67-year-old mother, sued the Klan with the assistance of the Southern Poverty Law Center. Back then, I did not understand the courage it took to do something like that. Like Mamie Carthan, the mother of the famous lynch victim Emmett Till, she wanted the world to know what the Klan had done to her innocent son. Donald won her civil lawsuit with the wrongful death verdict of $7 million. Unfortunately, the Klan filed for bankruptcy and gave her a fraction of that amount. However, they were forced to give her the deeds to their headquarters in Tuscaloosa, which she sold for $52,000. Just the thought of her owning their building always made me laugh.

Michael Donald, who worked in the mailroom of the *Mobile Press Register* where I later interned, had always dreamed of building his mother a home. Ironically, she used the settlement money to do just that. He was a devoted son, who was able to provide for his mother, even in death. Although she did not gain much financially, her point was made. Her son's life was valuable and his killers would not go unpunished this time. Sadly, she died shortly after. Her life's work was done.

Since then, the street where Donald was lynched has been renamed in his memory. He is also remembered in exhibits at the American Black Holocaust Museum in Milwaukee and the Civil Rights Memorial Center in Montgomery. And I remember him by sharing his tragic story with my students when I teach about Ida B. Well's anti-lynching campaign in History of Journalism. Whenever the teaching opportunity presents itself, I talk about him. And the more I say his name, Michael Donald, the boogeyman goes away.

The Mathematic Make-Up of SELF: The Self Within or An Examination of Our Being Through Numbers

Brother Fattah

Our community is one community, very similar to the human body. We have billions upon billions of cells, yet our body is one and functions as a unit. The concept of the "many" as an expression of "the one" is an ancient principle that carried the Original Man and Woman through many hardships.

The Black community in America is a string of disconnected organizations, mostly churches and other religious cloisters, with no constantly visible vehicle of unity. For the most part, the faith community of different denominations remains incestuous. Our European oppressors could never have enslaved us without attacking the natural tendency to see *ourselves* as one. Today, they maintain their brutal, psychological and pathological oppression by keeping us perpetually separated.

Self-hatred is the root of our problem. I can think of no other people who affectionately refer to themselves with negative terms like "nigga." We are so used to being oppressed, other nationalities within North America who are witnessing our poor conditioning feel free to use this term among themselves. The time is now for us all to begin to love ourselves and reclaim our dignity.

Dignity can only come when we love and activate the Divine gifts we were given. We must tap into the power of God within Self.

The Number 26:

The English Alphabet and the Power of "God" Within Self

311

What we yearn for is self-acceptance and knowledge. But what is the "Self?" I hope you will have a deeper understanding of that question after you finish reading this short essay. I will define "Self" according to its numeric component, or what we call its letters. A "letter" is not just a symbol representative of a single sound in the English language. To add an **"er" to** a verb is to make a noun. Without it, we have the verb **"let"** which means **to allow or permit,** according to most dictionaries. Implied is the idea that power to do so is present within the **"letter."**

There are "26 letters", or I say "26 powers" we can use to initiate our ability to communicate. Sound is the medium through which we bring into existence our creativity. According to the Book of Genesis, God's first word was **"...*Let*...."** The creator fashioned you and me in His and Her own image and we have the same ability to be divine producers. Psalm 18:21 says, **"death and life are in the power of the tongues: and they that love it shall eat the fruit thereof."** Do not underestimate the power of God within (your positive words) to shape your own reality.

The Many Numerical Definitions of the word "SELF"

Below is a simple chart defining the numeric value of each letter according to its position in the alphabet.

A	B	C	D	E	F	G	H	I
1	2	3	4	5	6	7	8	9

J	K	L	M	N	O	P	Q	R
10	11	12	13	14	15	16	17	18

S	T	U	V	W	X	Y	Z
19	20	21	22	23	24	25	26

The Full Numerical Value of "Self"

My concept of the Full Numerical Value of "Self" of any word is its comprehensive purpose as expressed in numbers. The resulting numbers for "Self" will unlock the value each individual person has to the community. Although "Self" is singular, we all have one and we even share the same "Self". Using the chart above, the numerical correspondence of "Self" is **"19+5+12+6"**. This equals a Full Numerical Value of **"42"**. These two digits speak volumes of the comprehensive purpose of "Self".

• Four (4) symbolizes *the inquisitive mind, asking questions, the capacity to search and discover all that is out here to find.* Think about it. There are four cardinal directions. We use these four directions to guide us in a time of confusion. It is the "inner compass" and it is manifest in our desire to *read, write, and define* our reality. We can also say it is *Literacy* and *Logic.*

• We have 4 physical elements (fire, air, earth, and water). As such, four (4) symbolizes *foundation* or *the state of preparedness*, which allows us to build on *stable ground*. Without these elements we would not have substantive matter. It also means understanding because just as a physical foundation of a house is the support for its infrastructure, so does understanding support our wise choices in life.

• Two (2) symbolizes *the state of dependence*. We know that "2" comes right after "1." This *dependence* is expressed fully in terms of the parent-child relationship, wherein children depend on the strength of their parents to provide nourishment and protection from the environment. We even see this principle in the concept of *faith in the divine, the community* and *brotherhood/sisterhood.*

• Two (2) also means *reflection*. Just as the moon (having no light of its own) *reflects* the light of the sun at nighttime, we have the mental capacity to *contemplate* or *reflect* on what we learn from our everyday experiences, family, and community.

As a unit **"42"** symbolizes the person actively engaged in the process of **"defining and discovering themselves through all sorts of literary pursuit" in order (4)** to make themselves an **"interdependent part of the community."** Discover your purpose and make your contribution to the uplifting of our people.

The Simplified Numerical Value of "Self."

The simplified Numerical Value of a word is its fundamental and basic purpose particular to the person, rather than the whole. Here, we unlock what the word's numerical value means for itself.

"Self" according to its Full Numerical Correspondence is **"19+5+12+6."** It is simplified into **"1+5+3+6",** making all digits single. The Simplified Numerical Value is **"15"**. One (1) symbolizes *leadership, focus*, and *determination*; it is our ability to make a decision in response to what must be done. We can also say it symbolizes the *gifts, skills* and *talents* we have to offer the world. Five (5) symbolizes *connection, relationship*, and the *ability to sense/observe.*

Together, **"15"** represents a person who knows what he has of value and is connecting him or herself to some avenue to express their value. We all desire to share what we have with the larger community; this is the nature we are created with. Join an organization that addresses your particular gift and express the beauty that God has put within you for our community.

The 4 Components of "Self"

S

"1"

One (1) symbolizes a healthy self-esteem. Being the first number, it symbolizes the initial component of self that allows every brother and sister the opportunity to mature into completeness. Having a healthy self-image or worth gives us the confidence to "step out on faith" toward any goal we set. We all have an "Inner Leader" who seeks to motivate us to do what must be done. The leading voice within just happens to sound like we do, except we do not hear it with ears; we hear it in our minds.

We can also say One (1) represents our gifts, skills, and talents we possess from the Divine. With your particular set of gifts and talents, you are recognized and praised for the wonderful things you do with them. Whether it is the ability to speak, run, calculate numbers, or even build fine structures, each one of us has something that makes us special and different. Properly cultivating your talents will give you the praise and admiration of your family and friends that naturally feeds a growing self-image.

The negative stereotypes our people are indoctrinated with are designed to damage our self-image. Whether it is our popular language (like "Nigga"), unnatural hair or hair color, or even images of unproductive or childish behavior ("sagging pants"), we are constantly being bombarded with unhealthy reflections of our own self-image.

E

"5"

Making Sense of Yourself and What You Have

314

The Mathematic Make-Up of Self

Five (5) is a numerical symbol for the faculty of observation. We observe through the sensory data received by our "5" senses. It represents all that can be known or perceived. As such, it is Knowledge; and like food, it sustains and satisfies our natural desire to grow intellectually as well as socially.

Five (5) also symbolizes the realization of what activities correspond to the gifts, skills, and talents we possess. It implies experimenting without talents to fully know who we are. From this deep sense of self, we pass from knowledge into intuition, which guides us into the path of what we desire without really knowing where we are going. Experimentation is the science of learning how to make "sense" of any subject. In this case the subject under study is you.

Just as our 5 senses connect us to the physical universe, five (5) also symbolizes our desire to form healthy relationships with others. Being among a true brother or sisterhood is food for the soul, keeping us grounded in times of confusion and doubt. Our families and friends offer guidance and satisfy the natural feeling of belonging. IN this sense, it can represent being a teacher or being taught, being consulted or being a counselor. We all must learn how to be friends to one another.

The word **"Five"** has a numerical correspondence *of* **"6+9+22+5"** and equals *"42,"* the same numerical value of **"Self."** This is a sign that the meanings we gather from the number Five (5) are the most important numeric components of Self. The willingness to translate our abilities into concrete action by coming to know ourselves is vital. The same is equally true of forming healthy relationships among one another.

L

"3"

The Warrior Within

Three (3) symbolizes the ability to handle difficult or stressful situations. There is an old saying, "Two is company and three is a crowd." Another is,"If at first you don't succeed, try and try again." The beauty in both is they symbolically teach that difficulty is associated with the number Three (3). Overcoming the stress of an external or internal threat is necessary to win the battles we face in life and is another vital component of "Self."

We can also say Three (3) represents harnessing control of

the mind, body, and soul. Notice the letter "L" is like unto a leg that holds any structure up. Having the courage to fight, protect, and to stand up or defend communities and ourselves makes one ready at all times to defeat negative aspects that exist within us. As children we were encouraged by our elders to stand up for ourselves when we were getting picked on. The same still holds true as we mature.

Every one of us must learn to be militant. Pain and suffering is natural and inescapable—there is no way around it. Only when we are ready to pass the threshold of pain will freedom to express ourselves grow. Out of this freedom comes an artistic sense that is the basis for the inner beauty we have within. Living without fear is like the sun, it shines regardless to whom or what. We must be the same.

A positive characteristic of fear or the presence of stress is its ability to make us aware of the necessities of life. Self-preservation is the first law of nature and—as the old saying goes, "necessity is the birth invention." Being pushed into a corner gives us the opportunity to show our creative and artistic capacities.

F

"6"

The Power of Attraction

The creator made us all Beautiful and He placed a demand and a command to work to express our Divine Beauty by applying our talents to attract all the necessities and righteous desires we seek from this Universe. Six (6) is a "1" that is pregnant with life, or is like a "1" whose belly (necessities and desires) is fully expressed. Everyone has the potential to put his or her ideas into material form. From creative productivity comes an internal sense of psychological security from leaving something of us on the earth, bearing witness to our presence.

Conclusion

My dear brothers and sisters, life is too valuable to go through it unaware of who you are. Make a list of the talents and skills you have and make a courageous attempt to find your place in the world. Regardless of your age, the Creator made you intelligent enough to make sense of what you have. All you need is the courage to be who and what God created you to be.

PART THREE

LEGACIES OF COURAGE

Achieving Victory Through Courage, Faith, and Determination

Nevil Shed

I was one of those five young Black men who walked on the basketball court at the University of Maryland Sports Arena on March 9, 1966, and confronted a hostile America that did not believe we could defeat the almighty, all-white University of Kentucky basketball team. We were playing for the national championship, and it was predicted that we would lose. After all, the great and legendary coach Adolph Rupp had made it known that five "coons" could not beat five fine white boys. That one game had more meaning outside the basketball arena than any other in the history of the sport. Its importance was a manifestation of what was happening in this country; it was linked to the civil rights struggle underway particularly in the southern part of the country. Black Americans, under the able leadership of Dr. Martin Luther King Jr. were demanding their most deserved and proper station in this country, and white Americans were determined to deny them their rightful place, based on some irrational notion of superiority. It had been that way for decades, and their argument was that it should not change.

As we went through our warm-ups, each of us had reasons why we could not lose. My reason was deeply etched into my memory bank and carried me back to my childhood days in New York City. For a moment I took my eyes off the court and looked up into the stands at my parents and knew they were my reason. Through their suffering I learned to respect courage. Both parents made extreme sacrifices that made it possible for me to be on that court, before a national audience, with the opportunity to make history, and in many ways become a legend in my time. How could I not win? What my teammates and I had to do was vindicate the hundreds of years of suffering juxtaposed against the same number of years filled with hope. We were their hope, and it was mandatory that we deliver a physical and measurable victory. Our victory would make it possible for millions of our people throughout this country to know they could win and that they were somebody.

Sitting on the bench, listening to the screaming fans and the bands playing from both schools, my mind flashed back on a time and incident that tore me apart when it happened and haunted me right until the moment before the tip-off. Once that ball went into the air and the game began, I knew I would erase the pain of that memory forever. With the beginning of that game, the past and the present merged and dictated a major change was coming for the future of Black people in this country. But it all goes back to that afternoon when I went down to Pennsylvania Train Station in New York to meet Dad who worked as a Pullman porter on the railroad.

As a Pullman porter, Dad would spend a lot of time traveling from New York to Chicago and from New York to Miami. When he made runs to Miami he would always bring back a lot of fruit, and I would meet him at the train station to help carry it home on the subway. When the trains would arrive, Dad, along with a number of Black red caps, would assist the white people off the train. First, however, they had to unload the luggage and move it far enough from the train so the steam that periodically exploded from the train wouldn't hit it. I would often help move the luggage away from the train while Dad helped the white folks off. It irked me to hear how they talked to him, calling him boy and all he could do was say "yes ma'am," or "yes sir." I finally couldn't take it anymore when one white man literally cussed him out for something that was not his fault. And that was the incident I momentarily thought about as I sat waiting for the game to start.

I stood there and watched Dad move the man's luggage away from the train; then I returned to the exit to help more people off. But for some reason one of the white men walked over to his luggage, picked it up and put it right next to the train. Within minutes, a blast of steam totally inundated his luggage with moisture. With a shocked and angry look on his face, the man ran over to Dad and began to blame him for the damage. He called him "nigger," "boy," and was all in his face. Instead of smacking that fool right in his mouth, Dad pulled out a towel, strolled over to the luggage and began to wipe it down. That wasn't good enough for the man. He followed Dad over to the luggage and continued to call him out of his name. Just about that time I wanted to go down there and slug the man in his mouth. But I didn't; instead I got angry with my father. I just couldn't understand how the man I most admired in life, the person who was my role model, could allow those men to talk to him that way. I respected him as a man, but he was testing that respect when he took that kind of abuse.

On the train ride home, I felt ashamed of my father. I turned my head and stared out the window because I didn't want to talk to this man who would allow that white man to talk to him in that manner. Finally, when we were all sitting in the living room, I exploded.

"Dad, how could you let that man talk to you like that?" I shouted with tears streaming down my face. "I love you Dad, and I don't want nobody talking to you like that. You're a man just like him and you shouldn't have to listen to that."

He let me finish blowing off steam, then got up, grabbed me by both my skinny arms, and pinned me against the wall. I knew he was angry by the manner in which he grabbed me, but I also knew he was hurt by the tears that streamed from his eyes.

"Boy, you think I like that man talking to me that way?" he asked, but did not wait for an answer. It was his turn to talk and mine to be quiet. "I'm your daddy and I got to take care of you. I got to put food in your stomach, clothes on your back, and a roof over your head." He paused because his emotions had him all choked up. He clenched his teeth and continued. "And I'll take that abuse as long as I know that my payoff is you'll have opportunities I never had and you'll take advantage of them so you'll never have to take that kind of abuse from no man, ever!"

Fast forward ten years later as the horn blew for the start of the game. I was in a position not to have to take that kind of abuse. The night before the game, Coach Haskins came into our rooms and repeated what Coach Rupp had privately told some friends.

"Ain't no way five coons can beat five white boys."

Before he could finish those words, I thought about that time Dad held me and with tears said his effort should pay off and I shouldn't have to take that abuse he took. But that racist coach

321

had done just that. The difference was that we could retaliate by winning. That would be more rewarding than punching him in his racist mouth. Mama drilled in our heads all the time that being successful was going after something you want to be and pursuing it until you got it. Right at that moment, I wanted to be a part of an all-Black basketball team that in forty-eight minutes would be crowned the national champions. Four other young Black men felt the same way. Kentucky really never had a chance. We could have beaten them with determination alone, and essentially not having to be the better basketball players, which we were, to the man.

Proper preparation was the primary reason we were destined for victory. The five of us had been preparing for that day for years. Even though we didn't know each other until we arrived at Texas Western University, we had an inevitable connection. We were destined to carry the weight of the entire Civil Rights Movement on the night of March 9, 1966. We were carrying the weight for Medgar Evers, gunned down outside his home on June 10, 1963; we carried the weight for four little beautiful Black girls killed in the Sixteenth Street Baptist Church bombing on Sept. 9, 1963, in Birmingham, Ala.; we carried the weight for three civil rights workers murdered in Philadelphia, Miss., in 1964; we carried the weight for Malcolm X, gunned down in a Harlem theater in February 1965; and we carried the weight for young heroes at the time like John Lewis, now a Congressman from Atlanta, Ga., James Clyburn, a current Congressman from South Carolina, Stokely Carmichael, who called on Blacks to organize because through unity came power; and we carried the weight for Robert Moses, who was beaten many times traveling throughout the South registering Blacks to vote. That night we carried the weight of over thirty million Blacks who had finally said enough is enough and were ready to lay their life on the line for freedom. They needed our victory as a physical manifestation of their struggle.

Through some distorted view of themselves, white people believed they were invincible when dealing with Black people, even though they had been proven wrong time after time. Jack Johnson proved them wrong when he beat their "Great White Hope" in 1915. Jesse Owens proved them wrong when he beat the best German racers in the 1936 Olympics. Thank God that we, as Black people, don't have to prove our value by diminishing that of another race. Our basketball team felt that way from the beginning of the game until the end. When Coach Haskins told David Latin, our overpowering and dominating forward, to slam-dunk the first opportunity he had and he did it, then the result was inevitable. But in all honesty, we dominated another basketball team and not a white basketball team. We saw opponents and not color. Once that whistle blew and the game started, the opposition could have been blue people from Mars. They were in for a whipping, because we had already made up our mind that the championship belonged to us.

I can practically replay that entire game in my mind. It was such an honor to be able to participate, and there is no way I will ever forget how we took on the powers that be and won. But the moment I remember most is when I walked to the free-throw line with the game tied and a chance for me to put us ahead. When the referee handed me the ball and I knew the entire Black community was watching. My biggest thrill was knowing that the man who had taken abuse for me was also sitting right there in the stands watching. It would have been too much out of character for a player at that moment to turn, look into the stands and shout, "Dad, this is for you." Instead, I bounced the ball a couple of times then sank the foul shot. After that we never did give up the lead. David dominated under that basket and Bobby Joe Hill dominated the rest of the court. He was so good that even a racist like Adolph Rupp had to acknowledge his superior skills that night.

When the final horn blew and the score read Texas Western 72 and Kentucky 65, our fans let out a loud cheer, and the celebration was on. I pointed to Dad and Mama. He knew exactly what I meant. He immediately stretched his arms in my direction. His years of abuse at the hands of men who believed the color of their skin gave them the right to do whatever they wanted were now vindicated with that score. All those years he had shown the courage to endure, and the reward was worth the pain and tears, many, I knew, he shed alone.

Both Grandma and Mama had prayed that the world would change and God would deliver Black people from the abuse and suffering they endured all those years. Grandma was no longer around to share that delivery from God, but Mama swore up and down that He had been right out there with us and because He was, there was no way we could lose. Because of the mornings that she would go without eating so that my brother, Dad, and I could, she is due the privilege to believe God was on our side.

However one wants to view that victory is fine, but what is not left to interpretation is that Black America shared a night of rejoicing that would carry on for years and culminate with election day in November 2008, when a Black man was elected President of the United States of America.

I can assure you that five young Black men were honoring their race, their culture, and their people's future with the victory that still resonates today within the Black communities throughout this country.

Reverend Fred Shuttlesworth: Lion of the Civil Rights Movement

Sephira Bailey Shuttlesworth

Reverend Martin Luther King Jr. called him "one of the most courageous freedom fighters in the South." In the 1961 documentary, *Who Speaks for Birmingham*? Howard K. Smith, a young CBS reporter called him "the man most feared by the southern racists." No annals of American history are complete without encompassing the contributions of this great man. He is, without doubt, an authentic American hero. His name is Rev. Fred Shuttlesworth.

He was born in Montgomery County, Ala. on March 18, 1922, to an unwed mother and the local watchmaker. His maternal grandfather moved the family to Birmingham when Fred was three years old. In Birmingham, his mother, Alberta, met and married William Nathan Shuttlesworth who adopted young Fred. An inquisitive, gifted learner throughout his schooling, popularity surrounded him like a spotlight. In his community, at church, and in school, he regularly heard, "Boy, I see something in you." He heard it so often that soon he thought he saw something in himself.

As a teenager, Fred showed extraordinary learning ability. He once read a four-page oration three times and committed it to memory. His fellow students and the teacher were awe-struck when he stood and recited it verbatim. Fred went on to graduate valedictorian of his high school class. By then, he had narrowed his choices of professions to doctor or minister. He has often said to me that while growing up, he knew more about what he *could not* be rather than what he *could* be. He married at age 19 and became a father at 21.

In his early twenties, Fred began to feel a call toward the ministry, studied the scriptures daily in preparation, and became a minister in 1943. However, for years something had been nagging him. He could not help wondering why, if God made us all in his image, Black people (then called Negroes) had no rights that white people had to respect. His wondering would later lead him to openly challenge the unjust laws of segregation that ruled the South.

Birmingham, Ala. was considered the most segregated city in the South, where segregation was not only accepted as a way of life, it was the *law*. Rev. Shuttlesworth began challenging those laws in the 1950's, first by asking that the city hire Black police officers to patrol the Black communities. His open challenge of the system quickly made him a target for the Klan and other hate-driven groups. History should be careful to record the dramatic exchange that unfolded from 1958 to 1963 between Fred and his nemesis, Eugene "Bull" Conner, Birmingham's notorious Commissioner of Public Safety. That public challenge eventually led to marches in the streets, boycotts, fire hoses and police dog attacks, bombings, arrests, mob beatings, murders, but finally the Civil Rights Act of 1964.

Shuttlesworth was the target of three bombings, including an explosion of his home in 1956 from which he miraculously emerged unscathed. He also survived a mob beating in 1957 as he attempted to enroll two of his children at an all-white high school. He was arrested more than 35 times and sued for millions because of his valiant attempts to lift his people.

Perhaps the most extraordinary thing about this man's work is the spirit in which he insisted on carrying out his tasks. In a document called the *Birmingham Manifesto*, co-authored by Shuttlesworth and Rev. Wyatt Tee Walker, they vowed, "not one hair on the head of one white person will be harmed in our struggle to be free." Although Shuttlesworth was a fiery preacher, who often times irritated both his friends and his foes with his sharp mind and his sharper tongue, he became respected as the courageous, grass-roots leader of the Birmingham movement.

During the spring of 1961, Rev. Walker, then the Executive Director of the Southern Christian Leadership Conference (SCLC), alerted Rev. Shuttlesworth that the Congress on Racial Equality (CORE) had organized the Freedom Riders to challenge the segregation laws on buses and in waiting rooms throughout the Deep South. Walker arranged for Shuttlesworth to be the primary contact for the Riders as they traveled throughout Alabama.

On Sunday, May 14, the drama began to unfold when Shuttlesworth received a phone call from James Peck apprising him of their arrival in Birmingham. The bus never made it to the city. Upon arrival in Anniston, Ala., some 65 miles away, the group was greeted by an angry mob that taunted and threatened the riders and slashed the tires on the bus. Eventually, the driver exited the bus, locked the door, and went for help. With the riders locked on the bus, the crowd began to break windows and tossed an incendiary device through one. The fire caused an explosion which blew the back section of the bus open allowing the riders to escape the fiery furnace right into the grips of the angry crowd.

When Shuttlesworth heard of the violence in Anniston, he organized a nine-car caravan to journey to the aid and rescue of the Freedom Riders. He housed the riders at his church, Bethel Baptist, and in the parsonage. He saw to it that the injured, including James Peck, received treatment. Over the coming days, he engaged in a series of negotiations with local and national authorities, including then Attorney General Robert Kennedy, asking the government officials to provide protection for the riders.

Rev. Shuttlesworth was arrested five times for his participation with the Freedom Riders. In his book, *A Fire You Can't Put Out*, Andrew Manis credits Rev. Shuittlesworth with playing a significant role in the Freedom Rides, acknowledging that the riders spent more time on his turf (Alabama) than any other place along the route. Manis wrote that Fred's role of "encouraging, housing, providing medical care for, and ferrying the riders to the bus station was indispensable."

Those were the days when Black men knew how to fight and who to fight. The enemy was the system that held so many of our people back, that kept the poor, always poor. The laws of the land even upheld the idea that a Black man was less than a man. And for once in our extended history, we came together to organize and force the doors of change open. *Why did we do it?* We did it for the children. Like Fanny Lou Hamer, most of us had gotten sick and tired of being sick and tired. We wanted, if not for ourselves, for our children to be able to pursue our dreams in the land of the free; for future generations to have the chance to self-actualize and become who they were intended to be. Like the greatest of our patriots, we too, longed for life, liberty, and the pursuit of happiness. And we were willing to pay with our very lives. And pay we did.

Fast-forward fifty years.... What about the children today? How are they faring. Did the sacrifice pay off? I suspect that our leaders of the ages would sing, in chorus, the praises of many of our young people for their tenacity, their stewardship, their scholarship, and their character. But together they would also cry out from the agonizing truth that too many of our young people have taken their eye off the mark.

I am reminded of the Biblical story of David and Goliath. David represented the youthfulness that often produces change. Where countless others feared the adversary, he was full of courage. Goliath represented a way of life, a system hinged on fear and destruction, anchored in evil. That system had existed since the beginning of time and it is still alive and well. More of our young people must remove their self-serving blinders in order to see the real challenges that beset our communities and families. From poverty to health care, education, sexism, economic disparities, injustice, crime, drugs, environmental issues, and our old enemy racism, the world is full of formidable foes to fight rather than to perpetuate the lingering attacks on each other. Where is the courage to lead the fight against the systems that threaten life as we know it as well as for generations to come?

I am convinced that it does not take courage to fight and/or kill your brother. Instead, it takes courage to slay life's giants. The bold truth is that when you take someone else's life you give up your own along with it. Multiple lives lost and multiple families in anguish and almost always over something frivolous. And all the while, the real Goliaths are running amuck. Too many of us have taken our eyes off the prize.

When we fail to harness our energies to address the needs of our fellow man (the community as a whole) we leave ourselves vulnerable to ultimately make decisions that hurt or destroy us. This is one of the tenets that our forefathers understood well. For men like Shuttlesworth and King, preparation for their life's work began early, and commitments were made to either kill the system or be killed by it for the good of the masses.

So what if with the same tenacity and determination that we

attack each other and vow to get even, we attacked injustice and disparity, vowing to even the playing field? And what if our young people could somehow see that having babies outside the family structure sets our race up to be slaves to another system that insures that our children are born weaker, learn slower, perform poorer, and struggle to the extent that they too, become wards of the system, perpetuating this cycle again and again to the destruction of our people? Is that what our ancestors gave their lives for? Is it really how we want our history to be written? A proud people who emerged from royalty and evolved to…what?

What will your legacy be? Are you a thug with a gun and proud of it? Or are you a leader, full of the kind of courage that won't let you sit idly by and watch the world destroy itself? Are you able and willing to find an unjust cause and apply your best efforts to rectify it? What we've learned from the past is that violence begets violence and courage begets courage.

On behalf of those very courageous men, women, and children, including my husband and many of his colleagues, we are asking you to prepare yourself in your youth for a cause greater than yourself. Learn all you can while you can. And if you really want to establish a legacy of courage, take others along with you. Inspire someone you know to improve their lives and plant seeds of prosperity and change in their community. Repeat this practice again and again. Remember, courage begets courage. The world is counting on you to make it better. Get on your mark! Keep your eyes on the prize! Stay the course! And run your race with grace and integrity! If you do that well, not even the wind can touch you.

"We Who Believe In Freedom Cannot Rest:"

What the Life and Work of Ella Baker Meant To Me

Margaret Richardson, M. A.

"Until the killing of Black men, Black mothers' sons, becomes as important to the rest of the country as the killing of a white mother's son, we who believe in freedom cannot rest."

Today, Ella Josephine Baker is forgotten. Her name is spoken only in circles of current leaders on the national stage. She is seldom written about in a history book, her profile in courage barely recorded among the many works detailing the Civil Rights Movement. Most of the work she did is attributed to others, some a little too eager to reap praise for work they did not have the stomach or fortitude to do.

Ella Baker's towering presence in the Civil Rights Movement has been made into a footnote after being taken over and consumed by the profiles of Martin Luther King Jr., Jesse Jackson, and others who captured the eye of the television camera. Maybe it was because Ella Baker worked from the sidelines, always in support of someone else. Or maybe, just maybe because that is the way she wanted to work. Ella Baker was a force of nature and touched every facet of the civil rights movement, from grassroots work to collective organization to social activism. She selflessly mentored and nurtured emerging young leaders like Diane Nash, Bob Moses, and Stokely Carmichael. Even though she is forgotten, Ella Baker made a definite impression on me.

As odd as it sounds, I was introduced to Ella Baker while I was looking for material for Kathleen Cleaver and Pauli Murray, other forgotten "sheroes" of the movement. While reading *Freedom's Daughters: The Unsung Heroines of the Civil Rights Movement From 1830 to 1970*, by Lynne Olson, I was impressed that Baker, who had been married from 1940 to 1959, had not taken the name of her husband. You ask: Why did this stand out to me? In a time when women were being told that their femininity was connected to a certain perception of womanliness, hour-glass silhouette, and staying at home to take care of house and home after World War Two, the fact that a Black woman could be married yet refuse to take the name of her husband symbolized to me that she was her own person. Not only that but many of those close to her never knew that Baker was married. I was fascinated by the example she set – she would not let herself be defined by being her husband's wife. Indeed this symbolized a greater significance because it is how Ella Baker lived her life, on her terms, refusing to be relegated to inferior status, even by those in the struggle who were not used to taking orders from a woman.

Ella Baker challenged and then helped to support Martin Luther King Jr. in establishing the Southern Christian Leadership Conference (SCLC). Created in the days after the Montgomery Bus Boycott, Baker seized the opportunity to take the momentum of the boycott and continue to the work of trying to register Blacks to vote. Even though King was the head of the SCLC and needed Baker for its day-to-day operations, he was uneasy having to depend on Baker. She was often the only woman in the room during discussions of organizing and planning, the only female in the sea of Black men who had assumed the front ranks of the Civil Rights Movement.

Baker was the SCLC's main organizer, secretary, and staff. She was the main reason for its effectiveness and success with registering Blacks to vote in the South. Also, she was the leading force behind the Student Nonviolent Coordinating Committee (SNCC). Now remembered primarily as the launching pad for the young Stokley Carmichael and for the controversial call for Black Power that pre-dated the creation of the Black Panther Party, SNCC was a leader in empowering students to action, to participate in the struggle that was also theirs to shoulder.

SNCC was formed in the days after the beginning of the sit-ins that took the world by storm. Quietly organized and executed by college students, the sit-ins were the very definition of the Baker philosophy of participatory democracy. The students themselves were doing the legwork of their organizing while assembling the leadership from their ranks to answer the call for direct action. Baker, while not their direct leader, was their unofficial godmother, providing guidance and supporting the students' efforts for them to provide their own direction. The Freedom Rides, also spawned as a result of the work by SNCC, found its origins in the example of direct action while retaining their independence of thought.

I can go on and on about the many decisions that were influenced by the presence of Ella Baker. But in the examples I have mentioned are perhaps two examples of how significant Ella Baker was to the Civil Rights Movement, to Black women in general, and to me in particular. Not only was she determined to control her own destiny but she was did not let anyone define who she was. She challenged anyone who attempted to put her in a box, not only through words but deeds. In fact, it would seem as if she worked harder just to prove that she had a place at the table and worked even harder to make sure others could benefit. In each of the organizations she worked with, Baker was the foundation that kept them grounded. She was the clay that held the mold together and she was the glue that kept many of these organizations together.

Ella Baker's body of service in the civil rights movement will never be chronicled as it should and certainly not given the space in this essay that it should. She devoted her life to the struggle and to the countless people she mentored, mothered, protected, and sheltered. That is perhaps, her legacy to me as an emerging leader in my community. The devotion Baker showed to the people she took responsibility for is a dynamic that I have only begun to understand and share. It is up to anyone who answers the call of direct action to understand the sacrifice, responsibility and blessing that comes with the job. It is also up to anyone who answers the call to remember that they have an obligation to share their resources with those coming in behind them. We as a community will never rise as long as some refuse to pass the torch or fail to take under our wing someone who needs nurturing. I may not ever have the opportunity to devote my resources as completely to the cause for uplift as Ella Baker did. But as God orders my steps, I realize that part of my path has already been prepared for me by the life and service of Ella Josephine Baker.

The Tuskegee Airmen and American Exceptionalism

Cary Clack

The eagle gets its name for the color of its plumage. The word "eagle" is a derivative from the Latin word, "Acquilus" which means, swarthy, dark-colored, or blackish. In the early 1940's there were a group of eagles down in Alabama who wanted to test their wings. These eagles were men whose plumage was swarthy, dark-colored, and blackish--men who other men didn't believe possessed the talent, the temperament, the intelligence, the reflexes, and the courage to fly.

From childhood, we are told that the sky is the limit. But for these swarthy eagles in Alabama, these men known as the Tuskegee Airmen, the cliché was a lie. The sky wasn't the limit. Like many places on the earth to which they were bound, the sky was off-limits because their skin, their plumage, had been darkened by the sun's kiss.

But one of the attributes of eagles is their vision. They possess extraordinary eyesight and can see things far into the distance. They have the ability to see things others can't. The Tuskegee Airmen, confident in the God given gifts, looked into the distance and saw themselves in flight, imagined themselves taking to the air in the finest aircraft in the world and fighting for their country, even as it denied them the freedom for which the country was at war to preserve.

They began World War II as outcasts whose talent was denied and not given a chance to flourish and ended it as heroes on their way to becoming legends. Officially known as the 332nd Fighter Group of the United States Army Air Corps, they received their

335

training at the historically Black Tuskegee Institute in Alabama. Nearly 1,000 pilots were trained in the program and the Tuskegee Airmen became world-famous as the United States' only all-Black unit of the war. They became subjects of lore, books, and movies, lionized as men who overcame obstacles of law and custom to achieve heights that surprised only those who doubted their gifts.

In 2007, President George W. Bush awarded the airmen the Congressional Gold Medal. The youngest of the airmen was in his 80's. In his remarks to the airmen, Bush said "Even the Nazis asked why African-American men would fight for a country that treated them so unfairly…these men in our presence felt a special sense of urgency. They were fighting two wars; one was in Europe, and the other took place in the hearts and minds of our citizens. That war taking place in the hearts and minds of Americans proved to be the more difficult of the two, but they won both wars.

For decades the amazing feats of the Tuskegee Airmen were coated with perfection. Perfection is an ideal dreamed about and pursued but rarely captured. It is so rare and out of reach that its elusiveness is used as an excuse for mistakes. When someone errs, it is dismissed with the reminder, "Well, nobody's perfect." Because most claims of perfection such as "He's the perfect husband" or "It's the perfect job," are subjective and exaggerated, the only things truly perfect are those that can be quantified by objective numbers. In bowling, a perfect game is a score of 300. In baseball, a perfectly pitched game is retiring 27 batters without allowing a base runner. (Although a truly perfect game would be getting 27 batters out on 27 pitches.)

For more than 60 years, the Tuskegee Airmen's perfect number was "0" as in the number of bombers lost to enemy fighters. But the day before they received the Congressional Gold Medal, an Air Force report was released that revealed that enemy aircraft had shot down at least 25 bombers escorted by the 332nd Fighter Group. The report proved just one thing: nobody's perfect, not even the Tuskegee Airmen. It didn't diminish their achievements, heroism, or trailblazing or remove from the record that they were so good that their services as escorts were requested by white bomber pilots who didn't know or didn't care that they were Black.

The report corrects numbers but can't rewrite the history of what these great aviators accomplished. Anyway, losing 25 planes in more than 15,000 sorties on 1500 missions made them close to flawless. The Tuskegee Airmen, those eagles out of Alabama, were men of extraordinary vision. They saw things and imagined possibilities others couldn't see or imagine.

When their government and fellow countrymen and women doubted them, they saw the bountiful gifts that God had blessed them with. When their country, the land of their births, treated them like second-class citizens and denied them justice and equality, they saw the immense promise of the Declaration of Independence and the Constitution. When society and custom demanded that they bow their heads in shame and submission, they lifted their heads, raised their eyes, and fixed their gaze on a far horizon that they knew was their destination.

And they took flight, made history, and became legends.

The night before he was assassinated, Dr. Martin Luther King Jr. cried out that he'd been to the mountaintop and seen the Promised Land. The Tuskegee Airmen flew over that mountaintop and carried all of us closer to that Promised Land. Perfection is in an ideal rarely achieved. The Tuskegee Airmen weren't called to be perfect. They were called to be heroic, they were called to be trailblazers, and they were called to fly into history.

The eagles answered that call magnificently.

Ida B. Wells-Barnett, The Crusader from Mississippi

Rhonda M. Lawson

There are some who throw up their hands in the face of adversity, feeling powerless against the wrongs of the world. Some might even ask, "What can I do? I'm only one person. I have no money. I have no influence. Who would even listen to me?"

Those words may possibly have crossed the mind of Ida B. Wells-Barnett at one time but instead of succumbing to those thoughts, she did the seemingly impossible—she overcame them. Today, she is most remembered for her journalistic efforts against the horrors of lynching and her crusades for women's rights.

Born in 1862, the daughter of two activists in Holly Springs, Miss., Ida rarely had time to dwell on being powerless. By the time she was sixteen, both her parents had died of yellow fever, leaving her on her own to take care of five brothers and sisters. Despite being a former slave, she had learned to read at a young age, so she was eventually able to find work as a schoolteacher. Later, she and two younger sisters moved to Memphis, Tenn., where she again taught school while attending nearby Fisk University. This move would soon change the course of her life.

Shortly after moving to Memphis, Ida planned a trip to Nashville, Tenn. The United States Supreme Court had just overturned the 1875 Civil Rights Law that banned discrimination in hotels and in transportation, ruling that the national government lacked jurisdiction where the facilities and transportation were under local and state laws. The state of Tennessee, as well as most southern states immediately began to enforce segregated quarters for Blacks on trains, and that was the case when Ida bought her ticket for first class travel. Having taken her seat in the first class car, the conductor promptly informed her that she would have to move to the Black section of the train, which was always in the front car because it was the hottest and where the smoke from the train settled. Ida adamantly refused to move. The conductor then tried to forcibly remove her, but she defended herself, biting him on the hand. He got help and with two other grown men, forcibly dragged her out of the car to the applause of the white passengers.

Because of the altercation, Ida sued the Chesapeake and Ohio Railroad, winning a five hundred dollar settlement, which was immediately overturned by the Appeals Court. She ended up paying two hundred dollars in costs. Ida's disappointment only lasted a moment. She began writing a series of articles about race and politics in the South under the pseudonym, "Iola." These articles spurred her career change from teacher to journalist.

Her articles attacked the unlawful lynching of Black men and women. When two prominent Black men were lynched, Ida put it on the front page of her newspaper. She advised Blacks to leave Memphis because it, "will neither protect our lives and property, nor give us a fair trial in the courts." She further encouraged Black citizens to avenge the lynching even if they had "to burn up whole towns." Ida encouraged all Blacks to arm themselves and protect their families. Her articles were so incendiary they caught the attention of both Black and white journalists. In 1887 the lady from Mississippi was named the most prominent Black correspondent at the National Afro-American Press Convention. She also bought one-third share in the newspaper, *Free Speech and Headlight,* becoming part owner and editor.

Soon, tragedy hit close to home when three male friends of hers, all successful businessmen, were accused of a crime and subsequently lynched. This so outraged Ida that she began an anti-lynching campaign through her newspaper. Her articles encouraged Blacks to boycott the city's transportation system. Her personal investigations uncovered other lynching injustices. She was so successful in motivating the southern Black populace that her newspaper was destroyed and her life threatened if she ever returned to Memphis (she happened to be visiting the Black publisher T. Thomas Fortune in New York when her press was burned). She stayed in New York and went to work for Fortune but continued campaigning against the atrocities of lynching in the South in New York and England. "Having lost my paper," she wrote in her autobiography, *Crusade for Justice: The Autobiography of Ida B. Wells Barnett,* "I had a price on my life, and been made an exile from home for printing the truth, I felt that I owed it to my race to tell the whole truth now that I was where I could do so freely." Her articles became so popular that Ida B. Wells' clubs sprung up in Chicago and other northern cities. Their goal was to eliminate lynching.

Her work brought her face to face with some of the most prominent figures in African American history, including Frederick Douglas, Booker T. Washington (she was very critical of Washington's accomodationist policies), and Dr. W.E.B. DuBois. She stood against both racial and gender injustices, helping to found the National Association of Colored Women. Even after moving to Chicago and marrying Ferdinand Barnett and giving birth to four children, her work for equality continued. She even ran for state senate in 1930, although her campaign was unsuccessful.

Ida died the following year of kidney disease, but her work in the pursuit of equality has never been forgotten. Today the Ida B. Wells Memorial Foundation and the Ida B. Wells-Barnett Museum in Holly Springs stand as a memorial to her work. Today, African American politicians and journalists, including President Barak Obama stand on the shoulders of giants like this young girl from Mississippi who dared to stare adversity in face and not back down.

A Sharecropper's Daughter
Brenner Stiles

No one possibly could have anticipated that a forty-one-year old uneducated sharecropper from the Mississippi Delta town of Rueville, Fannie Lou Hamer, would become one of the real heroes of the 1960's Civil Rights Movement. Fannie Lou was the youngest of twenty children born to her fiery mother who always carried a gun while working in the cotton fields. Early on in life she preached to Fannie Lou, "If you respect yourself enough other people will have to respect you also." To her mother the gun she carried in the cotton sack was the equalizer and brought her respect.

In order for the family to survive their miserable sharecropper's existence, Fannie Lou was forced to work the cotton fields right along with her siblings. Three quarters of all the Black residents in the Delta before 1970 lived below the poverty line. There was no time for school or a formal education. All the knowledge came in the fields trying to survive. But what Fannie Lou had more than most of the others was a strong "mother wit," and very low tolerance for injustice. These qualities would serve her well as she took on the forces of segregation and political oppression at the height of the Civil Rights Movement.

Rueville was a rural plantation town where the sharecropper population was the majority and if allowed to vote could have held every one of the elective offices. That is why the white landowners used every form of intimidation to make sure they never got the right to vote. One of the most effective forms was to evict any recalcitrant sharecropper who tried to vote, off his land. That method was quite effective with the farmers. Most of them refused to participate with Robert Moses and the Student Non-Violent Coordinating Committee when they showed up to register them to vote. That wasn't true with Fannie Lou when she first met Moses at a voter registration meeting held at the only Black church on the outskirts of the town.

Moses explained to the reluctant Blacks that the only way they could possibly break down the old tradition was to go with him to Indianola and apply for registration. Fannie Lou and a few other workers accepted the challenge and went to Indianola to register. Their registration request was not granted and she knew that the landowner would be right there to meet her with an eviction notice. She was right and he was waiting for her. The white owner told Fannie Lou that the Ku Klux Klan and White Citizens Council were harassing him because his field hands had been messing in politics. She had a choice, according to him: She could stop her meddling in politics or leave the land and cabin she had called home for the past eighteen years, which also meant leaving her husband, Pap Hamer. That night she left her family and found shelter in the home of a SNCC supporter.

There was no looking back for Fannie Lou. She was totally committed to the battle for justice. According to her, the refusal to vote and the denial of basic human rights in Mississippi may have been legal by the white man's standards but unjust by God's standards. She enrolled in SNCC's literacy classes under the leadership of another dynamic woman, Anne Ponder. Once she graduated from Ponder's class, she and four other students traveled to Tennessee to attend Septima Clark's intensive one-week teacher training class. It was when Fannie Lou and the other women started back to Mississippi along with Ponder, that she encountered the real brutal nature of racism.

They were traveling by Trailways Bus and when they stopped at the station in Winona, Miss., Ponder decided that she would test the new Interstate Commerce Commission regulation outlawing segregated facilities in interstate travel. She exited the bus and proceeded to walk into the white waiting room. Ponder and the others were arrested and taken off to jail, even though the students hadn't gone inside the waiting room. One of the arresting policeman promised that they would make the girls "wish they were dead."

Once inside the jail, they dragged Fannie Lou into a separate and empty cell. The police then forced two Black prisoners to beat her with a Billy club. One of the men held her down while they other inflicted the blows, then they switched and continued until her fingers went numb and skin on her back swelled up. But the beating did not have its intended effect. In fact, it did just the opposite; it made Fannie Lou more determined to change a system that allowed grown men, pledged to uphold the law, to break those same laws free from any punishment.

That beating in a Mississippi jail served as a catalyst to propel Fannie Lou forward. Afterwards she didn't want to just vote, but wanted control of the political apparatus in her county and town. With that in mind she helped to form the Mississippi Freedom Democratic Party (MFDP). A year prior to passage of the Voting Rights Act, these courageous Black sharecroppers joined forces with the SNCC and other Black civil rights leaders in the state of Mississippi to challenge the legitimacy of the established Democratic Party. Under the leadership of a sharecropper's daughter, the MFDP argued the moral imperative that they be seated at the National Democratic Convention in place of the established party.

To the chagrin of President Lyndon Baines Johnson, the MFDP took their case right to the convention when they were denied seats by the state delegation. Leading the charge was that sharecropper's daughter. They set up a boycott right outside the convention and were soon joined by such notables as Dr. Martin Luther King Jr., Stokely Carmichael, and the great Washington, D.C. civil rights lawyer Joseph Rauh. Dr. King argued that it was crucial that the convention recognize the MFDP because the entire free world was watching. It was an opportunity for the United States to demonstrate to oppressed people struggling for their own freedom "that somewhere in this world there is a nation that cares about justice."

The boycott in Atlantic City caught the attention of the entire world and infuriated President Johnson. When it was time for Fannie Lou to testify before the credentials committee, all television cameras zoomed in on her. She used this as an opportunity to strike back at the Winona Police Department by telling the world about the beating she took in a cell simply because she dared exercise her Constitutional right to vote. The apex of her testimony came when she pointed out that she was actually in jail being beaten at the same time that Medgar Evers was murdered in front of his home in Jackson, Miss. At that point, this sharecropper's daughter became the hero and everyone flocked to her after she ended her stirring rendition of a terrible example of America's injustice toward some of its people. *Jet magazine* reporter at the time Larry Still captured the scene in his column, "I felt just like I was telling it from the mountain," he reported Fannie Lou saying. "That's why I like that song, 'Go Tell It on the Mountain;' I feel like I'm talking to the world."

From that point on, this beautiful Black sister, who represented the tragic story of many of our women and men stuck in the mire of poverty, became a spokesperson for her race. In late 1964 Fannie Lou was invited to be the principal speaker at the Williams Institutional Christian Methodist Episcopal Church in Harlem. Malcolm X was present on the stage with her. Afterwards Malcolm X invited Fannie Lou to attend a rally of his new Organization of African American Unity, thus creating a bond between an east coast organization with a southern-based peoples' movement. For a very short period of time (Malcolm was assassinated two months later) Fannie Lou, an oppressed sharecropper from the South joined in coalition with an oppressed poverty stricken Black man from the North. They both had risen from the depths of what could be defeat to the heights of victory for their people, and thus demonstrated the excellence that is innate to African American people in this country.

Today, the heritage and legacy of Fannie Lou Hamer is carried on every morning, five days a week, on Sirius XM Radio on the African American talk show station by Joe Madison. He begins every hour with a quote from the sharecropper's daughter, thus assured that we will never lose the wise words of this knowledgeable woman. The quote is an excellent way to end this tribute to her. It goes as follows:

"You can pray until you faint, but if you don't get up and do something, God ain't going to put it in your lap. And there's no need of running, no need of saying 'honey, I ain't going to get in the mess.' Because if you're born with a Black face in America, you're already in the mess."

Reverend Claude Black Defends an Icon and Challenges a Giant

Taj Matthews

Writing as a young African American, I am very much aware of the tremendous responsibility that my generation will soon inherit from our elders. Now reaching the twilight years of their lives, they are the generation who stood their ground in the 1960's and 70's and fought against an entrenched, well-oiled racist machine throughout the South and in the North. After decades of humiliating social injustice, the Black men, women, and children of the civil rights years said no more.

Frederick Douglass, the great orator and abolitionist told Black people of his generation that "Power concedes nothing without a struggle. It never has and it never will." That was the case in the South when men like Dr. Martin Luther King Jr., Rev. Ralph Abernathy, and Rev. Fred Shuttlesworth took on Eugene Bull Connors, Commissioner of the Birmingham Alabama Police Force, and Governor George C. Wallace during that turbulent summer in 1963.

The one important quality these men possessed was courage. They faced the immense power of the racist machine and did not back down. But it wasn't only in Birmingham that this kind of courage existed. It was also present in San Antonio, Texas, manifested through my Grandfather, Rev. Claude Black. He never received the national recognition of a Dr. King or Rev. Abernathy but he displayed the same kind of courage as those other brave Black men. "He stood up during times that positions (on civil rights) were not safe and the politics not popular," is how Martin Luther King III described my grandfather.

Rev. Black's life was constantly threatened. A number of times he was accosted by hostile racists and his church was burned down, but he never wavered in his staunch commitment to equality for his people. "A person that can talk about justice should fight for it," according to Dr. Nick Carter, President of Andover Newton Theological Seminary. He went on to say, "In the Hebrews scriptures, that is what we call a righteous man and that is Reverend Black."

On two separate occasions, Grandfather put his courage right next to his convictions and did not back down from his detractors. The first time he was tested happened in 1952 when the famous cultural icon, Langston Hughes, was invited by local Blacks to read some of his poetry at the Colored Library Auditorium, which is now the Carver Community Cultural Center. The Black community was very excited about Hughes coming to San Antonio. On the other hand, there were quite a few in the white community that resented him because of his committed struggle against racial inequality. They did not want him to visit for fear that he would incite the Black population to take a stand against the city's segregated facilities.

Within days of Hughes's scheduled appearance the city attorney, with the assistance from the police department, forced the sponsoring group to cancel the event. Yes, if you can believe that in America, where freedom of speech is supposed to be protected under the First Amendment of the U. S. Constitution, a man was blocked by the awesome power of the local government from exercising that very guaranteed right. The reason given by the city officials was that he would incite a riot with his speech, supposedly tainted with a Communist message. That infuriated my grandfather. Against the advice of less courageous individuals, Rev. Black decided to address the all-white and segregationist city council to demand an explanation.

My grandfather entered the chamber at City Hall and was met with contemptuous looks from the whites attending the council meeting in anticipation of his appearance as well as the seven city council members, including the mayor. Despite the sneers and ugly stares, Grandfather took his seat and waited his turn to speak. He listened as the man testifying, Austin Hancock of the segregationist organization, The American Heritage Group, accused Hughes of being anti-American. He claimed that his appearance would cause an uprising among the local "Negroes."

When he finished his vicious attacks on this great Black American, Grandfather walked to the podium ignoring the jeers and taunts of being called "Communist, Communist." It was quite ironic that these people would accuse a man of God of being a Communist. I guess these fine citizens didn't understand that Christianity is anti-ethical to the Communist doctrine. Grandfather would later admit to me that he felt nervous standing there and vulnerable to a bunch of racists, who would just as soon see him hanging from a tree as standing there acting like an "uppity nigger." But he stood his ground and demanded that the council provide concrete proof that Langston Hughes ever had any Communist affiliations.

Members of the city council never addressed Grandfather but left that job to the city attorney. He provided Grandfather with no concrete evidence but simply stated that he was fearful that Mr. Hughes would incite a riot. He refused to further elaborate or to answer any of Rev. Black's questions in order to clarify his charges. During the entire deliberation not one city council member spoke up.

Just as Grandfather finished speaking, real trouble, in the form of five large white men, walked into the chamber and walked right up to the front, blocking Grandfather from leaving the chambers. It took five of them to confront one pacifist preacher. They showed their cowardly nature while, on the other hand, Grandfather brushed right around them, showing his courage. As he made his way to the back of the chamber, he heard one of the men shout, "Now what you all must understand is that not all the 'niggers' in this city are like this uppity 'nigger.'"

It was not surprising to Grandfather but somewhat appalling that the city council allowed this man to insult and demean a man of the cloth without one member objecting. But Grandfather did not back down. He marched out of that chamber and city hall with his chest stuck out, proud that he had stood up for one of the most basic Constitutional rights given to all Americans, and that is freedom of expression. In doing so, he also stood up for a great Black American icon, the poet, Langston Hughes.

Rev. Black's tremendous courage was on display again in 1958 when he single-handedly challenged the entire city's religious community and Rev. Billy Graham. The Black ministers of the city were asked to encourage their congregations to attend the Billy Graham crusade coming to San Antonio. Grandfather supported what Rev. Graham was doing in building a strong soul-saving ministry and he was willing to support his efforts. But that all changed when he found out that Price Daniel, a man who was running for Governor of Texas on a segregationist ticket, would introduce Rev. Graham at the revival. He felt that if he participated in the event, it could be interpreted that he supported the segregationist for governor. Grandfather went one step further than not participating in the event. He contacted the organizers for the Billy Graham crusade in San Antonio and complained about a segregationist being a part of a Christian service. Their response was that Grandfather needed to be a better Christian. He countered, saying it seemed being a Christian, according to them, did not require that we all fight for equal rights.

The committee continued to ignore his concerns so Rev. Black decided that he would mount a boycott of the crusade unless Daniel was dropped from the program. His question to the organizers, who all considered themselves dedicated Christians, was how could they possibly talk about God and love but accept racism, discrimination, and segregation? At that point, he believed that Rev. Graham had to take a stand against segregation. Grandfather contacted Dr. Martin Luther King Jr., A. Phillip Randolph, and Adam Clayton Powell Jr. and asked that they contact Rev. Graham in an attempt to persuade him to drop Daniel from the program. They all did contact him but to no avail. The only concession Rev. Graham made was to integrate the audience. He went one step further and found a Black minister willing to appear on stage with him and Daniel. They needed a "token," according to Grandfather, to show that all Blacks were not supportive of Daniel being dropped.

The crusade went on as planned and Grandfather refused to participate as did most of the other ministers. But their one Black minister stood on the platform with the segregationist and made a mockery out of what Grandfather and the others attempted to accomplish. Years later that same minister admitted to my Grandfather that it was a mistake on his part. An interesting aside is a few years later that same minister was beaten up by a group of racists and turned to Grandfather for help.

During that entire ordeal, the white ministers of the city attacked Rev. Black. They felt that his efforts were harmful to Rev. Graham's crusade for Christ. But just as Dr. King wrote in his "Letter from a Birmingham Jail" to a group of ministers who thought his actions in breaking laws were not Christian, and explained to them that being Christian called on all men of the cloth not to support unjust laws, my Grandfather told these ministers that it was his God-given duty to oppose any segregationist wherever he might appear, and that included a Billy Graham crusade.

On many other occasions, Rev. Claude Black put his life on the line as he constantly fought against the forces of evil in San Antonio and other parts of Texas. He was cut from the same cloth as other courageous Black leaders during those times of immense danger. These were men and women who stood for what was right and wouldn't let anyone back them down from their position. Just as the Black race has always had heroes to rise up to the crisis of their time, these brave men did the very same during the civil rights crisis. For that reason we must place them all in the category with such heroes as Nat Turner, Frederick Douglass, Harriet Tubman, Sojourner Truth, Dr. W.E.B. DuBois, and Ida B. Wells.

It is now important that my generation, the future leaders of the race, step forward like the brave men and women of the past, and take on the crisis facing us today. We must fight against all the negative influences in our community. Those of us who are the potential leaders must reach out to our peers and speak out when they are abusive to each other. We are compelled to tell our brothers to treat our sisters with respect; we are compelled to tell our brothers to leave the drugs alone, get an education and become productive participants in society. We are compelled to tell our brothers to pull up their pants, straighten out their attitudes, give up the gang mentality, and stop killing each other. If we do anything less, then we have dropped the ball and do not deserve to inherit the future of our culture and our people.

Moving From Obscurity to Prominence

Reverend James W. Sanders Sr.

I was born on September 17, 1929, in Union, S. C., a small, rural town located in the northern part of the state. The year I was born, over two hundred thousand people throughout the world died from an outbreak of influenza, the soft drink 7-Up was created, and two years earlier, Charles Lindberg had made his historical flight across the Atlantic Ocean in the Spirit of St. Louis. Most Americans had adopted the new age technology called the radio. It was a time when writers like William Faulkner, F. Scott Fitzgerald, and Ernest Hemmingway began to showcase their talent while the Harlem Renaissance was coming to an end. Harlem had seen the discovery and growth of immense African American talent readily on display in its music, art, poetry, and novels. A group of artists, led by the Harvard trained, Dr. W.E.B. DuBois, the Howard University Philosophy Instructor, Alain Locke; and by the young Bohemian writers, Langston Hughes, Wallace Thurmond, and Zora Neale Hurston, denounced the Euro-centric belief that all good literature must have a European connection and explored the African American culture in ways never done before.

Although I have traveled all over the world, I have never lived more than thirty miles from my birthplace. About the time I was born, Blacks were leaving the South in large numbers as a result of the push/pull phenomenon. The push was the escape from the horrendous conditions under which we were forced to live. Many Blacks refused to accept segregation and left for the North. The pull was the attraction of finding work in the north. Henry Ford had just introduced the Model T Ford, Andrew Carnegie had steel mills in Pittsburgh, and Blacks headed North to find work in these industries. Despite the poverty and racism, my family decided to remain right there in Union because that was our home and we refused to give it up to anyone for any reason. We were the Sanders family and that meant a lot to us.

Our pride emanated from Granddad, who was the greatest influence in my life. William Sanders was a no-nonsense man. He had a mill job as a painter. He was strong-willed, very tough, and because of his firm belief that all men should be treated fairly, he often took stands that put him in danger from the white establishment. One time he had an altercation with his supervisor on his job and the man called Grandpa a "nigger." Granddad punched the man right in the face and stood his ground in case any of the other workers wanted to take him on. They chose to leave him alone. In another confrontation he took on a lynch mob. His youngest brother was about to be lynched in the county courthouse yard for looking the wrong way at a white woman. Someone told Granddad and he went up to that place and asked what the problem was. After being told, he grabbed his brother by the arm, walked right through the crowd and said, "Come on let's go." Nobody did or said anything to him. That took a certain kind of courage that men possessed back then. This myth that all our Black men were cowards and ran from danger just isn't true. Granddad was proof of that.

Granddad also taught me about honor and pride among Blacks caught up in that horrible system. He told me early to always let your word be your bond. If you promise somebody something keep your promise. If you find you can't keep it, don't wait for them to come to you, go to them. If Granddad was your friend he would tell you, "I'm with you when you're right because you are right. And I'm with you when you're wrong to help get you right."

Every Sunday during my youth, he took me to church with him. As Superintendent of Sunday school at Corinth Baptist Church he was never late and would take me every Sunday during my youth to church with him. He was truly my role model, and every young boy in this country should have a role model just like him.

From him as well as my father, who was also my role model, I learned the importance of hard work. Poppa worked for the government during the Great Depression. President Franklin Roosevelt's administration established the Works Progress

Administration, designed to provide employment for unemployed workers. Although he only made $15.00 every two weeks Poppa managed his money so that we could make it. He taught me to never live above my means. He would often say, "If you desire something wait until you are able to pay for it." That advice stuck with me throughout my life. Mamma worked for several white families every day from 8:30 in the morning until 1:30 in the afternoon. She would wash and iron for five different families and still come home to take care of her family. She was a strong and beautiful woman.

School and education was an absolute necessity in our family. I was taught that our education should help us as well as others who would need our help. My parents wanted their children to accomplish more in life than what they had. Poppa would often say, "James, if you don't go any further than I did, I will consider myself a failure." I believed both my parents and after graduating from high school, I attended Benedict College in Columbia, S. C., from 1947 until 1951. Benedict College has a very rich history. Its first class consisted of ten emancipated slaves and one teacher, Reverend Timothy L. Dodge. He was a college-trained preacher from the North, who became president of the institute. The college had very humble beginnings. It was housed in a former slave owner's mansion in 1839 to train teachers and preachers.

By the time I began my college career, I had already given my life to the Lord. While in the tenth grade I began my public ministry. I was only sixteen at the time. Prior to my calling I had worked a number of jobs around Union. At twelve years old I worked in the afternoon and on Saturdays for Cleveland Five and Ten Store. I made $7.00 a week. I also worked a variety of jobs as dishwasher and janitor. In 1943 I got a job at the only hotel in Union. I worked as a dishpan washer and as a bell hop. But I had to give it all up when I received my calling. I had to dedicate all my time to the Lord. I preached my first sermon on June 9, 1946, at my home church, Corinth Baptist in Union. I continued the study of ministry at Benedict College.

I met my best friend whom God strategically placed in my life while attending Benedict College. He was a World War II veteran who had returned to college in order to better his life. He was not a bitter man over the racism that Blacks in uniform faced but was determined to take advantage of all opportunities presented to him as a result of fighting for democracy overseas only to return home and be denied those same democratic values. He had a car, and I was able to ride back and forth to school with him. Our friendship was a blessing from God, and what we shared as two Black men is what all Black men should share. We would never have called each other by the "n" word or "dawg." And we certainly would never have dreamt of taking a gun and aiming it at each other like these young kids do today. Loving each other as Black men struggling to survive in an oppressive world was a greater virtue than the hatred our youth feel today.

I was called to my first pastorate while still in college. I became minister of a very little church in Union County, eleven miles from my home. It was 1948 and I was only eighteen years old. The following year, while still in college, I was called to be the pastor at Bethel Baptist Church in Gaffney at the age of nineteen.

I didn't restrict my work to just the ministry. I worked for the Union County Educational System for nineteen years and eventually became Vice-Principal of Sims High School, my alma mater. My experience as an educator was interesting and challenging. When I became principal of a rural elementary school, there were three teachers including me. The schoolhouse consisted of two buildings. Children and teachers had to make fire from wood gathered from wooded areas around the school. Our pay was always much lower than that of the white teachers, our books were used, and the conditions for teaching were deplorable. After the Brown vs. Board of Education Supreme Court decision in 1954, conditions began to improve. But they were never equal to that of the white schools. Despite these obstacles, we were determined to teach our children because we all understood that education was the key to our future. We loved our children and believed they could achieve only if shown the love and commitment necessary for them to live healthy lives. This is missing with so many of our children today, and we must all make a commitment to change that problem. Regardless of all other problems our communities may confront, there is one thing no one can stop us from doing, and that is love our children.

The guiding hand in my life has always been God, and He has allowed me to soar to heights of success I never dreamt possible. Although I have never lived more than thirty miles from where I was born, I have accumulated a wealth of experience. I must proclaim that the Lord has blessed me immeasurably. One piece of advice I would like to leave with the young who read this anthology is that the road to success is always paved with commitment. One must be committed to God, to one's self, and to the job that one intends to do in life. There must be accountability, and you must always measure how well you are fulfilling your duty as a man or woman, father or mother and member of the greatest culture ever to come out of this country.

It is my sincere hope that this work will be an inspiration to those in need, those who are hurting, and those who want to learn from a man who has dedicated his life to the betterment of his people. It is through faith in God that I have persevered over the past eight decades and know that what I have accomplished has been as a result of hard work. We must all strive for excellence so the quality of what we do superseded the quantity of our works.

Postscript from the Editor: We lost this wonderful man on July 6, 2010. As he suffered with his illness, he was determined to finish his contribution to the anthology. He talked often with Toschia Moffett who is working on a biography of his life. During their talks he would constantly tell her not to worry because his works on earth had been blessed by God. His ministry at Bethel Baptist Church for over sixty-one years and as Senior Pastor at Island Creek Baptist Church for thirty-eight years had earned him a place in Heaven. But what he didn't articulate was that his works here in this world and for his people earned him a place as a legend among his people. His life is a compilation of all the stories that preceded his. Dr. Sanders is gone but not forgotten and will always remain a hero for all of us to emulate.

The Love That Forgives

Frederick Williams and Carrie Williams

On Sept. 15, 1963, less than a month after Dr. Martin Luther King Jr. delivered his historical "I Have A Dream" speech in front of thousands at the Lincoln Memorial and millions watching on television, four innocent, beautiful, and precocious Black girls entered the Sixteenth Street Baptist Church in Birmingham, Ala., for Sunday School services. Little did they know on that day they would enter martyrdom as a result of the most evil and atrocious act carried out against a race of people since Hitler's concentration camps.

Four young girls who didn't seek martyrdom, but only wanted a normal life, were denied that right because Birmingham in 1963 was anything but normal. It is difficult for us, now living in the 21st Century, to fully comprehend what it was like to be Black at the time these young ladies were killed. We take for granted what they, as well as thousands of other Black teenagers and adults, were forced to confront and challenge every day of their lives. For them something as mundane and simple as shopping in downtown department stores was an ordeal. For us it is a pleasure trip. They were not allowed to try on clothes unless they planned to buy the items; they were forced to endure the humiliation of drinking out of water fountains and using restrooms marked "For Colored Only," as if whites would catch some kind of disease if they shared those facilities with Blacks.

It was against these abuses that the Black children of Birmingham decided to do something that the adults refused to do which would ultimately lead to the brutal bombing incident at the Sixteenth Street Baptist Church. When many of the adults turned their backs on Dr. King and Rev. Fred Shuttleworth's call for massive demonstrations against apartheid in what many considered to be the most racist city in the country, the young folks showed up for the job.

On May 21, of that same year, three months before the fatal attack on the children, and a little after nine o'clock in the morning, over fifty young Black warriors marched out into the street ready to do battle with the white menace of apartheid. Those young warriors were determined to take their rights and freedoms guaranteed them in the Constitution. They were willing to stand tall and tell the world they were proud Black Americans, ready to confront the evil that would three months later prove just how demonic its forces could be toward other human beings.

Once the first fifty marched out of the church, were arrested, and thrown in the back of wagons to be hauled off to jail, another thousand followed close behind them. Once they were arrested, a third line, then a fourth line of young Black fighters, some only 6 years old, valiantly confronted the police knowing they would be arrested. There were so many demonstrators that the police literally had to bring in school buses to keep up with the flow of students.

Across the street in Kelly Ingram Park, Black adults watched in amazement as the children made a bold statement about freedom and liberty. Also looking on in a state of anger, to the point of insanity, was Eugene Bull Connors, Commissioner of Police and the personification of southern-style segregation. Unable to dissuade the children to disperse and end the demonstration, Connors finally gave the order to fire hose the young demonstrators, and also turned the vicious police dogs loose on America's children.

The more the dogs tore into the children and the more the power of the fire hose knocked them to their knees, the more determined they were, as they continued to show up in overwhelming numbers. A Black principal at the local high school actually locked the gates in an attempt to keep the students inside. But they would not be deterred by any obstacles, be it Connor's dogs or the principal's locked gates. They trampled the chain-like fence in order to be with their friends and allies.

The young Black Americans in Birmingham were essentially doing what young Blacks had been doing for decades. They were doing what a sixteen year old girl did in 1951 at R.R. Moton

The Love That Forgives

High School in Farmville, Va. Young Barbara Johns, the niece of the firebrand minister Vernon Johns, had summoned all 450 Black students to an assembly in the auditorium on the morning of April 23, 1951. Against the protest of the faculty, she stood in front of the student body and rattled off a series of complaints about the condition of their school. When the faculty attempted to remove her from the stage, she ordered them out of the auditorium. Just like the children in Birmingham, twelve years later, recognized the futility in trying to get adults to do what they should, she was determined not to let them stop her and the other students from eradicating evil.

She told her fellow students that Plessy v. Ferguson was nonsense and the white apartheid system would never comply with the decision that separate must be equal. Again, it was the children who became the warriors for justice. They made it known that they would no longer attend classes in tarpaper shacks, having to wear coats in the winter just to stay warm. They objected to being forced to ride in hand-me-down buses from the whites to schools that were not in their neighborhood. The buses often would not even start and if they did, would break down on the road. She told the students that they all should be outraged that their history teacher also had to drive the bus and had to gather wood and start the fire inside the school in order to keep them warm.

Barbara Johns shouted loudly for all to hear that young people demanded their rights as Americans. Since the adults couldn't get the job done, then the young people would. The white school board had rebuffed the demands of the adults to improve the conditions in the classrooms and reneged on a promise to build a new high school. The adults appeared impotent in their negotiations with the whites, so Barbara and her fellow students decided they would strike. They marched out of the school building and downtown, prepared for a confrontation with the power structure. The students then appealed to the National Association for the Advancement of Colored People for their legal help. A week later when officials from the NAACP arrived in Farmville under the assumption that it was the adults who had requested their assistance. They were surprised when they walked into the room full of students. The lawyers informed the students that their strike might be illegal, and they could be arrested. But just like the students in Birmingham twelve years later, they challenged the police to arrest them. They boldly stated that there was too many of them for the small jail in their town. But they were willing to be incarcerated in defense of their God given freedoms and liberties.

History inextricably connected these young Americans in a common bond over time. They were all marching toward freedom in their own time in their own country with a clear understanding there might be repercussions. They never dreamed just how vicious the forces of apartheid could be and the extent to which they would go to inflict pain, even on innocent young people.

When the bomb exploded at 10:22 a.m., four young ladies were in the basement lady's room talking about the beginning days of the school year. That particular Sunday happened to be Youth Day at the church and they were preparing to run the main service at eleven o'clock. The four girls, Denise McNair, Addie Mae Collins, Cynthia Wesley, and Carole Robertson, all dressed in white, were excited about the adult roles they would play in about twenty-five minutes. In a bitter twist of irony, a Women's Sunday School class, upstairs in the sanctuary, was discussing the topic for the week, "The Love That Forgives."

Actually, six young people died on that tragic day, the four little girls in the church and two young Black men who were shot dead for no apparent reason than riding on their bicycles. Virgil Ware was shot in the back by a racist policeman and Johnny Robinson was shot by a good old Eagle Scout, Alabama version, vintage 1963. The brutal killing of these two young men did not receive the same coverage as did the four little girls. But it was just as dastardly an act as was the killings at the church.

At the funeral days later for three of the girls (Carole Robertson's parents decided to have a separate funeral for her), Dr. King would reiterate and elaborate on what the women's group had been discussing when disaster struck. He would stress the value of love and forgiveness as requisite for the Christian church. Love and forgiveness were also critical components in Black America's struggle against evil. Why four beautiful young Black ladies and two vibrant young men had to die seemed to be a test of Black America's ability to love and forgive. The fact that an aggrieved Black population did not strike back and had the willpower to forgive the murderers is a testament of the goodness we possess as a people. It is a very special spirituality that is endemic to the Black race. Dr. W. E. B. DuBois wrote about it as a unique quality that Black America has given to all civilization.

The Love That Forgives

Our family members who were sacrificed at the altar of evil are a true personification of the forgiving nature of our people.

Their deaths served to connect the entire Black experience from the time our forebears first arrived in this country in chains until today and far into the future. Theirs was an awesome sacrifice that serves an awesome purpose. The four young ladies and two young men's legacy in death is our challenge in life so their existence will live on. It is quite obvious who occupies the moral high ground in this country, and the rest of the races can learn from our experience on how to be forgiving and actually believe that by loving your adversary, you also love yourself. For a few years after the tragedy at the church, Black folk turned inward and discovered who they were and how God had blessed them with an inordinate amount of courage and dignity through times of suffering.

We must never lose that special quality that is the foundation of our culture. We owe it to Denise, Carole, Addie Mae, Cynthia, Virgil, Johnnie, and all the other martyrs who have gone to their death at the hands of the evil that constantly tries to destroy the good that our race represents. It is now time for a new renaissance among our people. Like the great sphinx rising out of the ashes of destruction, we must rise once again and reject those forces of greed, narcissism, and nihilism that would bring us to a point of cultural annihilation. We owe it to our martyrs, our heroes, and ourselves.

Epilogue

Frederick Williams

Black America is at a crossroads as two distinctly different forces vie for control of its culture. The next twenty to twenty-five years will determine which set of forces will win out. If our culture is strong and unified behind the grace, beauty, and proud heritage of our past, then we will have confronted the negative forces of self-destruction and defeated them. Just like our ancestors confronted adversity and won, so can we also. But it is imperative that the youth take a stand against the prevalent nihilistic attitudes that are selfish and individualistic with no concern for the greater good of the race. Each author you have just read has, in their own way, delivered a message of hope for all our people. We have endured the worst in the past, and now it should be much easier as we move forward into our future. However, it will only be a smoother road if we remember that our ancestors brought us up "the rough side of the mountain" and opened doors they never were able to walk through. Our young people are freer and have more opportunities to achieve success than ever before in our history.

We must first, however, recognize that Black Americans are an excellent people with an excellent track record of achievements in the past. We must not allow certain forces, let loose in our communities, take advantage of the freedoms our ancestors suffered for us to have for their own individual and selfish gain. Those who make a fortune by producing music and literature that portrays our race and culture in a negative light must be rejected.

It is imperative that we all understand that our culture is on loan to us for a specific number of years and then is passed on to a new generation. While keepers of the culture we must continue to improve on the beauty, grace, and strength that our ancestors left as our heritage and legacy. A short trip down memory lane reveals just how skilled, talented, and determined were the many who went before us.

Blacks have excelled in sports for over a century. Soon after the end of slavery, Black excellence began to shine. In the sport of boxing, Jack Johnson forced white men to seek a "Great White Hope" to save their dignity. In the 1936 Olympics, Jesse Owens embarrassed the German dictator who had claimed the German runner was invincible, by defeating all of them in the 100-yard dash. In fact, Owens won four gold medals in the Olympics that year, proving that Black excellence was unstoppable.

A sport in which Black excellence in performance has been ignored for years is horse racing. For example the first winner in the Kentucky Derby was Jimmy Winfield, a Black man. In fact, 15 of the first 28 Derbies were won by Black jockeys. And the greatest jockey in the history of the sport was Isaac Murphy who won three Kentucky Derby races and 44% of all his races throughout his career.

Black exceptionalism does not end with sports, but can be found in academic circles also. There is no question that Dr. W.E.B. Dubois was the country's most gifted scholar of the 20th Century. He was the first Black man to receive a Ph.D. from Harvard University. He was a historian, sociologists, philosopher, novelist, and all around brilliant thinker. Dr. Alain Locke, also a philosopher, attained Phi Beta Kappa status and graduated magna cum laude from Harvard University. He was the first Black Rhodes Scholar at Oxford University and editor of the first Black anthology chronicling the changing nature of Black people in America, *The New Negro*. Jesse Fausett, was the literary editor for *Crisis Magazine* during the Harlem Renaissance. She was the first Black female to graduate from Cornell University and the first Black woman to achieve Phi Beta Kappa status. Dr. Ralph Bunche became the first African American to win a Nobel Peace Prize for his work toward bringing peace in the Middle East in the late 1940's. Today, we have Dr. Cornell West who is one of the most sought after scholars in the country. Dr. Condeleezza Rice was and still is an accomplished pianist and a scholar who has served as National Security Advisor and Secretary of State. Dr. Angela Davis is an accomplished scholar who has taught at the University of California at Los Angeles and wrote many political tracts critical of the oppression Blacks have suffered in this country.

Epilogue

In the field of music, Black Americans have excelled from their first arrival under the most horrendous conditions in this country. Spirituals became the slave's comfort and relief from suffering and as a code that a planned escape was imminent. Within those lyrics were the hopes and dreams of millions of men and women for release from bondage. Spirituals drew their parables from Biblical references. Moses' demand to the Pharaoh to "Let my people go" became the foundation on which spirituals were based. From out of those slave fields, our ancestors produced America's first original music in blues, ragtime, jazz, gospel, rhythm and blues, and rap. It is all American music, created, produced, and performed in the rural areas of the South as well as the cosmopolitan urban communities of all our major cities.

Black Americans have also excelled in the classical genre of opera. Marian Anderson was one of the most recognized stars from the 1930's until the apex of her career when she appeared with the Metropolitan Opera Company in New York, performing the role of Ulitca in Verdi's *Un Ballo in Maschera*. In 1939 after the Daughter's of the American Revolution refused to allow her to perform in Constitution Hall because she was Black, Ms. Anderson, with the assistance of First Lady Eleanor Roosevelt, performed on Easter Sunday that same year on the steps of the Lincoln Monument where 75,000 people came to hear her. According to Conductor Arturo Toscanini, Marian Anderson possessed a voice that "comes only once in a hundred years." She was another example of how Black Americans have never given up when faced with adversity but instead have risen far above the problem and came out the winner.

There is a genius of creation inherent within Black Americans that allows them to write music affecting the entire world. Michael Jackson was loved as much in Europe and Asia as in the United States. Before Michael, there was W.C. Handy, Eubie Blake, Louis Armstrong, Bessie Smith, Billie Holiday, Duke Ellington, Count Basie, and many more. Many female vocalists, Sarah Vaughn, Dinah Washington, and Etta Jones were precursors to Dianna Ross, Aretha Franklin, Gladys Knight, Tina Turner, and Patti Labelle, all who have in turn set the precedent for the contemporary female vocalist, Beyonce, Fantasia, Jennifer Hudson, and Kelly Roland. These ladies all represent a continuum of excellence in music that has always existed within the Black culture.

There are talented men also who have traveled that same

continuum. Roland Hayes, the son of a former slave, became one of the first Black men to sing classical music. Following in his legacy were greats like Paul Warfield, Paul Robeson, Ray Charles, Marvin Gaye, Lou Rawls, Luther Vandross, and Teddy Pendergrass. This is only a small representation of the men who have excelled and set a very high standard of excellence in the performance of Black music, which is American music.

Dance is also an expressive art form in which Black Americans have excelled for centuries. Our ancestors would dance to relieve the frustration and pain associated with slavery. Contrary to the misinformation found in many school history books, our ancestors did not dance to entertain their oppressors, but instead they danced because it was a natural way to find some joy in life. The Cakewalk was the first dance performed by our ancestors on plantations throughout the South. As often would happen with original works by Blacks, the white population adapted the Cakewalk and began to have competitions for best performance. Ragtime music was influenced greatly by the steps involved in the Cakewalk.

There is such an outstanding list of extraordinary dancers throughout American history it would take pages to name them all. But let us begin with the person who received awards for her performances both in the United States and France. Josephine Baker's career spanned over a fifty-year period and two countries, France and the United States. Katherine Dunham was both a performer and choreographer. She was so respected that in 1987 other dancers paid tribute to her when they performed, "The Magic of Katherine Dunham," at the Alvin Ailey American Dance Theater in New York. Besides her career as a dancer and choreographer, Ms. Dunham found time to earn a Bachelor of Arts, a Masters Degree, and a Ph.D. from the University of Chicago in Cultural Anthropology.

John William Sublet began dancing at the age of eight and created a dance routine, "Walking the Dog," that was emulated by Sophie Tucker. The Nicholas Brothers and Bill Bo Jangles Robinson set the stage for such great dancers as Sammy Davis Jr., Jackie Wilson, James Brown, Chuck Berry, and the late, great Michael Jackson.

There is a long list of Black Americans who have excelled in the field of literature. The early poets, novelists, and those who wrote slave narratives initially wrote about our ancestor's struggle to survive under the most horrendous system of oppression any people have been forced to endure. Most of the slave narratives were written by men and women who escaped bondage and were determined to tell the world how vicious slavery actually was and that no one was happy living under those conditions. Among the great writers were Olaudah Equiano, Frederick Douglass, William Wells Brown, Henry Box Brown, Harriet Jacobs, and William and Ellen Craft.

The Crafts' narrative reads like an exciting novel detailing how she, a very light skinned woman, disguised as an invalid, and her husband William, acting as her loyal servant, made their way through the South from Macon, Ga., to Philadelphia and finally Boston. They wrote of their exciting escape from slavery in a book, *Running a Thousand Miles for Freedom*. Henry Box Brown's escape story is just as exciting. He writes of how he and two white brothers, J.C.A. and Samuel Smith, who assisted him in his escape, constructed a pine box that was three feet long, eight inches deep, and twenty-three-and-a-half inches wide for Brown. They packed him into the box and mailed him to the Pennsylvania Anti-Slavery Society office in Philadelphia, Pa. He was in that box for more than twenty-four hours and arrived safely in Philadelphia.

William Wells Brown, who escaped bondage on New Years Day, 1834, also published the first novel by an African American, *Clotel,* in 1853. However, his was published in England. The first novel published by an African American in the United States, *Our Nig; or, Sketches from the Life of a Free Black, in a Two-Story White House, North. Showing that Slavery's Shadows Fall Even There*, was written by Harriett Wilson in 1859. Despite the laws prohibiting slaves from reading and writing, the sheer desire of our ancestors to educate themselves could not be curtailed. Regardless of the punishment that was inflicted if a slave was caught reading, they still pursued their God-given right to become literate. Their willpower prevailed and their natural acumen shined.

There were a number of significant and well-talented essayists, novelists, and poets in the years following slavery and into the beginning of the Twentieth Century. The prevalent theme among these writers was no longer the brutality of slavery and the quest for freedom but the brutality of apartheid and the fight for equality. Literacy was viewed as the gateway to social and economic equality. Still, there was an attempt on the part of the white dominant society to block these writers. But like their earlier predecessors they would not be denied. Ana Julia Cooper, an educator who taught at the famous Washington Colored School in Washington, D. C., wrote, *A Voice from the South: By a Black Woman of the South*. Charlotte Forten Grimke was educated in the North, but after the Civil War went South to help teach the ex-slaves to read and write. She chronicled her experience in, *The Journals of Charlotte Forten Grimke*. Frances W. Harper, an active promoter of equality for her people, wrote, *Iola Leroy, or Shadows Uplifted* in 1892. Elizabeth Keckley in her autobiography, *Behind the Scenes; or, Thirty Years a Slave, and Four Years in the White House*, covers her years as a slave and her burning desire to be free, as well as the four years she worked in the Lincoln White House as a free woman, but still plagued by a racist and sexist America. Finally, Pauline Hopkins, born in Maine just prior to the Civil War, introduced the subject of color prejudice, sexism, and uplift of the race in her novel, *Hagar's Daughter: A Story of Southern Caste Prejudice*. Ms. Hopkins was a strong advocate for self-determination and racial equality. She argued and fought against the debilitating affects of apartheid on her people.

Two writers who initially excelled in poetry and short stories, and later in life with novels were Charles Chestnutt and Paul Laurence Dunbar. Chestnutt, who had trained as a lawyer, wrote *The Conjure Woman* in 1899, which is a series of short stories highlighting the Black folk culture of the South. *The Wife of His Youth and Other Stories of the Color Line*, written in 1899, was very critical of race relations in the country. Two of Chestunutt's best works were *The Goophered Grapevine* and *Po' Sandy*.

Born the son of slaves, as were many of the early writers, Paul Laurence Dunbar became the most recognized writer of African American descent in the country at the turn of the century. Dunbar not only composed poetry in a southern dialect but also in traditional English. Dunbar was primarily recognized as a poet but also wrote novels, musical comedies, and short fiction. Some of his poems in dialect include, "An Ante-bellum Sermon," "When Malindy Sings," and "The Party." His most famous poem not in dialect and critical of how Black writers were blackballed if they wrote positive works on the race was, "We Wear the Mask." Late in his life, Dunbar turned to short stories to include such classic as, "The Strength of Gideon and Other Stories," "In Old Plantation Days," and "The Heart of Happy Hollow."

James Weldon Johnson bridges the gap between the early

nineteenth century writers and those of the Harlem Renaissance. He was productive as a writer during both periods. Johnson was the trailblazer of a most versatile group of men and women who had a very positive impact on our culture. Many have called him a Renaissance Man because of his numerous talents. He was a writer (*The Autobiography of an Ex-Colored Man*), a poet ("The Creation"), a songwriter ("Lift Every Voice and Sing"), a chronicler of Black history (*Black Manhattan*), and also the first Black Executive Secretary of the National Association for the Advancement of Colored People. Johnson became one of the major figures of the Harlem Renaissance because of his many different accomplishments.

It was the Harlem Renaissance that witnessed an explosion of Black poets and novelists. Such greats as Langston Hughes, Claude McKay, Jesse Fausett, Walter White, Wallace Thurmond, and Zora Neale Hurston wrote about the "New Negro" evolving as a result of the great northern migration of the Black population. The Harlem Renaissance, a period that lasted from 1920 to 1929, represents the flowering of the African American culture. It was a time when Black writers, musicians, poets, artists, political activists, and intellectuals came together in one small section of New York city and refined the heart and soul of Black America.

Richard Wright, Ralph Ellison, and James Baldwin followed in the footsteps of the talented authors from the Harlem Renaissance. Toni Morrison, who won a Pulitzer Prize for literature, Terry McMillan author of *Waiting to Exhale*, the novel that launched an avalanche of Black novelists, and Walter Moseley, have continued the long tradition of outstanding novelists right up to the present day.

The creative nature of Black Americans is apparent in the art of writing poetry. It has the longest history of literary expression taking us back to the 18th century and Phyllis Wheatley's poetry. Her poetry was written at such a high level of excellence that it was presented to Thomas Jefferson as evidence to disprove his assertions that Africans were inherently mentally inferior to whites. Other early poets included Jupiter Hammond, Lucy Terry, Prince, and George Moses Horton. Early 20th Century and Harlem Renaissance poets include, Paul Laurence Dunbar, Langston Hughes, Countee Cullen, and Claude McKay. Gwendolyn Brooks, Maya Angelou, and Nikki Giovanni followed in the footsteps of the earlier poets and continued the tradition of poetic excellence.

The natural creative talent of Black Americans is on display at many of the country's most prestigious art museums. Again, there is a long list of African Americans who have excelled in all fields of art. Romare Bearden began painting in the 1930's as a member of the Harlem Artists Guild and over the years gained the reputation as one of the leading 20th Century abstract painters. The one artist most associated with the Harlem Renaissance period was Aaron Douglas. In collaboration with the writers, he coordinated visuals to the messages in their novels and essays. In 1926, he worked with Langston Hughes, Wallace Thurmond, Zora Neale Hurston, and Bruce Nugent to do illustrations for the one time published magazine *FIRE!* It is now a classic publication. Douglas did illustrations for the *Crisis* and *Opportunity Magazines*. His most famous work is the murals, "Aspects of Negro Life," now housed at the Schomburg Center in Harlem. He also painted murals for Fisk University that dealt with African American identity and history. Douglas was often referred to as "the father of African American art."

Henry Ossawa Tanner was one of the first recognized African American photographers/painters. Tanner became famous for painting moving religious scenes and images of what he called the common man. Tanner's papers are now maintained in the Archives of American Art, Smithsonian Institution.

The essence of the African American culture has been captured over the centuries and decades by many other talented artists, of which Richmond Barthe, May Howard Jackson, Norman Lewis, Laura Wheeler Waring, and Charles Wilbert White are only a few.

Black Americans have also excelled in theater, movies, and television. *Shuffle Along*, featuring Florence Mills, Josephine Baker, and introducing the world to Paul Robeson, written and produced by Eubie Blake and Noble Sissle, is credited with jump-starting the Harlem Renaissance. Langston Hughes, after seeing the performance, knew he had to live in Harlem and be a part of the great outbreak of cultural identity stimulated by the musical, *Shuffle Along*.

Long before Denzell Washington won an academy award, Charles Sidney Gilpin won national acclaim for his portrayal of the lead character in Eugene O'Neil's play, *Emperor Jones,* in 1920. Rose McClendon also was recognized as one of the most accomplished and respected actresses of the 1920's and 1930's.

Epilogue

Cicely Tyson was nominated for an Academy Award for Best Actress in 1972 for her critically acclaimed performance in the film, *Sounder*. And who can ever forget her brilliant role she portrayed as a 110-year-old ex-slave, Jane Pittman when she made that historic walk up to the water fountain, marked for whites only, and graciously, with class and history on her side, took a drink of water. Ms. Tyson epitomizes the message in this anthology. She refused to play roles that did not portray strong, positive images of Black women. Unlike many other actresses she did her race proud by putting image above profits and fame.

Hattie McDaniel became the first African American to win an Academy Award. She won the best supporting actress award for playing a maid in the movie, *Gone With the Wind*. She was roundly criticized by some groups for playing the role of a maid that tended to stereotype Black women. Her response was, "It is much better earning $7,000 a week playing a maid than $7.00 a day being one."

Black filmmaker, Oscar Micheaux, produced more than 40 films, including the first all Black feature films, both silent and sound. Disgusted with the stereotyped portrayal in the plantation literature, Micheaux was determined to produce films as a counter-attack to Hollywood. His film, *Within Our Gates*, was a Black man's response to the racist film, *Birth of a Nation*. Micheaux did with his films what the writers of this anthology have done through literature and that is to paint a positive image of the race as counter to much of the urban street fiction that exists today.

The actor, intellectual, and political activist, Paul Robeson, represents Black excellence at its highest plateau. He excelled in every endeavor he undertook. At age 17, he won a four-year scholarship to Rutgers University. During his years at Rutgers he excelled in sports and academics. He was an All-American football player for two years in a row. He won letters in baseball, basketball, and track. Academically he was elected to both the Phi Beta Kappa Society and Cap and Skull. Robeson served as the Valedictorian for his 1919 graduating class. He went on to become an actor on stage and in movies, and an outstanding singer and spokesperson against a segregated military and against lynching.

Garland Anderson, with only a fourth grade education, became the first African American playwright to stage a full-length drama on Broadway, *Don't Judge by Appearance*, later shortened to

Appearance. Anderson's play had its debut at Broadway's Frolic Theater on October 13, 1925. It had a two-year run throughout the United States, re-opened for a second run in New York on April 1, 1929. The play had its international debut in London, England, in March 1930.

Black Americans have also excelled in motion pictures. One of the greatest all-Black movies was the classic, *Stormy Weather*, featuring Lena Horne, Bill "Bojangles" Robinson, and included such outstanding performers as Fats Waller, Katherine Dunham, Cab Calloway, and the Nicholas Brothers. Another outstanding movie was *Carmen Jones*, featuring Dorothy Dandridge and the great Harry Belafonte.

Black movie makers Spike Lee and Tyler Perry have continued the legacy of Oscar Micheaux with outstanding film productions. Both Lee and Perry have given us movies that create positive and strong images of African Americans. There is no doubt, Lee's classic production, *Malcolm X,* should have received an Academy Award.

Over the past fifty years, Black Americans have been extremely successful in television programs. Dihann Carroll in *Julia,* Esther Rolle in *Good Times*, Bill Cosby in *I Spy* and *the Cosby Show,* and Will Smith in *Fresh Prince of Bel-Air*, are only a few of the many Blacks who have excelled on television.

There is no question that the most successful television personality in the history of the industry is Oprah Winfrey. When writing about Black and excellence, she stands out above all others.

There are many fields of endeavor that I haven't even touched on that Blacks have displayed their genius. In the fields of medicine and science Blacks have excelled even before the turn of the 20th Century. This is reserved for another anthology.

Finally at the end of Lee's *Malcolm X*, a number of young children stand before their class and proclaim they are the descendants of some classic heroes of the Black Diaspora. Essentially what they are telling the world is the identical message in the pages of this anthology: We are Black and we are Americans, and that is an excellent combination.